*Fundamentals of U.S. Foreign Trade Policy*

# FUNDAMENTALS
# OF U.S. FOREIGN
# TRADE POLICY

## Economics, Politics, Laws, and Issues

### SECOND EDITION

Stephen D. Cohen

Robert A. Blecker

Peter D. Whitney

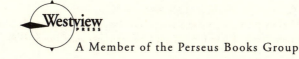

Westview PRESS

A Member of the Perseus Books Group

Copyright © 2003 by Westview Press, A Member of the Perseus Books Group

Westview Press books are available at special discounts for bulk purchases in the United States by corporations, institutions, and other organizations. For more information, please contact the Special Markets Department at the Perseus Books Group, 11 Cambridge Center, Cambridge MA 02142, or call (617) 252-5298.

Published in 2003 in the United States of America by Westview Press, 5500 Central Avenue, Boulder, Colorado 80301-2877, and in the United Kingdom by Westview Press, 12 Hid's Copse Road, Cumnor Hill, Oxford OX2 9JJ

Find us on the World Wide Web at www.westviewpress.com

A Cataloging-in-Publication data record for this book is available from the Library of Congress.
ISBN 0-8133-4027-6 (HC) ISBN 0-8133-9845-2 (Pbk.)
The paper used in this publication meets the requirements of the American National Standard for Permanence of Paper for Printed Library Materials Z39.48–1984.

10   9   8   7   6   5   4   3   2   1

# Contents

# Tables, Boxes, and Figures

# Preface and Acknowledgments

This is the second edition of a book published in 1996. The main reason for the new edition is the rapid rate of change and the increased complexity that have reshaped the international trading system in general and U.S. trade policy in particular since then. The world economy today is different in many respects from the situation and trends that existed in the early 1990s. The original version was therefore becoming increasingly obsolete. However, the broad conceptual approach and integrating themes that characterized the first edition are still applicable. While this version significantly updates and expands the contents of its predecessor, it retains the analytical framework that has held up well in explaining recent decisions and trends. The retention of this framework also preserves this book's distinctive identity in a crowded field.

As we said in the first edition, there is an abundance of good academic literature dealing with the foreign trade policy of the United States. Lack of time to read the thousands of books and articles written on this subject is the problem, not a lack of information. Nevertheless, this book still fills gaps in the academic literature. Works on U.S. trade policy produced by scholars and practitioners invariably have an "attitude." They are argumentative pieces praising or criticizing existing policies, usually on the import side. Economic theorists and political economists offer what they believe are better alternatives to existing policies: a more aggressive trade posture, a less aggressive trade posture, fewer restrictions on imports, more import restrictions, fewer export sanctions, more export sanctions, increased attention to labor and environmental issues, less attention to these issues, and so on. More recently, scholars have offered conflicting diagnoses about whether record-breaking U.S. trade deficits are a sign of weakness or strength. Other specialists write extensively on narrower subjects that tend to be considered in isolation from one another. Legal scholars have written hundreds of articles on the legal implications of U.S. obligations incurred from adherence to the rules of the World Trade Organization. Business specialists have written instructional books for would-be exporters and importers. Political scientists have written about the role of power in international commercial relations and about the prospects for one unified theory to explain trade policy decisionmaking.

What is still missing is a text that comprehensively and dispassionately explains the content of U.S. trade policy in an economic, political, and legal context. We hope to make a contribution to the understanding of this subject by emphasizing the distinctive theme that trade policy is the synthesis of mostly subjective choices by officials among legitimate, although competing, economic objectives and political constituencies. Decisions must reconcile the four components of foreign trade policy—domestic and external economics and domestic and external politics—each of which has its own priorities and its own policy agenda.

An appreciation of the dynamics of interactions among *economics, politics,* and *federal and international trade laws* is, we believe, a prerequisite for fully understanding the performance, objectives, limitations, virtues, and failures of U.S. trade policy. To a significant extent, the inevitable disagreements in the political process of determining which economic policy best serves the country's national interest (or the interest of its political leaders) are resolved either through the wording of a new trade law or through revisions to an existing one. These hypotheses are found only obliquely or not at all in other writings on this subject.

A second innovation in our approach is a commitment to objectivity throughout the book. To avoid being judgmental in all aspects of our study, no positions are taken on the logic or cost-effectiveness of trade policies adopted or proposed. Personal evaluations seem superfluous at best when another integrating theme of this study shows that trade policy is characterized far more by perceptions and values than by universal or absolute truths. U.S. trade policy is examined as it has been and is, not how we think it should be. Whenever applicable, all the major sides to a particular controversy are given equal treatment so that the reader can decide what he or she thinks would constitute "good" policy. We have tried throughout to avoid any indication of which policy options we personally think best serve the national interest of the United States. Even if we wanted to make evaluations and recommendations, disagreements among the authors about "first-best" policy would probably force us to abandon the idea in the interest of saving time and preserving harmony. No recommendations are made for changes in either the substance of trade policy or the decisionmaking process. This book is decidedly not a platform for the opinions of its authors. Instead, our purpose is to provide a uniquely insightful and integrated study that provides the reader with a knowledge of U.S. trade policy's many dimensions and nuances that is not available in any other single source.

The book begins with an overview of the nature and history of U.S. trade policy (Chapters 1 and 2). It next explicitly examines the principal elements shaping and moving trade policy: economics in Chapter 3 and politics in Chapters 5 and 6. The third principal element is law. Domestic U.S. trade laws are profiled in Chapter 7. International trade rules and the objectives, operations, and effects of the World Trade Organization are analyzed in Chapter 8. Chapter 4 differs from most academic studies of trade policy by examining in detail what at first glance may appear to the reader to be a counterintuitive premise: Trade policy usually has only a limited role in determining a country's overall trade balance. The chapter also discusses the nontrade policy factors most frequently cited as contributing to the large U.S. trade deficits. The purpose of Chapter 9 is to focus exclusively on the political economy and laws of U.S. export policy. This effort is necessary to avoid the all-too-common mistake of looking at U.S. trade policy exclusively or mainly as an import-oriented struggle between the champions of free trade and the advocates of protectionism. This is an overly narrow approach that is a necessary but not sufficient means of explaining the totality of trade policy. Export policy is too significant to be given incidental consideration or to be totally ignored.

The last section of the book examines in detail the U.S. responses to several of the most important issues in contemporary international trade relations. The common purpose of the case studies presented in Chapters 10 through 13 is to provide real-world examples that validate our hypothesis that the dynamic relationship among economics, politics, and laws is what mainly shapes U.S. trade policy. In keeping with our emphasis on objectivity, we do not take sides in the controversies inherent in all these major issues.

We hope that we have filled an important niche and produced a good textbook on the forces that make U.S. trade policy what it is. Trade relations affect many areas of national and international endeavors and many academic disciplines. This book is designed to be understood by people with a wide range of interests and occupations. It can be used at the university level for courses in economics, international relations, business, and law.

A deep expression of gratitude is extended to the graduate assistants of Stephen D. Cohen for their invaluable contributions to the preparation of this book. Mark J. Dunn, Meredith Montgomery, Joshua Carter, and Sara Ploskon provided incalculable amounts of excellent research and editing assistance. We also acknowledge and express thanks for the several legal insights contained in the two law chapters that are carried over from Joel Paul's contributions to the first edition of this book. A thank you is also extended to William Cromwell for his useful comments on the U.S.-European Union relations chapter and to Martha Whitney for her editing help with the WTO chapter. Needless to say, the authors take full responsibility for factual errors and all conclusions in their respective chapters. Stephen Cohen wrote the first, second, fifth through seventh, and ninth through fourteenth chapters. Robert Blecker wrote the third chapter and made significant contributions, especially on dumping issues, to the seventh. Peter Whitney wrote the eighth chapter. The fourth chapter was a collaborative effort by professors Cohen and Blecker. Each of us made many changes and corrections in the early drafts of our chapters as the result of suggestions from coauthors.

*Stephen D. Cohen*
*Robert A. Blecker*
*Peter D. Whitney*
*Washington, D.C.*
*March, 2002*

# Acronyms

| | |
|---|---|
| AD | antidumping |
| AFL-CIO | American Federation of Labor and Congress of Industrial Organizations |
| APEC | Asia-Pacific Economic Cooperation forum |
| ASEAN | Association of Southeast Asian Nations |
| CAP | Common Agricultural Policy |
| CBO | Congressional Budget Office |
| CEA | Council of Economic Advisers |
| COCOM | Coordinating Committee on Multilateral Export Controls |
| DISCs | Domestic International Sales Corporations |
| DSB | Dispute Settlement Body (of the WTO) |
| DSM | dispute settlement mechanism (of the WTO) |
| EAA | Export Administration Act |
| EC | European Community |
| ECB | European Central Bank |
| ECSC | European Coal and Steel Community |
| EEC | European Economic Community |
| EU | European Union |
| FCPA | Foreign Corrupt Practices Act |
| FDI | foreign direct investment |
| FSC | Foreign Sales Corporation |
| FTA | free trade agreement |
| FTAA | Free Trade Area of the Americas |
| GAO | General Accounting Office |
| GATS | General Agreement on Trade in Services |
| GATT | General Agreement on Tariffs and Trade |
| GDP | gross domestic product |
| GMO | genetically modified food |
| GSP | Generalized System of Preferences |
| H-O | Heckscher-Ohlin (trade model) |
| IEEPA | International Emergency Economic Powers Act |
| ILO | International Labor Organization |
| IMF | International Monetary Fund |
| IPRs | intellectual property rights |
| ITA | International Trade Administration (Commerce Department) |
| ITC | International Trade Commission |
| LDCs | less developed countries |

| MAI | Multilateral Agreement on Investment |
| MEA | Multilateral environmental agreement |
| MFA | Multifiber Arrangement |
| MFN | most favored nation |
| MITI | Ministry of International Trade and Industry (Japan) |
| MNCs | multinational corporations |
| MOSS | market-oriented sector-selective |
| MTNs | multilateral trade negotiations |
| NAFTA | North American Free Trade Agreement |
| NATO | North Atlantic Treaty Organization |
| NGO | nongovernmental organization |
| NICs | newly industrialized countries |
| NSC | National Security Council |
| NTBs | nontariff barriers (to trade) |
| NTR | Normal trading relations |
| OECD | Organization for Economic Cooperation and Development |
| OMB | Office of Management and Budget |
| OPEC | Organization of Petroleum Exporting Countries |
| R&D | research and development |
| RTAA | Reciprocal Trade Agreements Act |
| SII | Structural Impediments Initiative |
| SPS | sanitary and phytosanitary measures |
| TPA | Trade Promotion Authority |
| TRIMs | Trade-related Investment Measures (agreement) |
| TRIPs | Trade-related Aspects of Intellectual Property Rights (agreement) |
| TWEA | Trading with the Enemy Act |
| USTR | U.S. Trade Representative |
| VER | voluntary export restraint |
| VRA | voluntary restraint agreement |
| WTO | World Trade Organization |

Part One

---

# Overview

---

# 1   The Content and Context of Trade Policy

Foreign trade exists in two dimensions. Outwardly, it consists of economic transactions in which goods and services are exchanged for money (or other goods) by persons or entities in two countries. Inwardly, it is a political process in which difficult choices must be made among competing values, priorities, and interest groups. Whatever the level of analysis, foreign trade is important. The international exchange of goods and services has increased so much in value and volume that it has become pivotal in both the conduct of international relations and national economic performance. This chapter lays the foundation of the analytical framework used throughout the book.

## The Basic Nature of U.S. Trade Policy

Foreign trade policy is a convergence point. In the broadest sense, trade policy is the end product of governmental decisions that need to reconcile economic and political substance while seeking to advance governments' domestic and foreign concerns. These decisions are seldom taken independently of the numerous trade statutes and international agreements that play a critical role in determining the content of trade policy's substance and process. In the United States, the trade laws passed by Congress set guidelines and boundaries for the executive branch's conduct of policy. Although they are often a factor in shaping specific policy decisions, trade statutes have a larger significance: They represent a political interpretation of what good economic policy should be at a particular time.

The foreign trade policy of the United States consists of numerous pressure points but is constrained by domestic laws and international obligations. Its inconsistencies and shortcomings baffle and annoy casual observers. These negative traits can best be explained by understanding the multiple forces that constitute the guiding principles and influence day-to-day actions in U.S. trade policy. The objective of this book is to provide that understanding through a detailed explanation of what this policy is and why and how it takes the forms that it does.

*Our study's integrating theme is that the task of formulating and conducting U.S. trade policy is an important but inherently difficult and imprecise process that faces constantly changing circumstances. Trade policymaking involves reconciliation and trade-offs among a variety of economic goals and political necessities. To reach consensus on what constitutes "good policy," the executive and legislative branches of the government, as well as the private sector, inevitably must sort through numerous conflicting intellectual viewpoints, pure self-interest, domestic and international rules, and accumulated values. The necessity of making trade policy choices and promulgating rules is a political process, the economic substance notwithstanding.*

The methodology used to demonstrate this thesis and integrate the multiple components of formulating and conducting trade policy is based on synthesis. Our efforts to interpret facts and concepts rely on a diverse framework of political and economic analysis; it assumes that no single model of policymaking is universally applicable or consistently relevant to a comprehensive study of U.S. trade policy over an extended period. Depending on the issue, this book uses one or more of three vertical levels of political analysis: international, national, and individual. Similarly, the methodology uses the three major horizontal forms, or modes, of analysis in political economy: (1) rational, vigorous calculations of national or self-interests; (2) values and preconceived notions; and (3) rules and routines instilled into domestic and global institutions. As stated by Frederick W. Mayer in his study of the North American Free Trade Agreement, the overriding question is not which approach is correct, "but rather which ones are most useful for modeling the phenomena we seek to explain."[1] All these approaches play a role at different times in shaping the issues being studied here. Given our belief in the inherent heterogeneity of trade policy writ large, we prefer synthesis over pursuit of the so far futile effort to divine one integrated theory that would definitively explain past trade policy decisionmaking as well as accurately predict future policy.

U.S. trade policy pursues many goals, not all of them compatible with one another. The U.S. government (like its counterparts) professes to believe in free trade even when increasing its trade barriers. It professes to believe in a global trade regime based on universal rules while negotiating exclusionary free trade agreements with other countries. It also professes to believe in export promotion while restricting exports to one country after another. There is a method to the madness. The complexity and paradoxes of U.S. trade policy are due mainly to four principal factors, the first three of which are burdened by limited and often contradictory data:

1. the frequent conflict between economic logic and political necessity;
2. the conceptual disagreement among economists about whether an optimal trade policy is one that relies on free markets or one that incorporates repeated government intervention;
3. the intricate, ever-changing linkage between trade and other economic and political policy sectors, both domestic and foreign;
4. the diffusion of authority between the executive and legislative branches in formulating trade policy. Major limitations on presidential action are imposed by a voluminous, still-growing body of congressionally passed laws that affect all aspects of the conduct of U.S. trade relations.

The economics and politics of U.S. foreign trade policy are two distinct phenomena shaped and guided by different forces; they do not necessarily move toward the same goals for the same reasons. The disconnect between politics and economics is seen in the dramatic 1934 shift in U.S. policy priorities from a historical embrace of protectionism to a forceful pursuit of global trade liberalization. This policy about-face did not occur and continue because the scholarly output of economists succeeded in persuading official Washington that a liberal trade policy was in the national interest. Rather, the change was sustained by the emergence of a critical mass in the private sector's support for reducing U.S. trade barriers in return for enhanced opportunities to increase American exports.

In Hegelian terms, the economic thesis that a market-oriented global trading system was most compatible with U.S. economic interests started to grow increasingly dominant in the mid-1930s. The political antithesis that politicians elected to national office should protect constituents from import competition suffered a relative decline. The resulting synthesis was a reorientation of policy priorities that continues to the present. The emphasis on import barriers was abandoned. The new emphasis is on a series of legislatively approved trade liberalization initiatives, their perceived economic virtues partially constrained by legislated relief measures. The latter consist of relatively circumscribed, case-by-case provisions giving domestic interest groups the opportunity to petition for relief from alleged import-induced economic hardship or for the government's assistance in attacking foreign trade barriers.

In this chapter we establish the rationale for the content of subsequent chapters by reviewing the universal fundamentals of trade policy that influence its formulation and conduct. A concluding section deals with the unique characteristics of U.S. trade policy that differentiate it from worldwide concepts of trade policy.

## A Narrow Definition of Trade Policy

Throughout history, trade policy—in a literal, narrow sense—has consisted mainly of a constantly evolving series of official objectives, laws, and actions designed to influence the flow of imports and exports of goods and services in a manner different from what would otherwise occur in a free market. At any time, governments choose from a wide spectrum of trade policy actions that fall between total inaction and aggressive, comprehensive intervention. At one extreme, a government could adopt a completely free trade stance and consistently refuse to take any action that would directly affect the flow of its exports and imports. Under this scenario, a country would avoid all official import barriers and export controls or incentives. In addition, a country would dismiss the notion that the trade-restricting and trade-distorting policies maintained by its trading partners were economically injurious to it. Should a sovereign government ever choose this extreme policy strategy (none has), it would effectively choose to have *no* trade policy. At the other policy extreme, a government could essentially opt out of participating in the international economy by adopting pervasive, highly restrictive import barriers and by exporting little or nothing.

Defined in a narrow sense, trade policymaking in the United States (and in virtually every other country) is the act of determining the optimal point along the policy continuum illustrated in Table 1.1. Calculations of the optimal trade-off between market orientation and interventionism in pursuit of official goals must be made separately for imports and exports, the two core components of trade policy.

TABLE 1.1   Trade Policy Spectrum

| *Intrusive Government Intervention* | *Moderate Government Intervention* | *Free Market Orientation* |
|---|---|---|
| Extensive import protection; extensive export restraints; industrial policy supporting targeted industries | Ad hoc measures | Avoidance of import and export barriers; minimal governmental support of domestic industries |

*Import policy* determines the relative openness of the home market to competition from foreign-produced goods and services. It does so mainly by judging where the most economically advantageous and politically comfortable location is at any given time on a spectrum that spans two poles: (1) pursuit of "liberal" (or freer) trade based on an international division of labor; and (2) embrace of "protectionist" measures that shield some or all domestic producers from foreign competition so that existing production and jobs can be retained and, sometimes, new industries can be developed. Where on this spectrum governments and individuals decide their policy preferences lie usually reflects how they calculate winners and losers in trade relations. Economists tend to view trade as a positive-sum game in which all countries mutually benefit (see Chapter 3). Politicians and those whose profits or jobs may be threatened by imports tend to view trade as a zero-sum game in which someone gains at the expense of someone else. Erection of new import barriers under certain circumstances can be in full conformity with internationally recognized trade rules. Retaliatory import duties imposed when foreign exporters engage in recognized unfair foreign trade practices (described later in this chapter and in Chapter 7) and injure domestic producers are considered legitimate self-defense, not protectionism.

*Export policy* has three main components: (1) the use of government personnel and funds to promote foreign sales; (2) export controls that use domestic laws to restrict exports of certain goods to unfriendly countries; and (3) export enhancement efforts through the official pursuit of improved access to foreign markets. As with import policy, export policy for any given country at any given time is to be found on a continuum between a noninterventionist, free market approach and an aggressive, interventionist posture. The first approach allocates responsibility for export enhancement to the private sector and realignments of the exchange rate. The interventionist posture, in turn, can be tilted in one of two opposite directions. The first is an export-at-all-costs approach. In this instance, government officials adopt tunnel vision—to avoid being distracted by alternative strategies—and mount an extensive, expensive campaign to maximize overseas sales, presumably in an effort to achieve the largest possible trade surplus. A government tilted in the second direction embraces numerous export restraints because it places more importance on ethical and national security concerns than on maximum exports. This approach condones blocking shipments abroad as the means for pressuring foreign governments to alter what are deemed to be their undesirable political, military, or human rights policies.

Trade policy can also be divided between proactive and reactive actions. The former are initiatives conceived to advance a country's perceived self-interests. For example, a trade policy decision to impose a new import barrier to enhance a favored domestic industry is proactive (but a possible violation of the theory and practice of liberal trade). A "passive" variant of proactive trade policy would be decisions not to act; for example, rejecting pleas from a domestic industry for import protection. Sometimes, trade decisions can be considered reactive when they are taken in response to actions or policies originating in other countries (trade sanctions, for example).

Economists generally wish to maximize consumption, and virtually every one of them would agree that for maximizing efficiency and global welfare, an essentially open system that encourages trade flows is preferable to a tightly closed system that stifles trade. Nevertheless, for various reasons the political leaders of the United States and those of every other sovereign country are unwilling to accept a totally hands-off approach to trade flows. The desire of politicians to seek favor with the electorate is incompatible with their placing complete trust in the invisible hand of the market to determine the composition, volume, and value of its imports and exports of goods and services. The result is that an interventionist, market-altering strategy characterizes the conduct of all countries' trade policies. To achieve this strategy, government officials—in accordance with the terms of foreign trade statutes—make a steady stream of specific decisions, conduct endless rounds of trade negotiations with other countries, and introduce numerous operational programs to moderate imports, increase imports, promote exports, restrict exports, assist domestic producers to compete more effectively, and so on. Given constant changes in the political and economic environments, the import and export policies of the United States and most other countries are subject to constant evolution—and occasional revolution.

## Basic Trade Policy Options

All countries face the same limited menu of alternatives for a basic trade policy strategy. *Liberal or entirely free trade* policy seeks maximum reliance on market forces, rather than bureaucratic dictate, to determine the volume and composition of international trade flows. *Protectionism* seeks to maximize trade barriers. It reflects the beliefs that economic strength arises primarily from domestic production and that minimizing the social disruption associated with unrestrained competition from imports is more desirable than seeking the abstract ideal of economic efficiency. Although numerous rational alternatives exist between these two extremes, a foolproof process guaranteed to make an optimal policy choice among competing perceptions of "reality" has not been perfected.

Selecting an ideal trade policy mix is unusually difficult for the United States at the start of the twenty-first century. The unprecedented size of the trade deficit creates an enormous uncertainty concerning the degree of weakness (if any) in the U.S. trade position. Before trying to fix something, it is logical to confirm that something is wrong and then determine its source and severity.

Unfortunately, a number of unanswerable questions preclude making precise assessments of the nature and causes of a possible problem. No one knows at what dollar amount the trade deficit becomes "too big." Will the rising merchandise trade deficit eventually be offset by rising surpluses in services? Should the trade deficit be calculated primarily as a percentage of gross domestic product (GDP)? Is the size of the deficit a simple, inevitable derivative of the domestic saving-investment imbalance? If so, there is no foreign trade problem. Or is the deficit mainly the result of a secular decline in U.S. industrial competitiveness? If so, the correction once again lies not primarily in traditional trade policy tools but in internal reforms such as greater capital formation, larger increases in productivity, and improved education. Should international monetary forces, namely, dollar depreciation, be looked to as the primary means of reducing the trade deficit? How significant are foreign trade barriers, a core aspect of trade policy, and what is the best way to address trading partners' practices that are considered injurious? Different philosophies present at least three courses of action: Immediately replicate these practices in full (trade barriers, industrial policy, and so on); diplomatically request their termination; or unequivocally threaten and resort to retaliation if they do not cease.

The trade policy options that follow are offered in a nonjudgmental manner without advocating one over another and in no particular order. There is no reason to believe that U.S. trade policy needs to select just one of these options. Since the alternative choices described here are not always mutually exclusive, specific ideas from different policy scenarios are sufficiently compatible that they can be stitched together to form many combinations of overlapping foreign trade objectives and strategies. Space constraints preclude detailed discussion of potential changes in domestic policy that could or should complement potential trade policy changes.

Economists are still in the vanguard of those persons committed to the proposition that a *liberal (or free) trade* strategy makes the most sense. Liberal trade advocates believe that the theory of comparative advantage outshines all its rivals: Any country presumably maximizes its welfare by concentrating on those goods that it can produce relatively efficiently and cheaply and then exchanging them for goods that would be relatively expensive to produce at home. Free markets, not government fiat, would mainly determine the amounts, kinds, and sources of foreign-made goods available to domestic consumers. As the Nobel Prize–winning economist Paul Samuelson has written, "Free trade promotes a mutually profitable division of labor, greatly enhances the potential real national product of all nations, and makes possible higher standards of living all over the globe."[2]

The recommended action here is the pursuit of a more liberal (i.e., open) trading system through negotiations to dismantle the remaining barriers and distortions to trade. Free trade advocates argue that imposing import barriers, even if other countries do so, is tantamount to shooting oneself in the foot. The advisability of turning the other cheek to other countries' trade barriers is based on an economic argument traceable to Adam Smith in the eighteenth century: Since consumption is the sole end of production, consumers' interests come before producers' interests, especially those of relatively inefficient producers. Carried to its logical conclusion, this strategy recommends that the U.S. government take no action to offset the de facto subsidies provided to domestic consumers when imports are sold at prices below fair value. A relatively free flow of imports is also deemed beneficial because it is essential to aggressive competition in the private sector. Pressure to compete against foreign goods encourages ongoing cost reductions and productivity gains in domestic industry by reminding corporate executives and production-line workers that their future well being depends on their constant ability to innovate, increase efficiency, and produce high-quality goods.

From the end of World War II until the mid-1980s, the United States pursued freer trade exclusively on a multilateral basis within the General Agreement on Tariffs and Trade (GATT). The great virtue of multilateral trade liberalization is that by being all-encompassing, it is nondiscriminatory. Embracing *regionalism* in pursuit of freer trade is a relatively new strategy for the U.S. government (see Chapter 12). Although regional and bilateral free trade agreements risk trade diversion from efficient producers not members of a trade bloc, they are easier to negotiate (fewer countries are involved); they can completely eliminate traditional trade barriers; and they are more conducive to producing substantial agreements on new trade issues, such as free trade in services and environmental protection standards. Supporters of regional free trade areas argue that the benefits associated with their reductions of trade barriers outweigh the disadvantage of discrimination against nonmember countries.

Apparently encouraged by the idea that every and all success in reducing trade barriers is a net positive, the United States has concluded free trade agreements with Canada, Mexico, Israel, and Jordan. The potential exists for a long list of additional bilateral free trade agreements—above and beyond those under negotiation in early 2002 with Chile and Singapore—because sooner or later many other countries will consider the idea of locking in free access to the lucrative American market to be very appealing. In addition, the United States is actively participating in negotiations to create regional free trade areas in the Asia-Pacific region and in the Western Hemisphere.

Not everyone accepts multilateral and regional reductions in trade barriers as the best U.S. trade strategy. Some prefer a policy based on *protectionism*. Advocates of this approach believe that the alleged benefits of free trade are based on erroneous or anachronistic assumptions about the inescapable wisdom of the so-called invisible hand of the marketplace. Others argue that a broad-based industrial sector is a prerequisite for national economic stability and power. If one believes that domestic self-sufficiency or social harmony and equity are more important policy goals than economic efficiency and increased consumption, he or she will not likely embrace free trade.

Liberal trade skeptics in the United States caution that the elimination of remaining U.S. import barriers would disproportionately impose hardships on relatively unskilled, uneducated workers. This viewpoint does not necessarily lead to the open advocacy of comprehensive import restrictions. Instead, protectionist-leaning organizations and individuals want to put a hold on further market-opening measures and make it easier for domestic producers and workers to prove that injurious import competition justifies their getting temporary relief. No large or influential American group urges revisiting the pervasive trade barriers that spread around the world in the early 1930s, making a bad economic situation far worse (and giving protectionism a bad name).

A relatively recent policy proposal that sidesteps the negative connotations of straightforward protectionism is *managed trade,* an amorphous nonfree market trade philosophy advocating a more interventionist role in economic matters for government. One objective of managed trade is to prevent excessive import competition in a limited number of sensitive product sectors that are too important to put in harm's way from imports. U.S. supporters of managed trade claim that foreign governments' targeting favored industries for growth and protecting them from import competition have made obsolete the continuation of the allegedly misplaced U.S. commitment to a trade ideology based strictly on laissez-faire concepts. The futile effort by the United States to construct the elusive first-best policy of a universally free market–based international trading system, it has been argued, not only puts American industry at a disadvantage, but "also leaves the world trading system with a dishonest and inefficient blend of subsidy, suboptimal investment, and subterfuge."[3] U.S. acceptance of a managed trade strategy allegedly would add coherence to the existing U.S. pattern of imposing import restraints in a manner that many consider to be hypocritical and ineffective. Past and current departures by the United States from its liberal trade stance have been characterized as being implemented with guilt, poorly thought out, lacking in long-term strategic purpose, and "generally not helpful either to the trading system or to America's own economic self-interest."[4]

Not all trade policy is based on import strategy. *Aggressive unilateralism* (sometimes called bilateralism) focuses on the logic of the United States demanding "reciprocity"—the attainment of access to foreign markets comparable in degree to the presumably more open U.S. market (see the discussion of the Section 301 provision in Chapter 9). This strategy was an outgrowth of the assumption that the most effective means of eliminating the massive U.S. trade deficit is to increase exports, not reduce imports. Although it does include the genuine threat of retaliatory import barriers if other countries refuse to reduce their trade barriers, the clearly stated priority of U.S. efforts to gain improved access to foreign markets is to expand trade and secure more open markets overseas—not to close American markets.

Opposition to this strategy was and is based on the belief that it is an excessively aggressive approach in which the less-than-free-trade United States decides to act as plaintiff, prosecution, judge, and jury to decide unilaterally which foreign trade barriers are unacceptable and must be phased out. Most committed liberal traders abhor the possibility that failed diplomacy—a refusal of the targeted country to offer concessions—could result in a mutually injurious spiral of retaliation and counter-retaliation.

*Results-oriented trade policy* is another contemporary trade policy proposal; it combines the tenets of aggressive unilateralism and managed trade. All these proposals share the common intellectual heritage of being primarily a response to the "Japanese challenge." The anger and fear directed at Japan were by far the most important instigators of new U.S. trade strategy ideas devised between the mid-1980s and the early 1990s. Critics contended that the world's greatest contemporary industrial miracle—Japan—succeeded largely by combining a unique quasimarket variant of guided capitalism with a pursuit of adversarial, nonliberal trade practices. To them, the appropriate U.S. policy response was not simply to chant the mantra of free trade.

Results-oriented trade strategy (now largely ignored) "invited" the Japanese to accept a specific numerical target, such as a designated increase in dollar terms or in market share, for specified imported goods. The underlying theory is that Japan's market is characterized by so much collusion that traditional market opening measures (i.e., a change in the rules) generate insufficient increases in imports. Advocates of this strategy argue that it makes more sense to give the Japanese specific quantitative targets and tell them to achieve the stipulated import expansion in any way they see fit. The definitive example of U.S. fulfillment of a results-oriented trade policy was the bilateral semiconductor agreement signed with Japan in 1986. A key provision informally and secretly established a 20 percent market share target (approximately twice the existing figure) in Japan for foreign-made semiconductors.

Substituting quantitative targets for normative behavior has been criticized on several grounds. Allegedly, it fosters the creation of new foreign cartels to attain stipulated increases in imports; it wrongly presupposes that the U.S. government knows exactly what the appropriate minimum market share for a given product should be in a specific foreign market; and it arrogantly assumes that the United States need offer no quid pro quo to the other country.

Another quite different trade strategy, advocated less and less since the U.S. high-tech surge of the mid-1990s, would entail meeting the perceived threat of foreign government-business cooperation through a *proactive science and technology policy.* This option, a euphemism for "industrial policy," would seek to protect and enhance the international competitiveness of U.S. high-technology industries. The latter, according to "strategic trade" theory, are disproportionately important to the future strength of the U.S. economy because of high-tech's unrivaled contribution to private research and development (R&D) spending, unusually high social returns from innovations and technological advances that spill over to other sectors, the above-average wages they pay to their highly skilled workers, their above-average rate of return on capital, and so on. Government financial support is allegedly necessary to compensate for the extraordinarily high cost structure of cutting-edge high-tech industries, a result of the high risks of failure and the high fixed costs associated with developing new products.

Before becoming the Clinton administration's first chairperson of the Council of Economic Advisers (CEA), Laura D'Andrea Tyson summarized the argument for the interventionist option:

> Technology-intensive industries violate the assumptions of free trade theory and the static economic concepts that are the traditional basis for U.S. trade policy. In such industries, costs fall and product quality improves as the scale of production increases, the returns to technological advance create beneficial spillovers for other economic activities, and barriers to entry generate market structures rife with first-mover advantages and strategic behavior. A nation's competitive position in industries with these characteristics is less a function of its national factor endowments and more a function of strategic interactions between its firms and government, and between them and the firms and governments of other nations.[5]

Critics of the activist-government approach to enhanced U.S. industrial competitiveness dismiss the idea that the U.S. government can pick winners and losers in different economic sectors, a task allegedly best left to private markets. There are no unambiguous economic criteria for selecting economically strategic technologies and rejecting pleas of special interest groups for government nurturing. Opponents argue that an industry viewed as having a bright future can raise capital from private investors and is not in need of federal subsidies. Two Brookings Institution economists warned that given the nature of the U.S. political system, "any attempt to divide the pie would be based not on strategic economic and trade criteria, but on political trade-offs that would reflect lobbying skills."[6]

A major new option for trade policy is the incorporation of social issues into traditional rules governing imports and exports. The extent to which *environmental and labor standards* belong in future trade agreements, for the purpose of constraining the alleged harm unleashed by purely capitalist pursuits, is part of the larger debate over globalization and its effects (see Chapter 13). Pressure to make social issues an integral part of trade policy is a function of the growing activism and political clout of nongovernmental organizations.

No one in principle opposes the ultimate objectives of cleaner air, water, and land, or the prudent management of nonrenewable natural resources. However, there is a heated debate over whether the pure pursuit of economic growth and free trade unfairly skews income distribution in favor of a very few, very wealthy persons and dangerously pollutes the earth's environment. The "race to the bottom" thesis envisions trade flows being altered as companies shift production to countries that are relatively lax in enforcing laws to protect the environment and the basic rights of workers. Most environmental groups view the liberal trade orientation of the global trade rules, originally embedded in the General Agreement on Tariffs and Trade (GATT) and later incorporated into the World Trade Organization (WTO), as a threat to the enforcement of national environmental protection regulations. This fear was reinforced by several decisions of the WTO's dispute settlement mechanism (see Chapters 8 and 13). Environmentalists want the world trading system to incorporate a strong awareness of the potentially negative effects of commerce on the world's ecosystems, natural resources, and endangered species. They and their interest groups oppose an international regime that would force the United States to relax the enforcement of its environmental protection laws and descend to a lax, least-common-denominator global environmental protection standard.

Liberal trade advocates and most business advocates strongly disagree. They point to data showing that higher incomes in a given country are linked with increased popular pressure on behalf of antipollution efforts and the economic ability to pay for them. They claim that labor standards are best designed and enforced in the International Labor Organization (ILO), not the WTO where the requisite expertise and jurisdiction are both absent. In addition to questioning the inherent wisdom of incorporating these standards into trade agreements, this viewpoint warns that the pursuit of desirable social goals can be used as a subterfuge for a new strand of protectionism. Imports could be restricted not by traditional barriers but by having the wealthy industrialized countries diminish the competitiveness of developing countries by imposing vigorous, expensive-to-meet labor and environmental standards on them.

## Politics and Economics:
## Trade Policy As Inter-Disciplinary Phenomenon

If politics is about making important and difficult decisions affecting national welfare, then the trade policy process in the United States and elsewhere has been politicized. The foreign trade sector is an increasingly important variable in the performance of domestic economies, and the ability of national politicians to remain in office is closely linked to domestic economic performance, mainly the ability to deliver on promises of more jobs and less inflation. Conflicting opinions about optimal trade policies in response to an open-ended number of contingencies have assured a constant procession of difficult decisions. The foreign trade interests of industry, workers, farmers, consumers, foreign policy, and major campaign contributors seldom coincide. Should a government declare that one of these constituencies ought to be given priority attention, the nature of trade policy would move in certain preordained directions. In point of fact, modern U.S. trade policy has seldom made such an unequivocal designation of a favored constituency, and when it has, circumstances changed and the "most favored constituency" eventually was stripped of its status. Compromise has been the more frequent mode of policymaking, mainly because it is the most effective way to minimize anger and maximize at least grudging acceptance of official decisions by a majority of members of a majority of constituencies.

Inspired by certain cherished economic principles, observing the need to be responsive to domestic and foreign political pressures, and operating within legislative constraints, U.S. trade policymakers are confronted by the need to make an endless series of value judgments. Usually, these decisions must be made in situations where the "correct" response is more a perception than an empirically demonstrable or self-evident truth. Virtually every significant trade issue will generate two or more rational alternatives for the policy option that will best serve the national interest. Political necessity and economic logic frequently are not congruent. In a sense, trade policy is the cumulative outgrowth of responses by usually well-intentioned policymakers to a barrage of intellectual and emotional stimuli and to a nonstop array of unique circumstances. Consistency, coherence, and wisdom are therefore frequently in short supply in a process involving many difficult choices.

Jobs, incomes, production, profits, and investment decisions at home and abroad are inevitably affected by what is and is not imported and exported. Ostensibly economic actions therefore closely dovetail with the classic definition of politics: the determination of who gets what, and how, and when. Most major decisions on trade policy create winners and losers at home and in affected foreign countries.[7] The ability of consumers to enjoy inexpensive goods produced abroad that compete directly with domestic production comes at least partially at the expense of fellow citizens' jobs or salary levels. Conversely, import restrictions that prevent lower-cost foreign-made goods from disrupting favored domestic sectors are often tantamount to governmental subsidies bestowed on relatively inefficient producers. When consumers are forced to pay for more expensive domestic goods because cheaper imports are limited, the economic equivalent of a domestic tax has been imposed that also penalizes foreign producers. Foreign trade also affects global politics. Extensive commercial relations between countries create networks of interdependence, cooperation, and friendship. At the other extreme, the exclusion of commercial relations between countries can create divisiveness and hostility.

In the absence of applicable universally accepted truths about what constitutes economic logic, trade policy should be viewed as the end result of imperfect choices about economic options—a political process. Trade policy is a subjective thing. Even clear-cut decisions that are popular in one country may generate radically different opinions when evaluated by foreign cultures.

Trade policy dilemmas abound because any given trade action usually involves contradictory rather than complementary effects on political and economic as well as domestic and external objectives. In short, the impact of a typical trade action is favorable to some, detrimental to others. If one accepts the thesis that the "central feature of American politics is the fragmentation and dispersion of power and authority,"[8] it is obvious that the U.S. pursuit of a liberal trading system is perpetually saddled with policy compromises. Seldom explained in the traditional debate about freer trade versus protectionism is the U.S. government's political need to imbue its trade policy with a sense of fair play, balance, and equity that is sufficient to prevent the formation of an overpowering anti-import coalition of aggrieved interest groups.

The goal of maximizing economic efficiency is in constant tension with the political necessity of responding to the complaints of businesses and workers injured by import competition. All governments feel compelled to operate programs designed to assure that the losers from increased imports are not too numerous, do not suffer too much, and are not displaced too rapidly. Since the end of World War II, Congress has frequently taken it upon itself to expand and alter U.S. trade statutes to guarantee that domestic companies and workers have a credible opportunity to seek relief from import-induced injury. Congress has been equally concerned with assuring American companies the opportunity to request the executive branch to act on their behalf to reduce foreign barriers against their exports. Within these same trade laws, Congress has repeatedly delegated power to the administration to pursue the long-term goal of a more liberal international trade order.

Trade policy decisions are not made in a vacuum. The full scope of trade relations is best described as a diverse, expanding agenda of issues that is seen at the convergence of four critical policy spokes:

- domestic politics
- international politics (foreign policy)
- domestic economic performance
- international economic efficiency

Linkage is inescapable. Virtually every major foreign trade decision simultaneously affects the performance of the U.S. economy (in employment, income, price stability, etc.), other countries' economies, the welfare of domestic interest groups and factions, and political relations with foreign countries.

The already thin dividing line between trade policy and domestic economic policy management continues to blur. Trade policy now overlaps an expanding cluster of economic issues that have traditionally been considered "domestic." These issues include monetary and fiscal (tax) policies; industrial policy measures such as corporate tax incentives and research subsidies; regulatory provisions covering environmental protection, worker safety, and health standards; agricultural subsidies; labor conditions and training programs; and the enforcement of antitrust laws. The old foreign policy adage that countries do not intrude into the internal affairs of other countries is obsolete. Whether deliberate or inadvertent, these ostensibly internal economic measures influence the cost structure of a country's products and therefore the value and product composition of its foreign trade flows.

Another boundary that continues to blur is the one between national security ("high" foreign policy) objectives and international commercial ("low" foreign policy) objectives. There is a growing consensus that economic strength is now an integral part of the national security equation. Defense of domestic political values (e.g., opposition to human rights abuses) can lead to trade sanctions that could damage U.S. political and economic relations with other countries (see Chapter 9). A hardline defense of domestic U.S. industrial interests can put the United States on a collision course with a close overseas military ally. Consider the priorities of President George W. Bush's national security advisers in 2001 in responding to two new, sensitive trade matters. They feared that the imposition of escape clause-related trade barriers to help the distressed domestic steel industry would strain relations with steel-exporting countries, such as Great Britain and Russia, that were making major contributions to the American military effort in Afghanistan. Similarly, these national security advisers relegated domestic political concerns to second place in assessing the optimal U.S. response to a trade demand by Pakistan, another key ally, for which the hostilities in Afghanistan were an economic burden. The foreign policy perspective naturally endorsed the approval of that country's request that the U.S. government reduce tariffs on Pakistani textile and apparel exports to offset the rising tendency of American importers to cancel orders and look for more secure overseas sources farther away from a war zone.

The axiom that trade policy will be made in a manner consistent with the "national interest" is too vague to provide a sophisticated understanding of the subject. Government agencies seldom find it easy to agree on which policy in any given situation would maximize the national interest, and they must often adopt cumbersome compromises. Attaining a relatively open trading system that imposes few barriers to an efficient global allocation of resources while inflicting minimum dislocations on domestic producers is a good all-encompassing definition of the national interest in trade policy. However, it is too general and idealistic to provide a practical guideline for predicting or explaining individual policy decisions. In any event, economic efficiency must be viewed as only one possible priority in foreign trade. Social equity and national security are worthy contenders for top priority—depending on one's priorities and values.

Definitions of "good" trade policy are shaped by the value judgments of individual observers. To some, the international flow of goods and services is mainly an inherent part of domestic social and political policies; to others, it is mainly a dimension of foreign policy. Workers, business executives, and politicians tend to view trade as a zero-sum game in which domestic interests compete head-on with foreigners for sales and jobs. Economists have traditionally viewed trade as a positive-sum gain and a means of increasing efficiency by allocating the world's finite resources to their most productive use, thereby maximizing production and consumption. Foreign affairs specialists would identify with the perspective of Cordell Hull, U.S. secretary of state from 1933 to 1944, who maintained that the trading system either supports or threatens a peaceful international political system, depending on whether governments are moving toward a more open or a more restrictive flow of trade. In fact, trade policy is all of the above—and more. As already suggested, there are many layers of reality in international trade policy.

## Why Countries Import, and Why They Do Not

All countries import goods and services from others because every country realizes that the alternative, autarky (the heretofore unsuccessful pursuit of economic self-sufficiency), would leave its national economy relatively poorer and less efficient. All governments officially endorse foreign trade, but not on the basis of altruism. They believe that being part of what is known as the international division of labor is cost effective; that is, over time, more benefits are received than costs are incurred.

Nevertheless, bitter opposition inevitably arises among the political, business, and social leaders of all countries concerning the wisdom and equity of allowing the unlimited importing of goods made more cheaply in other countries. This explains the decision by all sovereign governments to impose some constraints on imports that compete with domestic production rather than to adopt the aforementioned option of a pure free trade policy.

On one level, economically advanced countries do practice a largely hands-off approach. Import policy is seldom applicable in situations involving "noncompetitive" imports—goods that either are not available in the home market or are deemed by economic planners to be something that could not practically be produced domestically. For example, to the extent that they can afford them, countries are usually content to import foreign-produced natural resources (e.g., petroleum) and manufactured goods such as supercomputers and jumbo jet passenger planes. Purely economic considerations usually dominate as long as imported goods cause no harm to domestic producers. The United States imposes no trade barriers on such goods as bananas, coffee, and manganese because there is no domestic constituency to plead for import relief.

The public's desire to import begins with the simple economic decision of domestic consumers to favor foreign-produced goods over domestic equivalents. One of the most common reasons for such a preference is a lower price, presumably the result of greater efficiency and lower production costs abroad rather than unfair business practices. Importing can also be motivated by the desire to obtain higher-quality goods or the need to offset goods in short supply relative to domestic demand (the United States is the world's largest oil importer despite being one of the world's largest oil producers).

Importing goods, competitive or not, indirectly serves two international policy objectives. First, there is the old axiom in international economics that trade is a two-way street. If other countries are to be able and willing to buy your goods, they must be allowed to earn foreign exchange by exporting to your country. Second, the basic foreign policy goal of enhanced political friendships with other countries is served through expanding trade relationships.

The so-called dynamic benefits of trade provide yet another rationale for a country to import. When countries join together in a free trade area and phase out trade barriers, the result, other things being equal, will be what economic theory sees as a virtuous cycle that enhances production efficiency over several years. Companies either sink or swim in an enlarged market that encourages the cycle of increased trade flows, stable or lower prices, increased real incomes, and increased domestic economic growth. Guesstimates of increases in GDP were regularly included in forecasts of the effects of creating the single European market and the North American free trade area.[9]

A government's desire to limit imports of goods and services that are in direct competition with domestic producers begins with a fundamental political reality: Foreigners do not vote in one's own country. Nothing in the theory of free trade says that *everyone* in a given country will benefit from it. In the short run, there are losers whenever imports increase fast enough relative to domestic production that they cause the loss of jobs, the bankruptcies of companies, or the decimation of entire industries.[10] No democratically elected government can continuously turn a deaf ear to pleas by workers and companies for protection from economic harm caused by imports. Nor can it totally ignore the social and economic costs involved when a community is threatened with the loss of its largest factory to import competition. It is therefore not surprising that international trade guidelines permit *temporary* import restraints when increased imports cause or threaten to cause "serious injury" to domestic producers. Countries have a clearly articulated legal right under the provisions of the WTO to invoke the so-called safeguard mechanism (see Chapters 7 and 8). Presumably, producers affected by import restraints will use their temporary respite from intensifying import competition to restructure and modernize themselves and emerge strong enough to hold their own against foreign competition.

The international trade regime countenances other contingencies involving *fair* foreign competition in which temporary import restraints are legally justifiable, including:

- the promotion of "infant industries," whereby governments seek to foster the creation and maturation of new industries that would otherwise have no chance to develop in the face of existing levels of import competition;
- the preservation of industries that a country deems vital to its national security;
- limitations imposed by a deteriorating balance of payments position, in which the declining earnings of foreign exchange inhibit a country's ability to pay for all its import needs.

Contemporary international trade rules also consider it legitimate and appropriate to impose import barriers to negate the three major *unfair* trading practices (see Chapter 7) by other countries that injure or threaten to injure domestic producers:

- dumping, or the overseas sales of goods at less than fair value, either because export prices are set below domestic market prices in the exporting country or because export prices are below production costs;
- governmental subsidies that distort market forces and allow exporters to reduce prices from levels that would have prevailed in the absence of such subsidies;
- violations of intellectual property rights, or the unauthorized use (in this instance by a foreign company) of a company's patents, trademarks, copyrights, and business secrets.

The use of import barriers for retaliatory and political purposes constitutes a final category of acceptable trade-restrictive behavior. Import controls have the effect of denying foreign currency earnings to countries guilty of such political transgressions as posing a military threat to others, violating the human rights of their own citizens, and flouting international law (such as Iran's seizure of U.S. diplomats in 1979). Import sanctions may be imposed in a range extending from a unilateral basis up to collective action taken by all member countries of the United Nations (such as economic sanctions against South Africa in the 1980s). Import barriers are also imposed tit-for-tat for commercial reasons (sometimes in conformity with internationally accepted trade practices and sometimes not) as retaliation against countries (e.g., Japan) for which import barriers have been judged deleterious to the exports of others.

## Why Countries Export, and Why They Do Not

A thriving export sector brings tremendous joy to political leaders. Although abandoned by most economists in the late eighteenth century, the theory of *mercantilism* (which equates a trade surplus with national wealth and power) is still embraced by almost everyone else.[11] Surpluses in the balance of payments no longer automatically trigger an offsetting inflow of shiny gold bars as they did under the gold standard, but the many positive economic trends associated with export growth explain why politicians (and workers) still maintain a love affair with exports. A sustained increase in the volume of exports will usually generate new jobs that pay above-average wages (because export workers usually have above-average productivity), increase corporate profits, increase tax revenues, encourage capital expenditures on new plant and capital equipment, and enhance the image of domestic economic vigor. Exports also add to foreign exchange earnings and support the strength of a country's currency in the foreign exchange market. Because exporters tend to be relatively large, efficient, and influential producers, politicians are happier (and, presumably, more re-electable) when these politically potent interests are happy.

In a world economy increasingly dominated by high-technology goods having high fixed costs (costly research and development [R&D] programs and expensive production facilities, for example), exports have another crucial economic role to play.

High-tech companies must achieve *economies of scale* through maximum production and maximum sales. The greater the sales volume, the easier it is for a company to amortize (i.e., spread) high fixed costs and to reduce unit prices. To realize maximum sales volume, manufacturers cannot be limited to one home market. The pursuit of economies of scale explains the move by all large industrial companies in all industrialized countries to adopt global marketing strategies. The disappearance of national markets is epitomized by the hypothetical Belgian producer of machine tools that cannot possibly achieve optimal sales volume by selling only in its small home market. Even the $10 trillion-plus U.S. economy is too confining to absorb efficiently the enormous fixed costs incurred by the high-tech producers of such capital-intensive goods as jumbo jets and supercomputers. In sum, a successful global marketing effort is a necessity for high-tech manufacturers wishing to enjoy growth, profits, and longevity. The almost certain alternative to generating a large volume of international sales is to watch lower-cost, higher-volume, globally active competitors steadily decimate a stay-at-home company's market share.

The recognized advantages of exporting have resulted in a standard array of official export promotion programs maintained by all industrialized countries. These programs differ only in their magnitude and effectiveness, which are largely determined by budgetary resources and the bureaucracy's commitment to the business community, respectively. Perhaps the most important export promotion program is officially subsidized export financing facilities (in the United States this function is rendered mainly by the Export-Import Bank). These programs provide the foreign buyers of a country's goods with guarantees of commercial bank loans and concessional, or below market, lending terms. If an export order runs in the tens of millions of dollars, as it would with jumbo jets and nuclear power plants, the buyer's ability to obtain a low-interest loan that requires a relatively small down payment and has an extended repayment period often determines which country gets the export order.

Governments also promote exports by sponsoring trade missions and trade fairs in foreign markets and by providing export awareness facilities at home to small companies that are new to exporting. Some countries provide direct funding or tax deductions to defray expenses incurred by companies in connection with overseas market development efforts. Commercial attachés stationed in embassies and consulates overseas provide expertise in how foreign markets operate to potential exporters, conduct overseas marketing surveys, and ferret out and address foreign import barriers. On a macroeconomic scale, governments can indirectly promote exports by minimizing the costs of capital through low interest rates, providing favorable corporate tax treatment, and keeping their currency low in value relative to other currencies. (Hence U.S. economic officials periodically made public statements in the 1970s and 1980s to "talk down" the exchange rate of the dollar by encouraging market sentiment to move against the dollar). Most pillars of industrial policy, such as subsidies and lax antitrust enforcement, can also contribute to export expansion.

On the other side of the coin are programs involving export restraints and embargoes, most of which are foreign policy measures designed to influence the political behavior of other countries. Except in special circumstances, however, this option is a disdained aspect of ongoing export policy—in every country except the United States.

The one purely economic reason in U.S. law to restrain or prohibit export shipments occurs in the event of anticipated or actual domestic shortages, when large foreign sales would aggravate rapidly rising prices at home. In addition to wanting to contain domestic inflation, a government may decide to conserve nonrenewable raw materials by limiting their export. Exports (usually of primary products) may also be limited to maintain or boost the price of goods. This ploy is best exemplified by the occasional efforts of major oil-producing countries to limit production and foreign sales.

Politicians and businesspeople are otherwise ecstatic about export maximization, but foreign policy practitioners, especially those in the United States, perceive a high-level national security need for a policy denying exports of goods capable of enhancing the military might of unfriendly countries. Although the industrialized countries agree that the spread of dangerous weapons should be restricted, there has been no agreement about how far to extend export controls to so-called dual-use goods such as computers, telecommunications equipment, and even trucks—all of which are commercial goods but can be adapted to military purposes. Export controls are also used as a middle-ground foreign policy strategy falling between inaction and military attack; as noted later, the United States has been the most frequent practitioner of this approach. In theory, the disruption of trade can wreak sufficient havoc on the economy of a targeted country that it is compelled to alter or cease certain domestic or external policies deemed by embargoing countries to be in violation of the norms of acceptable state behavior (e.g., human rights violations or state-sponsored terrorism).

Orderly marketing agreements are a final example of export restraints. In the 1970s and early 1980s, the United States and what was then known as the European Community frequently sought the middle ground of negotiated protectionism as a politically attractive compromise between free trade and unilaterally imposed import barriers. This tactic took the form of applying pressure on other countries, usually in East Asia, to agree "voluntarily" to restrain their exports of manufactured goods. In return for this concession, exporting countries secured a voice in establishing annual export ceilings. The alternative was to face harsher, unilateral restrictions imposed by countries deeming it necessary to restrain import growth for goods such as textiles, steel, and automobiles.

## The Unique Aspects of U.S. Trade Policy

There are several economic and political idiosyncrasies in U.S. import and export policies that differentiate them in many ways from the trade policies of other industrialized countries. As a consequence, the basic principles of U.S. trade attitudes and actions discussed in subsequent chapters cannot always be extrapolated to provide an explanation of how and why other countries formulate trade policies as they do.

In the first place, shared political authority imposes a unique balancing act in formulating and administering U.S. trade policy. The constitutionally mandated separation of powers among branches of government assures that the joint roles of the executive and legislative branches (and occasionally the judicial branch), as well as the number of laws guiding executive branch behavior, are unlike anything found in any other country. One of the most common misperceptions about U.S. trade policy is that the president is fully in charge and does as he sees fit. In fact, presidential trade power is legally limited to the authority Congress specifically consents to transfer through trade legislation (see Chapters 2 and 5).

The politics of U.S. trade policy are reinforced by the divergent, deeply rooted attitudes that the two branches of government harbor toward trade flows. When considering trade legislation, the legislative branch tends to place the burden of proof on interest groups trying to make a case for additional trade liberalization. The executive branch usually does just the opposite: It tends to place the burden of proof on interest groups trying to make a case for protectionist policies. Congress is relatively more sympathetic to complaints by domestic constituents alleging that they are being injured by increased import competition. Most members of Congress are amenable to assuring that administrative procedures (described in Chapter 7) are readily available for addressing "justifiable" demands from the private sector for import relief. Conversely, the executive branch is predisposed to favor the global priority of trade liberalization and to require groups seeking import barriers to make a convincing economic (or political) argument before acting on their behalf. On the export side, Congress has placed the burden of proof on those who advocate sanctions limiting foreign sales, while the executive branch has frequently put foreign policy ahead of promoting export shipments.

A second differentiating factor contributing to a unique U.S. approach to trade policy is that exports and imports expressed as percentages of U.S. GDP are still relatively small and remain the lowest of the major industrialized countries as well as one of the lowest in the world. Despite their large absolute size, external economic transactions do not loom nearly as large as a variable in influencing total domestic economic activity in the United States as they do in Canada, Western Europe, and Japan. Whereas U.S. merchandise exports accounted for just over 7 percent of GDP in 2000, the comparable figures for Germany and Canada were 29 and 39 percent, respectively.[12]

Three specific and unique aspects of U.S. import policy can be identified. The first is a relatively high receptivity to imports, the singular international role of the dollar, and the relative lack of U.S. domestic economic planning. Compared to most sovereign countries, the United States has a high marginal propensity to import (the proportion of an increase in national income that is spent on foreign goods) and a relatively high tolerance for imports that inflict dislocations on domestic industries. The first explanation of this unusual import receptivity (and of the even more unusual U.S. priorities in the export sector described subsequently) is the influence of the residual status of the United States as an international economic superpower. In pursuit of what political scientists call "hegemonic stability," global superpowers in the nineteenth and twentieth centuries—the United Kingdom and the United States, respectively—demonstrated a high degree of willingness to make foreign trade sacrifices by maintaining relatively low import barriers. Both hegemons used their influence to pursue a less restrictive trading system. A liberal trading order was viewed as cost-effective because it enhanced global political stability and economic prosperity without generating a significant increase in import competition into their own strong, competitive domestic economies.

Second, for more than half a century, U.S. tolerance of imported goods has been strengthened by an important international monetary phenomenon: the unique role of the dollar as the principal currency for international reserves and transactions. Foreign citizens and governments have been willing to hold dollar-denominated assets and then either invest portions of them in the United States or lend them back. The result is that the United States has assumed a unique financial position since the end of World War II: *It is the only country that can pay for all of its imports by using its own currency.* The United States does not have to earn foreign currency to finance a current account (goods and services) deficit. The rest of the world must earn hard currency (mostly dollars) to pay for imports the old-fashioned way by first exporting goods and services or by borrowing foreign currency. The United States is unique in the relative ease with which it can finance the difference between its imports and exports of goods and services; it simply attracts or borrows back from overseas the large amounts of its own currency, dollars, that have moved into foreign hands in payment for imports. Since President Richard Nixon closed the gold window in 1971, the country has not needed to fear the loss of gold reserves—even in the face of what have been the world's most persistent and largest current account deficits.

The dominant economic question here is whether significant dollar depreciation and higher interest rates—both economically undesirable trends—may become necessary to attract the net capital inflows from abroad required to finance the extraordinarily large current account deficits recorded since the mid-1990s. No problem existed (as of the early years of the new millennium) because of two factors. Foreign investors poured huge amounts of investment capital into the booming U.S. economy to buy stocks and bonds and to acquire companies. In addition, most other countries at least indirectly welcomed the contribution that the soaring American appetite for imports made to their GDP and exports. As long as adequate foreign capital continues to pour in, the United States faces no urgent need to reduce or eliminate its record-setting current account deficit.

A third unique characteristic of American import policy is that it is disconnected from domestic economic policy far more than it is in most countries. The U.S. government extends import relief only sporadically and usually only after domestic industries experience severe or unfair import competition. Relief is almost always provided in response to short-term problems and interest group pressures rather than as a long-term vision of domestic economic development. This situation is perpetuated in part by the U.S. ideological predilection toward free market competition, consumer sovereignty, and maximum consumption. Another contributing factor is the economic policy rule of thumb that a government maintains a cohesive, consistent import policy strategy roughly in proportion to the extent that the government is engaged in domestic economic planning and implementation of an industrial policy aimed at enhanced competitiveness and full employment. Because U.S. trade policies are less proactive and less comprehensive than those found in many other countries, they mirror the relatively low-intensity approach taken by the U.S. government toward the larger issue of domestic economic policy planning and intervention. If a government is uncomfortable about intervening to promote favored domestic industries, it is defensive about introducing policies providing import protection and export assistance to special interests.

Trade policies in countries such as Japan are afforded greater importance because these countries have a domestic "vision" and trade flows have a direct effect on achieving the country's top policy priority—a strong domestic economic performance. Conversely, the United States historically has responded to unacceptable import pressure through statutory provisions and spasmodic, often poorly reasoned, politically induced protectionist measures. The latter do not reflect an integrating economic theme or strategic plan to maximize industrial competitiveness.

The unique nature of U.S. export policy centers on the unusually schizophrenic nature of U.S. government attitudes toward it (see Chapter 9). All administrations in the post–World War II era have paid lip service to the goal of increasing U.S. exports. But these same administrations have repeatedly refused to make export promotion actions a top priority. Virtually every other country seeks to maximize exports with a feverish zeal that borders on overt mercantilism. But the U.S. government has been in a league of its own in two respects: (1) its willingness to subordinate export growth to restrictive export controls and trade sanctions intended to advance foreign policy and human rights goals, and (2) its reluctance to use government funds to provide subsidized export finance (i.e., generous loan terms) to potential foreign customers of U.S. goods. Much of the explanation for the uniquely relaxed U.S. government attitudes about the need to maximize exports comes from the same ideological, foreign policy, and international monetary reasons just mentioned as being responsible for the relatively high U.S. tolerance for imports.

Yet another distinction of U.S. export policy since the late 1970s has been the aggressive attacks on trade barriers restricting the access of certain American goods to foreign markets. Ironically, almost all these efforts (see Chapter 9), which include threats of retaliation if other countries refuse to respond to U.S. requests to reduce specified barriers, have been directed at countries friendly to the United States but unappreciative of unilateral U.S. judgments about what constitutes an appropriate degree of reciprocity (i.e., relative market openness in other countries).

## Conclusions

U.S. foreign trade policy encompasses economics and political science; it has flexible boundaries and an expanding content. Like all countries' trade policy, it demonstrates few absolute truths and many differences of opinion. Trade policy everywhere is an economic process in the first instance. However, it is ultimately a political process for several reasons. Trade policy puts a premium on judgment rather than on scientific vigor; it helps and hurts the fortunes of different sectors of the domestic populace; and in the United States, the complex formula for power sharing between the executive and legislative branches necessitates an elaborate system of negotiated consensus-seeking. Trade statutes exercise significant influence on the formulation and conduct of U.S. trade policy. Trade laws, however, are a subordinate variable. They are only a formal articulation of a consensus that has been shaped by the synthesis of the two dominant variables: political and economic forces.

To understand the objectives, successes, failures, inconsistencies, and limitations of U.S. trade policy, one needs to understand and never lose sight of the array of economic, political, and legal factors simultaneously involved. These include the economic logic for promoting and controlling imports and exports, the political realities affecting decisionmaking in what ostensibly is an economic realm, and the laws setting parameters for executive branch behavior in carrying out U.S. trade policies. After outlining the history of these policies, we provide a detailed examination of economic, political, and statutory fundamentals. We conclude the book by integrating these three themes in pursuit of comprehensive explanations—not criticisms—of the major contemporary trade policy issues facing the United States.

## For Further Reading

Bhagwati, Jagdish. *Protectionism*. Cambridge, Mass.: MIT Press, 1988.

*Brookings Trade Forum*. Published annually by the Brookings Institution.

Freiden, Jeffrey, and David Lake, eds. *International Political Economy: Perspectives on Global Power and Wealth*. 4th ed. Boston: Bedford/St. Martin's, 2000.

Gilpin, Robert. *The Political Economy of International Relations*. Princeton: Princeton University Press, 1987.

Krueger, Anne O. *American Trade Policy: A Tragedy in the Making*. Washington, D.C.: The American Enterprise Institute Press, 1995.

Krugman, Paul. "Is Free Trade Passé?" *Journal of Economic Perspectives* 1 (fall 1987): 131–143.

_____. *The Age of Diminished Expectations: U.S. Economic Policy in the 1990s*. Cambridge, Mass.: MIT Press, 1990.

Lawrence, Robert Z., and Charles L. Schultze, eds. *An American Trade Strategy: Options for the 1990s*. Washington, D.C.: Brookings Institution, 1990.

Low, Patrick. *Trading Free: The GATT and U.S. Trade Policy*. New York: Twentieth Century Fund Press, 1993.

Meier, Gerald M. *The International Environment of Business*. New York: Oxford University Press, 1998.

Spero, Joan Edelman, and Jeffrey Hart. *The Politics of International Economic Relations*. 5th ed. New York: St. Martin's Press, 1997.

Tyson, Laura D'Andrea. *Who's Bashing Whom? Trade Conflict in High-Technology Industries*. Washington, D.C.: Institute for International Economics, 1992.

Walters, Robert S., and David Blake. *The Politics of Global Economic Relations*. 4th ed. Englewood Cliffs, N.J.: Prentice-Hall, 1992.

## Notes

1. Frederick M. Mayer, *Interpreting NAFTA: The Science and Art of Political Analysis* (New York: Columbia University Press, 1998), 12–13.

2. As quoted in John Jackson, *The World Trading System* (Cambridge, Mass.: MIT Press, 1992), 8.

3. Robert Kuttner, *Managed Trade and Economic Sovereignty* (Washington, D.C.: Economic Policy Institute, 1989), ii.

4. Ibid., 2.

5. Laura D'Andrea Tyson, *Who's Bashing Whom? Trade Conflict in High-Technology Industries* (Washington, D.C.: Institute for International Economics, 1992), 3.

6. Robert Z. Lawrence and Charles L. Schultze, eds., *An American Trade Strategy: Options for the 1990s* (Washington, D.C.: Brookings Institution, 1990), 31.

7. In a specific example of the winners and losers phenomenon, the creation of a free trade area with Mexico has enabled many U.S. makers of high-value-added industrial goods and some agricultural producers to increase shipments to that country. Simultaneously, the North American Free Trade Agreement (NAFTA) is hurting some U.S. labor-intensive, low-tech sectors and some farmers by easing access to the American market for competitive Mexican goods.

8. Stephen D. Krasner, "U.S. Commercial and Monetary Policy: Unraveling the Paradox of External Strength and Internal Weakness," *International Organization* 31 (autumn 1977): 645.

9. Some economists would argue that the expected dynamic benefits from trade liberalization may not be reaped equally by countries that would mainly import manufactured goods and export agricultural and primary products.

10. Some of the trade theories reviewed in Chapter 3 imply that even in the long term, some groups, such as less skilled workers in the United States, may suffer permanently lower real wages, other things being equal. The result of a more liberal import policy can be a reduction in demand for their services and less negotiating leverage for some unions.

11. Keynesian macrotheory, however, implies that trade surpluses caused by increased exports can be good for employment in the short run, even though neoclassical microtheory disagrees.

12. Data sources: U.S. International Trade Commission, *Shifts in U.S. Merchandise Trade 2000,* July 2001; and the German Embassy, Washington, D.C. (by telephone). Trade as a percentage of GDP in member countries of the European Union is relatively high because of extensive intra–European Union (EU) trade, which some economists no longer consider as "foreign" transactions in the traditional sense.

# 2 Historical Survey of U.S. Trade Relations

U.S. foreign trade policy has passed through several identifiable periods. An appreciation of the causal factors responsible for the ebbs and flows of trade priorities from the beginning of the republic to the early years of the twenty-first century is essential to gain a full understanding of where we are today and why. In a brief review of the history of U.S. trade policy, this chapter analyzes both the fundamental changes and the persistent themes in economics, politics, and laws that have shaped the evolution of more than two hundred years of U.S. trade policies.

## A Conceptual Blueprint

In a democracy, trade policy over an extended period is the outcome of not always gentle clashes between two forces. The first consists of economic debates about the most desirable means to advance the long-term welfare of the country as a whole. The second force consists of political struggles among different ideologies and well-organized, well-financed, message-bearing interest groups. The history of U.S. trade policy tells of change and a continually shifting balance of power among the four main forces that constitute this policy: domestic politics, domestic economics, international economics, and international politics. The endless progression of shifting circumstances pertinent to each of these four factors, as well as the ever-changing dynamics of the trade policymaking partnership between the executive and legislative branches, perpetually alter the cost-effectiveness calculation of the import or export policy status quo. Policymakers must reconcile their perceptions of political necessities and economic logic within a constantly changing trade policy equation. Trade policy is therefore relatively fluid: The core question of how severe restrictions should be on imports and exports at any given time is constantly being answered in different ways by different people for different reasons and in different circumstances. Sometimes, experience is the best teacher, and lessons are learned only after major mistakes are made.

The broad concept that the substance of U.S. trade policy is the outgrowth of the need to reconcile competing ideas has been a constant. The United States prides itself on pluralism and participatory government. Therefore, it is not surprising that so many senior economic and national security policy officials, elected politicians, candidates for public office, economists and political scientists, businesspersons, labor leaders, consumers, lawyers, and demagogues have collectively contributed to the inconclusive debate about how the government should regulate trade flows.

At the heart of the political economy of trade policy is the perennial rule of thumb that most trade decisions create winners and losers, both in the domestic body politic and in the economies of trading partners. Few losing groups quietly accept their fate, content that their misfortunes are being offset by a greater good for a greater number. When imports are allowed to enter freely, consumers and foreign producers benefit, but domestic producers of goods sensitive to import competition usually suffer. To protect their interests, business executives and workers adversely affected by imports become a vociferous minority. They petition elected representatives for trade barriers that usually drive up domestic sales prices or reduce the availability of foreign-made goods, or both. When domestic interests succeed in their efforts to get import barriers imposed, they are the winners and foreign producers and domestic consumers usually are the losers.

As suggested in Chapter 6, success in convincing the U.S. government to impose import barriers (under conditions of fair foreign competition) usually depends upon five major recurring variables. The ability to predict over time whether import barriers will be erected is still somewhere between difficult and impossible. The relative importance of each recurring variable is constantly shifting and occasionally sui generis factors find their way into the policymaking equation. The first variable has been the preponderant economic philosophy and the assessments of political self-interests of the president and his senior advisers. The proximity of elections to the time when a trade decision must be made can be a subvariable. Second are statements and legislative actions by interested members of Congress. The third variable depends on the official perceptions of how severe the import competition is; that is, how important is the affected domestic sector and to what extent have rising imports caused, or threaten to cause, domestic bankruptcies and job losses. A related variable is the overall health of the economy at any given time. Increased imports are usually better tolerated when there is full employment and rising income than when job losses are mounting amidst a recession.

The fifth major variable is the relative strength at any given time of those domestic groups advocating protectionism and the domestic and foreign forces opposed to import barriers. Strength depends on the size of an industry's output and workforce, how much money is available for lobbying and campaign contributions, and good connections in Washington. Advocates of import protection enjoyed clout and a sympathetic audience in Congress until the disastrous global trade wars in the 1930s (discussed below).

Only after World War II did the balance of lobbying power in the United States shift to advocates of a liberal trade policy. The architects of U.S. efforts to promote postwar recovery in Western Europe and Asia had the luxury of global U.S. economic dominance in discarding protectionism as an option. By the early 1970s, the growing internationalization of U.S. industry caused the lobbying power of corporations with overseas subsidiaries to reach critical mass. These companies have little use for governmental limitations on their ability to move goods, services, and capital across national borders in accordance with their global marketing strategies. They oppose protectionism at home because it annoys their overseas customers.

The support of U.S.-based multinational corporations (MNCs) has provided critical political support for repeated official efforts to convene multilateral negotiations to reduce trade barriers. However, it has never been adequate to prevent repeated interventions to protect domestic producers and workers from the strains of fair import competition. MNC support has simply made the task harder for those American industries and workers seeking a protectionist-leaning import policy. Politicians always have and always will feel the occasional need to please vociferous interest groups and return political favors—even if the larger population is economically harmed. This is another way of stating our central premise: The formulation of trade policy is a political process with economic substance.

For countries other than the United States, an important sixth variable in embracing import restrictions is the strength of their balance of payments position and, more specifically, the availability of convertible foreign exchange (mainly dollars) necessary to pay for imports. Countries at risk of exhausting their monetary reserves must selectively cut back on imports; foreign exporters demand payment in cash and do not offer charity to potential importers who plead poverty.

Historically, the presence of controversy (and the absence of universal truths) has characterized U.S. trade policy. The first phase of U.S. trade policy started with a relatively nonpartisan disagreement between free trade and protectionist ideologies about how best to promote domestic economic prosperity in a new country. The second phase emerged in the early 1800s as a regional dispute between northerners and southerners. It in turn evolved into a new phase, lasting from the late 1880s until the 1920s, that was characterized by differences between Democrats and Republicans regarding the appropriate levels of tariffs (the former favored low levels and the latter favored high tariffs). The common denominator of this period is that the debate was exclusively about *domestic* economics and politics.

The modern era of U.S. trade policy was ushered in as the result of incredibly bad timing. The gradual (and unrecognized at the time) emergence of the United States after World War I as a major commercial and financial actor in the world economy collided violently with the decision in 1930 to adopt the most protectionist U.S. trade posture in history. A harsh lesson was learned: Closing the expansive, influential U.S. market to imports placed every country's economic growth at risk. This new link between domestic and international economic prosperity caused a radical redirection in U.S. trade policy in 1934. The quest for mutually beneficial reductions in barriers to the flow of trade became the guiding tenet of U.S. trade relations with other countries.

During the second half of the twentieth century, U.S. trade policy went through at least three distinct phases. In the years immediately after World War II, trade policy was subordinated to the unexpected new role of the United States as global political, military, and economic hegemon. By the 1970s, rising domestic economic woes and the economic recovery in Western Europe and East Asia turned policy priorities toward internal needs and concerns. After a period of flirting with traditional protectionism, U.S. trade policy by the late 1980s was actively debating the possible need for Washington to proactively administer industrial policy as a counterforce to government interventionism in Japan and elsewhere. A third phase quietly emerged in the early

1990s, its dominant characteristic being paradox. Despite the American economy's best performance ever, six decades of activist, decisive U.S. leadership in pushing for a more liberal world trading order degenerated into rhetoric and hesitation.

## The First Stage of U.S. Trade Policy, 1789–1929

The transcendent features of the first stage of U.S. trade policy were the absence of presidential discretion in conducting trade policy, a gradual ratcheting upward of U.S. tariff rates, and an indifference to how the global trading system operated. The first substantive piece of legislation passed by the first Congress in 1789 was a tariff act. The bill's main purpose was to raise revenue—a critical need for a new country that had not yet implemented any generalized income or sales taxes and was forbidden by the Constitution to impose export duties. Although protecting the country's fledgling industrial base was on the minds of Congress, imposing a low tariff rate of 5 percent meant that, by design, there was little discouragement of imports. Fiscal considerations remained a major, though declining, variable in the setting of U.S. tariff levels until the end of the nineteenth century. The simple reason for the tariff-taxation link was that until the twentieth century, tariff collections represented a high (at least 40 percent) proportion of total federal revenues.

Conspicuous by their absence for more than a century in the debate were two of the most basic concepts of trade policy: (1) concerns about trade theory such as comparative advantage; and (2) concerns about the impact of trade barriers on U.S. political and economic relations with other countries. Tariffs were viewed as a domestic matter. This disengagement by the United States from concerns beyond the water's edge went largely ignored until the 1920s owing to the limited external impact of a young country that accounted for an inconsequential percentage of world trade.

An intellectual tug-of-war over trade policy between political heavyweights quickly erupted in the wake of the country's first tariff bill. In 1791, Alexander Hamilton, the first secretary of the treasury, produced his *Report on Manufactures* after studying the efficacy of using protectionist measures to encourage the development of a domestic industrial base. The document strongly advocated activist economic policies incorporating the use of high tariffs as well as federal "bounties" (i.e., subsidies). Hamilton, in the best tradition of mercantilism (see Chapter 3) believed that "not only the wealth but the independence and security of a country appear to be materially connected with the prosperity of manufactures."[1] A thriving industrial base, he argued, would also increase domestic demand for home-grown agricultural goods, thereby reducing the allegedly dangerously high degree of dependence by farmers on sales to foreign markets. His recommendations were rejected. James Madison and Thomas Jefferson articulated the opposing views that carried the day. They argued in economic terms that prohibitive tariffs would not benefit the national interest. And they believed that politically, the delegation of additional power to the central government for any reason—including guiding industrial development—should be minimal.

Hamilton lost the battle but won the war. Over the next 140 years, Congress by fits and starts increased the average level of tariffs. Although the periodic need for additional tax revenue was often a factor, the overwhelming determinant of an increasingly protectionist U.S. import policy was the responsiveness of lawmakers to industrialists' demands for protection against import competition.

This upward spiral of the average U.S. tariff rate reflected the virtually nonexistent role of the executive branch in formulating U.S. import policy during the eighteenth century. The executive branch in trade matters was little more than a tax (tariff) collector. Regular negotiations among governments aimed at reducing trade barriers did not exist. The president had no legal authority—and sought none—to reduce U.S. trade barriers on his own. All trade agreements signed with other governments had to be ratified by Congress. (A few relatively minor, limited-duration bilateral treaties providing for small tariff cuts were concluded in the late 1800s and early 1900s.) Trade policy continued to be defined by a profusion of tariff laws that mainly raised the U.S. tariff schedule. These statutes, not presidential intent, determined the openness of the American market to foreign goods.

Conditions prevailing at the end of the War of 1812 led to the first of several legislated increases in the U.S. tariff schedule. The virtual absence of imports while the war was being fought had stimulated the domestic manufacturing sector, most of which was located in the northern states. The subsequent resumption of imports of British-made goods and the burdensome debt load incurred by the U.S. government from waging the war led to a sharp rise in import duties in the Tariff Act of 1816. At this point, the tariff became part of a larger historical phenomenon: Rising tariffs became an irritant in the widening gulf between the North and South that culminated in the Civil War.

The failure of the 1816 Tariff Act to blunt the British export drive set the stage for the passage in 1828 of the "Tariff of Abominations." This highly protectionist bill was the result of a major political miscalculation. On the assumption that the bill would become so odious that it would be rejected in the final vote, opponents of increased protectionism quietly encouraged major tariff increases on every manufactured good they could think of. The strategy backfired in the first major example of the inherent dangers of congressional logrolling in tariff legislation. Most members of Congress accepted large tariff hikes on goods (some tariffs were equivalent to 100 percent of the value of the import) as a trade-off for enlisting support among colleagues for higher duties on commodities that they pushed on behalf of their own constituents. The dark specter of this legislative version of "you scratch my back and I'll scratch yours" returned in 1930 to haunt U.S. trade policy in spades—see the next section.

Although tariff levels were subsequently reduced by Congress in 1833, politicians from the South did not abandon their heated opposition to the relatively high U.S. tariffs that were angering the countries buying their tobacco and cotton. Increasingly, Southern politicians felt they were being marginalized in the shaping of U.S. import policy. One historian wrote that Southerners saw the tariff dispute as a symbol of the North's attacks on their economic and social systems.[2] After Southern states began seceding from the Union in 1861, laws increasing tariff rates came pouring out of Congress for many years.

From the 1870s until well into the twentieth century, tariff levels were moved up or down in moderate degrees by a relatively rapid succession of new legislation. The direction of tariff modifications was determined mainly by which party controlled

Congress. After the Civil War, the two major political parties "fell into an almost perfect equipoise. As Democratic and Republican leaders worked to slide the balance in their favor, they developed opposing stands on the issues, sometimes for no other reason than to create an appeal among the voters."[3] In general, the dichotomy between the Democrats' advocacy of lower tariffs and the Republicans' embrace of higher tariffs amounted to an intellectually barren period in U.S. trade policy. As one study concluded: "No conclusive evidence exists that either high or low tariff rates greatly affected economic conditions in that period. The whole controversy was frequently more an exercise in political, rhetorical and partisan faith than a well-considered, profound discussion of conflicting economic and trade strategies."[4]

It was not until after World War I that great consequences emerged from the tendency of the United States to "internalize" import policy. Because the U.S. economy in international trade relations had always been overshadowed by the larger European countries, mainly Great Britain, the United States had been able to impose tariffs with little concern for their external effects. Beginning in the mid-1800s, the country became, to use a basic term in political economy, a "free rider." It was content to enjoy the benefits of eased European trade barriers embodied by Great Britain's repeal in 1846 of its highly protectionist Corn Laws without reciprocating with its own liberalization.

Great Britain was then playing the classic hegemon role in the international economy. Its economic and international political strengths allowed it to set a more liberal trade tone to the global economic order as it more willingly accepted imports. Britain's decision at this time to chart a more open trade policy conforms perfectly to the approach used in this book to explain the bottom-line of U.S. trade policy formulation: a political and intellectual struggle among government policymakers to determine who will be winners and losers. Britain's trade policy was transformed in 1846 just as that of the United States would be exactly one hundred years later. The political balance of power in Great Britain shifted from a land-owning aristocracy committed to smothering agricultural imports to industrialists who saw a connection among lower tariffs, expanding world markets, and the stimulation of their exports of manufactured goods.

The United States emerged in the post–World War I period as a bona fide industrial superpower, the world's number one exporter, and the world's most important import market for semifinished goods and raw materials.[5] The United States also became a major net supplier of capital to credit-hungry countries, moving in a relatively short time from international debtor to international creditor. Unfortunately, the quick resumption after 1918 of an isolationist foreign policy assured that U.S. trade policy decisionmaking would remain mired within the gravitational pull of purely internal considerations—the priority that had prevailed for more than a hundred years.

A disconnect resulted between the quick onset of U.S. international economic maturity and its continued international political immaturity: No longer would U.S. efforts to restrict imports have insignificant effects on global economic prosperity. The damage caused by the failure of the United States after World War I to become a progressive force in the international trade system was magnified by the economic inability of Great Britain to continue in its role of liberal trade–supporting hegemon. The worldwide spread of the Great Depression appears to have been made more severe than it would otherwise have been by the absence of an undisputed economic leader with a relatively open market. In the words of Charles Kindleberger, who popularized the thesis linking an open, liberal international economic order to the existence of an affluent hegemon: "When every country turned to protect its national private interests, the world public interest went down the drain, and with it the private interests of all."[6]

## Moving to Extremes: Revolutionary Changes in the 1930s

U.S. trade policy was irrevocably changed by its spectacular roller-coaster ride during the first half of the 1930s. The shift started unsensationally enough with an effort to accommodate U.S. farmers' demands in the 1920s for higher agricultural prices. This effort effectively short-circuited what might have been a possible shift by the United States in the direction of a more open trade policy. The Underwood Tariff Act of 1913 had cut import duties (the statute offset the revenue cost of lower tariffs by initiating the income tax). President Woodrow Wilson's Fourteen Points program for the post-war world order had included a call for the early removal "of all economic barriers and the establishment of an equality of trade conditions among all nations consenting to the peace."[7] But in the end it was business as usual as protectionism carried the day. Wilsonian foreign policy was rejected in the 1920 elections, a post–World War I economic boom fizzled, and the U.S. economy fell into recession.

The Fordney-McCumber Act of 1922 represented yet another embrace of the fallacious assumption that increased import duties could effectively address the farm community's distress over falling prices for agricultural goods, the main cause being excessive domestic production. The bill also doled out major tariff increases to industries, such as chemicals, that had flourished during World War I.

Although higher tariffs had consistently failed to revive the fortunes of the U.S. agricultural sector, President Herbert Hoover early in 1929 yielded to intensifying political pressures and endorsed higher tariffs on agricultural goods as a means of boosting food prices. The utter lack of a compelling economic justification for providing this protection opened the door to a veritable army of lobbyists clamoring to get in on the act by urging higher tariffs on manufactured goods. Organized labor added its support. The result was an unprecedented exercise in logrolling. Votes in the House and Senate were freely exchanged to provide higher tariffs in response to nearly every constituent demand for relief from import competition. When the stock market crashed later in 1929 and economic conditions deteriorated within the United States, Republican leaders in Congress accelerated efforts to pass the new tariff act. They hoped the bill would switch demand to domestically produced goods. President Hoover urged restraint and was reportedly unhappy with the protectionist-laden bill that emerged. But he did sign it, dismissing bitter foreign complaints on the grounds that tariff legislation was strictly an internal matter.

The Smoot-Hawley Tariff Act of 1930 was a disaster of major proportions. The only consolation is that the damage ultimately generated by the statute continues to scare policymakers around the world away from overt protectionism. To this day, the act remains a textbook example of what *not* to do in trade policy. The average U.S.

tariff duty was raised to 53 percent, an all-time high, and the number of dutiable items increased sharply. The bill was viewed abroad as an unjust and unfriendly action by an economically strong creditor country and as a symbol of U.S. isolationism.[8]

The timing of the Smoot-Hawley legislation could not have been worse. As the depression spread from the United States, other countries retaliated by imposing higher tariffs and quotas. A wave of fear and economic nationalism produced an unprecedented worldwide display of beggar-thy-neighbor policies in which all major trading countries were more or less trying simultaneously to dump their domestic economic problems on someone else. A proliferation of international financial controls and a series of competitive exchange rate devaluations further contributed to a phalanx of repressive international economic policies.

The ensuing global trade war produced all losers and no winners. As national economies spiraled downward, so too did the volume of international trade and the economic efficiency that comes with the international division of labor. Countries succeeded in reducing imports, but at the cost of decimating their export sectors, normally an economy's most productive and dynamic sector. Estimates peg the value of world trade in 1933 at just one-third of what it had been in 1929.[9] U.S. imports in 1932 had plunged by 70 percent from their 1929 level, but exports during this period also plummeted by about the same amount.[10] Although import-sensitive jobs were saved, relatively high-paying export jobs were lost.

The inevitable return to international economic sanity began when the traditionally low-tariff party, the Democrats, gained control of the White House and Congress in 1932. The Democratic platform presented what was then a unique critique of higher tariffs. It vigorously condemned the Smoot-Hawley Act as detrimental to U.S. industry and agriculture by causing a loss of foreign markets and increases in domestic production costs. The platform went on to endorse reciprocal tariff-cutting agreements and other efforts to revive international commerce.

Initially, President Roosevelt was not personally committed to acting on this initiative. The catalyst for change was the unwavering zeal of Roosevelt's secretary of state, Cordell Hull. He deeply believed that an open trading system fostered a peaceful, cooperative, and stable international political order, whereas a closed trading system produced international tension and conflict. Having won President Roosevelt to the cause, Hull was entrusted with the task of gaining congressional approval for reciprocal trade agreements in which the United States would lower tariffs in return for comparable concessions by other countries.

Selling Congress on approving tariff cuts in 1934 amid massive unemployment at home would have been difficult to impossible without the astute, pragmatic marketing strategy adopted by the administration. Rather than asking for a sharp departure from established trade policymaking, Secretary Hull sought temporary negotiating authority in the form of an amendment to the Smoot-Hawley Act. Unilateral tariff cuts were not part of the request; U.S. tariff cuts would approximate the value of tariff cuts made by trading partners. The export enhancing—and by implication, job creating—aspects of obtaining reductions in foreign tariffs were stressed. Little or no reference was made to economic theory extolling the virtues of a country's ability to import goods more efficiently produced abroad. Furthermore, the administration accepted a congressional amendment that limited its tariff-cutting authority to three years, at which time the Congress would review the administration's performance before deciding whether to extend presidential tariff-cutting authority. Many members of Congress were, and still are, happy to interpose the executive branch between themselves and special interest groups, letting the administration serve as the lightning rod for petitions from the private sector requesting import protection.

The Reciprocal Trade Agreements Act (RTAA) of 1934 is one of the major turning points in international trading relations. For the first time, the U.S. executive branch was given authority to *enact* reductions (of up to 50 percent) in tariffs as long as other countries reciprocated in kind. Previously, when the executive branch made trade policy promises to other countries, they were subject to formal approval by Congress. Also for the first time, an ongoing series of bilateral negotiations commenced for the expressed purpose of reducing barriers to trade as a step toward expanding global production, employment, and efficiency.

Immediately after passage of the RTAA, U.S. trade negotiators got down to business with their foreign counterparts. By the early 1940s, bilateral trade agreements with some twenty-five countries, mainly in Europe and the Western Hemisphere, had been concluded. Because the most-favored-nation principle was included in the act, the tariff cuts resulting from each of these agreements were automatically extended by the United States on a nondiscriminatory basis to all other countries. (This meant that the executive branch effectively was rewriting the U.S. tariff schedule.) The average ad valorem tariff rate in the United States fell from over 50 percent in 1930 to about 37 percent in 1939.[11] Never before had the direction of global trade relations moved so broadly and deeply toward reduced trade barriers.

Although commercial trade relations were totally disrupted during World War II, the new postwar environment would expedite the relatively modest momentum toward liberalization generated in the 1930s. Throughout U.S. history, wars had been the major causes of shifts in trade policy. World War II brought about many momentous changes, not the least of which was how American policymakers altered their views of the role that the United States played in the international trading system.

## The United States As Hegemon: Internationalism Prevails in the 1950s and 1960s

The end of World War II found much of Europe and Asia in political disarray and economically devastated. The search for a lasting peace to prevent a third world war became more urgent during the Cold War between the free world's capitalist countries, led by the United States, and the totalitarian countries behind the Iron Curtain, dominated by the Soviet Union. Economic growth in democratic countries became a transcendent U.S. international goal. To this end, international economic policy was commandeered as an instrument of U.S. foreign policy. Because the United States could afford commercial altruism on a global scale, the Truman and Eisenhower administrations were under no pressure to put domestic economic interests first. The unassailable strength of the U.S. economy in the initial postwar years made it immune to serious unemployment and declining domestic production traditionally associated with rising import competition.

By 1950, U.S. international economic policy was clearly defined and sharply differentiated to serve two separate national security strategies. Democratic countries in Western Europe and Japan received considerable financial assistance (eventually to surpass $30 billion) from the United States to rebuild their war-torn economies. The assumption was that economic progress in those countries would promote political stability and create a growing bulwark against the expansion of communism. The initial emphasis on aid was soon supplanted by efforts to maximize commercial relations, the objective being the integration of industrialized democracies into a thriving, harmonious, mutually rewarding, and nondiscriminatory international economic order. Later, the same strategy would be applied to friendly, less developed countries in Latin America and newly independent "emerging countries" in Asia and Africa.

The opposite policy strategy sought to deny trade, capital, and advanced technology to the hostile countries of the communist bloc. Export controls and the de facto excommunication of "expansionist" communist states from the international trading system by the United States and its allies became the economic dimension of containment during the Cold War (see Chapter 9). Some American policymakers viewed the minimization of trade as being far more costly to the former than to the latter.

U.S. trade policy toward friendly countries in the immediate post–World War II period was extraordinary in the degree to which it acquiesced to allies' discriminating against U.S. goods. U.S. long-term foreign policy goals generated an unprecedented international economic unselfishness that actively encouraged imports and ignored export expansion to an extent never before seen. The shortage of dollars in Western Europe and Japan sharply curtailed their ability to import, which in turn slowed their ability to rebuild the thriving, competitive industrial sectors sought by a "benevolent" Uncle Sam. Furthermore, their ability to penetrate the U.S. market was minimal in light of the physical destruction suffered by factories in these countries during the war.

The decision not to seek full reciprocity from trading partners in Western Europe and Japan was justified by the overwhelming U.S. economic dominance in the immediate postwar period. Some critics of contemporary trade policy contend that the U.S. government's approach toward export promotion has never progressed from the "Marshall Plan mentality" of the 1950s. In their view, the relatively low priority given by policymakers to export performance has been increasingly costly and out of sync with the decline in relative U.S. global competitiveness that became visible in the mid-1960s.

The executive branch's policy of actively encouraging imports and accepting the right of other countries to adopt quantitative and discriminatory import restrictions was vividly displayed during the 1947 negotiations to create the ill-fated International Trade Organization (ITO). State Department trade negotiators failed to liberalize Great Britain's Imperial Preference system of tariff preferences extended to Commonwealth countries. But in the apparent belief that an unbalanced deal was preferable to no deal at all, the administration signed an agreement that, in the words of one critic, "cracked open only one market—its own." The State Department acknowledged that Washington gained concessions at Geneva worth an estimated trade value of $1.2 billion but yielded concessions worth about $1.8 billion.[12]

The Senate and the U.S. business sector were deeply disenchanted by the numerous exemptions in the proposed ITO charter that would have permitted countries to impose quantitative and discriminatory (non–most favored nation [MFN]) import barriers, mainly for balance of payments and economic development purposes. "There are more exceptions than rules in the ITO charter" was the gist of the criticism. As one scholar noted, U.S. trade seemed "to be the object of more restrictions and discrimination than ever before."[13] The Congress failed to act in 1949 on the administration's initial request for ratification of U.S. membership. The atmosphere on Capitol Hill toward the ITO deteriorated so much that the Eisenhower administration decided it was pointless to resubmit the ITO charter to Congress. Now that the ITO was effectively dead, the administration signed the General Agreement on Tariffs and Trade (GATT), which included most of the terms of the ITO, as an executive agreement. No formal multilateral organization existed to administer the rules of the trading system until the World Trade Organization was launched in 1995 (see Chapter 8).

The United States actively supported various efforts at regional economic cooperation among West European countries (initially, the European Payments Union and later the European Union [EU]), even though they openly discriminated against exports of U.S. goods. Any effort to cement cooperation among West European countries was seen as a boon to the strength and solidarity of the Western alliance and therefore an acceptable price to pay for a few lost export opportunities. That European economic and political integration was viewed primarily in balance of power terms by the U.S. foreign policy establishment can be seen in the wording of President John F. Kennedy's speech of July 4, 1962: "We do not regard a strong and united Europe as a rival but a partner. . . . We will be prepared to discuss with a united Europe the ways and means of forming a concrete Atlantic partnership."[14]

An implicit deal had been struck in the 1950s. By holding most of its mounting net dollar inflows, Western Europe extended a nearly blank check to the United States government. It could then protect the free world without having to worry about the accumulating balance of payments deficits incurred, in part, from playing the expensive role of global superpower. The United States, in turn, condoned Europe's using the trade and monetary systems to promote the latter's regional economic prosperity, even if this meant losing some American exports.[15]

U.S. trade policy toward Japan in the 1950s incorporated essentially the same strategy used toward Western Europe. Memoranda declassified in the early 1990s show that the National Security Council (NSC) declared in 1952 and 1953 that the entry of Japanese goods should be "facilitated" because increasing access to the U.S. market was necessary to halt "economic deterioration and falling living standards" in Japan that "create fertile ground for communist subversion."[16] The Eisenhower administration accepted the need to negotiate trade agreements that were "favorable" to Japan and believed that "all problems of local industry pale into insignificance in relation to the world crisis." It therefore largely ignored the concept of reciprocity in favor of helping the Japanese resuscitate their economy and expand exports. One scholar has charged that the bilateral trade agreement signed with Japan in 1955 was an "egregious example of sacrificing domestic interests for foreign policy advantage." For national security reasons, it was "an unbalanced agreement" in which the Japanese "provided few major tariff concessions" while the United States "granted extensive tariff reductions covering almost all of Japan's major export items."[17]

The swan song for the State Department as head of U.S. trade negotiating teams occurred in the Dillon Round of GATT trade negotiations that concluded in 1962. (The round was named for C. Douglas Dillon, then undersecretary of state and chief U.S. trade negotiator.) The U.S. negotiating position put a premium on encouraging European economic integration (this was the first multilateral trade negotiation in which the EU, then known as the European Economic Community [EEC], negotiated as a single entity, supplanting national delegations from its member states). Seemingly oblivious of the need to protect domestic interests, the State Department–led U.S. delegation again apparently acted on the notion that the failure to agree was the worst possible scenario for trade negotiations. Rather than risk failure, the Kennedy administration agreed to several tariff concessions below the "peril point" levels recommended as the minimum necessary protection by the independent Tariff Commission (now known as the International Trade Commission [ITC]). In addition, it made only a perfunctory effort to negotiate a partial liberalization in Europe's highly protectionist Common Agricultural Policy (CAP), which had only recently been put into effect.

The failure of the Dillon Round to go beyond marginal tariff cuts sustained the administration's nightmare that the EU's Common External Tariff would devastate U.S. exports in their most important foreign market and interfere with the Kennedy administration's grand design of a more integrated Atlantic Community. This situation led U.S. officials to propose a "wholly new approach" to trade negotiations that may have been an instinctive realization that the era of U.S. economic hegemony was coming to an end. A uniting Europe made the need for reduced trade barriers all the more important to U.S. exporters. Aided by the slogan "trade or fade," the Kennedy administration quickly convinced Congress to grant it the most extensive tariff-cutting authority ever.

The Trade Expansion Act of 1962 authorized (on a reciprocal basis) across-the-board tariff cuts of up to 50 percent, with only a few exceptions; in a few instances, tariffs could be eliminated entirely. Passage of the bill set into motion the Kennedy Round of multilateral trade negotiations (named for President John F. Kennedy). After a flurry of last-minute dealmaking in 1967 (the Trade Expansion Act provided only five years of tariff-cutting authority to the executive branch), the two trade superpowers, the then European Community and the United States, concluded a deal that at the time was the largest single tariff-cutting agreement ever: about 35 percent on a worldwide basis.

The second innovation contained in the 1962 act emanated from Congress's refusal to allow the State Department to remain the chief spokesman for the U.S. government in trade negotiations. The perception (if not the reality) existed that the increasingly sophisticated overseas competition facing the U.S. economy called for tougher negotiators not beholden to cultivating the friendships of foreign governments. Congress demanded a more hard-nosed chief negotiator having a more balanced set of priorities, someone who would be willing to walk away from the negotiating table if unable to get a satisfactory overseas market access deal for U.S. producers. Accordingly, Congress created the post of Special Representative for Trade Negotiations in the Executive Office of the President, legislating that person's status as head of both U.S. trade negotiation delegations and interagency trade policy committees in the executive branch (see Chapter 5).

In hindsight, the conclusion of the Kennedy Round was the high point, at least through 1994, for liberal trade. By the end of the 1960s, momentous changes were surfacing in the international economy. Undisciplined macroeconomic policies were rapidly eroding relative U.S. economic strength, a trend that was hastened from another direction: the success of U.S. efforts to expedite the economic recoveries of Western Europe and Japan. The leadership provided by U.S. hegemony was in eclipse. The rising competitive threat from East Asia was beginning to alarm Europe and the United States. The U.S. balance of payments deficits went from bad to worse. On the foreign policy front, the threat that Western Europe and Japan might succumb to the "red menace" had disappeared, taking with it the national security justification for a soft-line U.S. acceptance of import barriers in these countries. The demise of internationalism-driven U.S. trade policy was at hand.

## The Agonizing Reappraisal in the 1970s

The end of the 1960s coincided with the start of the transition to a new phase of international economic relations in general and U.S. trade policy in particular. The size and strength of its economy, together with its military might, assured the United States of a continued global economic leadership role. But it was a challenge for policymakers in all countries to adjust to U.S. leadership based more on compromise and threats than unquestioned hegemony. U.S. trade policy, meanwhile, was strongly influenced by a diminution of U.S. international competitiveness. The latter was induced by a relatively high rate of inflation and the full return of Western Europe and Japan as major international competitors. Achievement of this status was accelerated by efforts to keep their currencies' exchange rates undervalued against the dollar.

The impact of these trends was clearly visible in the gradual but steady decline in the U.S. trade surplus. While U.S. export growth began to stagnate, imports grew rapidly as more foreign-made goods became price-competitive in the U.S. market. This perceived decline in American competitiveness generated growing doubts about the continued suitability of a liberal trade policy for the United States. As noted above, advocates of a liberal trade had marketed it as a device to sustain a U.S. trade surplus. Within months of the signing of the Kennedy Round tariff-cutting agreements, numerous quota bills were introduced on Capitol Hill in response to pleas from several manufacturing and primary product producers. Although nothing came of the 1968 offensive, the incoming Nixon administration's immediate move to limit imports of synthetic textile products (rayon, dacron, etc.) was a metaphorical lighted match tossed into a container of gasoline.

Frustrated with its long-running inability to convince the Japanese to adopt "voluntary" export restraints on these newly popular textile products, the administration surprised everyone by endorsing pending legislation that would have unilaterally invoked rigid textile quotas. The economic justification for such a harsh measure was dubious. Imports of synthetic fibers and apparel were indeed growing rapidly, but on a multilateral basis they still accounted for only about 8 percent of total U.S. textile consumption because domestic production was also growing rapidly. Nevertheless, political factors won out. Congress revived the mutual back-scratching that had not played a significant role in trade legislation since the Smoot-Hawley Tariff of 1930. The end result was arguably the most protectionist piece of trade legislation ever passed by the U.S. Congress. The Trade Act of 1970 included quotas on synthetic textiles, footwear, and various minor products. It also introduced a complicated trigger formula, which, if met, would have automatically extended escape clause relief to petitioners demonstrating that they had been "substantially" injured by import competition. Versions of the bill passed both houses of Congress, but the congressional session ended before differences in the two bills could be reconciled by a conference committee. The likelihood of a presidential veto was never clear.

Dissatisfaction with the trade policy status quo was vividly displayed in the radical Burke-Hartke bill introduced in 1971. The bill was never acted on, but it was significant in that it marked the formal conversion of the politically powerful AFL-CIO (American Federation of Labor and Congress of Industrial Organizations) to a protectionist stance. The labor confederation at this time was suffering from a net loss of members, part of which was attributed to jobs lost to rising imports and increased overseas investments by American corporations. The Burke-Hartke bill, largely written by the AFL-CIO, called for across-the-board import quotas and changes to U.S. international tax laws so sweeping that most foreign direct investment would have become immediately unprofitable for U.S. companies.

The probability that protectionist trade legislation would be enacted into law was reduced to nearly zero by a radical change in U.S. international economic policy orchestrated by President Richard Nixon. Frustrated with stagflation at home; jealous of growing prosperity, full employment, and surpluses in the balance of payments in Western Europe and Japan; burdened by large defense expenditures to protect its allies; alarmed by currency crises involving enormous dollar sales in the foreign exchange market; and angered by continued gold losses stemming from the deteriorating U.S. balance of payments, the Nixon administration determined that dramatic change was needed. The twenty-five-year policy tilt toward foreign priorities had become a prohibitively expensive liability that needed to be shed.

The policy pendulum now swung dramatically back toward domestic needs. The international components of the New Economic Policy, announced to a stunned world on August 15, 1971, centered on a 10 percent surcharge on all import duties and the termination of the U.S. obligation to convert dollars held by foreign central banks into gold at a fixed price. The international financial markets suffered four months of chaos as an unprecedented volume of dollar sales forced one central bank after another to suspend their obligation to keep exchange rates fixed. By initiating the largest multilateral exchange realignment in history, the Smithsonian Agreement of December 1971 permitted the return (at least temporarily) to fixed exchange rates. The dollar was devalued and surplus countries revalued their exchange rates upward in an effort to restore U.S. trade competitiveness. The Nixon administration also demanded and received a commitment by the other industrial countries to initiate another round of multilateral trade negotiations. When it came to trade barriers, the United States considered itself more sinned against than a sinner. The U.S. government therefore believed it would be a major beneficiary of additional global trade liberalization.

A new round of multilateral trade negotiations automatically requires the executive branch to secure additional legislated authority. Without it, the administration cannot *implement* whatever trade liberalization concessions it might agree to in a trade agreement. The Trade Act of 1974 became another example of the post-1945 trend whereby major trade legislation replaced war as the benchmark for observing turning points in U.S. trade policy. Although almost thirty years have passed, many contemporary trade policy issues are rooted in the bill's innovative provisions.

Broadly analyzed, its twin philosophies blazed the trail for the occasionally contradictory two-track import policy pursued ever since by the United States: trade liberalization on a broad sector basis and restraints on imports of selected, politically sensitive products. The Trade Act of 1974 contained yet another in a long-standing series of authorizations to the president to reduce tariffs. But in view of the success of past negotiations to reduce most tariffs to the "nuisance" level, it was recognized from the start that the new round of trade talks would have to address nontariff barriers (NTBs) such as quotas, health and safety standards, and government procurement policies. Congress refused the administration's request for carte blanche authority (including the power to revise existing statutes) to reduce U.S. NTBs on a reciprocal basis. Instead, the fast-track system was born. Congress would show "good faith" by guaranteeing a floor vote an administration's requests for new trade legislation within a minimum amount of time and without the option of inserting amendments (see Chapter 7).

On the protectionist side, the 1974 bill did not challenge the ideal of liberalized trade; it merely expanded the legal loopholes to the practice of liberal trade. The bill eased the qualifying language of the escape clause (a legislative provision providing temporary relief from fair foreign competition for companies able to demonstrate "injury" from rising imports) to make affirmative findings of injury or threat of injury much more likely. Congress tried to assure more leverage for domestic producers by voting itself the power to override all presidential decisions to ignore recommendations by the ITC under the escape clause for import relief. (The so-called legislative veto was subsequently declared unconstitutional by the Supreme Court.) In addition, the legislation introduced administrative reforms that favored U.S. plaintiffs in unfair foreign trade petitions filed under the statutes to protect them from dumping (sales of imports at prices below their production costs or below their sales price in the exporting country's market) and to impose countervailing duties (to negate the estimated value of subsidies received by foreign exporting companies from their governments). The bill also gave the president conditional authority to extend MFN treatment to countries not currently receiving it (the source of the complex situation with China, discussed in Chapter 10).

The first of two important legacies of the Trade Act of 1974 was the successful conclusion of the Tokyo Round of multilateral trade negotiations. In addition to agreeing to reduce tariffs in industrial countries that would drop them below 5 percent on average, participating countries concluded the first set of agreements to reduce non-tariff barriers to trade. They consisted mainly of "codes of conduct" regulating a number of internal government regulatory and administrative actions that can hinder trade flows, for example, health and safety standards. Another major breakthrough of the Tokyo Round agreement was the initial multilateral effort to deal with the special trade problems of the less developed countries by authorizing the industrial countries to extend "differential and more favorable treatment" to them.

The second legacy of the 1974 act was the extension of more protection to U.S. interest groups seeking import relief, usually from the rapidly intensifying competition of Japan and the newly industrialized countries (NICs) of East Asia: Korea, Singapore, Taiwan, and Hong Kong. In a compromise between the unilateral protectionism of the 1930s and the enthusiasm for trade liberalization of the 1960s, the United States and the EU became the principal practitioners of what is commonly called "the new protectionism." The latter is epitomized by so-called orderly marketing agreements, also known as voluntary export restraints (VERs).

The agonizing reappraisal of U.S. trade policy introduced a search that still continues for an economic and political equilibrium between the extremes of pre-1934 protectionism and post-1945 internationalism. The 1970s flirtation with legislated protectionism was rolled back by two developments: the sustained downward movement in the value of the dollar during the early 1970s and the willingness of the executive branch to impose ad hoc import restraints, unilateral and negotiated, on numerous products. The threat of widespread, overt protectionism was over, but new events and trends precluded a return to an unambiguous liberal trade policy.

## The 1980s and Early 1990s: Multidirectional Trade Policies

In the early 1980s, an activist U.S. trade policy featured several inconsistent themes because policymakers felt the need to attack foreign trade barriers, sponsor further initiatives to reduce barriers to trade, and negotiate ceilings on imports of sensitive goods. No single-minded focus or common denominator was present. At times the U.S. government was simultaneously pressuring foreign countries to "voluntarily" restrain certain exports to the American market; championing a new round of multilateral trade negotiations; threatening retaliation if other countries failed to reduce their foreign trade barriers; questioning whether the U.S. economy could compete with the Japanese model of industrial policy; and, for the first time, negotiating regional free trade agreements in the Western Hemisphere and the Pacific Basin. Critics of U.S. trade policy alleged that a new variant of protectionism emerged in the late 1980s: The Department of Commerce was accused of enforcing legislation dealing with allegations of unfair foreign trade practices (see Chapter 7) in a manner so arbitrary and capricious that it constituted de facto protectionism.

U.S. trade policy was deeply affected by the revolutionary changes in domestic economic policy introduced in 1981 by the adoption of "Reaganomics." Sharp reductions in taxes and a rising budget deficit resulted in national spending that exceeded production and in domestic saving that was increasingly inadequate to cover investment outlays. Secondary effects included a soaring trade deficit, high interest rates, and huge capital inflows. Despite the largest trade deficits ever recorded up to that time (peaking at $152 billion in 1987), the U.S. dollar continued to appreciate to levels that devastated the ability of many U.S. industrial and agricultural sectors to compete in the international marketplace. The Reagan administration obstinately preached the discipline of the free market when urged to "do something" about the rising dollar.

This obstinacy and the domestic implications of the rising trade deficit produced in Washington a political disequilibrium that triggered counterforces to nudge U.S. trade policy toward a more "centrist" orientation. In a stunning demonstration of how the separation of powers works in the U.S. government, Congress eventually forced the administration to alter its hands-off import policy by actively considering (but not passing) trade legislation increasingly biased against imports.[18] Fearing that a frustrated Congress would eventually pass a protectionist trade bill, the then treasury secretary, James Baker, took the lead in having the administration address the spiraling trade deficit. The Plaza Agreement of September 1985, concluded by the finance ministers of the major industrialized countries, changed market psychology and induced a significant drop in the dollar's overvalued exchange rate (thereby tending to make U.S. exports cost less in other currencies and to make foreign goods more expensive in dollars). Soon after, President Reagan announced a "get tough" trade initiative designed to force other countries to make their markets as open to imports as the U.S. perceived its market to be open to imports.

U.S. trade policy now had a new theme: reciprocity. The term originated in a bill introduced by Senator John Danforth (R., Mo.) that would have required the president to seek as much access to foreign markets as that provided to foreign goods by the United States. The Reagan administration placed reciprocity at the core of its new strategy of seeking to reduce the U.S. trade deficit by increasing exports rather than reducing imports. The willingness of the U.S. government to turn the other cheek to foreign trade barriers, as it had done in the era of U.S. hegemony, disappeared. Foreign barriers to increased American exports were now viewed as being prohibitively costly.

Congress thereupon embarked on a three-year initiative to pass comprehensive trade legislation with or without the cooperation of the executive branch. The end product was the Omnibus Trade and Competitiveness Act of 1988. This legal milestone in U.S. trade policy epitomized evolving U.S. trade philosophy as well as the tightening policymaking partnership between the executive branch and a more assertive Congress. The 1,000-page bill was devoid of unilateral restrictions on imports, a reflection of a remarkable consensus among politicians, economists, and the business community that protectionism was neither appropriate nor efficient in remedying U.S. trade problems. But like the 1974 trade bill, the new statute further institutionalized the two-track nature of U.S. trade policy. A continuing willingness to proceed with reductions of trade barriers coexisted with a continuing refusal to let market forces alone determine the magnitude and composition of American exports and imports.

The omnibus trade bill featured the usual delegation of authority to the president to reduce tariffs on a reciprocal basis in the impending round of multilateral trade negotiations. Desire for such negotiations only partly reflected a belief in the inherent virtue of further trade liberalization. It mainly reflected the belief that since other countries imposed higher trade barriers, they would be obligated to agree to more liberalization measures as part of a trade agreement than would the United States.

Angered by Japan's persistent barriers to imports, the 1988 trade act also placed unprecedented emphasis on achieving greater reciprocity, that is, more open markets overseas for U.S. goods and services. Most notable was the "Super 301" measure, a more proactive version of the Section 301 provision giving the president authority to retaliate if other countries refuse to reduce specific discriminatory actions against U.S. exports (see Chapters 7 and 9).

The growing fear that the United States was suffering a serious secular deterioration in its international competitiveness, mainly at the hands of Japan, translated into numerous provisions going well beyond the boundaries of traditional trade bills. These provisions established programs (in effect, a limited industrial policy) designed to strengthen U.S. productivity, technology, and workers' skills. This new approach to trade strategy was well summarized by Laura D'Andrea Tyson just before she became chairperson of President Clinton's Council of Economic Advisers: "Even the most sensible and effective trade policies cannot compensate for domestic programs that remain impoverished both fiscally and intellectually."[19]

The Uruguay Round, in addition to traditional tariff-cutting, produced more breakthroughs on new trade initiatives than any previous negotiation. For the first time, multilateral trade rules were established to deal with trade in services, trade-related investment measures, and trade-related intellectual property rights. The Uruguay Round also produced the blueprint for the WTO as the successor to the GATT (see Chapter 8). Despite continuing feelings of vulnerability to foreign industrial competition, the United States was compelled by its economic ideology and its superpower-driven geopolitical objectives to continue offering its vital leadership in concluding major international trade pacts.

## The Millennium Paradox: Policy Paralysis Amidst Prosperity

Academicians intent on constructing a model of U.S. trade policy that can demonstrate repetitive cause and effect relationships and correctly predict future actions were further set back by unfolding events as we moved into the new millennium. Several traditional import policy patterns ceased to exist as new issues emerged and the traditional debate between free trade and protectionism further dissipated.

The continuing upward spiral of U.S. trade deficits to record levels year after year brought no meaningful advocacy of import restraints. Americans were too busy enjoying an unprecedented prosperity. Unemployment neared record lows without unleashing inflationary pressures. Even the record highs, in dollar terms and as a percentage of GDP, the $450 billion U.S. merchandise trade deficit in 2000—an unheard of level in the 1980s and earlier—failed to elicit much emotion inside or outside of the United States. One long-standing pattern did remain: Increases in U.S. national income triggered a relatively strong increase in imports, a condition economists call a high-income elasticity of demand for imports.

The United States had no real reason to panic about the trade deficit. It was enjoying full employment. New products were continuously pouring out of high-tech centers; most of the import surge consisted of labor-intensive, low-tech goods and specialized components not made in the United States; and many U.S. services companies were enjoying unprecedented success in overseas markets. The steel and apparel sectors were the big exceptions to the rule that American industry was thriving in the greatest sustained growth in U.S. history, an import boom notwithstanding. America's trading partners were luxuriating in their booming exports to this fast-growing market. Foreign investors were so keen to invest in the United States that the dollar remained strong even though there was no end in sight for history's biggest trade deficits. In short, the situation could not have been more different than the anti-import backlash of the early 1970s that followed a relatively moderate deterioration in the U.S. trade balance.

A second deviation from a fundamental tenet of international political economy was the ongoing failure of Congress in the late 1990s—despite unprecedented U.S. economic prosperity—to act on administration requests for new authority to further reduce import barriers. While not stopping all new talks aimed at multilateral and regional reductions in trade barriers, the absence of presidential "fast-track" authority to *implement* new trade agreements put U.S. trade policy in the slow lane and threatened the continuation of U.S. leadership in trade liberalization (see Chapters 7 and 13).

The failure of Congress to sustain the tradition of being responsive to administration requests for new trade legislation that began with the Reciprocal Trade Agreements Act of 1934 had nothing to do with traditional protectionism. It was a matter of refusing to move forward on trade liberalization, not a backtracking into protectionism. Unusually acrimonious partisan politics between a Democratic president and a Republican Congress that intensely disliked President Clinton explained part of the new congressional intransigence. A second major contributing factor to the trade policy stalemate between the executive and legislative branches reflected an entirely new set of circumstances at the millennium that geometrically complicated consensus on the goals of U.S. trade policy. As part of the multifaceted backlash against the alleged evils of "globalization," influential special interests demanded that social issues, namely, environmental and labor standards, be added to the trade negotiating agenda (see Chapter 13).

## For Further Reading

Dobson, John M. *Two Centuries of Tariffs.* Washington, D.C.: U.S. International Trade Commission, 1976.

Hufbauer, Gary Clyde, Diane T. Berliner, and Kimberly Ann Elliott. *Trade Protection in the United States: 31 Case Studies.* Washington, D.C.: Institute for International Economics, 1986.

Kelly, William B., Jr., ed. *Studies in United States Commercial Policy.* Chapel Hill: University of North Carolina Press, 1963.

Lovett, William, Alfred Eckes, Jr., and Richard Brinkman. *U.S. Trade Policy—History, Theory, and the WTO.* Armonk, N.Y.: M. E. Sharpe, 1999.

Mikesell, Raymond. *United States Economic Policy and International Relations.* New York: McGraw-Hill, 1952.

Schattschneider, E. E. *Politics, Pressures, and the Tariff.* New York: Prentice-Hall, 1935.

Taussig, Frank W. *The Tariff History of the United States.* 8th ed. New York: G. P. Putnam's Sons, 1931.

U.S. International Trade Commission. *The Year in Trade.* Annual report on the operation of the Trade Agreements Program. Washington, D.C.: U.S. International Trade Commission.

## Notes

1. Reproduced in *Powernomics: Economics and Strategy After the Cold War* (Washington, D.C.: Economic Strategy Institute, 1991), 135.

2. John M. Dobson, *Two Centuries of Tariffs* (Washington, D.C.: U.S. International Trade Commission, 1976), 51.

3. Ibid., 56.

4. Ibid., 65–66.

5. Raymond F. Mikesell, *United States Economic Policy and International Relations* (New York: McGraw-Hill, 1952), 8.

6. Charles P. Kindleberger, *The World in Depression, 1929–1939* (Berkeley: University of California Press, 1973), 292.

7. Quoted in Dobson, *Two Centuries,* 31.

8. Mikesell, *Economic Policy,* 63.

9. Dobson, *Two Centuries,* 74.

10. John Parke Young, *The International Economy* (New York: Ronald Press, 1963), 35.

11. Mikesell, *Economic Policy,* 65.

12. Alfred E. Eckes, "Trading U.S. Interests," *Foreign Policy* 71 (fall 1992): 138.

13. Richard N. Gardner, *Sterling-Dollar Diplomacy* (New York: McGraw-Hill, 1969), 367.

14. Quoted in *European Community* (January 1970): 10.

15. Benjamin J. Cohen, "The Revolution in Atlantic Economic Relations: A Bargain Comes Unstuck," in Wolfram Hanrieder, ed., *The United States and Western Europe* (Cambridge, Mass.: Winthrop Publishers, 1974), 118.

16. Quoted in the *Washington Post,* 18 July 1993, H–1.

17. Eckes, "Trading," 139, 141.

18. For details of this process, see chapter 10 of Stephen D. Cohen, *The Making of U.S. International Economic Policy,* 5th ed. (New York: Praeger, 2000).

19. Laura D'Andrea Tyson, *Who's Bashing Whom? Trade Conflict in High-Technology Industries* (Washington, D.C.: Institute for International Economics, 1992), 2.

# Part Two

---

# Economics

---

# 3   Economic Theories of International Trade

As one prominent economist has written, the advocacy of free trade is "as close to a sacred tenet as any idea in economics."[1] In deference to most economists' strong views on this subject, political scientists, legal scholars, and editorial writers often take it on faith that free trade is the best policy for the nation and the world and view all departures from free trade as capitulations to special interests or nationalistic sentiments. Nevertheless, the economic theories of free trade are just theories: that is, conclusions that follow logically from certain underlying assumptions and principles. Rather than accept these theoretical conclusions on faith, it is important to understand their foundations—and their limitations.

Without exception, all economic theories imply that countries can obtain important benefits through their foreign trade. But this does not imply that a pure laissez-faire attitude of governments toward their nations' trade relations is necessarily the best policy. The argument for free trade is full of qualifications and exceptions: There are valid economic reasons for governments to regulate or promote particular types of economic activity among nations in specific ways under certain conditions. Moreover, understanding some of the subtleties of trade theory—such as the predictions about which groups (within a country) gain and which ones lose from free trade—can be extremely helpful for understanding the political economy of trade policy (e.g., who supports which policies and why).

By their nature, economic theories are highly abstract and simplified logical devices for analyzing the effects of open international markets versus various restrictions or interventions. For example, most trade theories contrast pure *free trade* (i.e., completely open markets with no government interference of any kind) with a hypothetical situation of *autarky* (i.e., a completely closed economy) or some specific form of intervention (such as a *tariff,* which is a tax on imports), assuming that the internal structure of the domestic economy (i.e., a country's *production possibilities*) would be the same regardless. In the real world, however, trade and trade policies can have feedback effects on the domestic economy (e.g., influencing which industries develop), and policy options are usually much less clear-cut than pure free trade versus protection. As discussed extensively elsewhere in this book (e.g., Chapters 2, 7, and 8), governments more commonly make decisions about *liberalizing* their trade in the sense of reducing—but not completely eliminating—tariffs and other trade restrictions.

Because many simplifying assumptions are used in constructing trade theories, important questions arise about how well these theories predict trade patterns and how useful they are for understanding the benefits and costs of alternative trade policies. This chapter presents the main theories of trade in roughly the historical order in which they were invented. The chapter starts with the earliest approaches, and emphasizes the debates about how applicable these theories are to the complex realities of contemporary global trade.

## Mercantilism

The first systematic thinking on trade issues was that of the *mercantilists*. Mercantilist ideas were developed between the sixteenth and nineteenth centuries by prominent merchants, political pamphleteers, and government officials. The mercantilists were strong nationalists who advocated policies to maximize the wealth and power of the nation (and especially the monarchy), rather than the well-being of ordinary consumers. Politically, the mercantilists represented the interests of domestic merchants and manufacturers who wanted protection from foreign competition and sought to convince their rulers that such protectionist policies were in the national interest.

The mercantilists believed that a country should strive to achieve a positive *balance of trade* (i.e., a surplus of exports over imports), which they believed would increase its national wealth. The earliest mercantilists thought that a country's wealth was measured by its monetary assets, which in that historical period consisted of precious metals (gold and silver *specie*). Because a trade surplus had to be balanced by a net inflow of specie in the simple balance-of-payments accounts of that era, a trade surplus would guarantee an increase in a country's monetary wealth. Presumably, such an accumulation of money would enrich the royal treasury (e.g., through taxation) and thus make the nation more powerful. Some early mercantilists even favored prohibiting exports of gold and silver to prevent "wealth" from leaving the country.

Later mercantilists were less interested in gold and silver inflows for their own sake and more interested in encouraging domestic manufactures. In this later view, a country enjoying a trade surplus would have prosperous domestic industries providing full employment for the laboring classes; a deficit country would have depressed industries and high unemployment. These later mercantilists favored protectionism for domestic industries deemed vital for economic progress to shield them from import competition and to help keep the balance of trade positive. Although these later mercantilists didn't focus as much on inflows of specie, they pointed out that restrictions on the export of gold and silver were unnecessary; they reasoned that a country that achieved a positive trade balance through other means would automatically have a net inflow of specie instead of an outflow.

All the mercantilists agreed that because unregulated markets could not be trusted to maximize national advantages in trade, some kind of government guidance and control was necessary. They also all agreed that each country could enrich itself only at the expense of its trading partners because one country's trade surplus had to be matched by another's deficit. Later economists criticized the mercantilists for assuming that trade was (in modern terminology) a *zero-sum game,* in which some countries (those with surpluses) could benefit only at the expense of others (those with deficits).[2]

The eighteenth-century philosopher David Hume also criticized the mercantilists for ignoring the possibility that trade surpluses could be self-correcting. Hume argued that the increase in the money (specie) supply resulting from a trade surplus would lead to inflation, which in turn would make a country's goods more expensive and less competitive, and so eliminate the surplus. This simple idea of an automatic adjustment process that would restore balanced trade became known as the *specie-flow mechanism.* Balance of payments adjustment is much more complicated today than in Hume's time, however, and trade surpluses (or deficits) do not disappear so easily (see Chapter 4).

## Classical Trade Theory and Comparative Advantage

The theories of the classical economists developed out of a critique of mercantilist ideas in the eighteenth and nineteenth centuries. Adam Smith devoted much of his 1776 book, *The Wealth of Nations,* to an attack on what he called "the mercantile system" (from which the name mercantilism was later derived). Smith argued that the true source of a nation's wealth lies in the productivity of its labor force, which was increased primarily by (1) the division of labor (specialization in different tasks); and (2) the accumulation of capital (investing in stocks of materials and equipment that could increase future production). In Smith's view, a productive labor force, not a large supply of gold and silver, was the key to economic prosperity.

Smith was interested in promoting the welfare of individual consumers rather than the wealth and power of the national government. For the most part, government regulation was unnecessary[3] because the force of market competition could be relied upon to compel self-interested individuals to serve each other's needs through the social division of labor. For example, the butcher would supply the baker with meat and the baker would supply the butcher with bread, both acting out of self-interest. The same principle also applied to foreign trade: No government intervention was required to restrict or to promote it; individuals in different countries would naturally specialize in the products they could produce most cheaply and exchange them with each other. The result of free trade would be the creation of an *international division of labor* that would make workers more productive and consumers more affluent in all countries. Consumers would benefit because more productive workers would make cheaper products that consumers everywhere could afford to buy in greater quantities.

Smith argued that because a nation could never grow rich by "beggaring" (impoverishing) its neighbors, trying to maintain a positive balance of trade was foolish. As Smith put it, "if foreigners, either by prohibitions or high duties, are hindered from coming to sell, they cannot then always afford to come to buy."[4] Moreover, the protectionist policies advocated by the mercantilists would not lead to maximum national wealth, according to Smith. Trade restrictions would force people to produce some goods domestically that could be obtained more cheaply abroad; the resources thus diverted could better be used in producing other goods that the country could make more efficiently. Only if producers were left free to choose which goods to produce would the *invisible hand* of the market lead them to specialize in the products they could produce most cheaply.[5]

## BOX 3.1   An Example of Ricardian Comparative Advantage

A simple numerical example will help to illustrate Ricardo's theory of comparative advantage. In this theory, comparative advantage is based on relative labor costs, which are measured by the person-hours of labor required to produce each unit of output. The example assumes that there are two goods, wheat and cloth, and two countries (or regions), America and Britain, whose labor costs for each good are as follows:

|  | *Hours of Labor per Unit of Output* | |
| --- | --- | --- |
| *Country* | *Wheat (per bushel)* | *Cloth (per yard)* |
| America | 8 | 9 |
| Britain | 4 | 3 |

These precise numbers are purely hypothetical, but in principle such labor costs could be calculated by measuring the total hours of production workers' labor in a factory or farm and dividing them by the number of goods produced. The amounts of labor time required in each country are determined mainly by its technology, but could also be influenced by any natural resources or capital goods used in production that lessen the amount of labor-time needed to produce the output.

Although Britain has lower costs in labor hours for both goods, it has a *relatively greater* advantage in cloth and a *relatively lesser* advantage in wheat (British labor is three times as productive as American labor in cloth but only twice as productive in wheat). Hence, Britain has a *comparative* advantage *only* in cloth. America, in turn, has a comparative advantage in wheat because its labor is *relatively* more productive in that sector. American labor is one-half as productive as British labor in wheat because it takes American workers twice as many hours to grow wheat (8 compared with 4). However, American labor is only one-third as productive as British labor in cloth because it takes American workers three times as many hours for each yard produced (9 compared with 3).

From this type of example, Ricardo concluded that a country does not have to have absolutely lower costs of producing a good to benefit from exporting it (and for the other country to benefit from importing it). Suppose, for example, that these countries can trade internationally at a 1:1 ratio (i.e., 1 yard of cloth per bushel of wheat). America gains by exporting wheat and importing cloth because, in the absence of trade, Americans would get only 8/9 of a yard of cloth per bushel of wheat (this is the relative labor cost of wheat in America); but by trading they can obtain 1 yard of cloth in exchange for each bushel of wheat exported. Britain also gains by trading: Without trade the British would get only 3/4 of a bushel of wheat per yard of cloth (the relative labor cost of cloth in Britain); but

**BOX 3.1 (continued)**

by trading they can get 1 bushel of wheat for each yard of cloth they export. In this way, *both* countries end up with more of both commodities to consume if they trade than if each country tried to produce both goods for itself.

To see the gains from trade from another perspective, consider an American worker who can spend her time producing either wheat or cloth. In 8 hours, the American can make 8/9 yard of cloth. But by devoting the 8 hours to wheat production, she can grow 1 bushel of wheat, which she can then trade for 1 yard of cloth (at the "world" price of 1 yard for 1 bushel). Thus, the American can get more cloth by producing wheat and trading it for British cloth than by making cloth in America. The same logic applies to a British worker. If he works for 8 hours growing wheat, he obtains 2 bushels. But if the British worker produces cloth, in eight hours he can make 2 2/3 yards, which he can then trade for 2 2/3 bushels of American wheat at the price of 1 for 1.

Although Smith's critique of mercantilist ideas was profound and influential, he did not invent a coherent *theory* of international trade—an explanation of which countries export which goods and why. His notion that countries should specialize in the goods they can produce most cheaply has been referred to as the theory of *absolute advantage.* But this theory has an obvious flaw: How can a less developed nation, which cannot produce any goods more cheaply than more advanced countries, have anything to export? Thus, although Smith made a strong argument against mercantilism and had interesting ideas about the benefits of trade,[6] he did not satisfactorily explain how all countries could gain simultaneously from trade (i.e., why trade should be a positive-sum game for *all* countries).

Later classical economists addressed these issues head-on. The most important of these was David Ricardo, whose *Principles of Political Economy and Taxation* was first published in 1817. Ricardo is best known for his theory of *comparative advantage,* which he formulated in terms of labor costs. Suppose that one country (say, Britain) can produce all goods more cheaply than another country (say, America), in the sense that in Britain each good can be produced in fewer hours of labor. Nevertheless, Britain may be *relatively* more productive in some goods (e.g., cotton cloth), and *relatively* less productive in others (e.g., wheat). Then Britain has a comparative advantage only in cloth, and America has a comparative advantage in wheat (for the reason that it has a smaller absolute disadvantage in wheat). Ricardo showed that if each country exports the good in which it has a comparative advantage, both countries will benefit from the trade even if one of the countries is absolutely more productive in both goods (see Box 3.1).

The logic of comparative advantage is irrefutable, but some important caveats are in order. First, although both countries always gain from trade by specializing according to their respective comparative advantage, one country may receive a relatively greater *share* of the mutual gains if the *terms of trade*—the ratio in which the products exchange—turn in its favor.[7] This means that the exporting country gets a higher price for its exports and the importing country has to pay more for its imports, such as occurred when oil prices rose in the 1970s and again in the late 1990s. In these situations, the importers and exporters of the product whose price increased still gain from the trade (compared with a hypothetical situation of "autarky," or no trade); but the exporters get a greater share of the gains and the importers get a smaller share.

Second, the theory of comparative advantage assumes that trade is balanced (i.e., exports equal imports in value) and that labor is fully employed, thus abstracting from two of the main concerns of the mercantilists. If trade is not balanced, the surplus country must be exporting some goods in which it does not have a "true" comparative advantage (e.g., because an undervalued currency makes the country's products artificially cheap), and therefore trade does not entirely follow comparative advantage. If there are unemployed workers, it is possible to increase exports without producing fewer import-competing goods (i.e., by hiring some of the unemployed to work in export production); and so increasing exports can create more total jobs, just as the mercantilists claimed. Thus, the theory of comparative advantage has to assume that macroeconomic policies and monetary adjustments (such as Hume's specie-flow mechanism, which Ricardo endorsed) succeed in keeping trade balanced and workers fully employed.

Third, the classical theory of comparative advantage assumes *capital immobility*, which means that domestic firms cannot go abroad in search of absolutely lower labor costs in other countries (a subject discussed later in this chapter). An even more fundamental qualification concerns whether the costs of production are fixed by unalterable conditions (e.g., scarcity of natural resources) in each country or could be changed by human effort. If, in our previous example, America could acquire improved technology and know-how from Britain (say, through the importation of textile machinery or the immigration of skilled textile workers), then America could potentially become more efficient in cloth production. It is even possible that, if the reduction in American labor cost in cloth production is large enough, America could achieve a comparative advantage in cloth.[8]

Thus, the policy recommendation that a country should always follow its current comparative advantage ignores the possibility that the country could improve its productivity in some import-competing sectors and so transform its comparative advantage in the future. In other words, critics of classical trade theory would argue that the comparative advantage of a country is not fixed and immutable, especially in manufactured goods. To achieve such a potential improvement, temporary protection of the import-competing sector (cloth in America, in this example) or other government intervention (e.g., a subsidy) to promote its development might be necessary if imports would otherwise wipe out the nascent industry and prevent it from getting off the ground. This is the famous *infant industry* argument for protection, which can also be thought of as *dynamic comparative advantage* (i.e., developing the industries that offer the greatest gains in the long run).[9]

# Neoclassical Trade Theory

Later economists found Ricardo's explanation of comparative advantage based on comparisons of relative labor costs too simple for the reason that goods are produced with other inputs besides labor alone. New generations of trade theorists, known as "neoclassicals," generalized the theory of comparative advantage by arguing that countries would export whatever goods they could produce with the relatively lowest *opportunity costs* (i.e., the amount of other goods they would have to sacrifice to produce a unit of the exported goods). In this view, comparative advantages could derive from relatively low costs of any *factor of production* (productive input), such as capital or land, not just from relatively low labor costs.

One specific explanation of why countries have comparative advantages in particular products was developed by two Swedish neoclassical economists, Eli Heckscher and Bertil Ohlin, in the early twentieth century. Heckscher and Ohlin observed that goods are produced by using different proportions of the various factors of production (such as land, labor, and capital), and that countries are differently "endowed" with supplies of these factors.[10] For example, in a comparison of clothing, wheat, and automobiles, one might say that clothing is relatively labor-intensive, wheat is relatively land-intensive, and automobiles are relatively capital-intensive. Comparing three countries, say China, Canada, and Japan, we could say that China is relatively labor-abundant, Canada is relatively land-abundant, and Japan is relatively capital-abundant. (Note that all such comparisons are inherently relative!)

Under certain conditions, these differences in factor supplies should determine the three countries' comparative advantages, and we should expect to find the following pattern of trade: China would export clothing, Canada would export wheat, and Japan would export automobiles.[11] This proposition has become known as the *Heckscher-Ohlin* (H-O) or *factor-proportions* theory of trade: A country will tend to export goods that are produced using relatively large amounts of the country's relatively abundant factor of production.

At first glance, this prediction seems almost self-evident, but it is not as simple as it first appears. As later theorists, discovered, among them Paul Samuelson, the H-O theory requires some very strong assumptions; without them, the theory is not even logically true. For example, H-O theory assumes that differences in *factor endowments* (relative factor supplies) are the *main* economic differences among nations. In other words, the theory assumes that differences in *other* characteristics (such as technological capabilities or consumers' preferences) are too small to influence a country's trade. Another key assumption is *constant returns to scale*. This means that there are no cost advantages (or disadvantages) from producing larger quantities of output in any given industry. However, economies of scale have become so important in today's world that they are the basis for new theories of international trade (discussed later in this chapter).

Given the strong assumptions required for the H-O theory to give valid predictions, it is not surprising that the theory has not always fared well in empirical testing of its predictive accuracy. In 1953, Wassily Leontief discovered that the United States imported capital-intensive goods and exported labor-intensive goods, which, assuming the United States was relatively capital-abundant, was contrary to the predictions of the H-O theory. This surprising finding, which was dubbed the *Leontief paradox,* led to many efforts to refine the H-O approach, especially by including more finely differentiated factors of production. Distinguishing between *more-* and *less-skilled labor* has proved especially helpful in explaining the U.S. trade pattern: The United States is relatively abundant in more-skilled labor (sometimes referred to as *human capital*), and many subsequent studies have shown that the United States exports more-skilled labor-intensive goods and imports less-skilled labor-intensive goods.

Nevertheless, over the past several decades, numerous studies of global trade, using more sophisticated computer models and more comprehensive data sets for more countries, have concluded that the H-O factor-proportions theory does not always give reliable predictions of actual trade patterns.[12] The reason H-O frequently fails to give accurate predictions is that several of this theory's assumptions are often violated in the real world. Contrary to H-O, international differences in technological capabilities and consumer preferences appear to be important determinants of nations' trade. In addition, the prevalence of economies of scale in many important global industries implies that the H-O assumption of constant returns to scale is also inaccurate. These and other empirical findings have motivated a search for new theories of trade (discussed later in this chapter).

## The Gains from Trade and the Costs of Protection

Traditional theories of comparative advantage (both classical/Ricardian and neoclassical/Heckscher-Ohlin) imply that free trade is the most beneficial policy for a nation's consumers in the aggregate. That is, with free trade a nation's consumers usually have access to the most goods at the lowest prices compared with any other trade regime (either partial protection or a completely closed market). Based on this logic, economists argue that protectionist policies cause substantial losses to consumers. For example, a 1994 study estimated that tariffs (taxes on imports) and other import restrictions cost U.S. consumers about $70 billion in 1990, or slightly more than 1 percent of the gross domestic product (GDP) at that time.[13]

There are important qualifications to such estimates, however. First, the *consumer* costs of protection are not the same as the *net national* costs, which are usually much lower. This is because most of what consumers lose (as a result of higher prices for protected products) is offset by gains to producers in the protected industries; and, assuming that the tariffs aren't high enough to block all trade, another part is captured by the government in the form of tariff (tax) revenue. Only the *difference* between the consumers' losses and the gains to other groups constitutes a net national loss to the country as a whole. Thus, for example, in the previously cited estimate of $70 billion in consumer costs of protection, only about $11 billion represents a net loss in U.S. national income, after deducting $59 billion for the gains of domestic producers (i.e., higher profits for companies and more wages for workers) combined with the tariff revenue of the U.S. government.[14]

A more recent study puts the net national welfare cost of "significant" U.S. import restraints at $12.4 billion in 1996, of which the vast majority ($10.4 billion) is attributed to textile and apparel protection that is slated to be phased out in the early 2000s.[15] These may seem like large amounts, but they are relatively small compared to the overall size of the U.S. economy. For example, the $12.4 billion estimated loss in 1996 amounted to less than 0.2 percent of the gross domestic product (GDP) in that year.

Although these net welfare losses from current levels of U.S. protectionism are proportionately small, the potential gains to protected producers and losses to consumers of the affected products are an order of magnitude larger. One could say that protectionism is, in effect, a gigantic transfer program that redistributes income from consumers to producers (and, if a significant amount of tariff revenue is collected, to the government as well). The relatively small net national costs of protection in the 1990s can also be attributed to previous decades of trade liberalization efforts, which have resulted in relatively low tariff rates; these costs constituted larger percentages of GDP when higher tariffs were in place earlier in U.S. history (the nineteenth century and the first half of the twentieth).

On the other hand, the benefits to consumers from trade liberalization may be underestimated in these studies because they fail to consider that increased trade can reduce the market power of domestic firms and make markets more competitive. In a protectionist regime, domestic firms may be able to exercise considerable market power and set artificially high prices (i.e., prices out of line with costs) because those firms don't have to compete with imports. Thus, removing import restrictions can result in lower prices not only because the imports themselves are cheaper but also because the imports can force domestic firms to behave more competitively. Indeed, trade liberalization can sometimes effectively transform a domestic *monopoly* (single-seller industry) or *oligopoly* (an industry with only a few sellers) into a competitive industry by exposing the domestic firm(s) to *global competition* with foreign firms.

Aside from the losses imposed upon consumers, protection from imports in some industries can also hurt producers in other industries, including export industries. For example, if the United States protects the steel industry, and steel becomes more expensive, this raises costs for domestic manufacturers of automobiles, farm equipment, and other steel-consuming industries. Also, by raising the prices of imported goods, protectionism creates incentives for a country's business firms to produce more of those goods and (if labor and other inputs are fully employed) therefore fewer other products—including exported goods. For this reason, import protection can diminish export production, emphasized as in the *Lerner symmetry theorem* (after economist Abba Lerner). This last effect may not be operative if there are unemployed factors of production that could be put to work in the import-competing industries.

The theories of comparative advantage (both classical and neoclassical) imply that liberalizing trade is always beneficial to consumers in any country, regardless of whether the country's trading partners reciprocate by reducing their own trade barriers. From this perspective, the emphasis on the *reciprocal* lowering of trade barriers in most actual trade liberalization efforts (as described in Chapters 2, 7, and 8) is misplaced. Some economists believe this insistence on reciprocity is based on a mercantilist view, in which sacrifices by U.S. producers in allowing liberalized imports have to be matched by similar sacrifices from foreign producers in opening up to more U.S. exports, rather than on the theory of free trade. To put it another way, actual U.S.

trade policies sometimes seem to place more importance on opening up foreign markets for U.S. exporters rather than on opening up the U.S. market for American consumers. Alternatively, the emphasis on reciprocity can be viewed as a political compromise with domestic producer interests that is necessary to form a majority coalition in favor of a relatively liberal overall trade policy.

## The Distribution of the Gains and Losses from Trade

Even if free trade policies bring positive gains to a country's consumers in the aggregate, opening up trade can also have profound effects on the distribution of income among different groups within a nation. Not all individuals share equally (or at all) in the aggregate gains that a country's consumers as a whole obtain from free trade. In this section, we identify some of the chief winners and losers from trade liberalization and discuss how these redistributive effects can explain resistance to free trade policies by adversely affected groups.

Trade redistributes income among different groups of people in the economy depending on how they are affected by a country's exports and imports. Usually, these groups are distinguished by their factor ownership; that is, individuals are grouped according to whether they are owners of capital, labor, land, or other resources. Sometimes, people are distinguished rather by whether they are producers or consumers of a particular product or by whether they are associated with export or import interests. In all these cases, there are losers as well as winners from opening up to trade, and the losers generally stand to gain from protectionism. Thus, although free trade usually brings aggregate gains to all consumers, this does not prevent some groups of consumers from being worse off with free trade. The redistributive effects of trade stem from the same source as the aggregate welfare gains; namely, countries are induced to reallocate their resources away from import-competing sectors and into export sectors. To put it colloquially, "no pain, no gain."

The most famous theory of how trade affects income distribution is based on the logic of the Heckscher-Ohlin trade model, which implies that owners of abundant factors gain from free trade but owners of scarce factors lose. To see why, recall that in the H-O theory, countries export the goods that are relatively intensive in their relatively abundant factors of production, and they import those goods that are relatively intensive in their relatively scarce factors of production. The reason for this is that the abundance of some factors of production makes them comparatively cheap (e.g., the low wages of labor in China), and therefore products made with relatively large amounts of these factors (e.g., labor-intensive clothing or toys) are cheaper and more competitive when produced with those cheaper inputs.

But as a country specializes in the goods that use an abundant factor relatively intensively, the demand for that factor rises and so does its *factor price* (wage rate for labor, profit rate for capital, or rental rate for land). At the same time, as the country imports the goods that use a scarce factor more intensively, domestic production of those goods is reduced, demand for the scarce factor falls, and the price of the scarce factor decreases. As a result, the owners of the abundant factors gain and the owners of the scarce factors lose when a country liberalizes its trade; the reverse happens if a country abandons free trade and protects its import-competing industries.

This implication of the H-O trade model—that free trade hurts the scarce-factor owners and protectionism benefits them—is known as the *Stolper-Samuelson theorem* (named after economists Wolfgang Stolper and Paul Samuelson). According to this theorem, the losses to the scarce-factor owners from free trade are absolute as well as relative; that is, the real income of the scarce-factor owners (as measured by how many goods they can afford to buy) is lower with free trade and higher with protectionism. In relation to trade politics, this theorem explains why the owners of scarce factors of production (e.g., landowners in Japan or less-skilled workers in the United States) are often in favor of protectionist policies. These distributional predictions of the H-O theory are summarized in Table 3.1.

**TABLE 3.1    Distributional Effects of Free Trade**

| *Theory (Perspective)* | *Winners* | *Losers* |
|---|---|---|
| Heckscher-Ohlin theory/Stolper-Samuelson theorem (long-run) | Owners of abundant factors of production | Owners of scarce factors of production |
| Specific factors theory (short-run) | Owners of factors of production stuck in export sectors | Owners of factors of production stuck in import sectors |
| Partial-equilibrium model (supply and demand in specific industries) | Consumers of imported goods; producers of export goods | Producers of import-competing goods; consumers of exported goods |

In the last two decades of the twentieth century, one of the most notable distributional shifts in the United States was a widening gap between the wages of more-skilled (professional and technical) workers and less-skilled (production and service) workers. According to some economists, this trend can be explained at least in part by Stolper-Samuelson effects. Because more-skilled labor is relatively abundant and less-skilled labor is relatively scarce in the U.S. (compared with other countries), increased imports of less-skilled labor-intensive goods from countries where less-skilled labor is relatively abundant (such as Mexico or China) would have a depressing effect on the wages of less-skilled workers in the United States. Other economists, while not denying that such an effect is possible in theory, claimed that trade was a relatively minor factor empirically in explaining the growing wage gap between more- and less-skilled labor in the United States in the 1980s and 1990s. These economists blamed the growing wage gap on other factors, such as technological changes that favored more-skilled workers and the increased immigration of less-skilled workers. Because different researchers using different methodologies and data sets have reached different conclusions, this issue remains unresolved.[16]

It must be emphasized that in spite of the losses to the scarce-factor owners predicted by the Stolper-Samuelson theorem, free trade normally yields aggregate (net) gains to the country as a whole. For this to be true, the gains to the winners (abundant-factor owners) must be greater than the losses to the losers (scarce-factor owners). This creates the possibility of *compensation:* The winners could pay off the losers; this way, the latter would be no worse off with free trade, and the former could still keep part of their gains. In this sense, free trade can *potentially* be what economists call a *Pareto improvement,* after the early twentieth-century sociologist Vilfredo Pareto. A Pareto improvement occurs when some people in a country are made better off and no one is made worse off. However, unless an effective compensation scheme is in place, free trade is not likely to be an *actual* improvement for all groups in society.

The reason for this disturbing conclusion is that there are severe practical difficulties in arranging compensation for those who would lose from free trade. First, there is no mechanism in a free market system that compels the winners to compensate the losers. Ironically, some kind of government intervention would be required to make the winners pay compensation in order to prevent free trade (which is otherwise a free market policy) from harming some members of society. Second, some kinds of compensatory policies could lessen the incentives for producers to specialize and thus would reduce the gains from trade overall. For example, a tax on the profits of the export activity would be a disincentive to produce for export.

Even leaving these difficulties aside, whether the losers from free trade deserve to be compensated at all is a value judgment that citizens and policymakers must make. If the losers are a wealthy class, such as a landed oligarchy, there is little moral justification for paying compensation. If the losers are members of a less affluent group, such as industrial workers or peasants, there may be a stronger moral reason for paying compensation to them. Whoever the losers may be, compensating them may be politically important for creating a majority coalition in favor of free trade.

Taking the Stolper-Samuelson logic to its extreme, it is theoretically possible that free trade could completely equalize factor prices in all countries, even if the factors themselves are not mobile between nations (i.e., even if labor or capital cannot freely cross international borders). This proposition, known as the *factor-price equalization theorem* (also developed by Paul Samuelson), says that free trade in commodities alone could make workers, capital owners, and landlords each receive the same real incomes for their land, capital, and labor (respectively) in all nations. But if any of the strong assumptions[17] of this theorem do not hold in practice, then trade will not produce a complete equalization of global income distribution. In reality, the world is still far away from complete factor-price equalization; this is evidenced especially by the persistent wide gaps in real-wage levels between rich and poor countries, which are mainly attributed to differences in technological capabilities that are ignored in the H-O theory.[18]

The H-O theory assumes that the factors of production are mobile between industries within a nation; that is, the same land, labor, and capital can be used in all sectors of the economy, although in different proportions. For this reason, the distributional effects predicted by the H-O model pertain to *all* owners of a factor, *regardless* of the sector in which their factor is employed.[19] But this assumption is not always realistic, especially in the short run. Many productive factors are adapted in some special way to a particular industry and cannot easily be transferred to another line of production (or would not be equally efficient if they were). For example, an autoworker cannot easily become a computer programmer, or a textile worker turn into an airplane mechanic—at least not without costly retraining. Similarly, most capital is invested in specific types of plant and equipment that cannot easily be converted from one use to another. In the long run, capital can be reinvested in other activities; but in the short run, a steel mill cannot be used to make computers.

To the extent that productive factors are specific to particular industries, the conclusions of the H-O theory must be modified. Instead, the *specific factors theory* (developed by Gustav Haberler) can be applied when factors are stuck, or *immobile*, between industries. This theory says that the owners of a factor that is not freely mobile across industries will gain or lose from trade according to whether the factor is used in an export sector or an import-competing sector, as shown in Table 3.1. Thus, skilled technicians who make jet airplanes (an export product in the United States) benefit from free trade, whereas equally skilled technicians who are employed in the automotive sector may lose from free trade (because automobiles are imported), if both groups' skills are industry-specific.

Finally, one can also analyze the distributional effects of trade policies in a framework of producer versus consumer interests. This analysis is based on a standard supply-and-demand approach, which economists call *partial equilibrium* ("partial" because it is applied to the market for only one good at a time). According to this type of analysis (also shown in Table 3.1), the producers (workers and business firms) in import-competing industries lose from free trade, because imports lower the prices at which they can sell their products and also take away part of their domestic markets. Consumers of the same products benefit from free trade, however, because it allows them to buy the imported goods more cheaply. In this same theoretical approach, producers in export industries gain from free trade because, by the logic of comparative advantage, they can command higher prices for their products in world markets than they could get at home if they didn't export them. Domestic consumers of exported goods lose, however, because they have to pay higher prices for these goods when the country is open to trade.

In theory, the overall gains to the consumers generally exceed the losses to the producers from free trade in import-competing sectors, and the gains to producers of exports exceed the losses to consumers of those products, so that there are positive net benefits of free trade in all industries. But political realities may still lead to protectionist outcomes, in import-competing industries. Usually, import-competing producers represent a concentrated set of interest groups, often located in a few regions of the country (such as the U.S. auto industry in Michigan). The consumers of imported goods, in contrast, are usually a widely diffused group of individuals for whom the extra costs of a particular protected product are not readily apparent. Thus, import-competing producers are more likely to base their votes and political contributions on support for protectionist policies, whereas consumers are more likely to base their political support on other issues and concerns that are more salient for them than trade policy. An exception occurs when the direct "consumers" are other ("down-stream") industries that are able to organize political campaigns against protectionism for their supplier industries (e.g., some steel consuming businesses have organized a coalition to oppose the American steel industry's demands for protection).

When so many groups in society stand to lose from trade liberalization, it is hard to obtain a political consensus in favor of *pure* free trade policies that would not allow for any exceptions for producers whose jobs or industries are adversely affected by imports. Nevertheless, export interests can be relied upon to strongly support liberal trade policies (see Chapter 6). Therefore, it is still possible to form a coalition in support of a relatively liberal trade regime in which a country is mostly open to imports but exceptions are made for those import-competing producers who mobilize to obtain protection for their specific interests (such as European farmers or U.S. apparel manufacturers).

## Exceptions and Qualifications to the Case for Free Trade

The theories discussed up to this point imply that free trade is in the interest of a country as a whole, even if it does not benefit all groups within the country. But there are some exceptions or qualifications to the case for pure free trade, even at the national level.

One important qualification to the theory of comparative advantage is the problem of *adjustment costs*. When we analyze the gains from trade in a comparative advantage model, we are essentially comparing an economy that has already fully adjusted to free trade with an economy that does not trade at all (or one that has restricted trade). This type of comparison does not take into account the social and economic costs of removing existing trade restrictions and making the transition to free trade. For example, after trade is liberalized in a country, some workers will lose their jobs, at least temporarily, and some capital equipment will have to be scrapped. If the new jobs and industries that emerge are located in different parts of the country, workers may be required to move and governments to provide new social infrastructure (e.g., high-ways and schools) in the booming areas. At the same time, tax revenues will be reduced, especially in the states and municipalities where factories are shut down and jobs are lost, thus making it harder to pay for the rising adjustment costs.

Adjustment costs are not considered a valid reason to maintain protected or ineffi-cient industries in the long run, but they can be an argument for gradualism in trade liberalization. Adjustment costs can also be ameliorated through domestic social poli-cies that help people through the hard times of the transition period, rather than by protecting their industries. Programs such as labor retraining, job placement services, and relocation assistance can help offset adjustment costs and make trade liberaliza-tion more politically acceptable. (See the discussion of U.S. adjustment assistance pro-grams in Chapter 7.)

Another exception is called the *optimal tariff* for a *large country*. If one country (or a group of countries combined into a cartel) holds a large share of the world market for the products it trades in, that country (or group) can drive up the prices of its exports and drive down the prices of its imports (in relative terms) by artificially restricting trade. Of course, if the large country restricts trade too much it won't benefit from the higher terms of trade (relative price of its exports). The trade restriction must set at a moderate level; in theory, there is some unique, positive tariff rate that would be "optimal" in the sense of maximizing the country's gains.

In practice, a large-country trade restriction does not have to be an import tariff. The best real-world example of such a trade restriction occurred when, to drive up the price of oil, the Organization of Petroleum Exporting Countries (OPEC) restricted oil production and oil exports, efforts that were most successful in 1973–1979. (Note also that OPEC is a cartel, not a single country.) Large-country trade restrictions are strictly beggar-thy-neighbor policies because they hurt the trading partners of the country or countries imposing the restrictions (e.g., the nations that imported oil from OPEC). Most economists believe that few individual countries (even the United States) are big enough to benefit significantly from such trade restrictions, and the collapse of oil prices in the 1980s showed that cartels like OPEC are not likely to be successful in the long run.

Yet another exception to the case for free trade is the problem of *market failures*. Market failures are situations in which Adam Smith's invisible hand fails to operate properly, and the self-interested behavior of individuals does not lead to the greatest social good. When market failures exist, free trade may not be the optimal policy even for a small country (i.e., a country that is too small to affect the prices of its traded goods). There are many possible types of market failures, but perhaps the most important for trade policy are *externalities*. Externalities are costs or benefits to some actors in the economy that are not accounted for in market prices.

Externalities can be either negative or positive, depending on whether they cause injury or bring benefits to the affected groups. A classic example of a negative externality is a factory that emits pollution and injures the health of people who live in the vicinity. Another example would be the ecological damage caused by deforestation when forest land (as in the Amazon basin in Brazil) is cleared for export-oriented agriculture. Positive externalities include beneficial *spillovers* from one activity to another. An example might be that knowledge generated in computer production can benefit producers in other industries if the computer firms that generate the knowledge are not fully compensated for the benefits they create for others.[20]

When externalities are significant, the free market gives the wrong "signals" to market participants about how much of the goods to produce, to consume, and to import or export. In situations with negative externalities market participants will produce too much because they are not forced to pay all the costs that their production creates. In situations with positive externalities (including infant industries), the free market will induce too little output because market prices do not fully reward producers for the benefits they create.[21] Whether governments should intervene in these situations is a separate question, but in theory the right government policies can improve on free market outcomes by correcting for the externalities.

Although government policies have the potential to improve on free markets in the presence of externalities, a *trade* policy (e.g., a tariff to discourage imports) is *not* generally the best way to solve the problem. Rather, the best solution (what economists call a *first-best policy*) is a policy that directly attacks the source of the market failure.

For example, a tax on the polluter's production or a subsidy to the computer firms generating positive externalities would be the best policies in the examples previously cited. These domestic policies may affect trade, but they are not trade policies; rather they are direct efforts to counteract the harmful externality or encourage the beneficial externality.

A trade policy is usually only a *second-best policy* in situations with externalities. If it is desired, for example, to encourage the production of an import-competing product that generates a positive externality, then a tariff that protects the industry would be effective. It would not be as good as a subsidy to the producers, however, because the tariff imposes extra costs on consumers of the product (the tariff increases the price of the product, whereas the subsidy does not).[22] This same point applies to infant industry promotion, which can be accomplished at a lower social cost through direct subsidies instead of import protection.

The same logic that enables us to rank policy options when markets fail allows us to rank policies when there is a *noneconomic policy objective* (but no demonstrable market failure). Suppose, for example, that there is overriding political pressure or a national security need to maintain domestic production in a certain import-competing industry. If free trade is not an option politically, economic theory teaches that it is better to subsidize the producers directly rather than use trade restrictions to keep out imports. The subsidy policy involves lower costs to society than trade protection (tariffs or quotas) because protectionism makes the goods more expensive for consumers and the subsidy does not.

But a subsidy is still a socially costly policy. Consumers must pay for the subsidies through higher taxes, even though in theory this costs them less than trade protection would. If the subsidized goods are exported, the subsidy also hurts producers in other countries who have trouble competing with subsidized imports. Under international trade agreements and U.S. trade laws, producers are entitled to obtain *countervailing duties* to protect themselves from subsidized imports under certain conditions (see Chapter 7).

Interestingly, countervailing duties are one of the few types of trade barriers that are endorsed by some pro-free-trade economists. Because subsidies are considered an interference with free markets to begin with, countervailing duties that offset foreign subsidies are seen as restoring the market to its natural equilibrium, and thus as making international markets work more efficiently. Paradoxically, from these economists' point of view, countervailing duties sacrifice domestic consumers' interests but increase global economic welfare by eliminating subsidy-induced "distortions" of international trade.

Some scholars of industrial development argue that most of the major countries that successfully industrialized—including (at different times) the United States, Germany, Japan, and most of the East Asian newly industrializing countries (excepting only Britain, the first country that industrialized, and later the former British colony of Hong Kong)—accomplished their greatest industrial growth historically behind protectionist barriers. To be sure, most of these countries promoted exports, but until recent decades they tended to be mercantilist traders who also protected their industries from imports. Some economists have questioned whether these countries could have done even better with more liberal trade policies, and other economists have complained about the injury allegedly caused to other nations by these countries' mercantilist practices. Nevertheless, the fact remains that import protection was the most politically feasible method of encouraging infant industries to grow up in the historical periods when these nations industrialized.

## New Trade Theories

The empirical difficulties of the H-O theory (discussed earlier) and new findings about contemporary international trade patterns have motivated a search for alternatives to traditional models of comparative advantage. This section will discuss several of the anomalies in actual trade patterns, compared with H-O predictions, and how new theories have been developed to account for the observed trends in actual trade.[23]

The "new" theories of international trade originated in the 1960s, but developed more rapidly in later decades when mainstream academic economists began to work out new models of trade based on new developments in economic theory (e.g., models of oligopoly and monopolistic competition that could be applied to international trade). Because the new trade theories are diverse and still evolving, it is difficult to generalize about them. What follows are brief summaries of some of the most important and influential versions and discussions of their policy implications.

### *Monopolistic Competition, Scale Economies, and Intra-Industry Trade*

This branch of the new trade theory evolved in response to three empirical findings. First, researchers discovered the importance of *intra-industry trade,* which means two-way trade between countries in *similar* types of products. This generally involves trade in different styles, brands, or models of the same products, usually manufactured goods such as cosmetics, pharmaceuticals, and automobiles. The simultaneous export and import of similar goods is not consistent with theories of comparative advantage, which imply that countries should specialize in *different* types of products. Yet typical estimates show that about 50 percent of U.S. trade in manufactures and as much as 70 percent in some European countries consists of intra-industry trade in similar goods.[24]

A second problem for the traditional theories is the importance of *economies of scale.* In many industries, it is cheaper to produce goods when there is a larger volume of output. Often, this is because a large fixed cost (overhead), such as expenditures on research and development (R&D) or heavy machinery, has to be incurred no matter how many units of output are produced. As a result, the average fixed cost per unit falls as output increases. This is often true in high-tech sectors, such as computers and aerospace, as well as in the older "smokestack" industries, such as steel and automobiles.[25]

Third, traditional theories of comparative advantage assume *perfectly competitive markets* in the sense that there are large numbers of sellers of identical products, each of whom is too small to influence the market price. This may be a good characterization of some markets (e.g., textiles and agricultural commodities), but it is clearly not true where some form of *imperfect competition* prevails. The type of imperfect competition that is most relevant to explaining intra-industry trade is called *monopolistic competition,* which occurs when there is *product differentiation* through brand-name identification or other ways of distinguishing the products of different firms. In this type of market structure, each firm is the monopolistic (sole) producer of its own brand or model, but still has to compete with the producers of different brands or models of the same (or similar) products.

New trade theories that incorporated these three elements (i.e., intra-industry trade, economies of scale, and monopolistic competition) were developed by Paul Krugman and others in the late 1970s and 1980s. These new theories imply two types of gains from trade that are not found in traditional theories of comparative advantage. First, consumers can get a *greater variety of products* to choose from because open markets give consumers access to other countries' brands or types of goods. Second, workers in *all* countries can get *higher real wages,* regardless of whether labor is an abundant or scarce factor in the H-O sense. The reason is that, with economies of scale, increasing output to serve world markets lowers the average cost of production; as long as prices are reduced accordingly, workers everywhere can afford to buy more of the cheaper products. Thus, in these new theories, no group loses from free trade as in the traditional theories discussed earlier; everyone can share in the benefits when unit costs are reduced by producing more goods for export.

Theories of trade with economies of scale *cannot* predict the *direction* of trade, however. With economies of scale, any country can *acquire* a cost advantage in an industry or product line by producing enough of a good to drive unit costs down to a competitive level. As a result, the pattern of trade in industries that have scale economies cannot be predicted by reference to intrinsic country and industry characteristics, such as comparative labor costs or factor endowments. The pattern of trade is determined by historical accidents, such as which country starts up an industry first; there are no inherent comparative advantages in goods with strong economies of scale. Nevertheless, this theory does predict that there will be intra-industry trade because countries can exchange differentiated versions of similar products (e.g., different models of automobiles or brands of toothpaste) with each other.

One still has to be careful in applying these new theories because they make just as many unrealistic, simplifying assumptions as traditional trade theories. For example, the new theories also assume full employment, without which one cannot be sure that all workers will receive the promised benefits of higher real wages as a result of free trade. In addition, these theories usually assume that each brand or type of good is made by one firm in a particular country, thus ignoring the role of multinational corporations and intra-corporate trade (discussed later in this chapter).

These same theories typically assume *free entry,* which means that it is costless for new producers to enter industries in which there are positive economic profits. In theory, the free entry of new firms must increase supply until prices are driven down to equal average total costs, and therefore economic profits are driven to zero. As a result, cost reductions from producing larger volumes for export are passed on to consumers as lower prices instead of increasing companies' profits. But if there are *barriers to entry,* an industry can become an oligopoly that is dominated by relatively few large firms (such as Boeing and Airbus in commercial jet aircraft production). The next section discusses new trade theories that are designed for oligopolistic industries.

## Oligopolistic Rivalry and Strategic Trade Policy

Another type of new trade theory deals explicitly with oligopolistic international markets in which there are few firms. Oligopolistic firms can reap excess profits (often called *oligopolistic rents*) by holding prices above average costs of production. Oligopolistic firms also act *strategically* in the sense that they take each other's actions into account in forming their competitive strategies. In oligopolistic markets, it becomes possible for government intervention (such as protectionism or subsidies) to increase national income by allowing domestic firms to capture a greater share of the excess profits in the global industry for the home country firm(s). This sort of intervention is called *strategic trade policy* because the policy intervention allows the domestic firms to gain a stronger position in their strategic interplay with their foreign rivals.

The type of government intervention required to give national firms a strategic advantage varies depending on the nature of the oligopolistic rivalry in an industry. In the Brander-Spencer model (named for James Brander and Barbara Spencer), for example, it pays for the government to subsidize export production by the domestic firms: Subsidization effectively lowers their costs and thus allows them to grab a larger share of the world market for themselves by underselling their rivals.[26] If the extra profits thus obtained exceed the cost of the subsidy, total national income is increased—at the expense of the foreign country, of course (although in this case global consumers benefit because more goods are available at lower prices).

Paul Krugman has analyzed a different situation in which a country can use import protection as a means of export promotion. This paradoxical type of policy requires strong economies of scale in addition to an oligopolistic market structure. If the government protects the home market for an oligopoly with strong economies of scale, the domestic firm may be able to increase its output and thereby lower its unit costs by enough to become a more competitive exporter, and thus take market share away from its foreign rivals.

In reality, governments often subsidize or protect oligopolistic producers regardless of whether economic estimates suggest that such a policy is in the national interest. A classic example was the European countries' subsidies of the jet aircraft consortium Airbus Industrie, which enabled this start-up firm to compete with the American behemoths Boeing and McDonnell-Douglas. Whether this policy has enhanced (or will eventually enhance) overall European economic welfare is impossible to determine, but it did succeed in creating a competitive jet airplane manufacturer and it had a profound effect on a global oligopolistic industry (eventually forcing McDonnell-Douglas to merge with Boeing, leaving only one U.S. firm producing large civilian jetliners).

Although the theory of strategic trade policy created great excitement when economists first developed it in the 1980s, it is important to be cautious in assessing the practical implications of this theory. For one thing, strategic trade policy is a nationalistic, beggar-thy-neighbor approach that usually benefits one country (if at all) only at the expense of its trading partners. This means that the use of strategic trade policies by some countries gives other countries incentives to retaliate (e.g., by subsidizing their own companies), which would be likely to negate the former countries' intended strategic advantage. Second, even if foreign countries don't retaliate, a strategic trade policy will work as intended only if actual industry behavior matches the theoretical assumptions required for that policy to be in the national interest. If the assumptions of the theoretical models do not hold in reality, the policies implied by those models may not help, and could hurt, the interests of a country that adopts them. Third, it is debatable whether a government could obtain the voluminous information that it would need in selecting industries for strategic trade policies and deciding which policies to use to help those industries (e.g., whether to use a subsidy, a tariff, or some other policy instrument; how high to set the subsidy or tax rate; etc.).

One important insight generated by the theory of strategic trade policy is the idea of a *prisoner's dilemma.* Each country can be better off if its government intervenes appropriately to support its own firms and its rival does not, but then the rival will suffer. But if both governments intervene, both countries are likely to end up worse off. To prevent the latter outcome—which is most likely if one country retaliates against the other's strategic intervention—the best option is international cooperation in the form of agreements to forswear the use of strategic policies. Thus, ironically, a theory that was developed to prove that government intervention in trade can sometimes be in the national self-interest has ended up providing a new argument in favor of trade liberalization.

### *Technological Innovation and the Product Cycle*

Although the Heckscher-Ohlin theory assumes that all countries have the same technological capabilities, much research has shown that this is not so. There are enormous disparities in technology levels between different countries, especially when one compares less developed countries with the industrialized nations. Indeed, international differences in technology are one of the main reasons why labor productivity and average wages differ so much between richer and poorer countries and why factor-price equalization fails to occur.

One trade theory that emphasizes technological change is the *product cycle model,* originally developed by Raymond Vernon in 1966.[27] This model is based on the recognition that some manufactured products are new and innovative (e.g., supercomputers) while others are older and more standardized (e.g., steel). According to this theory, a few countries such as the United States, Germany, and Japan are the technological leaders that export the new and innovative products; other countries are followers that can export only mature or standardized products. Trade in new and innovative products is thus explained by absolute technological superiority, sometimes referred to as *technological gaps,* on the part of firms in the exporting nation.

As products age, their production becomes more routinized and mechanized and no longer needs to be located in the original innovating country. According to Vernon, production shifts initially to other industrialized nations that are capable followers but not major leaders in innovation. The costs of production fall as there is greater use of labor-saving machinery and firms take advantage of scale economies. Eventually, the technology becomes completely standardized; production can then be shifted to less developed countries where wages are lower and costs can be minimized. In Vernon's theory, foreign direct investment by multinational corporations is an important vehicle for the transfer of technology for producing standardized products to less developed countries (an issue discussed below).

Still newer theories of trade and technology were developed in the 1990s. A major issue in these new theories is whether, taking technology factors into account, international trade helps the poorer countries grow faster than the richer countries and thus encourages international *convergence* (greater international equality); or whether trade leads to concentrated gains in the richer countries and leaves the poorer countries behind, which causes international *divergence* (greater inequality between nations). Convergence is more likely to result if a lot of technology is transferred to the less developed countries; divergence is more likely to result if technological innovation becomes highly concentrated in the already more advanced nations. Although no firm conclusions have been reached, theorists in this genre have shown that either convergence or divergence can result depending on factors such as the countries' initial income levels, the amount of education and training of their respective labor forces, and their institutional environments for promoting innovative activity.

## *Capital Mobility and Multinational Corporations*

Most new theories of trade based on imperfect competition as well as old ones based on comparative advantage assume that business firms are nationally based, and therefore a country's export potential and import propensities are primarily determined by such internal factors as factor endowments or scale economies. In reality, however, global trade today is largely dominated by large *multinational corporations* (MNCs) operating in two or more countries, and *intra-corporate trade* (i.e., trade that is conducted by affiliates of the same companies located in different countries) accounts for a large proportion of international exchanges.

In the United States, about 36 percent of goods exports and about 40 percent of goods imports are *internal* transactions or transfers between MNC affiliates located in the United States and abroad (counting both U.S. *and* foreign-owned companies). If one counts *all* MNC transactions, including sales to other companies and purchases from them, as well as internal transfers, MNCs account for about 71 percent of U.S. imports and fully 86 percent of U.S. exports of goods.[28]

The growing role of MNCs in trade has been accompanied by heightened *capital mobility:* the ability of firms to locate their productive facilities in different parts of the world, depending on where it is most convenient for access to foreign markets, sources of cheap inputs, or other competitive reasons. Capital mobility has been enhanced in recent decades by several factors, including trade liberalization, financial liberalization, the privatization (and reduced threats of nationalization) of enterprises, and the information technology and telecommunications revolutions that have made it easier to manage global companies. Thus, modern world trade is based to a considerable extent on the strategic internal planning of MNCs rather than the arms-length transactions of the marketplace.

As a result of these trends, the proliferation of *foreign direct investment* (FDI)— acquiring significant shares in enterprises, or ownership of them, in another country— is playing an increasingly important role in determining international trade patterns (see also Chapter 4 on how FDI affects overall U.S. trade performance). Competitive advantages in the production of today's sophisticated manufactured goods are influenced by variables such as technological sophistication, management savvy, the skill level of the labor force, product innovation, receipt by corporations of favorable government treatment, and the excellence of the transportation and telecommunications infrastructure. Many contemporary MNCs have created *global factories*, in which a finished product (such as an automobile or computer) includes parts and components manufactured and assembled in a variety of nations. Global factories consist of MNC subsidiaries and affiliates (either wholly or partly owned by the parent company) and local firms that produce for MNCs on contract, a relationship known as *outsourcing*.

The global spread of MNCs has helped many countries become capable of exporting products that they could not have produced by using their own internal resources and technology only. Ireland and Singapore are good examples of countries that have become successful exporters of sophisticated manufactured goods in a relatively short time almost entirely by attracting large inflows of FDI. MNCs account for the majority of manufactured output in Ireland and more than 80 percent of its manufactured exports. Foreign-controlled companies in Singapore produce more than two-thirds of manufacturing output and export sales.[29]

Costa Rica joined the elite ranks of exporters of highly sophisticated microprocessor chips virtually overnight, not because of inherent comparative advantage but because the Intel Corporation liked the corporate environment and built a semiconductor factory there. Although labor costs must always be part of a corporation's investment location decisions, many countries offer even lower wages than Costa Rica; therefore, minimizing labor costs alone does not fully explain this particular investment. Other factors, such as an educated labor force and a stable government, also helped to attract Intel into the country. The Intel operation in Costa Rica is especially interesting because a very high-tech firm, the world's dominant producer of microprocessors, decided to service global customers from an overseas location rather than by exporting from its U.S. home base.

China is another country whose export success is closely tied to FDI and MNCs. An estimated one-half of China's exports in 2000 came from companies with some foreign ownership; when the shipments from these companies are excluded, China falls from the world's ninth largest exporter to the fifteenth.[30] Similarly, companies with foreign ownership (minority or majority) account for about one-half of China's imports, mainly because so many unfinished goods are brought in for final assembly and then re-exported.

### *Low-Wage Competition and Export-Led Growth*

The rise of the global factory phenomenon suggests that the transfer of standardized manufacturing production to lower-wage developing countries, originally described in Vernon's product cycle model as a gradual process taking several decades, may be occurring at an accelerated pace. In today's world, both productive inputs (such as capital equipment) and technological knowledge are increasingly mobile. It is now possible to locate a factory in, say, China or Mexico, that uses up-to-date machinery and equipment and produces goods of world-class quality. Once the work forces are suitably trained, the labor in these transplanted factories can be just as productive or nearly as productive as that in similar factories in the United States, Europe, and Japan.

Yet the workers in the developing countries still earn much lower wages. In 2000–2001, total compensation costs (wages and employer-paid benefits combined) were about $2.50 per hour for Mexican manufacturing workers, about $1.50 per hour in some Central American and Caribbean countries, and less than $0.50 per hour in China, compared with about $20 per hour for U.S. manufacturing workers.[31] As a result, in production processes where labor costs are relatively important, there are clear incentives to move production to lower-wage sites when feasible.

One should not exaggerate this point and claim that all or most manufacturing jobs are in danger of disappearing from the United States. Corporations face limits in their ability to relocate production to low-wage sites. To attract (and keep) FDI or out-sourcing, those countries must have reasonably stable and honest governments, respect for property rights, and open capital markets. The low-wage countries also need adequate infrastructure, such as airports and seaports, roads or railroads, and reliable telecommunications facilities (which today include Internet access). Otherwise, transportation costs or lack of communication with suppliers could over-whelm the putative savings in labor costs.

These qualifications explain why the very poorest and lowest-wage countries in the world (e.g., in sub–Saharan Africa) have not become major export platforms for labor-intensive manufactures. Also, the logic of low-wage competition applies only for labor-intensive goods or the labor-intensive stages of production for which special skills and training are unimportant. In activities where either capital costs, raw materials costs, or *human capital* inputs (high skills and technical training) are more important than ordinary labor costs, it will not pay to move production to low-wage countries. Also, much FDI is motivated by other concerns besides the minimization of production costs. Most FDI has occurred in the industrial countries, probably because of a desire to locate the production of many goods closer to the more prosperous markets where there is greater demand for the products.

Nevertheless, there is considerable scope for low-wage competition to influence trade patterns, as the rapid growth of U.S. trade with countries like Mexico and China makes clear. By combining foreign capital and technology with domestic low-wage labor forces, these countries (and many others) can achieve *unit labor costs* (wage costs per unit of output) far below U.S. (or European or Japanese) levels in certain types of export-oriented production.

Traditional trade theory (based on the Ricardian model) discounted this possibility by asserting that wage differences among countries always reflect differences in labor productivity; thus, low-wage countries must also be low-productivity countries and therefore cannot gain overall competitive advantages by virtue of their low wages. There is still much truth in this view. Even in the new export powerhouses such as China or Mexico, technology remains relatively backward in large areas of the domestic economy (especially agriculture, services, and handicraft manufactures), and the low wages do correspond to low *average* productivity.

What is new, according to some authors, is the heightened mobility of capital and technology that makes it possible to create export platforms in developing countries in which labor productivity (in export production) is far above the national average. The enhanced productivity is limited mainly to export sectors; therefore, wages remain low relative to the industrial countries because of low productivity in the rest of the domestic economy (and possibly the repression of labor movements as well). Low wages *alone* are not a competitive threat, in this view, but low wages *combined* with high productivity in export activities are seen as a powerful stimulus to exports.[32]

In the long run, low-wage competition ceases to be a viable strategy for successful developing countries in which higher productivity becomes diffused throughout the economy and wages eventually rise. Thus, in countries such as South Korea and Taiwan, wages have risen so much that these countries are no longer competitive in the simpler labor-intensive manufactures, which are now moving to lower-wage sites (such as China and Malaysia). Following the earlier Japanese model, Korea and Taiwan are now moving into more advanced types of manufactures (such as appliances and auto parts) in which high quality and productivity make it possible to pay higher wages.

Meanwhile, other countries from Bangladesh to El Salvador are trying to imitate the East Asian countries' past successes in exporting labor-intensive manufactures. A major issue in the early twenty-first century will be whether the model of export-led growth that was so successful in the East Asian countries in the last several decades of the twentieth century can be duplicated throughout the developing world. Critics of export-led growth argue that, if large numbers of countries all try to export the same types of products to the same markets (especially the U.S. market) at the same time, they will suffer from a *fallacy of composition* and not all will be able to succeed.[33]

## Economic Integration and Trading Blocs

An increasingly popular option in trade policy today is the potential for two or more countries to enter into trade agreements that give the signatories trading preferences in each other's markets while excluding other nations from the same privileges. Such exclusive agreements are called *preferential trade arrangements* or *regional trading blocs.* The EU and NAFTA are examples of such preferential arrangements.

Recent trends toward the formation of more regional trading blocs are discussed in detail in Chapter 12; here, we restrict ourselves to the basic economic issues involved. Economic theory offers several perspectives on the advantages and disadvantages of preferential trading arrangements. One simple benchmark, originally proposed by Jacob Viner, is that joining a trading bloc is beneficial for a country if the gains from *trade creation* are greater than the losses from *trade diversion.*[34] Mexico's entry into a free trade area with the United States and Canada in NAFTA can be used to give some (purely hypothetical) examples of these types of gains and losses.

Suppose, for example, that Mexican construction companies formerly bought protected Mexican steel at $400 per ton (in U.S. dollar terms), but under NAFTA they could buy imported U.S. steel at $350 per ton. This is pure trade creation, which benefits the Mexican economy and Mexican consumers through cheaper steel and cheaper products made with steel.

Now consider a Mexican manufacturing firm that could choose between importing a Japanese machine that cost $1,000 and a qualitatively identical Canadian machine that cost $1,100. If Mexico (pre-NAFTA) had a tariff of 20 percent on imported machinery from *all* countries, the Mexican firm would have bought the cheaper Japanese machine for $1,000 (bringing the total cost to $1,200 including $200 for the tariff). After Mexico and Canada joined NAFTA and the Canadian machine became exempt from the tariff, the Mexican firm would have switched to the more expensive Canadian machine (again assuming that the Canadian machine was of equivalent quality). The Canadian machine, having a zero tariff, would cost the Mexicans only $1,100, while the Japanese machine would remain subject to a 20 percent tariff and would still cost $1,200.

In this example, the net gain or loss to Mexico is ambiguous. On the one hand, the Mexican firm pays $100 less for the Canadian machine than it formerly paid for the Japanese machine with the tariff and as a result can afford to buy more machines; getting more machines at a lower price represents a gain from trade creation, just as in the previous example. On the other hand, the Mexican government loses $200 in tariff revenue on each machine formerly imported from Japan; this is a loss due to trade diversion. Overall, whether Mexico benefits in this example depends on whether the gains from the trade creation are larger or smaller than the losses from the trade diversion.[35]

It should not be forgotten that nonmember countries can suffer losses from trade diversion, such as the Japanese machine company's lost sales to Mexico in the above example. Most studies have found that the diversionary effects of recent trade agreements are relatively small compared with the trade-creating effects, however.

The analysis of trade creation and diversion addresses only the static (one-time) gains from forming a preferential trade arrangement. Countries forming free trade areas also hope for dynamic (long-term) gains as a result of scale economies, induced technological progress, and competitive pressures to improve quality. Scale economies are especially important for smaller countries, such as Mexico in NAFTA or Belgium and the Netherlands in the EU. Producers in these countries can lower their unit costs by producing larger volumes for regional markets rather than just their own smaller national markets. Generally, the dynamic gains from scale economies and, more broadly, from rationalizing production in order to compete in a wider market are thought to far exceed the static gains from trade creation (i.e., merely obtaining cheaper imports).

Finally, a major impetus for some countries to join trading blocs is to attract FDI. A country that joins a trading bloc can serve as a base for foreign MNCs seeking to sell their products in all the member countries of the bloc. Joining the trading bloc can also serve as a signal to foreign companies of the country's commitment to trade liberalization and a market economy. Attracting more FDI was a major motive for Mexico's interest in forming NAFTA, and has also been an important source of gains for some peripheral European countries such as Ireland in the EU.

# Conclusion

After more than two centuries, economists have developed numerous theories of how international trade works, how nations gain from trade, and how the gains are distributed both among and within countries. Older theories emphasize the static gains from trade that occur when countries improve their efficiency by specializing according to their comparative advantages. Newer theories imply other types of gains, including the exploitation of scale economies and the dynamic gains that accrue from the international diffusion of new technologies.

Trade theories also imply that political conflict over trade policy is inevitable because the gains from trade are at best unevenly distributed and particular groups or sectors often lose from trade liberalization. Sometimes government intervention can theoretically be superior to free trade, as in the cases of externalities and strategic trade policy, for example; but the ability of governments to identify these cases and to apply appropriate interventions remains in dispute.

The very diversity of trade theories, old and new, suggests that international trade is multifaceted, and that no one theory can explain it all. The Heckscher-Ohlin model gives important insights into trade in those products whose production is tied to factor endowments, such as natural resource-based trade or trade in less-skilled labor-intensive goods. For trade in manufactures, the models of the product cycle and technology gaps emphasize that new products are exported by a small club of advanced nations whose firms have a virtual monopoly on technological leadership. The models of trade with scale economies and imperfect competition remind us that many competitive advantages in manufactures are essentially created advantages that derive from some set of historical accidents and sometimes even from government policies.

The increasing role of FDI in fostering competitive export sectors in a variety of countries moves us even further away from a world of inherent comparative advantage based on purely domestic factors within individual countries. Yet, when it comes to standardized manufactures, the classical Ricardian model comes back into its own: Nations tend to export those products for which they have relatively lower unit labor costs. Even here, we see a new twist: Advantages in labor costs may be created by acquiring new technologies from abroad, often imported via FDI or outsourcing by MNCs, a factor not considered by Ricardo.

Traditional models of comparative advantage emphasize how trade patterns are influenced by the internal characteristics of countries, which are taken as givens in the analysis. The newer theories suggest the potentially more interesting question of how the external trade relations of nations affect the development of their industries and the structure of their economies. How does immersion in a global system of production, exchange, and investment affect a country's internal development and thus condition or constrain its future ability to gain from trade? This kind of question will probably dominate international trade theory as it enters its third century.

## For Further Reading

Batra, Ravi. *The Myth of Free Trade: A Plan for America's Economic Revival.* New York: Scribner's, 1993.

Blecker, Robert A., ed. *U.S. Trade Policy and Global Growth: New Directions in the International Economy.* Armonk, N.Y.: M. E. Sharpe, Economic Policy Institute Series, 1996.

Cowling, Roger, and Keith Sugden. "Strategic Trade Policy Reconsidered: National Rivalry vs. Free Trade vs. International Cooperation." *Kyklos* 51, no. 3 (1998): 339–357.

Dosi, Giovanni, Keith Pavitt, and Luc Soete. *The Economics of Technical Change and International Trade.* New York: New York University Press, 1990.

Feenstra, Robert C. "Integration of Trade and Disintegration of Production in the Global Economy." *Journal of Economic Perspectives* 12, no. 4 (fall 1998): 31–50.

Irwin, Douglas A. *Against the Tide: An Intellectual History of Free Trade.* Princeton: Princeton University Press, 1996.

Kozul-Wright, Richard, and Robert Rowthorn, eds. *Transnational Corporations and the Global Economy.* New York: Palgrave, for the United Nations University/World Institute for Development Economics and Research (WIDER), 1998.

Krugman, Paul R. *Pop Internationalism.* Cambridge, Mass.: MIT Press, 1996.

Leamer, Edward, ed. *International Economics.* Worth Series in Outstanding Contributions. New York: Worth Publishers, 2001.

Markusen, James R., James R. Melvin, William H. Kaempfer, and Keith E. Maskus. *International Trade: Theory and Evidence.* New York: McGraw-Hill, 1995.

Pugel, Thomas A., and Peter H. Lindert. *International Economics.* 11th ed. Boston: Irwin/McGraw-Hill, 2000.

## Notes

1. Paul R. Krugman, "Is Free Trade Passé?" *Journal of Economic Perspectives* 1, no. 2 (fall 1987): 131.

2. In spite of their problematic views, the mercantilists' conceptualization of the balance of trade was an important development in the understanding of balance of payments accounting (see Chapter 4). It also foreshadowed twentieth-century Keynesian macroeconomics, which holds that a high level of exports and a low propensity to import are helpful for stimulating aggregate demand and national income. See John Maynard Keynes, *The General Theory of Employment, Interest, and Money* (New York: Harcourt, Brace, 1936), especially chapter 23 ("Notes on Mercantilism, Etc.").

3. Although Smith is famous as an advocate of free market policies, he did recognize legitimate areas for government activity, including national defense, public education, and infrastructure construction (e.g., highways).

4. Adam Smith, *An Inquiry Into the Nature and Causes of the Wealth of Nations,* ed. Edwin Cannan (London: Methuen, 1904; reprint Chicago: University of Chicago Press, 1976), 1:486.

5. However, Smith recognized some exceptional cases, such as protecting domestic industries deemed necessary for national security reasons, as well as exempting exported goods from domestic excise taxes. Smith also advocated that trade liberalization should be slow and gradual in order to mitigate adjustment costs.

6. Most significantly, Smith argued that by producing for a large global market, a country's producers could specialize more and thus increase the division of labor, which would make the nation's labor force more productive. This idea foreshadows the new theories of trade based on economies of scale (discussed later in the chapter).

7. In the example from Box 3.1, the international terms of trade of 1:1 means that it costs 1 yard of cloth to buy 1 bushel of wheat. If the price of wheat rises above 1 yard of cloth, the

terms of trade would be more favorable to the country that exports wheat (America) and less favorable to the country that imports wheat (Britain). Suppose, for example, that the terms of trade rise to 5 yards of cloth for every 4 bushels of wheat, or a ratio of 1.25:1. Both countries still gain from trade, but Britain gains relatively less while America gains relatively more.

8. In the example from Box 3.1, suppose America could lower its labor cost in cloth to 4 hours per yard. In this case, the comparative advantage in cloth would shift in favor of America, because its relative cost of producing cloth would fall from 9/8 to 4/8 = 1/2, which is less than the British relative cost of cloth (3/4).

9. However, protectionism is not necessarily the best policy for helping an infant industry to develop, as discussed later in this chapter.

10. Most standard expositions of this theory assume only two factors, such as capital and labor, for simplicity. But the theory was originally intended to apply to multiple factors of production, and most recent empirical studies have included more inputs (studies with about ten factors are very common; see, e.g., the source listed in note 12 below).

11. These examples were chosen to seem realistic and thus to portray the H-O theory in the best light. However, recent empirical studies show that the H-O theory does not generally give accurate predictions of trade patterns, as discussed later in this chapter.

12. See, for example, Daniel Trefler, "The Case of the Missing Trade and Other Mysteries," *American Economic Review* 85, no. 5 (December 1995): 1029–1046.

13. Gary Clyde Hufbauer and Kimberly Ann Elliott, *Measuring the Costs of Protection in the United States* (Washington, D.C.: Institute for International Economics, 1994).

14. Additional complexities arise if an industry is protected by a *quota* (quantitative limit on imports) or a *voluntary export restraint* (VER, which is a quantitative limit on foreign countries' exports) instead of a tariff. With a quota, the tariff revenue is replaced by *quota rents* that are captured by the importers who get the licenses to import the goods at the world price and sell them at a higher price domestically (although the government can recapture these rents if it charges a fee for the licenses). If an industry is protected by VERs, the foreign exporters capture the quota rents by selling artificially limited supplies in the U.S. market at a price above the world price. These complexities in turn affect economists' cost of protection estimates. For example, out of the estimated $11 billion net loss in U.S. national income found in the Hufbauer and Elliott study (see note 13), $7 billion was transferred to foreign exporters as a result of VERs. If tariffs had been used instead to protect the domestic industries in place of VERs, the net national loss would have been only $4 billion.

15. U.S. International Trade Commission, *The Economic Effects of Significant U.S. Import Restraints,* Second Update, Publication No. 3201, May 1999. Note that this study considered only legislated protection, and thus did not include the costs of "administered" or "contingent" protection in response to industries' legal actions for import relief under the unfair trade laws and the escape clause (see Chapter 7).

16. For a variety of perspectives and estimates, see Adrian Wood, *North-South Trade, Employment, and Inequality* (Oxford: Clarendon Press, 1994); William R. Cline, *Trade and Income Distribution* (Washington, D.C.: Institute for International Economics, 1997); and Susan M. Collins, ed., *Imports, Exports, and the American Worker* (Washington, D.C.: Brookings Institution, 1998). Among the notable economists in this literature who think Stolper-Samuelson effects are significant are Edward Leamer and Jeffrey Sachs, in addition to Wood.

On the other side are found such luminaries as Jagdish Bhagwati, Paul Krugman, and Robert Lawrence.

17. Some of these assumptions include identical technologies across countries, constant (nonincreasing) returns to scale, absence of transportation costs and other trade barriers, incomplete specialization, no factor-intensity reversals across countries, and perfectly competitive markets for goods and factors.

18. See Daniel Trefler, "International Factor Price Differences: Leontief Was Right!" *Journal of Political Economy* 101, no. 6 (December 1993): 961–987.

19. According to the H-O theory (Stolper-Samuelson theorem), if U.S. labor (of a certain skill grade) loses from free trade, those who work in export industries (e.g., farming or aerospace) would be included as well as those who work in import-competing industries (e.g., steel or apparel) because all workers of the same type would be competing with each other for jobs and therefore (in a perfectly competitive labor market) would have to receive the same wage.

20. Positive externalities are often cited as a justification for infant industry protection in developing countries. Note that an argument for government assistance to an infant industry must allege *either* (1) that the benefits are external to the firms so that they will not be reflected in private profits; *or* (2) that capital markets fail to allocate credit efficiently (perhaps because such markets are poorly developed). There is then a further question of whether protection or a subsidy is the best way to aid an infant industry, an issue that is discussed further below.

21. The quantities traded are also affected by externalities. For example, if a polluting factory is in an export sector, the country may be exporting too much of the product (thus creating too much pollution). Or, if an industry that generates a positive externality is in an export sector, then the country will export too little of the industry's product with free trade.

22. Similar principles apply in other types of market failures. For example, if a country imports a product that is socially harmful (generates a negative externality) through its consumption, such as cigarettes, the best policy is to tax consumption of the product rather than to restrict imports via a tariff. Or, if a country needs to develop a better-trained labor force, and private employers do not have sufficient incentives to provide enough training, the best policy is to subsidize training rather than to tax (or subsidize) the trade.

23. Some of these anomalies were anticipated by earlier theories of *economic imperialism* among dissident economists. For a survey, see Anthony Brewer, *Marxist Theories of Imperialism* (London: Routledge, 1980).

24. Based on data from Stefano Vona, "Intra-Industry Trade: A Statistical Artifact or a Real Phenomenon?" *Banca Nazionale del Lavoro Quarterly Review,* no. 175 (December 1990): 383–412, cited in Thomas A. Pugel and Peter H. Lindert, *International Economics,* 11th ed. (Boston: Irwin/McGraw-Hill, 2000), 101.

25. Some types of scale economies are *dynamic*, that is, they accrue only over time. For example, in industries where there are important *learning effects* (figuring out better ways to do things by experience), costs fall as the *cumulative* amount of production (past and present) rises. Also, some scale economies are *external* to individual firms—they obtain only at the regional or industrial level. For example, the training of skilled computer technicians benefits all the firms in a geographic area (such as the Silicon Valley) because the workers can easily move from one firm to another.

26. However, this particular policy only works with a type of behavior known as *Cournot oligopoly,* in which the rival firms, taking each other's output as given, choose their own quantities

of output and let prices adjust. If oligopolies behave differently (e.g., they set prices instead of choosing quantities), a subsidy policy would backfire and could reduce rather than increase national welfare.

27. Raymond Vernon, "International Investment and International Trade in the Product Cycle," *Quarterly Journal of Economics* 80 (May 1966): 190–207. According to Vernon, the innovative leaders must have certain characteristics. For example, they must have high income levels so that their consumers can buy expensive new products. They must also have high wages (which induce a search for labor-saving devices), good communications between consumers and suppliers, and well-functioning capital markets to provide finance for innovations. In Vernon's view, these requirements restrict innovative leadership to a handful of countries, principally the United States and a few other major industrialized nations.

28. These figures include the transactions of U.S.-based MNCs and their foreign affiliates as well as U.S. affiliates of foreign MNCs and their parents or other affiliates abroad. The authors' calculations were based on data from the U.S. Department of Commerce, *Survey of Current Business* (July 2000): 29; and (August 2001): 152.

29. See "Ireland," downloaded from www.irelandemb.org/econ.html/; and "Singapore: Background Notes," at www.tradeport.org/ts/countries/singapore/bnotes.html/.

30. See "China: Coping with Its New Power," *Business Week,* 16 April 2001, 32.

31. U.S. and Mexican data are from U.S. Department of Labor, Bureau of Labor Statistics, "International Comparisons of Hourly Compensation Costs for Production Workers in Manufacturing, 2000," Statistical Release, September 25, 2001. The exact figures are $19.86 for the United States and $2.46 for Mexico. Chinese compensation data are not available from official sources, but a figure of 43¢ per hour is cited by Ginger Thompson, "Fallout of U.S. Recession Drifts South Into Mexico," *New York Times,* 26 December 2001 (downloaded from www.nytimes.com), quoting economist John Christman of the Ciemex-WEFA consulting service. The latter source also cites costs to employers of $1.59 per hour in El Salvador and $1.53 per hour in the Dominican Republic.

32. Actually, the traditional (Ricardian) theory implies that labor productivity *should* be above average in export sectors because that is the meaning of comparative labor cost advantage. However, that theory assumes that capital is immobile and technology is indigenous, and thus comparative advantages can only be based on domestic production capabilities. For contrasting views on this issue see Mehrene Larudee and Tim Koechlin, "Wages, Productivity, and Foreign Direct Investment Flows," *Journal of Economic Issues* 33, no. 2 (June 1999): 419–425; and Stephen Golub, "Does Trade with Low-Wage Countries Hurt American Workers?" in Philip King, ed., *International Economics and International Economic Policy: A Reader*, 3d ed. (Boston: Irwin/McGraw-Hill, 2000), 132–143.

33. See Robert A. Blecker, "The Diminishing Returns to Export-Led Growth," in *The Bridge to a Global Middle-Class: Development, Trade and International Finance in the 21st Century,* ed. Glen Yago and James Barth (Norwell, Mass.: Kluwer Academic Publishers for the Milken Institute, 2002).

34. From a more mercantilist (or macroeconomic) perspective, however, trade diversion can be beneficial rather than costly to a nation joining a trading bloc. For example, giving a trading bloc partner incentives to buy more of a country's exports can help to improve the exporting country's balance of trade. This can create jobs in an economy that does not have full employment to begin with.

35. Generally, the more elastic the Mexican demand for machines (i.e., the more the quantity imported increases in response to the lower domestic price), the greater are the gains from trade creation. The larger the cost differential between imports from member and nonmember countries, the greater is the potential for losses from trade diversion. With small initial protection, trade diversion is less of a problem.

# 4 Trade Balances, Trade Performance, and Trade Policy

A country's trade balance may be a simple number, but it is a complex economic phenomenon. Trade policy is not synonymous with trade performance. A trade balance cannot be judged good or bad simply because it is in surplus or deficit. At the beginning of the twenty-first century, the U.S. trade deficit had soared to unprecedented levels. In 2000, the merchandise trade deficit hit the $450 billion mark, a record 4.5 percent of the nation's GDP (gross domestic product, or total goods and services produced). A broader measure of trade in goods and services, known as the current account, was in deficit by $445 billion, also a record. The continued growth of record-breaking deficits, with no end in sight, generated considerable controversy about their causes, costs versus benefits, and cure. Some pointed to the deficit's destabilizing effects; others welcomed the net inflow of real economic resources. From a technical standpoint, the huge U.S. trade deficit was not necessarily an indicator of domestic economic weakness. Similarly, as in the contemporary Japanese case, a huge trade surplus does not necessarily indicate economic health and vigor. The absolute size of a trade imbalance is less important economically than the underlying causal factors, the product composition (kinds) of goods and services that a country is importing and exporting, and the size of the imbalance relative to overall GDP.

This chapter first examines the many factors that collectively determine the volume and value of a country's exports and imports. The chapter then discusses how and why the political significance of trade balance numbers sometimes exceeds or distorts their economic importance. It will examine in particular the controversy over the causes of the rising U.S. trade deficit and will attempt to provide the reader with enough data to form an opinion on the seriousness of the deficit. The main, and perhaps surprising, themes of this chapter are that the trade balance alone is not an adequate measure of how well a country is competing in the global marketplace and that narrowly defined trade policy has only a limited influence on a trade balance.

## Short-Term Determinants of the Trade Balance

Unlike the general public and most politicians, few economists believe that trade deficits and surpluses are explained *primarily* by the competitiveness of a country's industries, foreign trade policies (e.g., protectionism and subsidies), or whether its trading partners' trade practices are "fair" or "unfair." Virtually all economists agree that macroeconomic factors such as exchange rates (currency values) and business

**BOX 4.1 The Trade Balance and the Balance of Payments**

There are several different measures of a country's trade balance, depending on what types of transactions are included. The table below shows the most important of these measures, using U.S. balance of payments data for 2000. The most common, although narrowest, measure is the "merchandise" balance, which is the difference between exports and imports of physical goods: agricultural and mineral commodities as well as manufactured goods of all kinds.

In today's world, trade in services has become increasingly important as well as trade in goods. By 2000, U.S. exports of services had grown to nearly 40 percent of the value of U.S. merchandise exports. Major examples of internationally traded services include transportation, tourism, telecommunications (including the Internet), insurance, banking services, engineering, education, advertising, and royalty payments for copyrights (e.g., movies and software). The balance of trade for goods and services combined is a more complete measure of how well a country's business sector is doing in the world marketplace than just the merchandise balance alone.

An even broader measure of a country's trade balance is the current account, which is the sum of the balance of trade for goods and services plus net international income receipts and unilateral transfers. "Income receipts" refer mainly to payments received from a country's investments abroad: remitted profits from overseas corporate affiliates, as well as interest and dividends on investments. Receipts must then be balanced against "income payments" made to foreign investors, as well as nonresident persons employed domestically. "Unilateral transfers" are financial gifts sent abroad by private citizens and vice versa, plus governmental grant aid.

The trade deficits shown in Table 4.1 were the largest in U.S. history at the time. However, measuring trade deficits nominally (i.e., in current dollars) can be misleading because this does not control for growth of the economy or increases in prices (inflation). Therefore, in making historical comparisons, economists usually express the trade balance as a percentage of GDP, which essentially shows the relative size of the trade surplus or deficit compared with the overall output of the economy at any point. Figure 4.1 shows that, no matter which measure of the trade balance one uses, the U.S. trade deficit was large and growing at the dawn of the twenty-first century.

---

cycles (growth or recessions at home and abroad) are two of the most important determinants of a country's trade balance, especially in the short run. They also believe that trade policies have only a limited impact in determining a country's aggregate exports and imports. Some economists argue that in the long term, the openness of a country's markets and the relative efficiency of its industries can contribute to persistent (or growing) surpluses or deficits; in effect, competitiveness and trade policies can set

TABLE 4.1    U.S. International Transactions: Balance of Payments in 2000

| *Balance of trade (in billions of U.S. dollars)* | |
| --- | --- |
| Goods (merchandise) | -452.2 |
| Services | 76.5 |
| Goods and services | -375.7 |
| Net income receipts | -14.8 |
| Unilateral transfers | -54.1 |
| Current account | -444.7 |
| Capital account (net financial inflows) | 444.0 |
| Statistical discrepancy | 0.7 |

DATA SOURCE: U.S.Department of Commerce, Bureau of Economic Analysis, News Release of June 21, 2001.

the *ranges* within which exchange rates and macroeconomic policies determine the specific level of a country's trade balance. Other economists believe that saving rates, including government budget surpluses or deficits, relative to investment outlays, are the main determinants of trade surpluses or deficits. In sum, there has never been unanimity on exactly how much of the U.S. trade deficit at any given time is caused by business cycles, exchange rates, saving relative to investment, competitiveness, and trade policies, and how much each of these factors needs to be altered to reduce or eliminate the deficit.

The short-run economic determinants of the trade balance can be grouped into two major categories, known as "income effects" and "relative price effects." Income effects relate to the level of *national income* at home and abroad, which influences how much residents of "Country A" are willing and able to spend on foreign goods and services (imports) relative to how much foreign residents are willing and able to spend on Country A's goods and services (exports). Relative price effects, in contrast, relate to the prices of domestic goods and competing foreign products, both in the domestic market and in export markets abroad. Because these price comparisons have to be made in a common currency (e.g., converted to U.S. dollars), relative price effects depend on *exchange rates,* the rates at which different currencies can be exchanged for each other. The next two sections will explain the income and then the price determinants of the trade balance. Later sections will return to discuss the roles of competitiveness and trade policies.

## Business Cycles and Income Effects

As a result of income effects, the domestic business cycle has a powerful impact on a country's demand for imports. During domestic economic booms, imports tend to rise in response to increases in aggregate demand, not only because more individuals can afford to buy more imported consumer goods but also because domestic producers require more imports of raw materials, intermediate (semifinished) goods, and capital goods (machinery and equipment). Sometimes, strong domestic growth may divert domestically produced goods away from exports and back to the internal market—unless domestic producers have enough excess capacity to supply the increased domestic demand while continuing to maintain or increase exports. Conversely, an economy in the depths of recession tends to import less due to declining rates of domestic production, employment, investment, and consumer spending. Business executives in a recession-plagued country that has a reasonably strong manufacturing base will try to increase exports to faster growing markets overseas to compensate for lost domestic sales.[1]

The effects of business cycles on the trade balance in the United States since the 1970s is dramatic (see Figure 4.1). In each recessionary period (1975, 1980–1982, and 1990–1991), the trade balance improved temporarily as demand for imports slackened.[2] Each time the economy recovered, the trade balance worsened again. When the economy began its recovery in 1992–1993, imports rose and the trade balance quickly deteriorated. Later, when the United States became the fastest growing major economy during the 1995–2000 period, it experienced rising, record-breaking trade deficits. U.S. GDP grew at an average rate of 4.2 percent annually between 1996 and 1999; GDP in Japan and the euro area grew at average annual rates of only –0.2 percent and 2.5 percent, respectively.[3]

Similarly, exports are affected by the business cycle in foreign countries. For example, U.S. exports have repeatedly suffered when important trading partners have gone into recessions. One such case occurred in the wake of the Latin American debt crisis of the 1980s. When the major debtor countries (Mexico, Brazil, and Argentina) began experiencing diminishing international creditworthiness in 1982, their access to new loans

**Figure 4.1  Three Alternative Measures of the U.S. Trade Balance, as Percentages of GDP, 1970–2000**

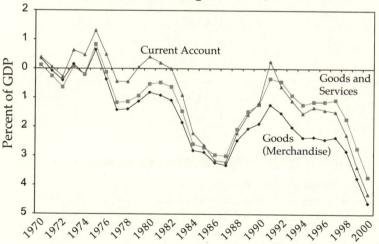

SOURCE: U.S. Department of Commerce, Bureau of Economic Analysis, National Income and Products Accounts, and authors' calculations.

from foreign commercial banks dried up. Under pressure from the U.S. government and the International Monetary Fund (IMF), the governments of the debtor countries adopted austerity programs designed to reduce trade deficits and reassure foreign creditors—but at the cost of declining national incomes and employment. The precipitous decline in their national incomes, combined with a commitment to continue servicing the interest due on their loans, triggered an immediate and sharp decrease in the ability of Latin American countries to pay for imports. Consequently, U.S. exporters suffered a significant decline in sales, through no fault of their own, to one of their major regional export markets. U.S. exports to Latin America declined in value by about 15 percent between 1981 and 1986. U.S. regional trade flows were further affected when dollar-hungry Latin American countries strove to increase exports to the U.S. market; U.S. imports from the region increased by 26 percent during the same period.[4]

A similar phenomenon occurred in the late 1990s. The outbreak of "Asian Contagion" caused several once-booming economies—South Korea, Thailand, Malaysia, and Indonesia—to suffer speculative attacks on their currencies, followed by precipitous capital outflows and dramatic drops in their exchange rates and stock markets. These countries were also important U.S. export markets. As it had in Latin America earlier, the IMF agreed to be the lender of last resort to most of those countries if they agreed to adopt restrictive monetary and fiscal policies, as well as reforms in business and banking practices, to counteract the financial panic devastating their economies. Table 4.2 illustrates that, once again, financial crises in emerging markets had a negative impact on U.S. exports, with short-term declines of up to 40 percent to some countries.

TABLE 4.2  **U.S. Merchandise Exports to Asian Contagion Countries, 1996 and 1998** (billions of U.S. dollars)

| Country | 1996 | 1998 |
|---|---|---|
| South Korea | 26.6 | 16.5 |
| Thailand | 7.2 | 5.2 |
| Indonesia | 4.0 | 2.3 |

SOURCE: U.S. Department of Commerce, Office of Trade and Economic Analysis.

## The International Monetary System and Exchange Rates

Events in the international monetary system in general and, more specifically, changes in the value of a currency relative to other currencies—its exchange rate—are important factors in determining the volume and direction of a country's import and export flows. A special link between trade and the international monetary system exists for the United States. Since World War II, the dollar has been the world's main international reserve and transactions currency. A major repercussion of the dollar's exalted status is that the United States has been the only country able to pay for all its imports with its own currency. Everyone else must earn foreign exchange (usually U.S. dollars) to pay for most of or all their imports. By the late 1990s, the continued desire of foreigners to accumulate dollar balances for international transactions was combined with a fast-rising desire of foreign companies and individuals to invest in the strong American economy. The result was that the United States was comfortably able to finance world record-setting trade deficits by attracting world record-setting net capital inflows. The latter reached $450 billion in 2000, an amount equal to 64 percent of the world's net capital exports.[5] If the United States should cease being able to attract large net inflows of private foreign investment, it would eventually face the same kinds of painful effects, namely, currency depreciation and higher domestic interest rates, incurred by any other country suffering a balance of payments problem. A second important trade-monetary link has been the frequency with which the dollar's exchange rate has increased in value despite a growing trade deficit, which in turn was further enlarged by a seemingly overvalued dollar.

Exchange rates strongly influence the local currency prices of a country's imports, which begin as foreign goods denominated in a foreign currency and are then quoted in a price denominated in the importer's local currency. Exchange rates also determine the prices of a country's exports through the conversion of prices quoted in the country's currency into the local currencies of overseas customers. A depreciating currency, all other things held constant, causes imports to become more expensive in local currency terms, and therefore less attractive, and allows a country's exports to become more cheaply priced when expressed in the currencies of foreign customers. Conversely, an appreciating currency, all other things held constant, causes foreign-made goods to become less expensive when priced in the stronger local currency. Exports become more expensive to foreign customers paying for these products (i.e., their imports) with their now weaker currencies. However, there are often exceptions to these "rules." For example, an exporter may reduce prices to offset the effects of a currency appreciation, and an importer or retailer might raise his or her profit margin by keeping the local prices of imported goods unchanged despite a currency depreciation in the exporting country.

Figure 4.2 illustrates the close, though not exact, correlation between the "real" (inflation-adjusted) value of the dollar and the U.S. trade deficit for goods and services (expressed as a percentage of GDP) over the period 1979–2000. Dollar appreciation in the early 1980s led to a rapid increase in the U.S. trade deficit. As usually happens, this change occurred after a lag of about two years because of the time it takes for physical import and export shipments to respond to exchange rate changes. After exchange rate changes occur, several months of lead time are required to negotiate new contracts and then produce and ship the goods ordered. Figure 4.2 also shows that the sustained dollar depreciation from 1985–1990 was followed by a reduction in the trade deficit as most imports became more expensive and most U.S. goods became less expensive in foreign markets, again after a lag of about two years. The trade deficit peaked and began to decline in 1987, two years after the peak in the value of the dollar. The correlation appears again in the late 1990s, when the dollar appreciation that began in 1995 was followed by a sharp increase in the trade deficit, especially after 1997.[6]

**Figure 4.2   The U.S. Trade Deficit for Goods and Services and the Real Value of the U.S. Dollar, 1979–2000**

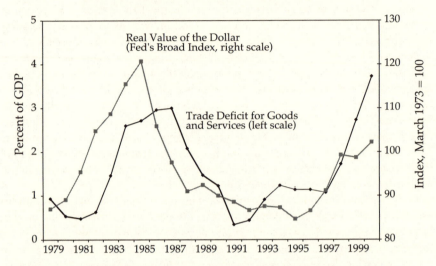

SOURCES: U.S. Department of Commerce, Bureau of Economic Analysis, National Income and Product Accounts; Board of Governors of the Federal Reserve System; and authors' calculations.

Since the late 1960s, the dollar, arguably, has been "overvalued" several times and for extended periods as measured by the international competitiveness of U.S. goods and services. In other words, a recurring disconnect has existed between the dollar's exchange rate at a given time and the rate that would be conducive to achieving equilibrium in the U.S. goods and services trade balance. The cumulative effects of periodic dollar over-valuation over the past four decades probably have had at least as much of a negative impact on the U.S. trade account as all foreign trade barriers combined.

Under the Bretton Woods exchange rate system that prevailed from 1944 until 1973, countries belonging to the IMF were obliged to keep their exchange rates fixed ("pegged") relative to the U.S. dollar. The dollar, in turn, was pegged to gold at the rate of $35 per ounce, and the United States was obligated to let foreign central banks convert their dollar reserves into gold upon request. A country was expected to main-tain its currency peg during normal fluctuations in its balance of payments. However, if it experienced a "fundamental" (i.e., chronic) balance of payments disequilibrium (deficit or surplus), a country was supposed to devalue or revalue its currency as part of a mix of policy changes needed to correct the disequilibrium.

As the other industrialized countries recovered from World War II, most of them steadily closed the competitiveness gap with the United States and their balances of payments steadily improved. The currencies of these countries should have, on aver-age, appreciated against the dollar. This was especially true for Japan and the former West Germany, which had the most successful industrial recoveries in the postwar period and by the late 1960s enjoyed consistent current account surpluses. Although, in principle, both chronic surplus and deficit countries should have adjusted their exchange rate pegs (surplus countries revaluing upward in value and the deficit countries devaluing), in almost every instance it was only the deficit countries that were forced to alter their exchange rates. (Surplus countries were reluctant to revalue their currencies, preferring instead to accumulate monetary reserves.) The deficit countries' mounting trade (and current account) deficits meant that prolonged efforts to defend their overvalued currencies eventually would have exhausted their foreign exchange reserves. Thanks to this surplus-deficit asymmetry in the international adjustment mechanism under Bretton Woods, the real (inflation-adjusted) exchange rate of the dollar steadily rose during the 1960s and early 1970s.

The negative effects of dollar overvaluation became painfully obvious only in the late 1960s, when U.S. inflation rates moved significantly higher than those of its major trading partners and caused a steady decline in the price competitiveness of many U.S. products.[7] Given the reluctance—if not refusal—of the major surplus countries to revalue, an increasingly overvalued dollar and a secular decline in U.S. competitiveness caused a steady diminution of the merchandise trade surplus in the late 1960s. The inevitable culmination of this trend materialized in 1971, when the United States suffered its first merchandise trade deficit in the twentieth century—a psychologically traumatic event that launched the agonizing reappraisal of trade policy discussed in Chapter 2.

Despite a major realignment of exchange rates and two devaluations of the dollar (in 1971 and 1973), the Bretton Woods system of adjustable pegs formally collapsed in March 1973; it was replaced by a system of floating (flexible) exchange rates.[8] The dollar depreciated further after the advent of floating rates, resulting in a cumulative nominal decline of about 22 percent in the dollar's value as measured against the other major currencies from 1971 through mid-1978;[9] this suggests just how much the dollar had become overvalued at the beginning of the 1970s. An improvement in the trade balance did follow in the wake of the weaker dollar during the 1971–1975 period, as well as when the dollar fell in value again in the 1977–1978 period.

Before 1973, it was generally assumed that floating exchange rates would induce an automatic adjustment in current account disequilibria. Currencies of surplus countries presumably would automatically appreciate and currencies of deficit countries would depreciate, eventually correcting trade imbalances and creating a tendency toward balanced current accounts. This presumption was proved wrong when floating exchange rates performed differently in practice.[10] Because of structural changes in the world economy, exchange rate movements under the floating rate system have usually not reflected the relative international commercial strength of countries, that is, their ability to sell goods and services in the global marketplace.

Although it was not immediately apparent, international capital flows have been the driving force behind most fluctuations in exchange rates since the mid-1970s. The phase-out of capital controls and the phase-in of modern computing and telecommunications technologies ended the era when merchandise trade or current account balances were the main determinants of exchange rate valuations. In the contemporary global economy, billions of dollars move in a matter of seconds, drawn by differentials in interest rates, foreign direct investments, purchases and sales of foreign stocks and bonds, and capital flight. Pure speculation about future exchange rate movements, that is, buying or selling a currency just because it is expected to rise or fall, respectively, is usually the largest source of foreign exchange transactions on any given day. Speculation is frequently responsible for swiftly driving rates well above or below levels suggested by a country's commercial competitiveness. When this occurs, trade imbalances tend to increase rather than contract.

The Bank for International Settlements estimated in 1998 that the turnover in the world-wide foreign exchange market averaged $1.5 trillion a day, making it the biggest market in the world.[11] Based on this figure, the amount of foreign exchange transactions necessitated by a year of world trade in goods and services equates to less than two weeks of transactions in the foreign exchange market. If poetic license is allowed, one can say that fifty full weeks of currency trading every year are devoted to international investments and pure speculation about future movements in exchange rates.

The dollar's exchange rate for many years has been linked less to U.S. international commercial competitiveness than to developments in international capital markets. Between mid-1980 and the end of February 1985, the dollar experienced the longest, most pervasive increase in value of any major currency in modern economic history. The genesis of this extraordinary currency appreciation appears to have been the advent of "Reaganomics," mainly the mix of expansionary fiscal policy (a large, growing budget deficit) and restrictive monetary policy (relatively high interest rates) that dominated the American economy in the early 1980s. The combination of a real interest rate differential in favor of U.S. financial assets; the relatively favorable business environment generated by the Reagan administration (including tax cuts and deregulation); and, especially after 1984, pure speculation on the dollar's continued rise caused an increase in dollar demand relative to supply. By one measure, the dollar's value jumped from an index number of 85 in mid-1980 to a peak of 165 at the end of February 1985, an extraordinary increase of 94 percent.[12]

For several years, the ensuing upward spiral of the U.S. trade deficit, discussed earlier, did nothing to discourage the rising hunger for dollar assets, and the dollar continued to appreciate. Booming imports and stagnant exports caused the U.S. merchandise trade deficit to swell from $28 billion in 1981 to $122 billion in 1985. Although other causal factors were involved—for example, the domestic saving-investment imbalance and an apparent secular decline in U.S. industrial competitiveness, to be discussed below—most analysts agreed that the significantly overvalued dollar was the leading proximate cause of the unprecedented deterioration in the U.S. trade account in the 1983–1987 period. The slow, gradual depreciation of the dollar that began in March 1985 accelerated in the fall of that year after speculators lost their ardor for buying dollars.[13] As noted above, after the usual two-year lag in the effect of exchange rate changes, the trade deficit peaked at a then-record $160 billion in 1987 before falling for the next four years.

As also noted earlier, the same syndrome reappeared in a somewhat less dramatic fashion in the late 1990s. The pursuit of relatively high returns on capital created a seemingly insatiable desire among foreigners to invest in the fast-growing U.S. market, the epitome of the so-called "new economy"; also contributing to this were relatively weak economic conditions in other countries. The dollar gradually appreciated against other major industrialized countries' currencies from 1995 into the new millennium. A double-digit dollar appreciation against the euro shortly after its inception in 1999 defied the widespread expectation that the new European currency would, from the beginning, more than hold its own against the dollar. Also, the 1997–1998 Asian financial crisis and the economic instability that followed soon after in Russia and Brazil led to massive capital flight out of "emerging market" countries and sharp drops in the value of their currencies relative to the dollar.

The main difference between this episode of dollar strength and that of the early 1980s is that the U.S. trade deficit was proportionately worse in the late 1990s, mainly due to the differences in growth rates (income effects) between the United States and its trading partners. Some economic estimates suggested that the dollar would have had to fall by about 20 to 30 percent to make a sizeable dent in the U.S. trade deficit of the early 2000s.[14] Nevertheless, two successive U.S. administrations (Clinton and Bush II) have argued that a strong dollar enhances the country's real income and standard of living by making imported goods and services cheaper and thus helping to hold down inflationary pressures.

## Underlying Causes of Trade Imbalances

Most *short-term* swings in a nation's trade balance can be explained by income effects (business cycles) and changes in relative prices (exchange rates). But these factors tend to reverse themselves over time: Cyclical upturns are followed by downturns, and vice versa; and currencies generally don't continuously rise or fall in real value (adjusted for inflation). Therefore, other factors have to be introduced to explain longer-term trends in trade balances; that is, why some countries, like the United States, have had persistently large deficits, and other countries, like Japan, have had persistently large surpluses. Considerable disagreement exists regarding the individual importance of these longer-term, structural causes of trade imbalances. This section discusses four factors that are commonly cited as influencing long-term trends in trade balances: the saving-investment balance, relative international competitiveness, trade policies, and foreign direct investment (activities of multinational corporations).

### *The Saving-Investment Balance*

A country that has a current account *surplus* must be a net exporter of capital to the rest of the world; that is, the country has a net capital outflow, or capital account deficit, as it acquires net foreign assets. A country that has a current account *deficit* must be a net borrower from the rest of the world; that is, the country accumulates international liabilities so that it can finance its trade deficits. Basically, a trade surplus/net lender country is one that has an excess of national saving over and above the requirements of financing domestic investment. A deficit country (net international borrower) has investment outlays that exceed its national saving so that it is forced to rely on net inflows of foreign saving. An immutable law of balance of payments accounting dictates that a capital account surplus must be offset by a current account deficit of approximately equal size (and vice-versa). Net capital inflows into the United States between 1985 and 2001 cumulatively exceeded $2 *trillion* to finance mammoth current account deficits. It is also possible that large net capital inflows can be at least a partial cause of a trade deficit. In any event, as measured by its net international investment position, the United States was transformed from the world's largest creditor country at the onset of the 1980s to the largest debtor country by the early 1990s.

The relationship between a nation's saving-investment balance and its current account balance is demonstrated by the following equation:

Current Account = Private Saving (corporate and personal)
plus Government Budget Balance (surplus or
deficit)* minus Domestic Investment

This equation is considered an accounting identity because in principle it must always be true (except for errors or omissions in the data). When a country invests more than it saves in a given period, by definition it is a net importer of capital from abroad, and its capital account surplus offsets the current account deficit. Conversely, when a country saves more than it invests, it is a net capital exporter, and its capital account deficit must be offset by a current account surplus.

The question of which variables in the saving-investment equation determine the others has bedeviled explanations of the U.S. trade deficit. In the early 1980s, the U.S. trade deficit (using the broadest definition, i.e., the current account) worsened dramatically after the Reagan administration's tax cuts and increased military spending led to large and growing government budget deficits (see Figure 4.3). This led to a popular notion at the time that the rising budget and trade deficits were "twins" and that the former caused the latter. The trade deficit, in this view, was simply the mirror image of the net borrowing required to finance the saving shortfall associated with the fast-rising budget deficit. Persuaded by this explanation, some observers erroneously assumed that eliminating the budget deficit was the only way to eliminate the trade deficit.

In retrospect, although the "twin deficit" hypothesis contained a germ of truth, it was exaggerated and oversimplified. The excessive focus on the growing federal budget deficit, seemingly sensible at the time, failed to recognize that private saving, investment and (as discussed below) competitiveness also play important roles in forging the overall numerical relationship between saving and investment. The fallacy of the twin deficit concept was empirically demonstrated by the sequence of domestic economic events beginning in 1992. U.S. economic growth picked up, taxes were increased, and the budget balance swung from a large deficit to record surpluses in the late 1990s through 2000. But instead of improving, the trade balance deteriorated during these years (Figure 4.3 clearly shows the U.S. budget and trade balance moving in opposite directions during this period). The explanation for this seeming paradox was that investment (most of it in new information technology and telecom-

---

*A government budget surplus counts as an addition to saving; a budget deficit represents government "dissaving" and reduces total national saving.

### Figure 4.3 Current Account and Government Budget Balances as Percentages of GDP, 1979 to 2000

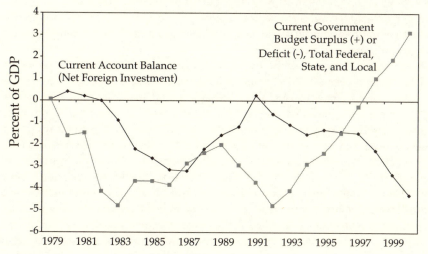

SOURCE: U.S. Department of Commerce, Bureau of Economic Analysis, National Income and Product Accounts; and authors' calculations.

munications equipment) increased by a larger amount than the budget turnaround, and private saving increased only moderately. As Robert Z. Lawrence has observed, "All current account deficits are not created equal."[15]

In sum, budget deficits and trade deficits do *not* have an automatic one-to-one relationship in the saving-investment equation. Even when there is a government deficit, private saving (corporate and personal) may be so large that it exceeds the sum of government dissaving and investment outlays. This explains why the twin deficit syndrome was *not* observed in Japan during the late 1990s and the start of the millennium, when that country was simultaneously running record budget deficits and the world's largest trade surpluses. Japanese private domestic investment was depressed throughout that period, and the famous high saving rate of Japanese households rose even higher, leaving the country unable to consume what it was producing and making the country a large net exporter of goods and capital. The depressed state of the Japanese economy contributed to both low tax revenue (and hence a large budget deficit) *and* low import demand (a contributor to the large trade surplus).

### Changes in International Competitiveness

As explained in the previous chapter, competitive advantage in the production of today's sophisticated manufactured goods (and even many agricultural products) is determined by more than a country's relative endowment of the three traditional factors of production, land, labor, and capital. International competitiveness, and therefore the composition of a country's imports and exports, are also functions of such new variables as technological sophistication, management savvy, the skill level of the labor force, product innovation, receipt by corporations of favorable government treatment, direct investment by multinational corporations, and the quality of the transportation and telecommunications infrastructure. Some old variables, such as a competent and honest government, still apply.

According to one school of thought, a lack of competitiveness can be an important variable causing persistent or growing trade deficits. Because roughly 80 percent of U.S. merchandise trade consists of manufactures, and manufacturing accounts for most of the non-oil trade deficit, qualitative shortcomings in the overall performance of the American manufacturing sector in domestic and foreign markets relative to other countries can be seen as a *contributing* factor to persistent U.S. trade deficits.

It is not easy to give an all-inclusive and meaningful definition of international competitiveness. From all that has been said thus far in this chapter, the trade balance *per se* clearly cannot be used as a precise indicator of competitiveness because it is influenced by too many other factors (business cycles, exchange rates, saving rates, fiscal policies, etc.). A widely accepted definition of competitiveness is the ability of a country to produce goods and services that meet the test of global markets while its citizens simultaneously enjoy a rising and sustainable standard of living.[16] According to one interpretation of this definition, a country is competitive if its exports are strong and growing relative to imports at the same time that domestic income and standard of living are rising. The American economy has a competitiveness "shortfall" under this standard because it has been unable to grow relatively rapidly without running large and growing trade deficits and incurring increased foreign liabilities to finance what conceivably could be unsustainable current account deficits.

In 1985, the President's Commission on Industrial Competitiveness declared that the "ability [of the United States] to compete in world markets is eroding" and there is "compelling evidence of a relative decline in our competitive performance."[17] Another policy report by three prominent economists in the late 1980s concluded that there was more to the U.S. trade deficit than the saving-investment imbalance, and that the basic economic adjustments facing the United States are "linked to the microeconomic issues of competitiveness in particular products and the general performance of U.S. exports and import-competing industries."[18] A widely read 1989 report issued by the Massachusetts Institute of Technology Commission on Industrial Productivity called attention to the "attitudinal and organizational weaknesses that pervade America's production system." This multidisciplinary task force found that the shortcomings of many American companies were symptoms of "systematic and pervasive ills," and argued that "the situation will not be remedied simply by trying harder to do the same things that have failed to work in the past. The international business environment has changed irrevocably, and the United States must adapt its practices to this new world."[19]

An empirical quantitative indicator of a U.S. competitiveness problem involves international differences in the *income elasticities* of demand for exports and imports. The income elasticity of demand for a product (good or service) is defined as the percentage by which the demand rises for each 1 percentage point increase in consumers' income. Thus, the income elasticity of American import demand is the response of U.S. imports to increases in U.S. national income. The income elasticity of U.S. export demand is the percentage change in U.S. export sales for each 1 percent increase in the national incomes of its trading partners. Statistical studies have repeatedly found that the United States has a much higher income elasticity of demand for imports than for exports. Most other industrial countries, especially Japan, have lower income elasticities for imports.[20] An example of the high income elasticity of U.S. import demand is seen in the fact that imports of goods and services (measured in real terms) increased by an annual average of more than 11 percent in 1998 and in 1999, which was more than twice the average real GDP increase of 4.3 percent in those years (thus indicating an income elasticity of roughly 2.5 for imports, while most estimates of the income elasticity for U.S. exports place it at slightly over 1).

The implication of this difference in income elasticities is that in a world where all countries are growing at an equal rate, the United States will tend to have a constantly growing trade deficit; but a country enjoying more favorable elasticities (higher for exports than for imports), such as Japan, will have an ever-growing surplus. To prevent constantly widening trade imbalances, then, there are only two kinds of conventional solutions.[21] One solution is to have continuous depreciation of the U.S. dollar and continuous appreciation of the surplus countries' currencies, thus maintaining trade balance through adjustments in relative export and import prices. As noted earlier, however, currencies do not necessarily (or usually) move in the direction required for correcting trade imbalances. The second solution would be painful for the United States: income adjustment through relatively slow growth. The alleged need to choose between these unpleasant alternatives to prevent rising trade deficits is seen by some as indicating that a "competitiveness problem" is one of the underlying causes of the U.S. merchandise trade deficit.

It is ironic that even though the trade deficits of the late 1990s and early 2000s are larger, absolutely and as a percentage of GDP, than the trade deficits of the mid-1980s (see Figure 4.1 above), the competitiveness hypothesis has fallen out of favor. The reason is that the notion of the United States as uncompetitive was hard to square with the general impression of its booming "new economy" in the 1990s. Indeed, it was not easy to pinpoint specific competitive failures of American industry at the turn of the millennium. The major quantitative indicators were relatively favorable: rapid growth of productivity and capital investment, high rates of innovation in advanced technology, stable unit labor costs in manufacturing, repeated corporate downsizings that supposedly made companies more lean and efficient, full employment with rising real wages, and so on. A further indication of a relatively strong American competitive position at the start of the new millennium was the widely watched global competitiveness rankings compiled annually by the Institute for Management Development, a Swiss business school. Based on 286 criteria used by the school and its 35 collaborating institutes worldwide, the United States was judged the world's most competitive country anually from 1997 to 2001.[22] Some analysts have suggested that U.S. industrial competitiveness would look much better if measured "properly"; they argue that extensive sales by American corporate subsidiaries overseas should be added to export figures. Given the heavy reliance by U.S. companies on foreign direct investment to sell their goods and services to foreigners, two Wall Street ana-lysts asserted that "concern about the swollen trade deficit" is "overblown," even a "dangerous obsession."[23]

Despite dramatic improvements in cost-cutting and product innovations since 1990, U.S.-based producers still seem to lag when it comes to beating foreign com-petition in winning sales both inside and outside the United States. Simply stated, the much-praised, much-admired American economy in the late 1990s and early 2000s was not making enough of the goods and services that domestic and foreign cus-tomers wanted to buy, at least not in domestic factories. The bottom line explanation may simply be that the economic and technological dominance of the United States in the 1950s and 1960s is a thing of the past. Other parts of the world—led initially by Germany and Japan, later joined by smaller European economies such as Italy and Ireland, and then by the "newly industrialized countries" in the developing world (such as Korea, China, and Mexico)—can now produce many high-quality goods at lower costs than their American counterparts. Some of this more efficient foreign pro-duction is the result of direct investment by U.S. multinational companies abroad or the licensing of U.S. technology to foreign producers through outsourcing arrange-ments (see the discussions of globalized production in Chapters 3 and 13 and the sec-tion on foreign direct investment below).

Some critics of the competitiveness hypothesis contend that this view is inconsistent with the saving-investment balance equation discussed above. According to what might be called the saving-investment determinism view, whether a country has a trade surplus or deficit depends only on whether its national savings (including the effects of the budget surplus or deficit) exceed its domestic investment and has virtually nothing to do with competitiveness. This argument seems to overlook the fact that causality is *not* identified in the saving-investment equation, which is only a statistical identity. Therefore, a trade deficit could be caused by a country's lagging competitiveness, which would discourage exports, encourage imports, depress employment and saving, reduce tax revenues, and increase welfare spending.[24] Conversely, strong competitive perform-ance can stimulate exports and national income and create high-wage jobs. These changes will then tend to increase private saving by domestic businesses and households, increase tax revenue, and reduce welfare expenditures, all of which would raise the coun-try's level of saving. Strong competitive performance also stimulates investment demand, of course; but *if* the industrial sector generates enough saving to pay for invest-ment needs, the country does not have to borrow or run a trade deficit.[25]

Perhaps the most fundamental criticism of the attention paid to the competitive-ness of a country is the allegation that the concept is devoid of meaning because it essentially means the same thing as productivity, that is, a country's efficiency in pro-ducing its output. Paul Krugman has argued that a competitive economy is simply a highly productive or efficient economy, and an "uncompetitive" economy is an inef-ficient one, that is, one showing slow productivity growth relative to other countries. He further asserted that most of the benefits of being highly productive are purely domestic: A very efficient economy is one that can support a high standard of living for its citizens; therefore, the impact of international trade on domestic living stan-dards in most countries allegedly is of negligible importance.[26]

## International Trade Policies

No sovereign government in the world adheres to an absolutely free trade policy. Despite repeated multilateral, regional, and bilateral trade liberalization agreements since the 1930s, no government (or the collective European Union) entrusts private markets completely to determine either the volume or the composition of trade flows into and out of the country. Furthermore, almost all governments intervene at least occasionally in the marketplace through an explicit or implicit industrial policy designed to influence the patterns of trade and domestic production.

For these reasons, it is often assumed that official trade policies are a major factor in determining a country's trade balance and overall trade performance. Although there is consensus that government intervention can help or hinder individual industries at the sectoral, or "micro" level, the impact on the "macro" level is the subject of ongoing disagreement. Import barriers and government-funded assistance to favored producers can and do affect the amounts and kinds of goods and services, product by product, that a country imports and exports. It is less clear whether and to what extent trade policies (and industrial policies) affect total national trade performance.

A popular view holds that overseas barriers to U.S. exports, subsidies to foreign exports targeted at the U.S. market, and the "unfair trade practices" of foreign exporters are a *major* cause of the U.S. trade deficit. This subsection will explore the arguments and counterarguments concerning the importance of such trade policies and practices in determining a trade balance. American exporters, like those in all countries, are confronted by a worldwide array of foreign tariff and nontariff trade barriers, both direct and indirect, which probably reduce potential U.S. exports by tens of billions of dollars annually. The extent of foreign trade barriers is suggested by the length of an annual report on the subject issued by the U.S. Trade Representative's Office. The 2001 edition contains 465 pages describing import barriers maintained by more than fifty-five countries and the European Union. Quantitative estimates have been made of potential exports lost to foreign trade barriers; for example, in a 1993 study of U.S.-Japanese trade, two pro-free-trade American economists concluded that at the time "limitations on foreign access to the Japanese market due to structural and sector-specific considerations may be curtailing US exports by $9 billion to $18 billion annually."[27]

The oldest forms of barriers are tariffs (taxes or "duties" on imports) and nontariff barriers, such as quotas (quantitative restrictions), both of which are imposed at the border. Other, less visible trade barriers include more indirect, inside-the-border practices such as official acceptance of collusion among domestic businesses, distribution systems that discriminate against foreigners, and restrictive government procurement practices. One of the most notorious instances of unduly restrictive safety and health standards was the onerous set of technical specifications that Japan imposed on imported skis in the early 1980s on the grounds that Japanese snow was different from that of other countries.

A different type of export impediment arising overseas consists of violations of U.S. companies' intellectual property rights—patents, copyrights, and so forth, by foreign companies. Counterfeit goods produced in foreign factories, many of which operate illegally, deprive American companies, such as software producers, of billions of dollars annually in overseas sales and royalties. Finally, some foreign governments are alleged to subsidize extensively many of their export industries, thus giving them an "unfair" edge in global competition with U.S. producers. Although overt and explicit subsidies are rare in today's world, indirect or implicit subsidies, such as preferential credit terms and cheap public utility rates, are commonly and legally used throughout the world. (See Chapter 7 for a discussion of what are acceptable and illegal subsidies under the WTO).

Foreign trade barriers can only be considered a *significant* cause of the U.S. trade deficit if foreign barriers to U.S. exports are, on average, greater than the trade barriers imposed by the United States on imports. Although most Americans believe that aggregate foreign barriers are higher, the amount of U.S. exports lost as a result of these barriers at any given time is difficult to pinpoint. The extent to which reductions in foreign trade barriers lead to increased exports in the short term is directly tied to macroeconomic conditions in the domestic economy. If an economy is operating near full employment and has little unused industrial capacity, the export stimulus of overseas trade liberalization would be limited until such time that additional production capacity could be brought on line. If the United States or any other country was in the midst of a recession, a much more simulative effect of reduced foreign trade barriers would result. There is also a political reality to be considered: As a quid pro quo for lowering their import barriers, other countries often demand a reduction in U.S. import barriers and/or a cutback in the use of the antidumping and antisubsidy statutes.

Despite its proclaimed faith in free trade principles, the United States does protect and aid its own industries through a variety of devices. To discourage specific imports, the United States, like all other countries, has erected an outer defense perimeter that consists of a broad array of tariffs and nontariff barriers (NTBs). As in all other industrialized countries, ordinary tariffs are now relatively low in the United States: 4.8 percent on average in 2000. If nondutiable goods are included in the calculation, the average duty imposed on all U.S. imports is 1.6 percent.[28] But, as is true of all averages, this statistic obscures some very high rates; for example, 30 percent and higher on some imports of clothing and footwear.[29]

With most tariffs reduced to minimal, nonrestrictive levels, NTBs have been the main impediment to international trade since the 1970s. Examples of American NTBs are the tariff-rate quotas (higher tariffs triggered after specified quantities of goods are imported each year) imposed on a handful of primary products, most notably dairy products, sugar, cotton, meat, tobacco, brooms, and peanuts. In addition to explicit protection on the import side, the United States has been accused of imposing nontariff distortions on the export side. The most commonly cited are indirect and hidden assistance to some major export industries, such as aerospace and agriculture, in the forms of government-sponsored R&D and price subsidies, respectively.

The outer ring of defense from foreign competition is not always adequate to prevent domestic producers from seeking protection under various U.S. trade laws for relief from what they claim is import-induced injury. Given the aforementioned low level of U.S. tariffs and relatively low incidence of NTBs outside agriculture and textiles, contemporary U.S. actions against imports mainly take the form of ad hoc administrative procedures that address the allegedly injurious domestic effects of import surges in particular products. When the U.S. government considers taking steps to restrict imports, it relies on an array of relatively transparent administrative actions established by trade statutes (discussed in Chapter 7). These domestic laws largely conform to international trade law, as codified in the WTO and other trade agreements (see Chapter 8). Nevertheless, the U.S. government's administration of its national trade laws has generated a great deal of displeasure among many U.S. trade partners (see Chapters 7, 8, and 14).

Some U.S. (and European) industries have been protected at various times in recent decades through negotiated "voluntary" export restraints (also called orderly marketing agreements) with other countries. Unlike unilateral actions, voluntary restraints give the exporting country a limited say in the quantitative ceiling to be imposed on annual exports of the product in question. Still, voluntary restraints act like quotas in arithmetically restricting the volume of imports (no matter what their prices are) of particular products (and they may allow foreign exporters to reap the excess profits ["quota rents"] created by selling artificially limited quantities at high prices in a protected market).[30] During the 1970s and 1980s, the U.S. government made extensive use of this device to limit imports of various goods, including automobiles, steel, machine tools, color televisions, and footwear. No new export restraint agreements have been signed by the United States since the early 1900s. The reasons were a diminution in the perceived need for import limits in a booming U.S. economy; an agreement in the Uruguay Round to forsake such agreements; and a U.S. government effort to encourage domestic companies and unions to rely more on the import relief laws. At the beginning of the twenty-first century, the United States was participating in only one significant export restraint agreement, the multilateral Agreement on Textiles and Clothing, (successor to the Multifiber Arrangement) covering LDCs exports of textiles and apparel, which is due to be fully phased out in 2005 per the Uruguay Round agreement.

On the export side, despite large and persistent trade deficits, U.S. policymakers have not significantly eased the restrictions and obstacles, onerous relative to all other countries, that have long reduced potential U.S. exports by amounts estimated to be billions of dollars annually. As we discuss in Chapter 9, the world's most extensive system of export controls and licensing procedures has been legislated and applied in pursuit of what many if not most Americans would regard as admirable goals. Since 1949, the U.S. government has sought to enhance national security by limiting the proliferation of weapons of mass destruction and by withholding military and advanced technology goods from potential adversaries and governments that support terrorism. U.S. policy has also employed export restrictions to penalize governments that systematically violate human rights and to limit overseas shipments of hazardous substances. The deleterious effects of export impediments on American companies have been judged an acceptable cost in pursuit of goals judged by many to be more important than increased wealth.

The significance of large *bilateral* trade disequilibria with particular countries is another controversial trade policy issue. One side urges the U.S. government to deal aggressively with the bilateral deficits long incurred with Japan and China because of their size, duration, and the alleged retention by both countries of significant import barriers (see Chapter 10). This viewpoint further argues that as long as these two countries account for a disproportionate share of the multilateral U.S. trade deficit, it cannot be significantly reduced unless other trading partners, such as Western Europe, Canada, and Mexico, accept significantly more American exports. Yet these are the markets that already have done the most to reduce trade barriers. The other side of the "bilateral debate" points to the truism that all countries will have trade surpluses with some countries and trade deficits with others. This viewpoint concludes that the total, or multilateral, trade balance is a far more important statistic.

In sum, despite the passions and political rhetoric inspired by trade impediments imposed by the United States and its trading partners, these barriers and distortions on the whole are only secondary factors in determining a country's aggregate trade balance. Their impact is felt most directly on a sectoral basis; that is, in particular industries and occupations. No matter how well U.S. trade negotiators pursue trade grievances against foreign governments, such efforts by themselves will not eliminate all or even most of the current U.S. trade deficit. Unless other issues such as unequal growth rates between the United States and its major trading partners, saving-investment imbalances, competitiveness problems, and exchange rate misalignment (the allegedly overvalued dollar), are addressed, trade policy alone can play only a limited role in closing the immense gap between U.S. imports and exports that existed in the early 2000s.

Despite its limitations, trade policy is a necessary and appropriate vehicle to reduce import barriers at home, to convince other governments to reduce their import barriers and halt unfair foreign export practices, and to stop overseas violations of U.S. intellectual property rights. The pursuit of a more open, market-based trading system less hindered by government barriers is inherently desirable for economic reasons having nothing directly to do with trade balances. To the extent that the world economy is based on an international division of labor reflecting comparative advantage and a relatively free flow of international commerce, economic theory tells us that the results will be increased levels of efficiency, output, and living standards. To the extent that domestic companies anticipate large and growing export sales, political theory tells us that a government will be less inclined to impose protectionist trade measures and thus risk foreign retaliation.

## *Foreign Direct Investment*

One of the most significant trends in the contemporary international trading system is the growing impact of foreign direct investment (FDI) in determining which goods a country does or does not export and import (see Chapter 3). FDI is defined as the ownership by a corporation located in one country of at least 10 percent of voting stock in a new or existing company in another country; such ownership provides the potential for influencing the management of the company. According to one Wall Street analyst, the international production networks of MNCs have proliferated to the point that "foreign direct investment has become the primary means by which firms compete in markets. And particularly in the case of the United States . . .

exports and imports are increasingly dictated by the strategies of both U.S. and foreign multinationals."[31] Indeed, overseas production by some 23,000 foreign affiliates is slowly eclipsing exporting as the major means by which American companies (and those of other advanced industrial countries) sell goods and services to foreign customers.

The scope of FDI proliferation globally can be gleaned from a few basic statistics. MNCs' (of all countries) percentage share of world trade and world production has grown rapidly because for many years worldwide FDI has grown much faster than either world trade or world GDP. The stock, or market, value of all foreign affiliates grew nine-fold between 1982 and 2000; world trade and world GDP both increased during this time only three-fold.[32] Exports by foreign affiliates of all MNCs were about $3.6 trillion in 2000, an amount equaling about one-half of world trade. Estimated sales of all foreign affiliates in that year were $15.7 trillion (a figure that includes sales within the country of production), more than twice the value of annual global trade in goods and services. The total book value of FDI was an estimated $6.3 trillion in 2000. Some 800,000 overseas affiliates have been established around the world by more than 60,000 parent firms.[33]

The value of U.S. direct investment overseas was estimated at $1.45 trillion (on the current cost basis) at year-end 2000. The sheer volume of this outward FDI poses one of the biggest conundrums in analyzing the U.S. trade performance: whether the extensive overseas production by U.S. MNCs displaces, enhances, or does not substantially affect the aggregate value of American exports. Some export shipments are inevitably displaced at a microeconomic (company-by-company) level after an overseas subsidiary is established. Conversely, moving production overseas may be a defensive move to protect market share that might otherwise have diminished or disappeared if exports had remained the only marketing vehicle. Sometimes, exports are increased when foreign subsidiaries import parts and product models from their U.S. parent that are not being made overseas. Exports also increase when foreign subsidiaries import the same American-made capital equipment used by their American parent. It is probably not a coincidence that U.S. exports to Western Europe have remained strong despite a large, growing U.S. MNC presence since the 1960s. Nor is it likely a coincidence that exports of manufactured goods have traditionally lagged to Japan, a country in which U.S. industrial FDI is minimal.

For the first time in the post–World War II era, FDI in the United States at year-end 2000 ($1.37 trillion on the current cost basis) was close to equalling the value of U.S. FDI abroad. An increasing number of big foreign manufacturers want to have a physical presence in the world's largest national economy. Some foreign companies, for example, Japanese auto makers, built assembly plants in the United States so that they could leapfrog U.S. trade barriers. The boom in FDI in the United States also resulted from the wave of corporate merger and acquisition activity between companies in different countries or because U.S. production costs are sometimes lower than foreign costs (e.g., average U.S. wages in the manufacturing sector are lower than comparable wages in many West European countries).

The effects of inward FDI on U.S. trade are complex and not subject to precise measurement. On the one hand, "transplant" production by foreign MNCs undoubtedly replaces some imports, especially of finished goods, thus moderating the U.S. trade deficit. Gross sales of goods and services by majority-owned affiliates of foreign companies operating in the United States reached $2 trillion in 1999, an amount well in excess of the $1.2 trillion in total U.S. imports in that year.[34] On the other hand, some foreign-owned companies operating in the United States run exceptionally import-intensive operations, buying large amounts of semifinished goods from their parent companies abroad. Estimated imports by U.S.-based affiliates from their foreign parents were $226 billion in 1999, accounting for about 22 percent of total U.S. imports.[35]

An important result of the proliferation of MNCs both at home and abroad is the growing need to distinguish between *country* competitiveness and *company* competitiveness when analyzing trade flows. The gross sales of goods and services by majority-owned foreign affiliates of American companies (other than banks) were $2 trillion in 1998.[36] This figure is more than twice the $933 billion value of U.S. exports of goods and services in that year. Thus, traditional import and export data are increasingly incomplete indicators of the total global marketing power of American companies. After taking into consideration domestic sales by foreign-controlled companies operating in the United States, a U.S. goods and services balance measured by traditional trade flows *plus* local sales generated at home and abroad by FDI would have registered a small surplus through the late 1990s. The U.S. merchandise deficit grew so large by 2000 that including foreign affiliate sales would reduce the deficit but no longer produce a U.S. surplus.

The rise in the volume of intracorporate foreign trade, which is trade originating in transactions between subsidiaries of MNCs located in different countries, suggests that, in the aggregate, FDI is *not* always a substitute for exports, at least not in the United States.[37] The U.S. International Trade Commission has characterized foreign affiliate sales as the "predominant mode of delivering" goods and services produced by U.S.-controlled companies to foreign customers. This conclusion is based on data showing that in 1997, majority-owned foreign affiliates accounted for 68 percent of such deliveries, while exporting accounted for only 32 percent. Sales by U.S. subsidiaries in the European Union accounted for 82 percent of total U.S. corporate sales in the European Union in 1997.[38] According to the U.S. Commerce Department's definition, $438 billion, or 64 percent, of total U.S. exports of goods in 1998 was "U.S.-MNC-associated." More specifically, 27 percent ($185 billion) of U.S. merchandise exports during that year was classified as intracorporate trade; that is, shipments by U.S. parents directly to their foreign affiliates.[39]

## The Significance of the Trade Balance

The size of a country's trade surplus or deficit is usually viewed by the general public and most politicians as a disproportionately important measure of the "success" or "failure" of a country's trade performance. Most people see a trade surplus as an absolute positive, and the bigger the better. Similarly, a prolonged trade deficit often unleashes widespread distress that often leads to anguished political debate about falling competitiveness and the need for more aggressive trade policies. However, as the economic theory in this chapter has argued, a trade surplus is not unequivocally rewarding for a country and a trade deficit is not necessarily harmful. The underlying causes of a trade imbalance and the product composition of trade tend to be more economically significant than the arithmetic of a trade balance. Trade imbalances can be a source of international political friction if they redistribute wealth or jobs in favor of surplus countries.

## Basic Principles

As discussed in Chapter 3, economic theory asserts that the primary purpose of engaging in international trade is to provide consumers with the benefits of imported goods and services produced more efficiently, that is, more cheaply, overseas. From this perspective, rising imports and a merchandise trade deficit are not automatically undesirable and damaging to a country's aggregate welfare, and trade surpluses are not necessarily a sign of economic strength. The jump in the U.S. trade deficit in the late 1990s, as noted previously, was mostly attributed to two positive factors. The first was the relatively high economic growth rates of the American economy relative to its major trading partners; the second factor was the strong confidence of foreign investors in the United States, which led to massive inflows of capital. In some unknown combination, these two factors offset and contributed to the growing trade deficit. Another example of a country's being better off with a trade deficit than with a surplus is when a less-developed country increases its economic base and production efficiency by financing net imports of real economic resources (capital goods, food, medicine, etc.) through net inflows of capital in the form of foreign investments, grants, and loans. Trade deficits *should* be of concern if they are symptomatic of flawed domestic policies, threaten to have a negative impact on a country's industrial development or income distribution, or require so much external borrowing that they jeopardize financial stability.

Some governments, such as Japan's, are alleged to embrace a mercantilist trade philosophy that believes surpluses enhance a country's economic wealth and political power; these governments are therefore happy to run continuous trade surpluses. In some circumstances, however, a trade surplus must be viewed as an unwanted consequence of undesirable economic trends. Surpluses can be generated by a recession and/or a sudden shortage of foreign exchange associated with a balance of payments emergency. Mexico experienced this malady in the mid-1980s (in connection with its external debt crisis) and again in the mid-1990s (after the peso crisis). Other Latin American debtor countries besides Mexico suffered similar hardships from externally imposed austerity programs that resulted in trade surpluses during the slow growth, "lost decade," of the 1980s.

## Conflicting Evaluations of the U.S. Trade Deficit

Although it is an empirical fact that the U.S. trade deficit reached record levels at the turn of the millennium, opinions on whether such a large deficit is really a serious problem differ widely. An example of the polarized thinking on this issue can be found in the final report of the U.S. Trade Deficit Review Commission, issued in

2000. This bipartisan commission was established by the Congress in 1999 to determine the causes and consequences of the trade deficit and to recommend appropriate policy responses, if any. Although trade policy has been largely a nonpartisan issue in the post–World War II era, the Democrats and Republicans on this commission ended up issuing two conflicting reports in one volume. The Republican commissioners took a benign view; they argued that the large and growing trade and current account deficits of the 1990s were principally the outcomes of relatively strong U.S. economic growth. In their opinion, government intervention to block imports would be counterproductive because "economies that are open to international trade generally have far better records of economic growth and better living standards than those that are less open." In contrast, the Democratic commissioners warned of the long-term costs of the trade deficit, including "job loss and increased economic insecurity for U.S. workers as well as downward pressure on [their] wages." The Democrats further claimed that "persistent trade deficits have also contributed to the erosion of the U.S. manufacturing base and the loss of long-run competitiveness."[40]

Optimists, such as the Republican members of the Trade Deficit Commission, argue that, to the extent that unemployment is low, capacity utilization in the industrial sector is high, and the dollar is stable, a trade deficit inflicts little or no immediate damage on the American economy. As an advocate of free trade has declared, "By virtually every measure, U.S. economic performance during years in which the trade deficit rises is superior to that during years in which the deficit shrinks."[41] (The measures referred to included such indicators as low unemployment rates, full employment, and high economic growth.) This claim is based on the generally agreed upon fact that, as a result of "income effects" (i.e., business cycle factors discussed above), imports tend to rise and the trade deficit naturally worsens during periods of relatively rapid economic growth. However, this claim does not prove that growing or sustained trade deficits are always desirable or that deficits caused by other factors besides rapid growth are always benign.

Pessimists, including the Democratic members of the commission, argue that the U.S. trade deficit is not benign because it disproportionately harms an important sector of the U.S. economy: manufacturing. This viewpoint believes that because manufacturing wages tend to be above-average for the whole economy, a large deficit in manufacturing means a net loss of relatively high-paying jobs for blue-collar workers in the United States. These critics cite studies showing that workers who are displaced from manufacturing by imports tend to end up in lower-paying jobs in the service sector, so that even if the total number of jobs in the economy is not affected, the trade deficit allegedly has caused a shift in the composition of employment toward lower-paying jobs.[42] In addition, some who believe that the trade deficit is a serious problem argue that the deficit causes lasting harm to U.S. competitiveness by discouraging companies from investing in new facilities or spending on research and development at U.S. locations.[43]

On the financial side, as long as foreigners accept payment for their exports in dollars and are willing to invest more than $400 billion (net) annually in the United States, as they did in 2000 and 2001, the large U.S. trade deficit can be sustained at its current level indefinitely. But further increases in or continuation of these deficits run the risk of provoking an eventual loss of confidence on the part of foreign investors.[44] Such a change in market sentiment could result in a free fall in the dollar's exchange rate that could seriously undermine international economic stability. If, instead of investing in the United States, exporters in surplus countries liquidated their dollar earnings en masse, Americans would face a painful adjustment in which the rapid depreciation of the dollar and higher interest rates adopted to try to prevent further depreciation would gradually choke off growth and possibly cause a serious recession. Although the resulting fall in U.S. expenditures would cut the demand for imports and thus probably improve the trade balance, the consequences for the domestic U.S. economy would be lost jobs, slower growth, a reduced standard of living, and more expensive imports. To the extent that slower U.S. economic growth and a reduced demand for imports hurt the global economy, U.S. exports would be adversely affected and could decline.

Many of those who are optimistic about the overall U.S. trade deficit point to a large and growing surplus in services trade between the late 1980s and the mid-1990s that partly offset rising merchandise trade deficits. The surplus in services meant that the overall U.S. goods and services deficit was smaller than the merchandise (goods only) deficit (see Figure 4.1, above). In fact, to present a more complete (and more positive) impression of overall U.S. trade, the U.S. Department of Commerce shifted during the 1990s to emphasizing a goods-and-services balance in its monthly statistical reports, rather than just the merchandise balance. The relatively innovative, efficient, and expanding American services sector led some observers to predict that exports of services could expand fast enough to be the means of restoring equilibrium to the overall trade balance. But such optimism may have been premature. When the services surplus peaked at $91 billion in 1997, it offset nearly one-half of the merchandise deficit of $197 billion in that year. But by 2000, while the merchandise trade deficit hit a record of $452 billion, the services surplus *fell* to only $77 billion, or barely one-sixth of the merchandise deficit. Thus, the combined goods-and-services deficit rose sharply from $106 billion in 1997 to $376 billion in 2000, nearly a four-fold increase.

## Conclusions and Outlook

The economic importance of a country's trade balance is easy to exaggerate, even though total exports and imports of goods and services have become important variables in a country's economic performance. Trade surpluses or deficits can be useful barometers of national economic health if their causes and consequences are adequately and accurately understood. The effects of the business cycle (the impact on a country's foreign trade of growth or recessions) and fluctuations in exchange rates usually explain most of the short-term swings in trade surpluses or deficits. In the long term, underlying factors such as saving-investment balances, relative industrial competitiveness, trade policies, and foreign direct investment affect the *direction* of a country's trade balance to some degree. There is no one dominant explanation of all trade surpluses or deficits that is valid at all times and for all countries. Nor is there a single panacea for reducing trade deficits.

A major theme of this chapter is that a trade surplus or deficit should not necessarily be interpreted as a good or bad sign, respectively, about a nation's trade performance and the health of its domestic economy. A moderate trade deficit that is financed by a manageable amount of international borrowing can be beneficial to a country, especially if the funds borrowed from abroad are invested in improving the capacity and productivity of the domestic economy and in enhancing export capabilities. A deficit that results simply from rapid growth relative to that of trading partners can certainly be considered benign. However, a large deficit that requires unsustainable borrowing, results from a chronically overvalued currency, hurts key domestic industries, or is used to promote consumption rather than investment, may bode ill for a nation's future. A trade surplus that results from positive causes—competitive export industries, a high saving rate, and a realistic exchange rate—indicates a vibrant economy. Conversely, a surplus that results from depressed domestic demand or credit constraints imposed by a debt crisis is definitely not to be envied.

Future trends in the U.S. trade deficit in goods and services can only be guessed at. It is theoretically possible, though not likely, that foreigners will perpetually exhibit an insatiable desire to accumulate dollar assets. Given uninterrupted net inflows of private capital of sufficient size, the United States could sustain a large trade deficit indefinitely. A second scenario is a gradual contraction in the deficit caused by some combination of faster economic growth among major U.S. trading partners, a steady upward spurt in the international competitiveness of American industry, a moderate depreciation of the dollar, and a large increase in U.S. services exports. A third scenario unfolds with massive sales of dollars by speculators and investors around the world. A relatively large contraction in the U.S. trade deficit would be a likely outcome of resulting unfavorable economic forces: a growth-choking increase in U.S. interest rates and/or large price increases for imports as the dollar's exchange rate plunges.

No matter which scenario unfolds, trade policy will be a secondary, not a critical, variable in generating major changes in the U.S. trade deficit. Even though trade barriers do alter and distort some trade flows, the ability of narrowly defined trade policy under normal circumstances to alter a nation's export-import balance is circumscribed. In the meantime, the current cost-effectiveness and long-term threat of the U.S. trade deficit can't be known with certainty. These issues will continue to be perceived in different ways and conflicting policy prescriptions will continue to be proposed.

## For Further Reading

Blecker, Robert A. *Beyond the Twin Deficits: A Trade Strategy for the 1990s.* Armonk, N.Y.: M. E. Sharpe, Inc., 1992.

Blecker, Robert A., ed. *U.S. Trade Policy and Global Growth.* Armonk, N.Y.: M.E. Sharpe, Inc., 1996.

Bosworth, Barry. *Saving and Investment in a Global Economy.* Washington, D.C.: Brookings Institution, 1993.

Dertouzos, Michael, Richard Lester and Robert Solow. *Made in America: Regaining the Competitive Edge.* MIT Commission on Industrial Productivity. Cambridge, Mass.: MIT Press, 1989.

Graham, Edward M., and Paul R. Krugman. *Foreign Direct Investment in the United States.* Washington, D.C.: Institute for International Economics, 1991.

Krugman, Paul R. *Pop Internationalism.* Cambridge, Mass.: MIT Press, 1996.

Mann, Catherine L. *Is the U.S. Trade Deficit Sustainable?* Washington, D.C.: Institute for International Economics, 1999.

Morici, Peter. *The Trade Deficit: Where Does It Come from and What Does It Do?* Washington, D.C.: Economic Strategy Institute, 1997.

U.S. International Trade Commission. *Examination of U.S. Inbound and Outbound Direct Investment.* 2001. Available at www.USITC.gov.

U.S. Trade Deficit Review Commission. *The U.S. Trade Deficit: Causes, Consequences and Recommendations for Action.* November 2000. Available at www.ustdrc.gov.

Vernon, Raymond. *In the Hurricane's Eye: The Troubled Prospects of Multinational Enterprises.* Cambridge, Mass.: Harvard University Press, 1998.

## Notes

1. An increased need to export appears to have induced Japan, Russia, and other relatively depressed economies during the 1990s to divert output of some industrial commodities, such as steel, to faster-growing markets, mainly the United States. See Box 7.1 on the long-standing steel-import problem in the United States.

2. The small current account surplus in 1991 was an aberration due to the inflow of positive unilateral transfers from U.S. allies to help pay for the Persian Gulf War. The other trade balances remained in deficits, in 1991.

3. Stefan Papaioannou and Kie-Mu Yi, "The Effects of a Booming Economy on the U.S. Trade Deficit" (research paper, Federal Reserve Bank of New York, February 2001), 1.

4. Data Source: International Monetary Fund, *Direction of Trade Statistics,* various issues.

5. Data source: International Monetary Fund, *Finance and Development,* September 2001; accessed at the IMF web site: www.imf.org/.

6. The correlation between the exchange rate and the trade deficit is not observed at times when other factors, such as income effects, play a more dominant role. For example, in the period 1992–1995, the U.S. trade deficit increased even though the dollar did not appreciate (and even depreciated slightly) because of the strong economic recovery from the 1990–1991 recession as noted earlier. Also, the increase in the trade deficit in the late 1990s is greater than what would be expected from the dollar appreciation alone; the difference is mainly identifiable to the unusually large (and positive) growth differential between the faster growing United States and the other major economies.

7. Most economists believe that price increases were triggered by President Lyndon Johnson's futile effort to have guns and butter simultaneously while waging two wars, one in Vietnam and one on domestic poverty, without paying for them through tax increases. The inflationary situation was further aggravated by what, in retrospect, was considered an overly accommodating monetary policy.

8. Most less-developed countries retained fixed exchange rates even after the collapse of Bretton Woods, with their currencies pegged to major "hard" currencies such as the U.S. dollar. Also, many western European countries later banded together to re-peg their currencies to each other in the European Monetary System, a precursor to the euro.

9. Computed from unpublished Federal Reserve Board data for the weighted average value of the dollar, March 1973 = 100.

10. See Robert A. Blecker, *Taming Global Finance: A Better Architecture for Global Equity* (Washington, D.C.: Economic Policy Institute, 1999) for an extensive discussion of how theories of flexible exchange rates have been invalidated by the behavior of wide-open capital markets and speculative currency trading.

11. Data accessed at the BIS web site: www.BIS.org/.

12. Data source: Federal Reserve Board statistical release H.10, 1 March 1985. Dollar appreciation is measured in nominal terms.

13. In September 1985, the Plaza Agreement successfully changed the prevailing psychology in the foreign exchange markets. The pact demonstrated a high degree of commitment by the industrial country governments to a realignment of exchange rates centering on a lower dollar exchange rate for the dollar.

14. See Robert A. Blecker, written statement on *The Causes of the U.S. Trade Deficit,* U.S. Trade Deficit Review Commission, Hearing of 19 August 1999; accessed at www.ustdrc.gov.

15. Testimony to the U.S. Trade Deficit Review Commission, December 10, 1999; accessed at www.ustdrc.gov/.

16. See, for example, Laura D'Andrea Tyson, *Who's Bashing Whom? Trade Conflict in High-Technology Industries* (Washington, D.C.: Institute for International Economics, 1992), 1. See also the discussion of Michael Porter's more microeconomic view of competitiveness of specific sectors in Chapter 3, above.

17. President's Commission on Industrial Competitiveness, *Global Competition: The New Reality* (Washington, D.C.: Government Printing Office, 1985), 1, 5.

18. Rudiger Dornbusch, Paul Krugman, and Yung Chul Park, *Meeting World Challenges: U.S. Manufacturing in the 1990s* (Rochester, N.Y.: Eastman Kodak Company, 1989), 9. Co-author Krugman later disavowed this view, however, as discussed below.

19. Michael Dertouzos et al., MIT Commission on Industrial Productivity, *Made in America* (Cambridge, Mass.: MIT Press, 1989), 166, 8.

20. Estimates of the relatively high income elasticity of U.S. demand for imports are discussed in Robert A. Blecker, *Beyond the Twin Deficits* (Armonk, N.Y.: M. E. Sharpe, Inc., 1992), 62–64.

21. This paragraph is based on the analysis in Robert A. Blecker, "International Competitiveness, Relative Wages, and the Balance-of-Payments Constraint," *Journal of Post Keynesian Economics* 20, no. 4 (summer 1998): 495–526.

22. The Institute for Management Development's rankings assess how a country's total environment "sustains the competitiveness of enterprises." A summary of the *World Competitiveness Yearbook* was accessed at www.imd.ch/.

23. Joseph Quinlan and Marc Chandler, "The U.S. Trade Deficit: A Dangerous Obsession," *Foreign Affairs* (May/June 2001); accessed at www.foreignaffairs.org.

24. This argument about reverse causality in the saving-investment balance equation is made by Robert A. Blecker, *Beyond the Twin Deficits: A Trade Strategy for the 1990s* (Armond, N.Y: M. E. Sharpe, Inc., 1992); and Robert A. Blecker, "The Trade Deficit and U.S. Competitiveness," in *Competitiveness Matters: Industry and Economic Performance in the U.S.,* ed. Candace Howes and Ajit Singh (Ann Arbor, Mich.: University of Michigan Press, 2000).

25. An exception can occur when a highly competitive export sector generates excessive euphoria among investors, leading to an over-investment boom fueled by large capital inflows and a widening trade deficit, as occurred in Thailand, Korea, and other East Asian countries in the late 1990s.

26. Paul R. Krugman, *Pop Internationalism* (Cambridge, Mass.: MIT Press, 1968), 6–8.

27. C. Fred Bergsten and Marcus Noland, *Reconcilable Differences? United States–Japan Economic Conflict* (Washington, D.C.: Institute for International Economics, 1993), 202.

28. Data Source: U.S. International Trade Commission, *Value of U.S. Imports for Consumption, Duties Collected, and Ratio of Duties to Values, 1891–1999,* March 2000.

29. In extreme cases, U.S. tariffs can reach 350 percent when imports of some agricultural products and tobacco exceed certain quantitative ceilings; these are known as "out of quota" tariffs.

30. In the standard economic analysis, which assures competitive international markets, ordinary quotas keep the excess profits, or "rents," at home. If the government gives out import quota licenses to domestic import merchants free of charge, they earn the "quota rents" by buying cheap in the world market and selling dear at home. Alternatively, the domestic government can capture the quota rents by selling the licenses to the importers via competitive auctions. See the discussion in Chapter 3 of how estimates of the costs of protection are affected by the form of protection.

31. Joseph Quinlan, *Whose Trade Deficit Is It, Anyway?* Morgan Stanley Dean Witter research report, 13 October 1999.

32. Data Source: United Nations Conference on Trade and Development (UNCTAD), *World Investment Report 2000;* accessed at www.unctad.org/en/docs/wir00one.en.pdf.

33. Ibid.

34. Data Source: U.S. Department of Commerce, *Survey of Current Business,* August 2001.

35. Ibid.

36. Data Source: U.S. Department of Commerce, *Survey of Current Business,* July 2000.

37. For a different perspective finding that U.S. foreign direct investment overseas was damaging on balance to U.S. employment, see Norman J. Glickman and Douglas P. Woodward, *The New Competitors: How Foreign Investors Are Changing the U.S. Economy* (New York: Basic Books, 1989), 156–187 and 317–324.

38. Data Source: U.S. International Trade Commission, *Examination of U.S. Inbound and Outbound Direct Investment,* January 2001, 5–1, 5–2.

39. Data Source: U.S. Department of Commerce, Bureau of Economic Analysis, *Survey of Current Business,* July 2000, 29.

40. U.S. Trade Deficit Review Commission, *The U.S. Trade Deficit: Causes, Consequences, and Recommendations for Action,* November 2000, 122, 88.

41. Daniel T. Griswold, "America's Record Trade Deficit: A Symbol of Economic Strength," Cato Institute Trade Policy Analysis, February 2001; accessed at www.freetrade.org/pubs/pas/tpa–012es.html/.

42. See, for example, Robert E. Scott, Thea Lee, and John Schmitt, "Trading Away Good Jobs: An Examination of Employment and Wages in the U.S., 1979–94" (Washington, D.C.: Economic Policy Institute, 1997); accessed at www.epinet.org.

43. See, for example, Peter Morici, *The Trade Deficit: Where Does It Come from and What Does It Do?* (Washington, D.C., Economic Strategy Institute, 1997).

44. Even if the U.S. trade deficit is financially sustainable, at least for the time being, from a global viewpoint it does not seem equitable for one of the richest countries on earth to be a net taker (importer) of both real resources and capital from the rest of the world. Rich countries as a group need to be net exporters of real economic resources and capital so that poor countries as a group can be net importers and obtain the additional real economic resources necessary for development.

# Part Three

## Politics and Law

# 5 The Formulation and Administration of U.S. Trade Policy: Who Does What

Process affects substance. The organizational means by which a government makes trade policy often has an impact on the nature of that policy. Broad national values, in turn, affect the structure of decisionmaking. Decisions are sometimes bewildering unless one is familiar with the elaborate process involved. It begins when policymakers assemble the relevant information and then outline the various options. Next, there is an assessment of the costs and benefits to the country and to elected politicians if the government were to respond to pressure from one constituency at the expense of another. Finally, a decision or strategy is agreed upon at the appropriate level in the chain of command.

In this chapter we identify the relevant players in the U.S. government and the private sector, describe what they do, and explain how they go about doing it. Implicit throughout this discussion are two themes. The first is the argument that different government actors bring different priorities, institutional cultures, and constituencies to the policymaking process. The second theme is that the inherent nature of trade policy precludes objective, consistent, and rigidly disciplined decisionmaking. The next chapter moves to the second stage: a review of the various theories employed to explain why policymaking dynamics function as they do.

## The Organizational Dynamics of U.S. Trade Policy Decisionmaking

At least five operational guidelines are essential for conceptualizing the complex and heterogeneous process by which the U.S. government makes trade policy. The first guideline refers to the point emphasized in Chapter 1: Trade is not just an economic phenomenon; in the final analysis, it is a political phenomenon. Inevitably, actions affecting the flows of imports and exports produce winners and losers among domestic workers, companies, and farmers; foreign interests; and competing economic theories. Politics can be succinctly defined as determining who gets what, when they get it, and how they get it. Trade policy regularly determines whether certain kinds of jobs and production stay at home or go to foreigners in the form of imports or lost export opportunities. Trade flows, in turn, affect price levels, consumer choice, and competition among corporations.

At least two fully rational and legitimate points of view about priorities are advanced in connection with virtually every decision that will result in a significant increase or decrease in imports, retaliation against a major trading partner that is discriminating against American goods or services, or the imposition of export controls. Trade policy-makers in all countries must make difficult, subjective choices among conflicting priorities based on value judgments and perceptions, not scientific methods based on absolute truths. Every sovereign government has exercised its right to interfere with free market forces. The pursuit of economic efficiency and the practice of free trade are inevitably tempered by concerns of social stability and equity, not to mention the assumption that popularly elected officials are supposed to be responsive to the desires expressed by their constituents—and the votes of foreigners do not count.

The political process inherent in choosing among different values would be inescapable even if trade policy were made by a group of politically unaccountable economics professors. There may be general agreement on the broad virtues of free trade in the abstract. However, no academic unanimity exists on exactly which economic theories should prevail with regard to such issues as which criteria to use in determining which industries are deserving of temporary import protection, how to calculate when a trade deficit grows "dangerously" large, and how to measure U.S. international competitiveness.

The second operational guideline is the recognition that different modes of decisionmaking exist because trade policy decisions vary in their nature, importance, political impact, breadth, and complexity. Sometimes decisions involve broad policy strategy on issues of dramatic importance and have significant long-term impact. Examples include drafting major new trade legislation, articulating U.S. negotiating objectives in multilateral trade negotiations, and determining whether to negotiate a bilateral free trade agreement with Mexico.

The majority of trade policy decisions are not of epic proportions. They involve either narrow, relatively low-impact initiatives or they result in minor incrementalism, that is, marginal modifications of existing policy. Examples are decisions on annual funding requests for ongoing export promotion programs and the U.S.-Canadian agreement in 2001 on inspection standards to assure that U.S. imports of potatoes from Prince Edward Island do not contain potato wart disease. Most issues do not materially affect the policy status quo, and they are handled at the working level by office directors or division chiefs.

Some decisions relate to one-time matters of limited duration such as whether to impose temporary import relief recommended by the International Trade Commission following an escape-clause investigation. A decision may involve proactive initiatives by the U.S. government, but it is more likely to be a defensive reaction such as retaliation against unfair foreign trade practices. Some decisions go beyond economic issues and involve sensitive national security matters. The latter include whether and how to limit steel imports from Russia, or convincing other countries to join the United States in imposing trade sanctions against a country engaged in some form of offensive behavior. Other decisions are primarily domestic and involve U.S. government dealings only with American companies, for example, whether to proceed with oil exploration in Alaska to reduce growing U.S. dependence on imported oil, and whether to approve a company's request for an export license on a high-tech piece of equipment.

The third operational guideline is the need to appreciate fully the limits of presidential power in formulating and implementing U.S. trade policy. Trade policymaking in the United States is unique in the partnership of virtual equals between two branches of government. No other legislative body in the world has as much influence and authority in trade policy relative to the executive branch as does the U.S. legislative branch. Congress possesses the sole authority to pass trade legislation. Many of the daily activities of U.S. trade policy bear the subtle—and sometimes not so subtle—genetic imprint of densely written trade statutes seeking to reconcile divergent congressional and presidential views on trade priorities.

The legislative branch is a direct or indirect factor in virtually every politically significant U.S. trade policy decision. As explained below, no administration can alter import barriers, restrict exports, fund export promotion programs, or pay the salaries of trade negotiators without statutory authority from Congress. No administration takes a major trade action without giving some consideration to the likely reaction among members of Congress. Senior trade officials understand that if an administration too frequently acts in a manner contrary to prevailing congressional sentiment, it invites interbranch retaliation. The more a majority of members become alienated, the more likely they are to refuse an administration's requests for new trade statutes or to pass legislation that the administration did not ask for and does not support.

The fourth guideline for conceptualizing the multiple patterns of trade policymaking is the extraordinary degree of decentralization in the executive branch's trade policymaking apparatus. No one agency is "in charge" of foreign trade policymaking (indeed, there is not even a *branch* of government in charge). Different bureaucratic actors will assume leadership roles depending on the issue at hand and the strength of personal relationships between agency heads and the president's inner circle. Given that no single executive branch actor can monopolize a major trade policy decision and that the president rarely unilaterally dictates trade policy decisions, coordination among many executive branch departments and agencies is the most common vehicle of U.S. trade decisionmaking. The ubiquity of interagency collaboration means that the larger organizational question is how many executive branch entities (there can be as many as two dozen) have a compelling reason to participate in the interagency committees and working groups dealing with dozens of categories of trade issues. (The Trade Policy Staff Committee operated more than sixty-five subcommittees and task forces in 2000). Private sector lobbyists, not-for-profit nongovernmental organizations, and foreign interests regularly exploit the U.S. government's belief that everyone affected by public policy has the right to be heard, especially in trade policy—which, after all, is administered overwhelmingly on behalf of the private sector and consumers.

The decentralization syndrome also exists in the legislative branch inasmuch as most standing committees have jurisdiction over some facet of trade policy: import restraints, export restraints, export promotion, high-tech competitiveness, agriculture, foreign direct investment, and so on. When there is extensive overlap, coordination can take the form of joint hearings of two or more committees drafting sections of the same statute. A specialized form of coordination between congressional committees is the conference committee, used to reconcile differences in bills passed by the Senate and House.

The final operational guideline is the propensity of the various bureaucratic actors to bring different perspectives and priorities to the interagency deliberative process. As explained more fully in the next chapter, none of the executive departments or congressional committees has been created to focus on the totality of U.S. interests or to represent all economic constituencies: consumers, industry, labor, agriculture, foreign interests, the financial sector, and so on. Instead, each department and committee represents narrowly defined constituencies, that is, different parts of the policy waterfront. Monolithic thinking in defining the national interest on trade policy is not a characteristic of the governments of any large industrialized democracy.

The notion that government seek only to advance their "national interest" is a gross generalization and not a useful guide to explaining or predicting individual decisions in trade policy. Reference to the national interest ignores the inherent difficulty of objectively determining case-by-case which of two or more compelling but mutually exclusive trade policy options would most benefit the nation as a whole. Is free trade with Mexico on balance good or bad for the United States? Should most-favored nation (normal trade relations) with China be extended unconditionally or only if China modifies at least some of the actions that offend Americans? These are just two examples of hotly contested and unresolved debates about which trade policy option would best serve the overall national interest.

In sum, the organizational dynamics of U.S. trade policy decisionmaking is inescapably shaped by interactions between two phenomena. The first is the procedural reality that many bureaucratic actors imbued with different perspectives and priorities participate in such decisions; the second is the intellectual reality that virtually every important decision in trade policy has at least two contending points of view about what is "good" policy. The resulting synthesis means that U.S. trade policymaking far more frequently consists of pursuing compromise and accommodation than of embracing extreme, daring, or unconventional tactics. This synthesis is also the reason inconsistencies in U.S. trade policy over time are far more evident than an unswerving allegiance to one guiding ideology.

## The Executive Branch

The passage of the Reciprocal Trade Agreements Act in 1934 delegated significant authority to the executive branch for the first time in American history to formulate and administer trade policy, mainly in the form of negotiated reductions in trade barriers. Then and now, the executive branch's power in trade policy exists only to the extent specified by congressionally passed legislation. The U.S. Constitution mandates that presidential authority in this area is solely derived from the legislative branch (see the next section). In transferring the authority to conduct trade policy, Congress in effect designated the executive branch to be the primary recipient of political pressures from interest groups making demands concerning import and export flows.

The executive branch's machinery to make trade policy is composed of three administrative entities: the Executive Office of the President, the line departments and agencies, and interagency coordinating groups. Although the president is formally in charge of all three realms, this does not necessarily mean that over the decades he has been a hands-on participant throughout a trade policy decisionmaking exercise. Only on a few occasions have presidents taken time away from more pressing (and more appealing) matters of domestic politics and national security to take a hands-on initiative in an important trade matter. Usually, direct presidential involvement in trade policymaking comes late in the process and consists of approving a cabinet-level recommendation or arbitrating relatively rare cabinet stalemates.

Outside the Oval Office, five White House groups are heavily involved in formulating trade policy and make up a separate layer of bureaucracy paralleling the cabinet departments, an organizational idiosyncrasy found only in the United States. First is the *Office of the United States Trade Representative* (USTR). The cabinet-level person who heads the office, the U.S. Trade Representative, is the titular head of "overall" trade policy formulation, "chief" trade negotiator for the U.S. government, and designated "representative" of the United States in the major international trade organizations.[1] The USTR plays a major role in managing interagency coordination below the cabinet level, serves as the designated chief liaison with Congress on trade matters, and has overall managerial responsibilities for the government's three-tiered network of private sector advisory committees on trade policy. The agency was described by an insider as seeing itself mainly as a policybroker and a problemsolver.[2]

The rationale for creating the USTR speaks volumes about the linkages between economics and politics, process and substance, and lawmaking and policy administration that collectively form the essence of U.S. trade policy. Although located within the Executive Office of the President, the USTR is literally a creature of Congress. It was created because legislators in 1961 decided that the State Department needed to be replaced as the head of U.S. trade delegations by a more hard-nosed, domestically sensitive bureaucracy that was not predisposed to free trade and avoiding clashes with other governments. One part of the "institutional culture" of USTR fully embraces the antiprotectionist tenets of the WTO and the wisdom of negotiating agreements to promote a more liberal world trading order. The other major part of its culture embraces the need to be sensitive to prevailing sentiments about trade on Capitol Hill.

Allegiance to its congressionally mandated heritage explains why the USTR has never allowed itself to become a dogmatic advocate of free trade or a miniature foreign ministry. On occasion, it has supported relief for import-impacted domestic industries. Similarly, it has not backed away from aggressively pursuing U.S. commercial interests overseas, even if that meant threatening retaliatory trade actions against a close political ally such as Japan.

The USTR is at the administrative center of gravity between Congress's predisposition to give a sympathetic ear to the foreign trade grievances of constituents and the predisposition of presidential administrations to give priority to trade liberalization and diplomacy. Congress has rewarded the USTR's mutual desire for a "special relationship" by loudly and angrily opposing occasional presidential proposals to collapse USTR operations into the Commerce Department or to strip its head of cabinet rank.

The USTR's role as primus inter pares among executive branch agencies charged with the development of U.S. trade policy has two important limitations. First, it has never been able to take the leadership role on all trade issues. The lines of command are sufficiently ambiguous and the USTR's staff sufficiently limited that other agencies sometimes take the lead, either through a bureaucratic power grab or by mutual agreement. Congress elevated the head of the Office of the USTR to cabinet status in the Trade Act of 1974, but the staff is still so small (about 150 full-time staff members) that it regularly uses the greater resources of the cabinet departments to supplement its limited personnel. Second, as a presidential office, the USTR by design has not been given "line" authority to administer major programs affecting U.S. foreign trade relations (see the discussion of the Commerce and Agriculture Departments later in this chapter).

A second key White House player is the *cabinet-level coordinating group for economic policy* used by U.S. presidents since Richard Nixon. Created by executive order and having various names, such as the Economic Policy Group and the National Economic Council, this operation represents collaborative policymaking at the highest political level. Usually, the president is the formal chairman, but in practice he attends meetings only occasionally. Each iteration of these coordinating groups has had roughly the same membership and the same indispensable responsibility: development of consensus among the ten or more members of the cabinet and senior presidential advisers having jurisdiction in formulating economic policy. For all but what are judged the most crucial issues in trade policy on which the president takes direct control, this is the final decisionmaking stop for international and domestic economic policy. Typically, a designated official of the senior coordinating council for economic affairs sends a memorandum to the president outlining its consensus recommendation, summarizing alternate options, and asking for his formal approval. On the rare occasions of cabinet deadlock, the president is asked to arbitrate and select one of the conflicting policy proposals.

Three other relevant White House offices exist to provide advice directly to the president of the United States. The *National Security Council* (NSC) is charged with coordinating international political and military policy (mainly between the State and Defense Departments) and providing independent advice on foreign policy to the president. The person on the NSC's professional staff in charge of economic affairs has been an integral part of interagency trade policy coordination when the subject under discussion deals with an international economic issue affecting the interests of U.S. national security. It had been a commonplace occurrence over the years for the NSC and the senior economic policy group to engage in turf battles to determine which one would assume responsibility for managing interagency decisionmaking for internationally sensitive issues in trade policy. The Clinton and Bush II administrations successfully minimized this organizational jealousy by having the same person serve as both the NSC's senior staff member for economic affairs and the economic policy coordinating group's senior staff member for international economics.

The *Council of Economic Advisers* (CEA) has a mandate to provide the president with nonpolitical, technical advice on economic issues affecting growth, employment, and price stability. Because trade policy affects domestic economy in so many ways, the CEA member (usually an academic) having responsibilities for international economic policy or a senior staff member joins the interagency process when major issues in trade are under deliberation.

The fifth and final White House entity having jurisdiction in trade policy, the *Office of Management and Budget* (OMB), is best known for its budget-setting responsibilities and is not visible in every day trade policy. Most of its international activities focus on defense and foreign aid. OMB's leadership and staff economists exercise clout in trade deliberations whenever governmental expenditures or lost revenues are a consideration (e.g., officially subsidized export financing and reductions in tariff duties). The office can also be influential in formulating trade policy by virtue of its responsibility for coordinating and clearing all responses from executive branch agencies to bills introduced into Congress and all testimony to congressional committees.

Line departments and agencies constitute the second realm of executive branch bureaucracy. By virtue of its domination of domestic economic and international financial policies, the *Treasury Department* has gradually assumed the role of number one voice in U.S. international economic policymaking as a whole. In the specific area of trade relations, its main function is to determine which trade actions would be best for its wide-ranging constituent: the overall domestic economy. Because import barriers tend to be inflationary, the Treasury Department usually joins the other economics-oriented agencies, the CEA and OMB, in preferring maximum competition from abroad. The department is especially influential in international agreements covering official export financing and in the interagency committee screening new foreign direct investment in the United States for possible threats to national security. (Treasury was less charitable toward imports when the U.S. balance of payments deficits were soaring in the final years of fixed exchange rates. The department now looks to faster economic growth abroad and realignments in exchange rates to induce equilibrium in the U.S. current account.)

The *State Department* conducts the country's foreign policy and thereby has responsibility for assessing the probable effects of U.S. trade actions on other countries, be they friendly or hostile. The unique role of global superpower requires the United States to place a relatively high priority on foreign policy concerns in the equation of trade policy. National Security objectives in national security more often supercede economic goals than in countries having no ambitions in global or regional leadership. Whereas domestic agencies in Washington see trade issues mainly through the prism of their impact on various sectors of the domestic economy, the State Department is charged with assessing the consequences of trade policy for relations with other countries and for the overall global atmosphere judged most conducive to American interests. The validity of giving priority to external factors depends in part on how important one thinks a friendly and peaceful global setting is for assuring prosperity to the American economy. It also depends on how "national security" is defined, for example, the extent to which one views a weak domestic economy as a threat to the continued projection of American power worldwide. The State Department monitors trade policy from its regional bureaus as well as from its Bureau of Economic and Business Affairs. Extensive commercial negotiations and reporting are conducted by its economic officers stationed overseas in embassies and consulates. Although the State Department was long ago stripped of its status as chief negotiator and coordinator of trade policy, it still takes the lead in international aviation and maritime negotiations and is one of the three major departments running the export control program.

The *Commerce Department* lacks the broad policy clout of State and Treasury, but plays an essential supporting role in trade policy by virtue of its administering a majority of the government's major trade programs and its speaking on behalf of the industrial sector (manufacturing and services) in interagency groups. Whereas USTR has the lead in "macro" trade policymaking, Commerce is influential in sectoral, or micro, policymaking and occasionally maneuvers its way into a position of leadership on industry-specific trade issues such as steel and auto parts. On the import side, it administers the antidumping and countervailing duty laws. This responsibility involves investigating complaints filed by domestic producers to determine the existence of these two unfair foreign commercial practices: selling goods in the United States at less than fair value and governmental subsidies to exporting companies, respectively. Commerce officials then calculate the amount of import duty needed to neutralize the unfair trade practice if one is found to exist—and if material injury to the domestic industry is proved (see Chapter 7). The department also has people monitoring compliance by foreign governments with the more than two hundred active international trade agreements signed by the U.S. government. These agreements cover improved overseas market access for American goods and "voluntary" restraints on other countries' shipments of textiles and apparel to the United States.

The Commerce Department also administers the two extremes of export programs. On the one hand, its U.S-based advisers and overseas commercial attachés provide marketing data and advice to help U.S. businesses expand exports. On the other hand, Commerce has a major role in administering U.S. export control laws, especially for high-tech nonmilitary goods. The department's influence is also felt through its administration of several programs designed to enhance U.S. high-tech competitiveness (e.g., research funding from the Advanced Technology Program). Commerce also provides the main executive branch expertise on the state of individual domestic manufacturing and service sectors and the impact of import competition on them.

The *Agriculture Department* assumes a leadership role when actions affecting imports or exports of agricultural commodities are the subject at hand. Expertise and statutory authority to administer domestic farm programs assure this department the lead in agricultural trade decisionmaking and in setting the U.S. agricultural negotiating agenda in international trade talks. The Agriculture Department has a clearly defined constituency, but it has a problem in pleasing an agricultural community that is split between farmers who are import-sensitive (e.g., dairy, meat, sugar, and peanuts) and those who are highly efficient, successful exporters oriented toward free trade (e.g., soybeans, corn, and wheat). Operationally, the department monitors import quotas on agricultural commodities, administers three separate government-funded export-financing programs for farm goods, and runs the Foreign Agricultural Service.

The *Labor Department* oversees the interests of workers as they relate to international trade and foreign direct investment. Actual or potential increases in unemployment as the result of rising imports or additional U.S. foreign direct investment are of primary concern to the department. Its sole operational role in trade policy is administering the cash and the retraining benefits provided under the adjustment assistance program to qualifying workers whose jobs have been lost to imports (see Chapter 7 ).

A definitive list of all executive branch departments and agencies having a limited, specialized jurisdiction in trade policy would be very long. To keep things manageable, what follows is a partial summary of those bureaucracies that are occasionally significant in formulating trade policy when certain narrowly defined issues are under consideration.

The *Energy Department* provides the primary source of expertise in dealing with international energy policy in general and in particular with issues related to the rising U.S. dependence on imports of petroleum and on the global outlook for energy supplies and prices. The *Defense Department* is concerned about trade issues having immediate effects on military and national security matters; it is a key player in regulating exports of military-related and dual-use goods. Negotiations involving international shipping and civil aviation bring in the *Transportation Department.* Because competition policy is a new issue on the international trade negotiating agenda, jurisdiction over antitrust laws will make the *Justice Department* a more frequent participant in trade policymaking.

The growing nexus between trade policy and environmental concerns has brought the *Environmental Protection Agency* into the mainstream of U.S. trade policymaking. It provides specialized expertise both to interagency decisionmaking and to the U.S. trade delegations to international trade discussions, most notably the free trade agreement with Mexico. The *Export-Import Bank* operates a multibillion-dollar program to provide subsidized financing and commercial loan guarantees to promote the export of U.S.-manufactured goods. As proof that virtually no agency is exempt from becoming an actor in trade policymaking, the *Federal Communications Commission* had an impact in the mid-1990s when it determined which of several proposed technologies would be the standard for all high-definition television (HDTV) sets sold in the U.S. market. The commission opted for a new, digital-based technology developed in the United States that was incompatible with the analog standard already used in Japan, the acknowledged world leader in consumer electronics. This decision effectively pulled the plug on billions of dollars worth of potential imports of Japanese-style HDTV sets.

The *International Trade Commission* (ITC) is statutorily independent of the executive and legislative branches and has no formal role in policymaking. It does have an important investigatory role in trade relations. Acting as a nonpartisan investigator, it is responsible for determining whether petitioners for import relief under the escape clause, antidumping, and countervailing duty statutes are in fact being "injured," as defined in each of these laws. If a qualified majority of its commissioners do find injury or threat of injury, the result may be the imposition of new U.S. import barriers (higher tariffs, quotas, or a combination of the two).

The ITC is headed by six commissioners who are nominated by the president and confirmed by the Senate; no more than 3 commissioners can be from the same political party. The commission's decisions are made in response to petitions for import relief and can exert a major influence on U.S. trade relations, especially when billions of dollars worth of an import such as steel are at stake. The ITC also conducts investigations under what is termed the Section 337 provision to determine the truth of allegations that certain imports are violating U.S. intellectual property rights (patents, trademarks, copyrights, etc.). If such a violation is found, an exclusionary order is issued and the offending imports are barred from entering the country. The ITC also conducts several major studies annually on technical trade issues such as the impact of reduced trade barriers and the current health of a particular industry. Because these studies enjoy a reputation for objectivity (the commission is administratively independent and does not have policymaking responsibilities), ITC trade analyses are widely respected in Washington and often influential.

The executive branch's third administrative realm of decisionmaking consists of the interagency coordinating groups in which all relevant bureaucratic actors have the opportunity to advance their policy recommendations and to shape the search for consensus. Coordinating bodies start at the office level and extend up to the aforementioned cabinet-level council. Virtually all trade-related decisions are made in one of them. On the import policy side, the most active are the Trade Policy Review Group (membership is at the level of undersecretary and assistant secretary) and the Trade Policy Staff Committee. Three additional interagency groups deal with export controls, and the Trade Promotion Coordinating Committee attempts to bring cohesion to the government's decentralized export expansion programs scattered among more than six agencies.

## The Legislative Branch

Article I, Section 8 of the U.S. Constitution empowers Congress "to regulate commerce with foreign nations" and to "lay and collect taxes, duties . . . and excises." This provision has been interpreted throughout American history as meaning that the legislative branch is unequivocally in charge of setting the course of U.S. trade policy. For almost 150 years after the founding of the republic, Congress possessed a virtual monopoly on the formulation of trade policy through the passage of statutes, the result being a progressive ratcheting upwards of U.S. tariff rates. The executive branch's role until the mid-1930s was mainly to collect the designated tariffs. After belatedly realizing the prohibitive costs of succumbing to pressures for intensely protectionist trade legislation in 1930, Congress has allocated considerable authority in trade policy to the executive branch. The reasoning was that the latter would better be able to balance the pressure from special interest groups for higher import barriers against the economic doctrine that says reduced barriers maximize efficiency and provide the greatest good for the greatest number.[3]

Congress has not abdicated control over trade policy. Rather, it has "subcontracted" authority to the executive branch to adjust import barriers (up and down) and to impose export controls. For example, legislation has consistently delegated authority for trade liberalization only for a circumscribed, limited period of time, usually three to five years. The executive branch is not an independent actor in trade policy. First, it must comply with the detailed directions of statutes passed by Congress. Second, all administrations know they must periodically seek the renewal of existing authority as well as the passage of new authority by Congress in connection with new international trade negotiations.

The formal role of Congress in trade policymaking is manifested in four phases of legislative activity:

- passage of trade legislation (or refusal to pass legislation requested by the administration);
- approval of agency and program budgets and appropriations of funds;
- confirmation of senior policymakers; and
- general review and evaluation (known formally as "oversight") of existing and evolving policies and programs.

If the focal point of trade policy decisionmaking in the executive branch is the interagency coordinating group, the focal point in the legislative branch is the committee. Jurisdictional overlap occurs in both branches. As trade legislation becomes more complex, the instances of overlapping committee jurisdictions increase. The epitome of this reality occurred when the conference committee was convened to finalize the text of the Omnibus Trade and Competitiveness Act of 1988. It consisted of 199 members representing fourteen House and nine Senate committees.

Just as the majority of executive branch departments are involved at some point in formulating or conducting trade policy, a majority of congressional committees have at least some role in drafting foreign trade legislation. The contours of committee jurisdiction reflect random historical events more than they reflect an administratively logical formula. The major actors in import policy are the House Ways and Means and Senate Finance Committees. Jurisdiction over specialized import issues, export control policy, and export promotion programs is scattered among the agriculture, appropriations, banking, commerce, energy, and foreign relations committees in both houses. The jurisdiction of a House committee does not always parallel the jurisdiction of its counterpart in the Senate. The Joint Economic Committee has no legislative duties, but it provides a unique forum for long-range examinations of trade issues as well as the links between trade and international financial and investment trends.

More than any other legislative body in the world, the U.S. Congress has given itself the capability, independent of executive branch resources, to collect economic data, analyze economic trends, draft trade legislation, and critically evaluate trade policies. The drive to enhance its capabilities in the trade policy sector was inspired first by the larger congressional disenchantment in the 1970s with what was then dubbed the imperial presidency, and second, by the increasing politicization of trade policy. Members of Congress care about their constituents' concerns, and trade has become a pocketbook issue to many voters. This attitude mirrors the slow but steady growth of foreign trade as a percentage of U.S. GDP and the steady intensification of import competition in relation to American-made goods. In addition to more professional staff personnel on standing committees, members of Congress can draw on trade policy research and advice from hundreds of specialists working in three legislative support agencies: the Congressional Budget Office, the Congressional Research Service, and the General Accounting Office.

U.S. trade officials now spend a considerable amount of time listening and lobbying on Capitol Hill. Members of Congress have made it clear that they are not content to be brought into trade policy formulation only at the very end of the process (to use Washington jargon, they want to be "involved in the takeoff as well as the landing"). Congress long ago ceased to be willing to rubber stamp proposed trade legislation and trade agreement implementation authority drafted by the administration without advanced consultation with key committees. As part of its efforts to be better informed and to maximize dialogue, Congress has initiated an increased number of subcommittee oversight hearings on all aspects of international commerce. These hearings provide a semiofficial forum to hear administration officials, business representatives, unions, nongovernmental organizations, and academic experts defend or criticize current and proposed policies and programs, expound on international economic trends, and make proposals for adding new items to the trade policy agenda. When administration witnesses appear at oversight hearings, they are typically asked pointed questions about everything from basic philosophy to technical and intricate aspects of trade policy. This scrutiny in turn discourages perpetuation of policy by inertia.

To this day, Congress successfully cultivates the institutional image of an ardent protectionist even as it has granted a long succession of administration requests for new authority to reduce U.S. import barriers on a reciprocal basis. It assiduously seeks to play the role of "bad cop" as counterweight to its willingness to allow the administration to act as the "good cop" in U.S. trade relations. Congress still remains a de facto court of last resort for domestic interest groups to argue that the executive branch is too ideologically committed to free trade and is ignoring their plight. Congress is like a parent: Through its watchful eye, it is indulgent of the desires of its offspring, but only up to a point. If the substance of U.S. trade policy is more pragmatic than consistent, part of the cause is that ever-changing congressional sentiment must be incorporated into the executive branch's trade strategy equation.

Predicting the trade policy orientation and voting behavior of individual members of Congress is a tricky process requiring detailed information about what each member is hearing from constituents back home. Traditional trade issues long ago ceased being a partisan issue. Partisanship returned in the 1990s in the form of a schism between (most) Republicans who oppose the inclusion of environmental and labor standards in trade agreements and (most) Democrats who argue in favor of such inclusion. The trade philosophy of a senator or representative is predictable neither by party affiliation nor by his or her position along the political spectrum of liberal to conservative. (Political conservatives tend to favor liberal—that is, unobstructed—trade.) Attitudes of congressional members on trade issues are shaped mostly by prevailing economic conditions in their respective states or districts.

As the saying goes, all politics is local, and members of Congress tend to correlate the national interest with trade policies that benefit the majority of the people who elected them. Representatives having export-oriented multinational corporations and competitive high-tech companies in their constituencies favor liberal trade policies. Members from apparel manufacturing districts are more amenable to protectionist measures. Senators and representatives from states in the southwestern United States were favorably disposed to free trade with Mexico because the geographical proximity of those states would give them excellent opportunities for increased exports to that country. Representatives from soybean-growing areas tend to be more liberal trade–oriented than those from dairy farm–intensive areas (soybeans are a major export commodity, and dairy products are sensitive to import competition). The presence of large-scale incoming foreign direct investments is a new variable that tends to reduce a legislator's protectionist ardor.

Despite their desire to be responsive to workers and companies injured by import competition, few members in recent years have been philosophically committed to widespread protectionism as a basic trade strategy. The bottom-line result is that congressional concerns about large U.S. trade deficits have emphasized the same broad corrective strategies favored by the executive branch: increased domestic competitiveness, reduced foreign trade barriers, and faster overseas economic growth. Even as the U.S. trade deficits were reaching historic highs at the beginning of the twenty-first century, minimal support emerged for turning to comprehensive import barriers as an answer to America's trade problems.

## The Private Sector: Special Interest Groups and Lobbying

What do owners of refrigerated warehouses, alligator farmers in Florida, ladder builders, radio talk show hosts, operators of bed-and-breakfast inns, and lobbyists have in common? All have their own trade associations. These groups are among the more than 20,000 trade, professional, and nonprofit associations in the United States currently in operation for the purpose of promoting public opinion and official actions favorable to their viewpoints and self-interests.

When it comes to trade policy, the private sector is an informal partner in policy-making in all democratic countries. Special interests have organized themselves to be pivotal actors in the contest of ideas to determine what is and is not "good" trade policy. Because the practical business experience of the relatively small number of U.S. trade officials is limited, and because trade policy is conducted more on behalf of the private sector than on behalf of national security, no one asserts that the government should make trade policy in isolation. There is widespread consensus that trade policymakers should pay careful, yet detached attention to what spokespersons for hundreds of different special interests are recommending.

The private sector provides two invaluable sources of expertise in trade relations. The first is hands-on knowledge of current business conditions at the sectoral and individual corporation level. Aggregate domestic economic and foreign trade statistics are too general and impersonal to assure that foreign trade actions or inactions do not have unintended consequences on a given industry or company. U.S. trade officials publicly acknowledge their reliance on the private sector to inform them of overseas trade barriers that warrant governmental efforts to have them reduced or eliminated. The negotiating agenda seeking improved market access in Japan has been largely written by a steady stream of U.S. corporate complaints about that country's trade practices. Industry coalitions successfully argued in the 1980s that the U.S. government needed to add reduction of trade barriers to services and protection of intellectual property rights to the trade negotiating agenda. The second source of expertise consists of former government officials who become Washington lobbyists and who often have detailed knowledge and institutional memory of programs and legislation exceeding that of incumbent officials.

Day-to-day lobbying consists mainly of two relatively innocuous endeavors. The first consists of simple public relations efforts (web sites, speeches, seminars, and so on) designed to project a favorable public image for a given special interest group. The second is nothing more dramatic than trying to keep fully and immediately informed by carefully gathering information on what relevant institutions and people at home and abroad are saying and doing that might affect the agenda of a special interest group. When either an administrative action or a vote on a trade matter is pending in Washington, any number of interest groups will be directly affected and lobbying action intensifies. Using the right of free speech, groups present impassioned arguments, assemble data favorable to their arguments, make allusions to their ability to deliver votes in the next election, and (also in conformity with law) make cash contributions to politicians' campaign war chests—all as part of an effort to assure that impending administrative and legislative actions are favorable to their individual causes.

The effort to influence trade policy in Washington is a crowded but still growing profession. It can be safely asserted that no significant interest group or social cause is without organized, professional representation in some form. Every manufacturing and services sector, virtually every major corporation, farmers, unions, importers, exporters, environmentalists, consumers, and major foreign exporters to the United States have a permanent presence in Washington. Efforts by interest groups to convince policymakers and the public at large that their particular desires and needs are the most complementary to the broad definition of the national interest come from trade associations, political action committees, coalitions, alliances of coalitions, Washington representative offices, embassies, and such "hired guns" as attorneys, public relations specialists, and assorted public policy consultants.

The pervasive presence and prodigious lobbying efforts of interest groups in general can be observed from the outside by surfing some of the thousands of web sites maintained by interest groups or by reading some of the thousands of testimonies to congressional committees, special studies, articles on newspaper op-ed pages, and news releases that are produced annually. An internal headcount indicates that at the end of 2000, the Senate had received registrations from 16,000 persons employed by about 4,800 firms and organizations that were lobbying on behalf of just under 14,000 clients. For the House, registered lobbying groups totaled some 3,800 and clients represented exceeded 13,200.[4] The Justice Department provides a "census" of lobbyists acting on behalf of foreign interests in its annual report on the Foreign Agents Registration Act; the most recent report shows that nearly 3,000 firms, organizations, and individuals have reported such activities.[5] The extensive, high-powered pro-and-con lobbying campaigns undertaken in connection with the proposals to create a free trade agreement with Mexico[6] and the debate about whether to attach conditions to extension of MFN tariff treatment to China exemplify the inescapable— and appropriate—linkage between argumentation provided by private advocacy and trade policymaking.

The influence of the private sector as an informal power center in trade policy also can be observed in the operation of the permanent three-tiered network of private advisory committees statutorily created by Congress. They are composed of approximately 1,000 unpaid participants representing all parts of the private sector, including labor, environmental, and consumer interest groups. At the top of the organizational pyramid is the President's Advisory Committee for Trade Policy and Negotiations, which considers trade policy and negotiations in a broad context. The second tier is composed of six policy advisory committees dealing with such issues as agriculture, labor, and trade and the environment. Twenty-six groups deal with more specific functional, geographic, and sectoral issues.[7] The advisory committees are charged with counseling the administration's trade officials on details of the private sector's attitudes toward U.S. negotiating objectives and bargaining positions in international trade negotiations.

U.S. trade law formally stipulates that before the executive branch can submit trade legislation to Congress for approval under the fast-track process (see Chapter 7), the advisory committees must first produce written evaluations that assess whether the proposed agreement is in their judgment compatible with U.S. commercial interests. Because Congress is highly unlikely to enact legislation implementing a trade agreement that has been lambasted by a majority of the influential members of the private sector, members of the advisory committees collectively possess a de facto veto over key trade agreements (e.g., NAFTA and the Uruguay Round). No sensible administration would agree to a trade pact violently opposed by this legislatively created sample of informed opinion from the private sector: Congress would assuredly reject it.

The important, bottom-line question about the impact of lobbying by business, labor, and nongovernmental organizations on the substance of U.S. trade policy over the years is discussed in the next chapter.

## Conclusion

A close reading of this chapter reveals several implicit suggestions that human beings, not organizations, make decisions on policy. Knowledge of who does what in trade policy is not equivalent to fully understanding the reasoning behind decisionmaking, just as knowledge of the human skeleton and circulatory system is not equivalent to understanding human behavior. In the next chapter we examine "causality" by explicitly identifying the forces that tend to govern the behavior of government officials and that partially explain why U.S. trade policymaking functions as it does.

### For Further Reading

Cohen, Stephen D. *The Making of United States International Economic Policy.* 5th ed. New York: Praeger, 2000.

Destler, I. M. *American Trade Politics.* 3d ed. Washington, D.C.: Institute for International Economics, 1995.

Destler, I. M., and John S. Odell. *Anti-Protection: Changing Forces in United States Trade Politics.* Washington, D.C.: Institute for International Economics, 1987.

Dryden, Steve. *Trade Warriors: USTR and the American Crusade for Free Trade.* New York: Oxford University Press, 1995.

Lewis, Charles. *America's Frontline Trade Officials.* Washington, D.C.: Center for Public Integrity, 1990.

Pastor, Robert A. *Congress and the Politics of U.S. Foreign Economic Policy, 1929–1976.* Berkeley: University of California Press, 1980.

*The United States Government Manual.* Published annually by the U.S. Government Printing Office; available at www.access.gpo.gov/.

## Notes

1. "Office of the U.S. Trade Representative," undated, photocopied paper prepared by USTR.

2. Not-for-attribution interview with USTR official, spring 1994.

3. This theme is well developed in chapter 2 of I. M. Destler, *American Trade Politics* (Washington, D.C.: Institute for International Economics, 1995.)

4. Data sources: the Senate Office of Public Records and the House Legislative Resource Center, both by telephone.

5. The Foreign Agents Registration Act report was accessed at www.usdoj.gov/criminal/fara/.

6. See, for example, the report issued in 1993 by the Center for Public Integrity (Washington, D.C.) titled *The Trading Game: Inside Lobbying for the North American Free Trade Agreement.*

7. Data source: Office of the U.S. Trade Representative. Website: www.ustr.gov/.

# 6 Decisionmaking Explained: The How and Why of Policymakers' and Legislators' Behavior

What makes the process of U.S. trade policymaking tick? What explains the behavior of the U.S. government as it formulates and implements foreign trade policy? Why have the institutions described in the previous chapter acted as they have? All-inclusive or permanent answers to these questions do not exist. There does not appear to be any one or permanent variable or official operating procedure that can be used to explain all the major trade decisions made throughout U.S. history or even in the post–World War II era.

Decisionmaking is art, not science. U.S. trade policymakers must act on their perceptions of reality because the reality of "good trade policy" is open to interpretation. In the words of a classic study of American foreign trade politics, even "the theory of self-interest as a complete and all-embracing explanation of behavior breaks down when we realize that self-interest is itself a set of mental images and convictions."[1]

The subjective determination of which of several legitimate, competing priorities should be judged "first among equals" inevitably links substance with process. This chapter analyzes the complementarity between these two broad components of trade policymaking. The nature of how trade policy is made—process—should be consistent with our central thesis that the substance of trade policy is the end product of a process of reconciling varying perceptions of domestic and foreign economic and political factors. The analysis that follows attempts to verify this consistency by reviewing the nature of trade decisionmaking, defined here as the process by which the government absorbs hard data and abstract perceptions (input) and converts them into concrete policy actions (output). This process, in turn, can be described as consisting of two main components: the influences on policymakers and the organizational mechanisms by which decisions are made.

## The Inevitable Diversity of Trade Policymaking

The absence of fixed, predictable procedures and patterns of behavior is not surprising given the nature of U.S. trade policy. There is a constantly changing cast of policymakers who are coping with constantly changing economic and political circumstances. Fashionable policy modalities come and go: Protectionism in the early 1930s, open markets to allies in the early Cold War years, dollar depreciation, industrial policy to compete with the Japanese juggernaut, and so forth. Balances of power among competing groups and ideas are also constantly shifting so that different groups and values have different degrees of influence in Washington, D.C., at different times. Yet another cause of trade policy's dynamism is that it requires a delicate balance between a country's internal and external goals, most of which shift over time in substance and relative importance. Academics use the term *two-level negotiations* to describe the phenomenon that trade agreements come into being only after policymakers have consulted and reached accommodation with domestic constituents (in the United States, the former are the president and the Congress, and the latter is the the private sector) on one level, and their foreign counterparts on another level. The bottom line is that there is no one variable that is a constant determinant of human behavior when U.S. government officials make trade policy. In other words, decisionmaking is too disparate and dynamic a process to produce a permanent, iron-clad paradigm of cause and effect.

Whereas the surface content of international trade relations is economic in nature, there are several reasons for arguing that the process of formulating trade policy is political in nature. Policymakers inevitably must select priorities from a number of logical but competing economic arguments. Given the absence thus far of economic absolutes and irrefutable econometric equations, trade policymaking is effectively an exercise in value judgments that at any given time will help some people and groups and hurt others. By influencing who gets production, jobs, and profits, trade policy meets a classic definition of politics. A detailed understanding of international trade theory is a useful but not sufficient factor in comprehending the art of compromise and the accommodation of "second-best" economic policies in the context of political necessity.

Scholars using the analytic techniques of political science have created a large body of international political economy literature in the effort to explain the forces that produce U.S. trade policy. The result is diversity, not a definitive explanation. Several theories focusing on quite different phenomena have been advanced.[2] Sometimes trade policymaking is categorized as a specialized form of foreign policymaking and sometimes it is viewed as a specialized form of domestic economic policymaking. Some models view government structures as the controlling, or independent, variable determining policy output. Others look to the policy environment, both domestic and foreign, as the ultimate determining factor. Still other models attempt to synthesize these two approaches. There is no intent here to praise the relevance of some models and dismiss others. Nor is the intent to express concern that the existence of what are often largely incompatible theories diminishes our ability to comprehend the act of trade policymaking.

Rather, the purpose here is to argue that all the explanatory models cited later in this chapter have *some* relevance over time in explaining a complicated phenomenon having many variations. The central thesis of the analysis that follows is that no one concept can explain the totality of the complex and fluid process of trade policymaking. No one model developed thus far can do more than explain what determined *some* import policies and perhaps some export policies as well. No one model identifies a constant relationship of cause and effect, individually or collectively, among the vast array of past import and export policy actions. Nor has any one model demonstrated infallibility in predicting future trade policy. The use of selective case studies to demonstrate the applicability of a given model is not inconsistent with the thesis that trade decisionmaking cannot be anything other than a diverse, multidimensional policy process. It continues to defy a single explanatory formula, as one study of U.S. import policymaking concluded:

> The models focusing exclusively on short-run, direct self-interest are insufficient for explaining the wide range of behavior patterns observable in the trade policy area. Models that include behavior based either on long-run self-interest or concern for the welfare of other groups and the state are also necessary to account for the actions of voters and public officials.[3]

Admittedly, a finite number of variables are inherent in reaching decisions on trade policy. There is a set of basic guidelines and, to use a phrase of Max Weber's, "general laws and events" that can be used to identify recurring patterns in the behavior of those who make U.S. trade policy. Policymakers must be responsive to, among other things, the economic ideology and political needs of the president and his senior advisers, the foreign policy objectives of a global superpower, public opinion, and the forcefully articulated demands of interest groups. The dominant economic ideology of U.S. foreign trade policy since the late 1930s is easy to identify: liberal trade—the pursuit of reduced barriers to the flow of international commerce. However, a solitary decisionmaking model placing primary emphasis on this belief system is not plausible in view of the many exceptions to a market-oriented trade policy that have consistently appeared in U.S. import policies. A solitary model based on the presumption that large, well-financed interest groups are able to dictate U.S. trade policy is also implausible by virtue of the frequency with which policymakers have ignored such pressures.

The dynamics of trade policymaking would be better understood if clear answers existed to two critical questions. Which domestic or international economic or political consideration will dominate in a particular policymaking situation? What is on the minds of policymakers at any given time that causes the interests of one perspective to triumph over others? Unfortunately, the most likely answer to both questions is hopelessly general: It depends on the combination of personalities and the circumstances at hand. So many combinations are possible in a decisionmaking exercise that the relative importance of a given variable is in a constant state of flux. So, too, is the U.S. government's trade policymaking apparatus, which is somewhere between haphazard and ultra-flexible.

The key to understanding the functioning of the trade policymaking system is to recognize that intangibles and circumstances vary from issue to issue, suggesting that in a given decision, different actors will assume leadership, different behavioral patterns will emerge, and different constituencies and perceptions will be given priority by different administrations. The process that has evolved to reconcile the conflicting interests associated with trade decisions lacks—appropriately—the precision, single-mindedness, and conformity always to use identical criteria and a fixed set of procedures in calculating which needs and objectives receive priority.

Theories of trade decisionmaking do not even agree on a basic frame of reference. At the risk of some oversimplification, the analysis that follows divides the main explanatory theories into two categories. The first consists of those that emphasize outside political and economic pressures on policymakers. These theories focus on preexisting forces that allegedly heavily influence governmental deliberations to resolve a specific trade issue. The second category (examined separately) encompasses theories that emphasize the discretionary role of the state and focus on organizational mechanisms within the government. To the empiricist, it is not a matter of either/or; an examination of the historical record shows that both theoretical approaches correctly assess policymakers' behavior in *some* instances.

# The Government As Reactive Decisionmaker

By law, government officials are in charge of creating and conducting trade policy. However, this does not automatically mean that they possess sufficient freedom to be autonomous, independent actors in trade policymaking. One theoretical approach is to identify the most important external force shaping the actions of trade officials. This approach has resulted in the construction of several models pinpointing different dominant factors that have at various times been instrumental in shaping the thinking of policymakers. Three of the major identifiable influences on policymakers are discussed here: domestic political forces (interest group politics), global political and economic structures (international regime constraints), and the state of the economy (market conditions).

## *Interest Group Politics*

Activism in the private sector affects virtually every decision in U.S. trade policy to some degree. The occasions when the U.S. government eliminates existing restrictions or imposes new import barriers on a major product can have a sizeable economic impact and therefore attract a relatively large amount of interest from the private sector. All things considered, a somewhat exaggerated, oversimplified viewpoint has emerged that portrays U.S. trade policymaking over the years as being ultimately controlled by organized domestic political forces demanding and receiving protection from import competition. U.S. trade policy is viewed by this theory as being less shaped by resolute, activist politicians than by a Darwinian struggle among special interest groups. The sources of policy are the outcomes of the raw exercises in political power by these groups and the success of their intellectual efforts to convince legislative and executive branch officials that their interests are synonymous with the national interest. Carried to its logical conclusion, this model portrays the U.S. government as a "disinterested referee," providing, but not controlling, a venue for lobbying by interest groups. In the end, governmental agencies are seen to be acting as mere conduits between the private sector's trade demands and foreign governments. This is an exaggeration even though in a few extreme instances representatives of the private sector have been allowed to write portions of proposed trade statutes.[4] U.S. government demands for specific market-opening measures by Japan almost always originate from specific private sector complaints.

Some scholars assert that "money talks" and that "policy outcomes on any particular issue are a function of the varying ability of groups to organize and give their interests prominence in the policy process."[5] Examples of this extreme interpretation do occasionally materialize but they are so limited that this theory is open to the criticism that it can be nothing better than a partial explanation. Overall, the direct impact of special interest groups on U.S. trade policy in the 1990s is laced with nuance. Extensive empirical evidence of a *pervasive,* lobbying-induced protectionist bias in contemporary U.S. trade policy does not currently exist. Less competitive, import-impacted industries have, on occasion, converted political clout (or genuine economic injury) into trade barriers that benefit the few and penalize the many. However, since the late 1980s, new U.S. import restrictions against *fair* foreign competition have *not* been commonplace. More often than not, the combination of economic ideology and interest groups advocating a liberal trade stance has caused the U.S. government to resist demands for import protection (against fair foreign trade practices) even by such industrial behemoths as the apparel, steel, and automobile sectors.

Sometimes, when interest groups pursue enlightened self-interests, they can simultaneously perform a broader public service, most notably by educating unaware Washington officials about unfair and restrictive foreign commercial practices. In two important instances in the 1980s, interest group agitation inspired the U.S. trade policy agenda to adopt new objectives for which there was no domestic opposition or criticism. The U.S. government became concerned with the protection of intellectual property rights only after it was educated in the matter. Two coalitions of adversely affected companies demonstrated through lobbying how U.S. industry was annually losing tens of billions of dollars in sales to foreign violators (typically illegal, "back alley" operators) of U.S. copyrights, patents, trademarks, industrial designs, and so on. In the same vein, efforts by lobbyists from companies in the services sector educated U.S. trade policymakers about the reality and heavy cost of foreign barriers against their exports, a situation not previously recognized in government circles. The result was that priorities in U.S. trade policy expanded during the Uruguay Round to include the economically sound goal of including services as well as goods in the definition of trade liberalization. Another contribution was made by environmental groups, when, beginning in the 1990s, they sensitized trade officials in many countries to the links between trade policy and efforts to protect the environment. As a result, environmental standards were added to the trade negotiating agenda.

Further clouding any simple model of protectionist policies derived from interest group politics is the relatively recent surge in private sector activism opposing protectionist trade policies.[6] The emergence of an energetic, politically significant lobbying effort on behalf of a more liberal world trading order, mainly by large American MNCs, is one of two all-important explanations for the relatively limited U.S. recourse to protectionism since the 1980s, despite a long run of gargantuan trade deficits. (The other is the widespread acceptance of the economic principle that market-directed trade flows lead to increased efficiency, output, and price stability.) These companies adopted active lobbying in the early 1970s when the U.S. infatuation with protectionism became serious in political terms. MNCs seek profit maximization on a global basis with little concern about political borders and thus disdain restrictive national measures. Another reason that restrictions imposed by the U.S. government on international trade and investment flows are anathema to MNCs is their fear that these measures will trigger retaliation by foreign governments against their exports and foreign subsidiaries. More recently, the liberal trade lobby in Washington has grown to include many foreign corporations, especially Japanese, that spend freely to hire talented local lobbyists to point out the costliness of depriving U.S. consumers and companies of maximum product choice in the marketplace.

The potential ability of liberal trade advocates to end the protectionist lobby's near monopoly in shaping U.S. trade legislation was recognized as early as 1963: "The stereotype notion of omnipotent pressure groups becomes completely untenable once there are groups aligned on both sides. The result of opposing equipotent forces is stalemate."[7] To the extent that both sides of a trade issue are pressed by high-powered interest groups, diametrically different positions will be supported by politically powerful interest groups having conflicting economic interests. Trade policy lobbying efforts in Washington have become so extensive that "lobby gridlock" periodically materializes. When conflicting lobbying efforts effectively neutralize each other on a specific issue, the administration and Congress are more able to concentrate on their own values in deciding what is optimal trade policy.

One version of industry-versus-industry conflict regularly arises when "downstream" users of intermediate goods oppose protectionist measures that would increase their production costs. The desire to have unfettered access to imports of raw materials and components opened a new business lobbying niche in Washington. The Consuming Industries Trade Action Coalition, representing some forty companies and trade associations, campaigns for liberal U.S. trade policies that take into account the competitive needs and economic importance of domestic industries dependent on foreign-produced intermediate goods.

Fearful of their own import competition, end-users of steel, such as makers of construction equipment, have long lobbied against restrictions on steel imports or demands for "voluntary" export restraint agreements with other countries. (To the extent that domestic manufactures of finished goods made of steel do not have the same access to cheap foreign steel as do their foreign competitors, they lose price competitiveness.)

Another example of the end-user phenomenon was the public cleavage in the U.S. electronics industry twice displayed in the intense struggles in the late 1980s and early 1990s by domestic assemblers of personal computers to reverse dumping duties imposed on two price-sensitive components: memory chips and flat-panel display screens. Rather than risk losing market share in a fiercely price-competitive market, several U.S. personal computer companies warned of the need to move their production offshore. If they did so, they could buy low-priced Japanese components abroad and avoid U.S. dumping duties. Although imports of an individual component might be subject to U.S. antidumping duties, such goods would be exempt when imported as parts of an assembled final product. The dynamics of interest group confrontation among corporations were also exhibited when the U.S. retail industry campaigned several times against limitations on imported apparel. Barriers in the form of "voluntary" export restraints by less developed country (LDC) suppliers against foreign-made apparel reduce American retailers' ability to provide customers with relatively low-priced (despite some high markups) and therefore better-selling clothing.

The limits of the interest of "big business" are further demonstrated when corporate lobbying fails. Not even the united position of American industry could convince Congress to approve the Clinton administration's repeated requests to restore authority for fast-track trade negotiating (see Chapter 13). Many of the largest U.S. corporations have spent decades trying unsuccessfully to coax Washington to minimize export controls and sanctions and bring them into line with those of Western Europe and Japan. For example, in late summer 1993, Iran Air was reported to have placed a $1 billion order for jumbo jet commercial aircraft with Airbus Industrie because the Clinton administration had refused to approve export licenses for the U.S. aircraft originally eyed by the Iranians.[8] The White House's anger with Iran's alleged support of international terrorism overruled an unusually powerful lobbying effort by the Boeing Corporation, the number one U.S. exporter, and the General Electric Corporation (the would-be supplier of engines for the 737 aircraft) that at the time was one of the country's largest companies and the third-largest exporter.

Assessments of the impact of special interest group lobbying are further clouded by the inherent difficulties of quantifying effective rates of protection. It is not as easy as it appears to declare certain interest groups the victors in their efforts to squelch import competition. Liberal trade advocates regularly complain about the ability of the textile and steel industries to garner considerable import protection. The domestic steel industry sees the situation in a completely different light. It perceives itself as being under siege from widespread foreign dumping and government subsidies that allegedly stay several steps ahead of the U.S. government's efforts to enforce laws against these unfair trade practices (see Chapter 7). The U.S. textile and apparel industries lament that they have been the recipients of a loophole-ridden import restraint program. They can point to trade statistics showing that, despite the Multifiber Arrangement and, after 1995, the Agreement on Textiles and Clothing, imports of textiles and apparel have steadily increased, both in absolute terms and as a percentage of total American consumption (Commerce Department data show that U.S. imports of apparel and fabricated textiles soared thirty-fold, from $2.3 billion in 1973 to $68 billion in 2000).[9] Indirect restraints of U.S. textile and apparel imports have many loopholes. Export restraint agreements do not apply to members of NAFTA, and special legislation has exempted designated countries in the Caribbean and Africa. Countries signing export restraint agreements can legally evade them by shifting shipments to textile products not covered by their agreement, or illegally evade them by exporting textile products through covert transshipments by way of third countries. Furthermore, the demands of the LDCs in the Uruguay Round led to the industrial countries' agreeing to a multiyear phase out of all textile and apparel export restraint agreements, the protests of the large U.S. domestic industry notwithstanding.

The outcome of lobbying efforts to affect the substance of U.S. trade policy is often inconsistent with the popular notion that only a large, financially powerful company or industry can induce the government to extend it protection from import competition. The power of a small but determined and well-organized group to buck the larger public interest is clearly evident in long-standing U.S. import quotas on sugar. These quotas are imposed at great cost to domestic consumers—an estimated $1.4

billion annually in higher prices, according to one study.[10] Food processors, a much larger industry, oppose limits on imports of cheaper foreign-produced sugar because of added production costs. (The makers of LifeSavers candy announced in early 2002 that they were shifting production to Canada to have access to cheaper sugar.) American foreign policy also suffers in that several friendly, relatively poor countries, mainly in the Caribbean, are hit by a sharp curtailment of their potential sugar exports to the United States. The only winners are about 15,000 U.S. sugarcane and sugarbeet growers concentrated in a handful of states.

Finally, a case study suggests that the political clout to influence U.S. trade policy can be wielded by a cleverly orchestrated, well-financed alliance of domestic importers and a large foreign company. After a huge lobbying effort in 1987 and 1988, Congress backed down from its stated intention to punish the Toshiba Corporation for what was perceived to be a serious national security transgression. (A subsidiary of Toshiba had violated Japanese export control laws and sold sophisticated machine tools to the Soviet Union that were used to make quieter submarines.) The proposed five-year comprehensive import ban on Toshiba products wilted when, in a well-orchestrated uproar, U.S. companies voiced concerns about the dislocations they would incur if unable to continue importing components from that company. Managers at Toshiba's American subsidiaries initiated a successful program to convince rank-and-file workers to tell their senators and representatives that their jobs would be at risk if the proposed import sanctions were enacted.

An objective, scholarly assessment of the impact of interest groups on U.S. trade policy substance leads to another set of imprecise conclusions. The dynamics of interest group politics, like all other models of trade policymaking, are neither uniform nor predictable in any given situation. Powerful pressure groups from the private sector seeking either to erect import barriers or to relax export controls are regularly rejected by independent-minded policymakers because of economic ideology, national security, or some other sui generis consideration. At other times, such as the extension of MFN[11] tariff treatment for China, a united business community's forcefully articulated sentiments effectively determine what policy will be. Continuously changing variables seem to determine on a case-by-case basis the nature of decisionmakers' responsiveness to the policy advice of interest groups. An important first question is which branch of government is being lobbied. Congressional responses to constituent pressures on trade issues frequently have a warmer, more empathetic tone than executive branch responses. Other important variables are whether only one interest group is intensively lobbying and what would be the costs (if any) to society as a whole if a policy decision bowed to the entreaties of a small minority of the population. If two or more powerful lobbying efforts are offering contradictory recommendations, the equation is very different.

## *International Regime Constraints*

Another model of trade policymaking argues that decisions in trade policy are ultimately grounded in interactions among sovereign states, all of which seek to use international economic relations to maximize their wealth and influence. Because an anarchic trading system is unlikely to benefit the majority of countries, there is a natural inclination to establish rules for acceptable state behavior. There is widespread agreement that the discipline that has resulted from the creation of an international trade regime is a positive-sum game that constrains aggressive behavior and encourages countries to cooperate. Foreign trade is a continuous process, not a one-shot event to be won or lost; thus long-term efforts to cooperate within the framework of liberal trade-oriented rules enhances global prosperity. U.S. trade officials, like their foreign counterparts, regularly subordinate domestic considerations to international standards of trade behavior, most of which they fully agree with in principle. Countries join the WTO (see Chapter 8) because they believe it is in their interests to do so, not because it is mandatory. Some argue that international regimes make cooperation rational in what is essentially a confrontational world of sovereign states. Respect for international rules is only a small part of the reason that sovereign countries usually conform to the WTO's many nonprotectionist provisions, which are not absolutely binding. More important is the desire of trade policymakers not to act in a way that might encourage other countries to adopt protectionist trade policies or erect retaliatory import barriers of their own.

A calculation of the costs associated with breaking an international trade rule is part of the equation when trade officials resist domestic political pressures to adopt protectionist measures inconsistent with WTO-imposed obligations. China exemplifies the desire of many countries to join the WTO as a means of institutionalizing market-based economic reforms. On occasion, U.S. trade rules have been modified to meet international norms. The U.S. government responded in 1979 to intense foreign pressure and added an injury test to its 1897 countervailing duty statute designed to protect domestic interests from imports receiving foreign government subsidies (see Chapter 7). Imposing countervailing duties solely on the basis of having detected an illegal subsidy was judged inconsistent with the international standard of requiring that both injury and a subsidy be demonstrated before the importing country can legally retaliate.

A country's preference for an international trade regime can be shaped by its position in the hierarchy of the global order. Most notable and demonstrable are the two instances of international political and economic hegemons, Great Britain in the nineteenth century and the United States in the twentieth. At the height of their power, both countries identified their interests with creating and supporting liberal (nonrestrictive) trade regimes—in part because of their power to export, in part because of their desire to enhance international political harmony and stability.

## *Market Conditions*

Yet another approach to explaining policy substance is to focus on market conditions. One version of this theory argues that changing international market conditions can make it "economically irrational for a government to continue prevailing policy."[12] This approach explains the need for radical changes in U.S. trade policy in 1971 and 1985, when distortions in the exchange rate caused a sharp deterioration in the level of American industrial competitiveness and in the trade balance.

The market conditions model is appropriate to explain the tendency for most governments to be relatively resistant to protectionist pressures during periods of high domestic economic growth and low unemployment. Full employment was the critical factor behind the fact that no outbreak of protectionist sentiment was evident anywhere in the U.S. government, even after a decade of progressively worse, world record–setting trade deficits in the 1990s. This model also explains why most governments are more predisposed to imposing protectionist measures during periods of slow or negative growth, a propensity best illustrated by the beggar-thy-neighbor policies employed during the Great Depression years of the 1930s. Yet another example of the utility of this model is that it apparently explains why the U.S. government did not react harshly to Japan's failure in fall 1994 to relax internal market regulations impairing the ability of U.S. automobile companies to export to Japan. The U.S. automobile industry at the time was producing at full capacity in an effort to meet unexpectedly strong domestic demand. A check of market conditions would have suggested that there were relatively few U.S.-made cars readily available for incremental exports, no matter what the Japanese government did.

## The Executive Branch As Active Decisionmaker

When U.S. governmental entities convene to formulate general policy or to make a specific decision, they cannot escape being influenced by a varying mix of external stimuli: the previously described constraints as well as perceived opportunities. Decisionmakers cannot and do not act in a value-free vacuum. Nevertheless, it is not a given that these stimuli are the independent variables in determining policy substance. A second, broad school of thought just as convincingly argues that the controlling variable is the manner in which government entities organize themselves to sort out the various constraints, opportunities, conflicts, trade-offs, and perceptions that are inherent in making trade policy.

The substance of trade policy is often a direct by-product of what a number of officials collectively determine is good for the country, favored constituencies, the global economy, and their personal situations—not necessarily in that order. Few persons aspire to the senior levels of U.S. trade policymaking for the money. Their usual motivation is a combination of ambition and confidence in their well-above-average intellects and problem-solving abilities. They also tend to possess a conscious or subconscious enjoyment in exercising power. For these reasons, the vast majority of U.S. trade officials view themselves as capable of making reasoned and calculated choices, not as being prisoners of externally imposed constraints.

There is no standard operating procedure by which the U.S. government formulates and executes trade policy. The choice of exactly which of several possible organizational procedures is used can have implications for policy substance. The delicate balance among the four components of trade policy—domestic and international economics plus domestic and international politics—can be tilted in one direction or the other depending on which government entities are involved and which assume leadership roles.

The purpose of this section is to introduce the three most widely used government organization-oriented models of decisionmaking in trade policy. The determination of which one of these models is used depends on yet another set of variables associated with the issue to be decided. The variables include the issue's political and economic importance, notoriety (at home and abroad), complexity, legal implications (if any), and whether it creates new policy or merely refines an existing one.

## *The Presidential Fiat Model*

The simplest, most dramatic model of U.S. trade policymaking consists of the relatively rare phenomenon of the president's taking an early and dominant role. Presidents are usually too preoccupied with national security and domestic social and economic issues to get deeply involved in the arcane details common to most trade dilemmas. When they do get involved, they usually arrive late in the process to approve a cabinet recommendation, to mediate an irreconcilable intra-cabinet disagreement, or to make public statements on behalf of the administration's position. Only on a few occasions, typically in response to dramatic issues, have presidents intervened at the onset of an international trade issue by making a forceful declaration of policy intent that immediately and unequivocally dictated subsequent U.S. actions. Staff work and interagency consultations are minimal to nonexistent before the declaration of a pure presidential fiat. The president speaks first, and then the bureaucracy is ordered into action to provide the support necessary to implement the president's publicly stated position. Criticism may be directed toward the substance of the policy produced by this model, but not its lack of clarity and quickness. In studies of national security policy decisionmaking, clear-cut control of the policymaking process by the head of government is known as the unitary, or rational actor, model.[13]

Examples of the presidential fiat model in the international trade realm include President Nixon's ordering his senior economic aides to join him at Camp David on an August weekend in 1971, where he guided and approved dramatic overnight decisions that reversed several major domestic and international economic policies. The so-called New Economic Policy imposed a 10 percent surcharge on all tariffs and terminated the ability of foreign central banks to convert dollars into gold—after only a cursory calculation of the likely international impact and repercussions. A second example is the personal anger and shock when the Soviets invaded Afghanistan that led Jimmy Carter immediately to order an economic retaliation by banning the export of 17 million metric tons of wheat previously ordered by the Soviet government, a move that financially hurt U.S. farmers as well as Soviet consumers.

A few weeks after the 1993 inauguration, the Clinton administration issued a detailed blueprint for greater government support for and involvement in the effort to strengthen the U.S. high-technology sector, an endeavor aimed mainly at increasing U.S. international competitiveness. This technology initiative originated in the White House because it was a direct outgrowth of Clinton's and Vice President Al Gore's personal economic philosophy, graphically spelled out in their campaign promises to upgrade the competitiveness of American industry.

Incumbent presidents are far more likely—except in the weeks immediately before a vote to determine whether they get reelected—to respond to deeply held, preexisting values, ideologies, and concerns for the country's broader, longer-term interests than they are to purely self-serving political manipulations on behalf of one segment of the political spectrum. Because each Oval Office incumbent possesses a different mix of personal beliefs and experiences, there is no preordained tilt in import or export policy philosophy when the presidential fiat model is used. George Bush (senior) took the lead in articulating his administration's support of an unconditional extension of MFN status to China mostly because of his earlier experience as ambassador to that country.

## The Bureaucratic Politics Model

The presence of top-down leadership in the form of active presidential involvement in U.S. trade policy decisionmaking has been and still is the exception rather than the rule. Because presidential time and energies normally are concentrated in other policy sectors, most decisions in trade policy are made at or below the cabinet level by an interagency group, sometimes having representatives from more than twenty agencies. As the impact of the growing trade sector has impinged on more domestic economic sectors, more agencies are participating in deliberations on interagency trade policy.

Interagency trade committees and working groups in the U.S. government ultimately operate as meetings of institutions possessing different missions, constituencies, priorities, and bureaucratic cultures. These groups share the common human traits of wanting to maximize their power, influence, and prestige. Nevertheless, they seldom have the benefit of an unambiguous, self-evident strategy to guide them in moving toward an optimal policy decision that is sure to maximize the national interest, the definition of which usually defies quick consensus.

Decisionmakers are usually confronted with the need to reconcile conflicting policy proposals that normally emerge from the departments and agencies in the absence of a specific directive from the president. Repeatedly, bargaining involving compromises and trade-offs among strategies becomes central to the process of interagency trade decisionmaking.

When the absence of quick consensus leads to interagency brokering of decisions, decisive strategy and brilliantly conceived tactics tend to be more the exception in trade policy than the rule. The dynamics of bureaucratic politics explain why most interagency decisions ultimately produce trade policy that more closely resembles a "line of least resistance"—accepting something all participants can live with—rather than breakthrough innovations and inspired brilliance.

But why, exactly, is the interagency coordinating process usually afflicted with disagreement rather than blessed by an easy consensus? In the first place, no official of executive branch trade policy, except the president and vice president, represents all constituencies and has responsibility for the entire policy spectrum. All trade officials work for bureaucratic entities that work on behalf of specifically defined constituencies, not the country as a whole. Various departments and agencies have been created specifically to manage issues relating to the industrial sector, foreign policy, agriculture, the labor force, the environment, and, in the case of the Treasury Department, the domestic economy in general. An important part of job performance evaluations for employees of line departments and agencies is how well individuals represent their chosen employers in interagency policy deliberations (see Chapter 5).

An analogous form of bureaucratic politics is practiced in Congress. Quite literally, constituents influence members' votes. The economic interests of the district or state that voted members into office, not political ideology or party, usually determine their outlook on trade issues. Advocates of import barriers do not come from districts with numerous high-tech, export-oriented industries.

The core principle of the bureaucratic politics model of decisionmaking is that "the government" is not a unitary actor and seldom engages in monolithic thinking.[14] In a policy field having few absolute guidelines, ministries and agencies supporting divergent missions, agendas, and priorities all bring to the process of interagency coordinating their distinctive mindsets about defining the optimal course of action. From ministers down to the junior staff level, officials in government agencies in all countries tend to perceive a linkage—self-serving but usually genuinely believed—between the defense of their arguably very important constituency's needs and the enhancement of the overall national interest. Nominees for U.S. cabinet posts judged unsympathetic or antagonistic to the constituency that they would represent have little or no chance to pass Senate confirmation (which explains why Wall Street bankers do not become secretary of agriculture and Kansas farmers do not become secretary of the treasury).

The bureaucratic politics model does not necessarily suggest venal or inappropriate behavior. There has never been and probably never will be unanimity about a clear, fixed order of U.S. trade policy priorities. What is the relative importance of economic efficiency versus social equity? How important are increases in domestic prosperity relative to achieving a stable global economic and political environment? Is the clear and present threat of U.S. retaliation a cost-effective method of forcing other countries to buy more U.S. products? Can temporary protectionist moves be beneficial in the long term by allowing an import-impacted industry to restructure itself into a world-class competitor? Is it appropriate for the United States to express its dislike for the policies of the Iranian government by denying Boeing export licenses to that country for potentially hundreds of millions of dollars of commercial aircraft shipments—aircraft the European makers of Airbus can and will happily sell to Iran? These are all rhetorical questions. Few universal truths are associated with the major issues of trade policy.

The bureaucratic politics model predicts a consistent general pattern of organizational behavior, but its appearance in a given decisionmaking exercise does not preordain specific policy substance. There is no way of knowing beforehand whether one viewpoint will dominate and, if it does, which one. The intraexecutive branch balance of power ebbs and flows as in all political arenas. Leadership is a critical variable in determining institutional influence, and some cabinet-level officials play the Washington power game better than others. The appearance of inconsistency in U.S. trade policy happens in part because no department or coalition of departments has sufficient power or resources to claim permanent authority to establish priorities in U.S. trade and to determine winners and losers in the private sectors at home and abroad.

Usually, institutional attitudes toward trade issues are consistent and predictable. Certain agencies invariably view trade policy mainly as an instrument of foreign policy, in other words, something that affects the attitudes and actions of other countries, friendly and unfriendly. The foreign affairs bureaucracies, namely, the State Department and the National Security Council, typically support liberal import policies because an open trading system would best promote a stable international economic order and harmonious political relations among like-minded countries. In addition, the strategic concerns of these two agencies and the Defense Department lead them to support a vigorous program of export controls as well as trade sanctions to punish foreign governments for what is thought undesirable or aggressive behavior. Officials in the foreign affairs bureaucracies are not totally insensitive to the well-being of domestic workers and companies. However, they know that they are not paid to worry primarily about domestic constituencies and that no one else in the bureaucracy can be expected to speak out on behalf of a global political environment compatible with American values—one of several legitimate concerns in making "good" trade policy.

It is necessary to examine the institutional "essence" of the coordinator of U.S. trade policy, the Office of the U.S. Trade Representative, to understand its sometimes paradoxical behavior. Its primary mission is to negotiate successful reciprocal trade liberalization agreements with other countries. Engaging in trade acts that would anger other governments is hardly conducive to encouraging such agreements. Nevertheless, the U.S. Trade Representative (USTR) takes a hard line on demanding reductions in overseas barriers to U.S. goods, and on occasion it sides with the protectionist faction in debates on import policy. As noted in the previous chapter, the USTR's bureaucratic behavior is rooted in the mutually accepted concept that it was born of congressional initiative and that it could be terminated by Congress if it loses touch with domestic constituencies. Translation: It must occasionally recognize the need to limit the injury inflicted on U.S. producers by severe import competition and provide a safety net for those adversely affected by reduced U.S. import barriers. Furthermore, most USTR officials feel that they alone are responsible for generating executive branch consensus on policy and are not supposed to impose a particular point of view.[15]

The growing linkage between domestic economic performance and the foreign trade sector means that in sheer numbers, the contemporary U.S. trade policymaking process is dominated by so-called domestic agencies that have specific, sometimes competing, jurisdictions. The macroeconomic agencies—the Treasury Department, the Council of Economic Advisers, and the Office of Management and Budget—generally advocate liberal trade positions, but for reasons different from those of the foreign policy bureaucracies. The economic policy agencies are dominated by professionally trained, free market–oriented economists. They tend to believe their mission to strengthen the overall U.S. economy is aided by a relatively unrestrained flow of imports. The latter increases competition and price stability within the domestic economy, whereas import barriers tend to do just the opposite.

The perception of its having an institutional predisposition toward tolerating increased imports was the reason Congress pressured the Carter administration to strip the Treasury Department of its authority to investigate allegations of dumping and foreign governmental subsidies. The Commerce Department, viewed as being institutionally more sympathetic to the domestic industries that are affected by unfair foreign practices, was given authority to administer these laws in the 1980 reorganization of the U.S. trade policymaking apparatus. An earlier example of Congress acting on its perception of bureaucratic politics occurred in 1962. A provision in a new trade law it enacted divested the State Department of its long-standing authority to lead U.S. trade delegations because Congress perceived it as being too soft on foreign interests at a time when U.S. international competitiveness was waning. Legislation passed that year created the USTR to perform this leadership role.

The bureaucratic perspectives of Commerce and Agriculture are simple to describe: Both departments advocate policies that strengthen and benefit what are arguably vital sectors of the economy. For the Commerce Department, this means manufacturing and services; for Agriculture, it means the agricultural community. When they confront individual trade decisions, however, their mission is complicated by the dichotomy in both their constituencies. Some subsectors, such as the information technology industry and soybean farmers, are internationally competitive and export-oriented; others are relatively inefficient and import-sensitive, such as apparel and dairy farmers. The result is that these departments sometimes vigorously support liberal trade policy options, but also selectively recommend exceptions in the form of import restraints on specific goods. There is much less ambiguity on the export side: Both Commerce and Agriculture are wholeheartedly supportive of export expansion. They dislike domestically imposed export controls and vigorously oppose trade barriers maintained by U.S. trading partners.

When participating in trade policy deliberations, officials of the Environmental Protection Agency are sensitive to the physical and legal need to temper economic considerations when necessary to assure conformity with domestic environmental protection laws and international agreements. For them, the national interest is measured primarily through limiting air, water, and land pollution, not through conventional trade theory, the utility of lower trade barriers, or the financial health of the private sector.

Clear-cut examples of bureaucratic politics abound in the annals of U.S. trade policymaking. The trifurcated approach long taken by the executive branch toward trade relations with Japan is symptomatic of the "internal harmony" that links a bureaucratic culture, a constituency's interest, and perception of what actions would most likely serve the national interest. The macroeconomic agencies, for the most part, believe that retaliatory import barriers would, on a net basis, hurt the U.S. economy and view imports as beneficial to the economy as a whole. The national security agencies soft-pedal aggressive trade actions because their primary goal here is to prevent commercial squabbles from damaging political relations with a key ally. Last, the "trade warriors" of the USTR and the Commerce Department retain their long-held advocacy of a hard-line trade policy to force, belatedly, Japan's allegedly unfair import and export practices into conformity with their broad definition of "national security" to include economic and technological strength.

In 1981, a cabinet-level task force in the newly elected Reagan administration quickly split into two predictable factions when formulating a response to the deteriorating financial condition of the big three U.S. automobile makers, which was partly being caused by a steep rise in Japanese imports. The "industry faction," consisting of the Commerce, Labor, and Transportation departments, felt that only a ceiling on imports could give the companies the essential "breathing space" they needed to adopt an $80 billion retooling effort that would improve their overall production efficiency and their ability to make more small, gas-efficient cars. The Treasury Department, the Council of Economic Advisers, and the Office of Management and Budget believed that the large inflationary impact of an artificial reduction in the supply of imported cars would inflict far more harm on the American economy than benefits. The USTR at the time, William Brock, hedged by publicly refusing to endorse either a free trade or a protectionist strategy.[16] In the end, a middle approach acceptable to both sides was adopted when the Japanese government was quietly pressured to unilaterally announce that it was "voluntarily" imposing a ceiling on the number of cars annually shipped to the American market.

A schism between those bureaucracies inclined to favor liberal trade and those leaning toward protectionism has frequently appeared when the executive branch— regardless of who is president—is deciding whether to restrict imports under an escape clause proceeding (presidential discretion is allowed because no unfair trade practices are involved) or whether to renew a voluntary export restraint agreement. During a 1976 deliberation on the possible imposition of barriers on footwear imports, the usual pattern of factional dissent was joined by an unusually animated Defense Department, not an agency that normally gets excited about run-of-the-mill trade issues. Its conclusion that the free trade approach would serve the national interest was based on a classic example of "segmented prioritizing." Spain and Italy, two major shoe exporters, were sites of important military bases (furthermore, the Communist Party in Italy, an ally of the North Atlantic Treaty Organization (NATO), was making significant advances at this time). Constituency needs dictated that Defense be more concerned about the health of the Italian and Spanish economies than with the problems of the American footwear industry.

Contradictory perceptions hampered the decision in early 1989 about whether to extend for another five years the voluntary export restraint agreements that had been negotiated with major steel-producing countries. The agreements had been signed in the mid-1980s on behalf of the U.S. steel industry and would begin expiring in the fall of 1989. Some agencies felt that the steel industry had received too much protection for too long. The opposing faction urged continued import restraints on the grounds that many foreign steel producers had not abandoned unfair trade practices (dumping and governmental subsidies), and that the domestic industry had taken great strides toward completing efforts to become more productive and internationally competitive. The steel situation was so ambiguous that President Bush was called upon to break the resulting cabinet deadlock. His decision to prolong the restraints for two and one-half years makes sense only in arithmetic terms. It was the half-way point between the two major policy recommendations: no extension of the restraints and a full five-year extension.

Bureaucratic wrangling over trade policy priorities and definitions of the national interest is not ubiquitous in interagency decisionmaking. Occasionally, there is easy consensus. This happened when the decision was made to retaliate against Japan when it was deemed to be violating conditions agreed upon in the 1986 semiconductor agreement.[17] On other occasions, one agency or one policymaker so dominates an issue that others quietly back off. Treasury Secretary John Connally's being designated by the White House to take the lead in setting international economic policy strategy in the wake of the New Economic Policy pronouncement in 1971 exemplifies this situation.

## Congress and the Interbranch Dynamics Model

A significant percentage of U.S. trade policy emanates from Congress's insistence on operationalizing its blueprint for the acceptable boundaries of presidential authority in this field. The extent to which trade policy consists of the executive branch's dutifully carrying out the spirit and letter of laws written by the legislative branch is one of the unique aspects of the U.S. system of political checks and balances. Unlike the situation in a parliamentary form of government, the president as head of the executive branch has little legal scope to act on his own in conducting trade policy. He depends on Congress for legal authority to commit the United States to trade agreements that reduce import barriers. If the administration flagrantly disregards strong congressional trade sentiments, it risks retribution through passage of statutes that it opposes or congressional refusal to pass legislation it seeks.

The use of U.S. trade policy decisionmaking models that consider only the executive branch (or only the private sector) are inadequate. Even though it dominates the *administration* of trade policy, the executive branch's ability to do so is dependent in the first instance on authority delegated to it by Congress. The cumulative effect of extensive statutory language written on Capitol Hill is limited discretion for an administration to act as it sees fit in the realm of foreign trade. The modern-day partnership between Congress and the administration and the uneasy fusion of their distinctive institutional perspectives embody a uniquely complex, multifaceted trade policymaking process.

Delegation of power is not the same as abdication. In the final analysis, the legislative branch maintains considerable control over policy outcomes. Virtually all important delegations of presidential authority in both import and export policies are extended on a temporary basis, meaning that key statutes have to be periodically renewed by Congress. The Omnibus Trade and Competitiveness Act of 1988 consisted of more than 1,000 pages of often detailed congressional guidance for executive branch behavior. Key provisions seek to increase the likelihood of (but not absolutely require) presidential retaliation against discriminatory foreign trade practices. Passage of these initiatives reflected a uniquely congressional sentiment that certain trade policy changes—mainly in the form of greater presidential resolve to attack foreign trade barriers—had become necessary. The act also seeks to enhance U.S. industrial competitiveness.

The legislative and executive branches remain uneasy about, and at times distrustful of, the perceived bias in the other's trade policy inclinations. Congress is unlikely ever to cede unequivocal dominance over trade policy to the other branch because it perceives the latter tilting permanently and too much in the direction of globalism and free trade and too far away from limiting trade-induced injury on the workers and companies whose interests members of Congress have been elected to represent.

Congress's decision to write and insert the Super 301 provision (see Chapter 9) in the 1988 trade bill was an outgrowth of the long-standing belief on Capitol Hill that all presidents, past and present, lean too much in the direction of internationalism. Many members of Congress have long perceived an ongoing presidential reluctance either to anger foreign friends or to be branded as a protectionist. This alleged tilt adversely affects domestic producers seeking relief from strong import competition and exporters burdened by foreign trade barriers. The trickiest part of drafting the market-opening provisions in this bill was finding the exact statutory language that imposed the maximum feasible amount of inflexible negotiating backbone (minimizing "wiggle-room," to use Washington parlance) on the president in pursuing overseas market-opening demands. If the language was too restrictive, it would trigger a veto on grounds that it excessively usurped presidential discretion in administering trade policy.

Sharyn O'Halloran has argued that Congress has effectively converted trade policy into regulatory policy that incorporates influence from interest groups. The result has been the enfranchisement of Congress and interest groups into the negotiation and implementation of trade agreements.

> Advisory committees must be consulted before and during [trade] negotiations. The president must hold public hearings. . . . And Congress holds hearings in which experts and representatives from affected industries have the chance to voice any concerns. As a result, in many cases the president will be forced to accommodate the demands of certain interests in order to assure final passage of the implementing legislation. . . . Thus, instead of allowing the president to remain above the fray . . . these procedures enmesh him in the parochial interests of legislators and force him to accede to protectionist demands.[18]

Congress began delegating authority to the executive branch to administer trade policy as the result of its economically disastrous yielding to the seemingly endless protectionist demands of special interest groups in the Smoot-Hawley Tariff of 1930. To avoid a repetition of its mistakes of 1930, Congress relinquished *some* of its constitutional power to the executive branch and to the independent International Trade Commission. By design, Congress has seen to it that the executive branch takes most of the heat in carrying out the delicate task of determining how to respond to the unending procession of demands from the private sector for trade actions that favor their interests. Congress's bottom-line assumption was that the relatively more internationally oriented executive branch was in a better position to just say no. As I. M. Destler has observed: "The system allowed members so inclined to advocate, even threaten, trade restrictions, while nicely relieving them of the need to deliver on their threats. Indeed, its main result was not protection for industry but protection for Congress—insulation of its members from trade pressures."[19]

To this day, Congress uses trial and error to codify into U.S. trade laws just the right tension between the broad pursuit of trade liberalization and the conditional availability of import relief measures and retaliatory sanctions. Whenever delegating trade authority to the executive branch, strings are attached. Congress is an unabashed advocate of "fair" trade, a pleasant-sounding concept lacking both opponents and precise meaning. The trade legislation passed since 1934 is equipped with an intricate set of counterweights and shock absorbers. Legislators since then have encouraged the executive branch to pursue a basically liberal trade policymaking strategy—but only up to a point. The post-1934 trade policy system has used an intricate system of congressionally designed political pulleys and levers that aim to sustain what is designed to be perceived as an equitable system meant to block, unofficially and informally, the reemergence of the once-dominant protectionist coalition. At the same time that trade barriers are being reduced, Congress has mandated that Americans who are losers as the result of import flows are assured an impartial hearing about their eligibility for legislated relief.

The substance of export policy is also affected by Congress's strings-attached approach to delegating trade power. First, it seeks to placate frustrated American exporters by pressuring the administration to be more aggressive than it might otherwise be in threatening consequences for trading partners that discriminate against U.S. commerce. Congress has also handed the executive branch the politically charged duty of deciding on which goods to impose export controls and on which countries to impose trade sanctions. An examination of the evolution of U.S. export legislation (see Chapter 9) demonstrates patterns similar to those that characterize import legislation: modest interbranch differences in trade philosophy and congressional efforts to restrict the executive branch's freedom to maneuver outside Congress's perception of the national interest.

As for exports, Congress is sensitive to business complaints about lost overseas sales opportunities, whereas administrations have repeatedly opted to impose export restraints in pursuit of foreign policy goals. While being careful not to usurp the administration's power to decide when to impose export controls for purposes of national security and foreign policy, Congress has progressively put the burden of proof on executive branch officials advocating restrictions. The Export Administration Act (previously named the Export Control Act) was amended several times by Congress in response to complaints by major exporting companies that they had lost billions of dollars in overseas sales to foreign competitors operating under much more relaxed export control systems. Specific changes have included reductions in the list of controlled items and the requirement that the overseas availability of an item be taken into account when an export license is being reviewed.

The interbranch dynamics model of trade policymaking is visible in four permutations. The first is the harmonious variant in which the two branches bargain cooperatively with one another. No bill submitted under the so-called fast-track authority had been defeated at the time that it expired in 1994. Because this procedure calls for an all-or-nothing, yea-or-nay, no-amendments vote on legislation to ratify proposed trade liberalization agreements, informal interbranch negotiations have always been conducted before the administration submits such legislation. Administrations have made the concessions and adjustments thought necessary to assure congressional passage before formally submitting such legislation. Cooperation was also evident in the form of literally hundreds of informal visits paid by administration officials to key congressional members to give private consultations while the Uruguay Round and NAFTA trade negotiations were still in progress.[20]

Informal interbranch cooperation has occasionally been displayed in the "good cop/bad cop" tactic used to increase U.S. negotiating leverage while making trade demands on foreign governments.[21] In its role as "bad cop," a seemingly furious cadre of congressional leaders threatens to abandon self-restraint and reason, and pass highly protectionist legislation. As noted in the earlier reference to the Reagan administration's effort to persuade Japan to voluntarily restrict automobile shipments, an angry Congress was a big reason the Japanese government decided to cut a deal with the ostensibly more reasonable, less protectionist executive branch.

Interbranch relations on other occasions become adversarial. Congress's repeated refusal to grant the Clinton administration's requests for renewal of fast-track negotiating authority is one of the more important examples of its ability to partially derail an administration's trade agenda. On occasion, Congress passes trade legislation actively opposed by the administration. President Carter's imposition of import duties on petroleum in 1980 was repealed outright by legislation banning it. The restrictive provisions in the 1974 trade bill governing extension of MFN status to countries not yet receiving it were judged excessive by the Ford administration and almost resulted in a presidential veto of this major piece of otherwise acceptable legislation.

A third variant of interbranch dynamics has occurred when Congress passes a statute containing trade-related provisions disliked by the administration, but not to the extent that the presidential veto is used. Purely congressional initiatives explain two relatively controversial measures in U.S. trade policy that were created in somewhat flukish circumstances. The Cuban Liberty and Democratic Solidarity Act (see Chapter 9) called for extending sanctions in legally questionable directions and would probably have been vetoed in March 1996 except for an unusual coincidence in timing. Hostility toward the Castro government was running high in Washington because a few weeks earlier it had shot down two unarmed planes flown by Cuban exiles resident in the United States. President Clinton also signed an omnibus appropriations act in October 2000 despite the presence of a non-germane provision called the Continued Dumping and Subsidy Offset. The so-called Byrd amendment (for its chief sponsor, Senator Robert Byrd [D, W.Va.]) mandates that import fees collected by the U.S. government from imposing antidumping and countervailing duty fees (see Chapter 7) be distributed to the American companies injured by the imports subjected to these penalties. Internationally, this provision immediately attracted criticism because it allegedly violated WTO rules. Domestically, the amendment was criticized because of a procedural peculiarity: It was inserted into the legislation during the conference committee (to reconcile differences between the Senate and House versions) without having received committee consideration in either house.[22]

On a few occasions, a fourth variant of the interbranch model appears when executive branch positions are taken, partially or totally, to influence future congressional action. This strategy may be designed to avoid Congress's passing legislation opposed by the administration. For example, the Reagan and Bush administrations secured a tightening in voluntary export restraints under the Multifiber Arrangement mainly by persuading exporting countries that this action was essential to sustain (i.e., preserve) presidential vetoes of unwanted textile quota bills passed by Congress. The latter seem to have been passed mainly to induce an administrative tightening of imports, not with the expectation or desire of being enacted into law. The Reagan administration chose the protectionist option of imposing higher tariffs in an escape clause decision involving shakes and shingles from Canada. Because this action was taken in the midst of negotiations for a free trade agreement between the two countries, it appeared on the surface to be a case of bad timing. This decision makes sense, however, when one learns that it came, not coincidentally, on the very day that the House was voting on protectionist amendments opposed by the administration.[23] Many observers assumed that the Bush administration's decision in June 2001 to request initiation of an escape clause investigation of alleged import-induced injury to the steel industry was at least indirectly related to its broader strategy of eliciting congressional support for renewing fast-track negotiating authority.

## Conclusions and Outlook

Trade policymaking in the United States is a decentralized process composed of a relatively large number of officials in many bureaucratic entities addressing issues of varying importance and difficulty. The conceptual models described in this chapter have tried to prove the thesis that the U.S. government formulates trade policy in several ways, depending on circumstances surrounding the issue at hand. These decisionmaking models will reappear in the last section of this book, which analyzes the major issues in contemporary U.S. trade policy. In a word, the decisionmaking process is inconsistent (a characteristic that is not necessarily good or bad). An integrated theory of policymaking that can accurately predict cause and effect relationships still has not been constructed, and may never be.

The system is often cumbersome and tentative. It sometimes speaks with more than one voice. This is not an accident and not caused by ineptitude. The U.S. trade policy decisionmaking process reflects the country's values, system of government, and the complex, fluid mix of political and economic elements that define individual trade issues. Trade officials are overwhelmingly sincere in their efforts to produce "good" policy. The problem is that this is an inherently subjective concept. When stripped to its core, the unavoidably imperfect decisionmaking process is a search for consensus among legitimate but conflicting priorities held by different constituencies that can seldom demonstrate an absolute truth.

The search for trade policy consensus in Washington is arguably the most complicated in any country in the world because of the special demands placed on it. First, the superpower status of the United States superimposes concerns of national security on the traditional confrontation between interest groups supporting trade liberalization and those demanding protection from import competition. Second, a basic American value dictates that all relevant viewpoints be given an opportunity to be heard in the policy formulation process. In addition, the separation of powers principle assures a unique, sometimes strained partnership in U.S. trade policy between two branches of government. The executive and legislative branches frequently disagree about which one has the greater wisdom in deciding what U.S. trade policy should be. A major strength of the U.S. trade policymaking process is that its flexibility and diversity enable it to do a reasonably good job in accommodating to the rules it must play by. The entrenched lack of rigidity also has the advantage of discouraging the retention of obsolete strategies, the creation of unassailable power centers, and permanent winners and losers.

One of the biggest shortcomings of the U.S. trade policymaking process is that its lack of fixed procedures and seemingly unlimited configurations create confusion in the American private sector and among foreign governments. Problems of communication are compounded when the system speaks with more than one voice, as usually happens when various elected and appointed U.S. government officials simultaneously go public in their efforts to influence final decisions in trade policy. Because it is part of a government that shuns economic planning, U.S. trade policymaking is frequently reactive and equivocal—just like the policy itself. To repeat, process affects substance. And a nation's history and values affect the process that makes policy.

## For Further Reading

Baldwin, Robert E. *The Political Economy of U.S. Import Policy.* Cambridge, Mass.: MIT Press, 1985.

Bauer, Raymond A., Ithiel de Sola Pool, and Lewis A. Dexter. *American Business and Public Policy.* Chicago: Aldine-Atherton, 1972.

Goldstein, Judith. *Ideas, Interests, and American Trade Policy.* Ithaca: Cornell University Press, 1993.

Ikenberry, G. John, David A. Lake, and Michael Mastanduno, eds. "The State and American Foreign Economic Policy." *International Organization* 42 (winter 1988), special issue.

Odell, John S. "Understanding International Trade Policies: An Emerging Synthesis." *World Politics* 43 (October 1990): 139–167.

O'Halloran, Sharyn. *Politics, Process, and American Trade Policy.* Ann Arbor, Mich.: The University of Michigan Press, 1994.

## Notes

1. Raymond A. Bauer, Ithiel de Sola Pool, and Lewis A. Dexter, *American Business and Public Policy,* 2d ed. (Chicago: Aldine-Atherton, 1972), 226.

2. Two excellent syntheses of this literature are G. John Ikenberry, David A. Lake, and Michael Mastanduno, eds., "The State and American Foreign Economic Policy," special issue of *International Organization,* vol. 42 (winter 1988); and John S. Odell, "Understanding International Trade Policies: An Emerging Synthesis," *World Politics* 43 (October 1990): 139–167.

3. Robert E. Baldwin, *The Political Economy of U.S. Import Policy* (Cambridge, Mass.: MIT Press, 1985), 174.

4. See, for example, Stephen D. Cohen, *The Making of United States International Economic Policy: Principles, Problems, and Proposals for Reform* (New York: Praeger, 2000), 122.

5. G. John Ikenberry, David A. Lake, and Michael Mastanduno, eds., "Introduction: Approaches to Explaining American Foreign Economic Policy," special issue of *International*

*Organization* 42 (winter 1988): 7. Also see Mancur Olson, *The Rise and Decline of Nations* (New Haven: Yale University Press, 1982).

6. See, for example, I. M. Destler and John S. Odell, *Anti-Protection: Changing Forces in United States Trade Politics* (Washington, D.C.: Institute for International Economics, 1987); and Helen Milner, *Resisting Protectionism: Global Industries and the Politics of International Trade* (Princeton: Princeton University Press, 1988).

7. Bauer, de Sola Pool, and Dexter, *American Business,* 398.

8. "Iran Seeking Jets from Airbus Industrie," *Washington Post,* 8 August 1990, D9.

9. Bernard Gelb, *Textile and Apparel Trade Issues,* Congressional Research Service report, 20 March 2001, 2.

10. U.S. General Accounting Office, "Sugar Program: Changing Domestic and International Conditions Require Program Changes" (Washington, D.C.: U.S. General Accounting Office, April 1993), 3.

11. As noted previously, the U.S. government, mainly for public relations reasons, now refers to this old trade concept as "normal trade relations."

12. John S. Odell, *U.S. International Monetary Policy: Markets, Power, and Ideas As Sources of Change* (Princeton: Princeton University Press, 1982), 18.

13. See, for example, Graham T. Allison, *Essence of Decision: Explaining the Cuban Missile Crisis* (Boston: Little, Brown, 1971).

14. See, for example, Morton H. Halperin, *Bureaucratic Politics and Foreign Policy* (Washington, D.C.: Brookings Institution, 1974); and Stephen D. Krasner, "Are Bureaucracies Important? (or Allison in Wonderland)," *Foreign Policy* 7 (summer 1972): 159–179.

15. Not-for-attribution interview with USTR official, summer 1994.

16. Stephen D. Cohen, "The Route to Japan's Voluntary Export Restraints on Automobiles: An Analysis of the U.S. Government's Decision-Making Process in 1981," January 2000, accessed at www.gwu.edu/~nsarchii~NSARCHIV/japan/scohenwp.htmlHTM/.

17. Stephen D. Cohen, *Cowboys and Samurai: Why the United States Is Losing the Battle with the Japanese, and Why It Matters* (New York: HarperBusiness, 1991), 62.

18. Sharyn O'Halloran, *Politics, Process, and American Trade Policy* (Ann Arbor, Mich.: The University of Michigan Press, 1994), 182.

19. I. M. Destler, "Protecting Congress or Protecting Trade?" *Foreign Policy* 62 (spring 1986): 98.

20. Not-for-attribution interview with USTR official, fall, 1993.

21. No hard evidence exists of formal pre-planning between the executive and legislative branches to enact the good cop/bad cop scenario. Usually, experienced legislators and their staff instinctively know when to initiate saber-rattling.

22. William H. Cooper, *Trade Remedy Law Reform in the 107th Congress,* Congressional Research Service report, 12 April 2001; accessed at www.cnie.org/nle/econ–78.html/.

23. Not-for-attribution interview with USTR official, spring 1987.

# 7 U.S. Legislation Regulating Imports and Exports

The broad outlines of U.S. trade policies are determined by a body of laws passed by Congress. These laws regulate the flow of imports and exports, implement trade agreements negotiated with other countries that in the main reduce trade barriers, and provide the legal authority to executive branch and independent agencies to carry out assigned trade-related responsibilities. Collectively, these laws set the rules, objectives, and obligations of import and export activities affecting consumers, producers, and workers in the United States and in its trading partners. U.S. trade legislation is the final product of a complex political process involving many different philosophies and self-interests held by the executive branch, the legislative branch, the private sector, and interested foreign parties. Trade laws can therefore be considered a vehicle for codifying compromise and consensus among competing ideas about what trade policy should be. A commercial transaction can be characterized as the outcome of a successful political negotiation between buyer and seller. The enactment of a U.S. trade law can also be characterized as the outcome of a successful political negotiation.

Trade laws operate in two spheres. Within the nation-state, the legal order applies to persons subject to the jurisdiction of the national government. The second sphere is at the global level, where rules and procedures apply to sovereign governments that are voluntary signatories to bilateral, regional, or multilateral agreements. Congress's collective attitudes towards trade issues and the implications of its decision to delegate trade policy authority to the executive branch were analyzed in the previous chapter. Here, the dynamics of the first operational sphere are examined: what Congress, the constitutionally designated regulator of U.S. foreign commerce, has established as the legal guidelines for the conduct of trade policy. The key provisions of the major trade laws will be outlined and then related to the larger political and economic context in which they function. The trade rules of the second sphere, the multilateral trading system, will be examined in Chapter 8. It should be noted that the trade laws of the United States are written to conform to its international obligations. When legislation is passed that implements a new trade agreement signed with other governments, existing laws are amended as necessary.

The first section of this chapter outlines the laws enacted by Congress since 1934 to give presidents the authority to reduce import barriers. The second and third sections explain statutes delegating authority to the president to restrict or discourage imports. These laws are the means to address the domestic political necessity and economic advisability of providing limits to the degree of internal damage inflicted by a liberal trade policy. Two sections are necessary to correspond to the generally accepted distinction between providing protection to domestic producers and workers from injury induced by "fair" foreign competition and injury induced by "unfair" foreign competition. The laws, economic principles, and rules governing remedies differ significantly according to whether the source of the increased import competition in question is classified as fair or unfair. The final section of this chapter summarizes the key provisions of relevant statutes and regulations covering the major aspects of export policy: promotion and overseas market-opening measures as well as export controls.

## Trade Liberalization Measures

Beginning with the 1934 Reciprocal Trade Agreements Act, the U.S. Congress has repeatedly passed statutes authorizing the president to conclude bilateral and multilateral trade agreements reducing U.S. barriers to trade on a reciprocal basis (meaning that U.S. liberalization measures can be taken only in return for comparable measures by other countries; see Chapters 2 and 8). Although the Constitution gives Congress the exclusive power to regulate import and export restrictions, Congress may delegate this power to the president if it prescribes when and how he may raise or lower tariffs. Although the executive branch has inherent authority to negotiate with foreign governments, it lacks the power to implement international trade agreements without explicit statutory authorization from Congress, either before or after such negotiations are concluded. It is no coincidence, therefore, that since the 1950s, the passage of major trade legislation extending presidential implementation authority has usually coincided with the initiation or conclusion of major trade negotiations involving the United States.

Examples of legislation designed to expand trade include the Trade Expansion Act of 1962, the trade acts of 1974 and 1979, and the Omnibus Trade and Competitiveness Act of 1988. The Trade Expansion Act of 1962 authorized the president for five years to negotiate and implement reciprocal reductions of up to 50 percent in most tariffs, and it specified that some tariffs could be eliminated entirely. The Trade Act of 1974 gave him a maximum of five years to negotiate and implement reciprocal reductions in certain tariffs to zero and others by 60 percent. The 1979 Trade Act facilitated the reductions in nontariff barriers (NTBs) negotiated in the Tokyo Round of the GATT. Almost all tariffs are imposed as a specified percentage of the value of an import, in which case they are called "ad valorem" tariffs. NTBs take such forms as arithmetic quotas, onerous health or safety standards, restrictive government procurement practices, and orderly marketing agreements (also known as voluntary export restraints) in which other countries reluctantly agree to limit their exports to specified levels.

In the 1974 trade act, Congress first authorized the president to negotiate reciprocal reductions in tariffs and NTBs by granting him "fast-track authority," a major departure from normal legislative procedures. A basic modification in trade liberalization legislation was needed. By the 1970s, tariffs on most manufactured goods had been reduced so significantly in previous negotiations that NTBs would have to be at the top of the agenda in future talks aimed at further reducing impediments to trade. Whereas cutting tariffs is mainly a matter of simple arithmetic (i.e., by what percentages they can be reduced), NTBs are heterogeneous. To reduce or eliminate them requires case-by-case changes in any number of statutes and regulations (e.g., health and safety standards).

Fast-track authority authorizes the president to submit legislation that implements just-concluded international trade agreements for congressional approval under extraordinary procedures. First, members cannot introduce any amendments to the legislation submitted under this authority. Second, Congress is obliged to vote on the proposed bill within a limited period of time; no parliamentary maneuvers to delay the legislation from reaching a floor vote are allowed under fast-track. These are self-imposed limits on the rules by which both houses of Congress operate. (Either house of Congress could terminate the fast-track rule by a simple majority vote restoring the usual rules of procedure.) Legislation to implement the U.S.-Canada Free Trade Agreement, the North American Free Trade Agreement (NAFTA), and the Final Act of the Uruguay Round, among others, was submitted to Congress under this provision.

The reasoning was and is that a complex trade liberalization bill affects so many special interests that it would attract a great many amendments under regular legislative procedures. If amendments were allowed, it was argued, the original agreement-implementation bill would likely emerge from the legislative process in a radically altered state, having attracted protectionist measures or changes in U.S. demands under the agreement, or both. The mere threat of such an outcome has generally discouraged other governments from investing the time and energy to negotiate a major trade pact with the U.S. executive branch if they believed that extensive congressional amendments to the enacting legislation would force them to revise what presumably had been a finalized agreement. A different point of view advocates permanently eliminating fast-track authority because the threat of amendments by Congress provides needed assurance that the president will fully address the concerns of members and their constituents in trade talks. Proponents of this view also claim that trade agreements can be, and sometimes have been, concluded while this authority had lapsed. Fast-track supporters argue that these agreements were relatively minor, as in the case of the free trade agreement with Jordan.

Fast-track authority expired (again) in 1994. Like all congressional delegations of trade liberalization authority, this provision was temporary. Fast-track is deliberately given an expiration date so that Congress can decide whether there is a compelling reason for renewing it. Every administration since 1974 thought there was; none wanted to take the risk of Congress's rejecting or substantially modifying a bill to implement a trade agreement. As described in Chapter 13, the Clinton administration tried repeatedly, but could not orchestrate a renewal. The Bush (II) administration in its first year in office was unable to convince Congress to renew fast-track even after adopting the somewhat more marketable term *Trade Promotion Authority.* The delay was mainly the result of the continuing disagreement over the extent to which U.S. trade negotiators should be required to demand the inclusion of environmental and labor standards in future trade agreements and by concerns over the power of dispute settlement panels in the WTO and NAFTA (see Chapters 8 and 12).

The president has been given authority by congressional statute to grant duty-free access to the American market for designated products exported from qualifying beneficiaries among less developed countries (LDCs). The concept of a generalized system of tariff preferences (GSP) emerged in discussions that began in the 1960s between the LDCs and the industrialized countries about the relative desirability of trade versus foreign aid as the best means to increase foreign exchange earnings by poorer countries. To deal with the latter's complaints about their inability to compete successfully in the international trading system, a broad consensus emerged that the fundamental principle of nondiscrimination should be altered. The result is that industrial countries maintain individual schemes that provide preferential (duty-free) tariff treatment exclusively to imports from LDCs, mainly manufactured goods. Receipt of GSP treatment by an LDC requires no reciprocal concession because this program is designed more to stimulate economic development than to advance global trade liberalization.

From the beginning, the favorable impact of the U.S. GSP program was limited because it excluded certain important but politically sensitive LDC exports, mainly textiles, apparel, and footwear. In addition, a relatively few advanced developing countries have always accounted for a disproportionately high percentage of GSP-eligible imports (sometimes, only ten countries have accounted for 80 percent of total U.S. imports entering under the GSP program). This situation was only slightly ameliorated by the forced "graduation" from the program of such countries as South Korea, Taiwan, and Singapore. In 2000, only 1.4 percent of total U.S. imports entered duty-free under the GSP program, and even that number would be substantially lower if certain petroleum products are excluded from the calculation.[1]

Section 9082 of the U.S. Harmonized Tariff Schedule is a statutorily-based provision that waives tariffs on goods coming back into the country that were originally manufactured in the United States and then exported for assembly. When the finished goods (e.g., apparel) assembled in other countries with U.S.-made components (e.g., fabrics) are imported, they are subject to a tariff only on the value added during the assembly of the final product, that is, the total cost of the good minus the value of the American-made parts. It is usual for this kind of assembly to take place in export processing zones that allow foreign parts to be imported duty-free for incorporation into goods that are then exported. A mutual benefit results. Section 9082 allows U.S. components producers to gain sales that might otherwise be displaced by imports that are 100 percent foreign-made, and allows low-wage countries to gain labor-intensive jobs. In this version of comparative advantage, the prices of the goods given favorable tariff treatment are presumably lower than they would be if assembled with higher-paid labor in the United States.

## Legislated Relief from Fairly Priced Imports

Competitive pressure is widely regarded as healthy in a market economy so long as prices are determined by genuine market forces rather than by manipulation. An unequivocal belief in free markets and free trade would lead one to oppose any legislation that restricted or raised the price of imported goods. If the welfare of consumers were given absolute priority over the interests of the minority injured by import competition, a country would not need legislation to prevent or minimize import-induced injury. However, *no* sovereign country conducts trade policy solely on the basis of consumer welfare or free market economics.

Import remedy legislation exists because of perceived political and social necessity, and sometimes for economic and legal reasons. Important constituencies in every country demand that the government provide some degree of protection from import-induced injury, either because they are being financially harmed or because they believe that equity and social stability are the most important criteria for determining trade policy. Significant support by Americans for liberal trade is contingent on knowing that relief is potentially available from serious dislocations caused by intense foreign competition, both fair and unfair. Other reasons that trade statutes are not based exclusively on the quest for economic efficiency include governmental efforts to enhance: national security by fostering domestic self-sufficiency in sensitive industries; deter the infringement of domestic trademarks, patents, or copyrights; protect the public from fraudulent or dangerous products; and pressure exporting countries to change their policies or political leaders.

The rules of the WTO, as incorporated from the GATT's articles of agreement, recognize the right of countries to impose temporary import barriers when imports of particular products are increasing fast enough to cause or threaten to cause "serious injury" to domestic producers. After imports of a particular product have taken a large share of the market, domestic producers may be forced to cut back production or lower the price of their goods in order to remain competitive. In either event, domestic producers may experience reduced profits, may be forced to lay off workers, and may even face bankruptcy because of imports.

Domestic producers of a good losing market share to imports may need to redesign their own products, increase the efficiency of their production methods, strengthen their marketing efforts, or do all these things to preserve and reinvigorate sales in their home market. Alternatively, the domestic producers may decide to shift into an entirely new line of products rather than face overwhelming foreign competition. These adjustments may take months or even years to complete. Meanwhile, the loss of profits and jobs may weaken domestic producers to the extent that they can no longer afford the necessary adjustments; the domestic company or even an entire industry could disappear in such circumstances. Temporary import restraints under the so-called safeguard mechanism are not considered an end in themselves. Rather, they are a means to provide a breathing space to allow domestic producers a limited time to adjust to intensifying foreign competition.

The equivalent of the safeguard mechanism that is now part of the WTO agreement, the so-called escape clause is authorized in U.S. law by Section 201 of the Trade Act of 1974 as amended. If the U.S. International Trade Commission (ITC) determines that an increase in the designated imports is a "substantial" cause of serious injury or a threat of serious injury to the domestic producer(s) of a "like or directly competitive" product, they will make a nonbinding recommendation to the president that temporary relief from import competition be provided to help the domestic producers adjust to this competition.

Despite changes in the statute's original language, Section 201 still imposes a heavy burden and high legal fees on domestic producers to convince the ITC that it meets the legal qualification for import relief. The ITC has often ruled against the domestic petitioner. Even when the ITC does find injury, the administration often exercises its prerogative *not* to act on a recommendation for import relief. Presidents may reject the idea of erecting new import barriers in this situation for such reasons as a philosophical attachment to liberal trade, foreign policy considerations, or the belief that the injured industry cannot regain competitiveness during the limited period that higher import barriers are in effect.

The growing belief that the odds were against success by domestic petitioners in escape clause cases led to a steep drop, beginning in the 1980s, in requests for protection under the statute. This perception contributed to an increase in domestic petitions for relief from unfair trade practices, especially dumping (discussed below), where presidential discretion to reject imposition of higher import duties is significantly less than in escape clause cases and the statistical probability of obtaining government-mandated import relief is higher. In some years between 1990 and 2000, no new escape clause cases were initiated. At the end of 2001, the United States maintained import barriers under the escape clause on only two commodities: steel wire rod and welded line pipe. Despite the trend away from the escape clause, one of the biggest investigations ever was completed in 2001. The ITC found that sixteen steel product categories were being injured, a ruling directed at U.S. imports valued at more than $10 billion annually. President Bush subsequently decided to grant most of the higher tariffs recommended by the ITC as discussed below.

A domestic company or industry seeking relief from import competition under Section 201 must first demonstrate that the imports in question are "like or directly competitive" with its product.[2] It must also prove that these imports are increasing, either in absolute terms or as a percentage of domestic consumption. A major requirement is for the domestic producer(s) to demonstrate that it has suffered a "serious injury or threat thereof." This means that there must be convincing proof that the affected American company or industry is suffering adverse economic conditions that would include some or all of the following: reduced output, significant job losses, idle factories, an inability to earn reasonable profits, a declining share of the U.S. market, increasing inventories, and an inability to raise capital by selling new stock or borrowing from banks. Because there is no absolute definition or precise quantitative indicator of what is sufficiently "serious" to warrant action by the ITC, the judgments of the commissioners, together with the staff investigators and lawyers who advise them, are usually the major variable in the ITC's final determinations.

Finally, a domestic petitioner must demonstrate that increased imports are a "substantial cause" of the injury. In determining causation, the ITC weighs all factors contributing to economic injury to the company or industry filing the complaint. A "substantial" cause is defined as one that is "important" and is not less important than any other single cause of injury. Thus, the ITC must find increased imports to be *at least* as important a cause of injury to the domestic petitioner as any other contributing factor. If, for example, increased imports account for 35 percent of injury, a shift in consumer preference accounts for another 35 percent of injury, and other factors account for the remaining 30 percent of injury, then increased imports are no less important than any other cause, and this part of the injury claim is satisfied. If changes in consumer tastes or another domestic factor are estimated to have caused at least 51 percent of injury, the petitioner automatically loses because import-related causes arithmetically could not be at least as important as this factor. Conversely, in theory injury could be found under the statute if increased imports are judged to be, say, 20 percent of the total cause of the domestic industry's problems, but no other individual factor is assigned a larger percentage share. Inevitably, subjective judgment, not precise calculations, plays a large role in making such determinations.

The escape clause is often defended as a means of buying time for a domestic industry to adjust to changes in the global marketplace that have put them at a competitive disadvantage. To obtain import relief, producers are encouraged to show that over time they can restructure themselves to regain competitiveness, but this is not an absolute requirement. If the administration determines that an industry cannot adjust and become competitive internationally in the foreseeable future, it is supposed to deny the industry relief. Critics maintain that few companies receiving escape clause protection have been able to reinvent themselves and then compete successfully against import competition.

The process for obtaining a 201 remedy is outlined in the statute. A business firm, trade association, certified union, or other entity representing a U.S. industry may file a petition requesting relief from alleged import-induced injury with the ITC (see Chapter 5), an agency that is independent of the legislative and executive branches. In addition, the commission can act at the request of the president, the USTR, specified congressional committees, or on its own initiative. The ITC has 120 days (extensions are possible in complex cases) after the filing of a petition to hold public hearings, conduct an investigation, and determine whether the injury and causation criteria have been met and import relief is merited.

If at least three of the six commissioners determine that an increase in imports is a "substantial cause of serious injury" or threat of serious injury to a U.S. producer of a like or directly competitive product, the ITC will recommend to the president a course of action that should provide appropriate relief from increased imports and assist in "positive adjustment" by the industry to import competition. The list of possible Section 201 import relief measures that the ITC can recommend includes imposing new or higher tariffs, tariff-rate quotas, arithmetic quotas, adjustment assistance (discussed below), or some combination of these measures. The ITC is not bound by its own precedents, and commissioners can use contradictory principles to decide similar cases over time. The president is free to accept or modify the suggested relief actions, or to reject the recommendation and do nothing if he believes that would be in the national interest. Before agreement was reached in the Uruguay Round to phase them out, "voluntary" export restraint agreements with other countries were regularly used by the United States in response to injury findings involving steel and color television sets, among others. This tactic was viewed as an attractive political compromise between unilateral action and no action.

If import relief is provided, it can be imposed for up to four years and then extended, but restrictions cannot last for more than eight years. When a WTO member imposes safeguard (escape clause) measures that are more than three years in duration against imports from other WTO member countries, the latter have the right to demand compensation in the form of lower barriers against other goods. Compensation is designed to give affected foreign countries the opportunity to increase the exports of other goods that are roughly equivalent in value to the losses caused by the safeguard barriers imposed on the product(s) found to be causing domestic injury. The ITC's decisions can be reviewed by the New York–based Court of International Trade; its decisions in turn can be appealed to the Court of Appeals for the Federal Circuit in Washington, D.C., and from there to the U.S. Supreme Court.

Virtually every U.S. Section 201 decision from the late 1990s to 2001 that resulted in the granting of import relief to American companies and workers drew allegations from affected countries that the United States was in violation of WTO rules. This string of complaints was encouraged by the regularity with which WTO dispute resolution panels ruled against the United States in these cases. Panels consistently agreed with the "plaintiffs" that the United States had violated at least one international trade rule when imposing higher trade barriers on imports of wheat gluten, lamb meat, and welded line pipe; these actions had been taken following escape clause findings that the domestic producers of these three products had been injured by rising import competition. The immediate announcements by several countries of their intention to request a WTO ruling against President Bush's decision in early 2002 to impose escape clause duties on several steel products (discussed below) were encouraged in part by these successful efforts to challenge U.S. use of one of its import remedy laws.

Producers of goods demonstrably related to "national security" can apply for protection from import competition under Section 232 of the Trade Expansion Act of 1962. Under this provision, an interested party representing a domestic industry or the head of a U.S. government agency or department can request the secretary of commerce to conduct an investigation to determine whether imports of a specified good threaten the national security. If the secretary does make a recommendation to the president to restrict imports, the latter has authority to take any remedial action he feels necessary to "adjust" imports. In 1959, President Eisenhower invoked Section 232 to impose import quotas on oil out of concern that the country's increased dependence on foreign oil was threatening the domestic oil industry and thus U.S. security in the event of a disruption in foreign oil supplies. This quota remained in effect through 1973.

A very different program offering government relief to producers and workers adversely affected by fair foreign competition is known as "adjustment assistance." It is a distinctive approach in that it seeks to provide financial compensation to assist import-displaced workers find new jobs and import-impacted companies adopt remedial business practices rather than restrict the inflow of sensitive imports. Adjustment assistance was established by the Trade Expansion Act of 1962 for the purpose of providing financial assistance to the relatively few workers injured by import liberalization policies that were judged to benefit the majority. The program also had the practical effect of helping to enlist the support of organized labor for this trade bill and the subsequent Kennedy Round of trade negotiations.

Adjustment assistance is provided for workers who are able to prove to the Labor Department that import competition "contributed importantly" to the loss of their jobs. Changes in the law now direct that instead of simple cash payments to the unemployed, the program is to emphasize job retraining and relocation benefits designed to help workers find new, more productive and higher-paying jobs. More recently, Congress established a special assistance program to provide benefits to workers whose jobs were lost as a direct result of increased imports from the NAFTA countries (Mexico and Canada). Total annual expenditures for worker assistance in recent years has been in the $400 million range. Approximately 100,000 workers (out of a total U.S. work force in excess of 130 million) were certified as being eligible for adjustment assistance in fiscal year 2000.

The statutory provisions governing adjustment assistance to import-impacted companies also have evolved. Firms that can demonstrate to the Commerce Department that increased imports "contributed importantly" to decreased sales and job cuts become eligible for government-funded technical assistance. Now that direct loans have been phased out, adjustment assistance to firms consists of twelve Trade Adjustment Assistance Centers around the country dispensing technical advice in the hope of restoring economic vitality to these companies. Typically, the business turn-around consultants hired by these centers provide advice on improved marketing and sales strategies, improved production techniques, new sources of financing, and so on. In a typical year, about 160 to 180 firms (usually small to medium-sized) are certified as eligible. Governmental outlays for corporate adjustment assistance in the early 2000s amounted to only a little more than $10 million annually.[3]

Special government-funded benefits for workers whose unemployment results from foreign competition are difficult to defend in some respects because far more workers are idled by recessions, domestic competition, technological change, and corporate downsizing. Nevertheless, most economists support adjustment assistance as a relatively efficient and constructive alternative to import restraints to relieve the impact of import-induced dislocations. In some specific instances (e.g., automobiles in the early 1980s), analysts have calculated that using government funds to maintain the incomes of workers laid off because of increased import competition would be far less than the total cost to consumers from higher prices due to new import restraints.[4] On the other hand, critics have long alleged that adjustment assistance has lacked the focus and funding necessary to adequately assist its intended beneficiaries.

### Steel: A Case Study in Four Decades of Import Relief

The steel industry provides an important case study of the recurrent use of U.S. import relief legislation. In March 2002, President George W. Bush imposed tariffs of up to 30 percent on the majority of U.S. steel imports, culminating an escape clause (Section 201) case he initiated the previous year (June 2001) under political pressure from the domestic steel industry. In between, following the administrative procedures outlined earlier in this chapter, the ITC investigated the industry's claim that increased imports were "a substantial cause of serious injury" to domestic producers and ruled in the industry's favor on about 80 percent of steel products (by value).

It was not surprising that an industry that had long been one of the most frequent users of the U.S. trade laws would seek additional import relief when many companies were going bankrupt and thousands of workers were in danger of losing their jobs. But it *was* surprising that a president who was personally committed to free trade, and who was simultaneously asking the Congress to reauthorize Trade Promotion Authority (formerly known as fast-track), would actively support the industry's request for protection. The story of how this decision came about perfectly illustrates this book's theme of how trade policy is formulated through the interaction of economic, political, and legal forces.

This new import relief for the American steel industry was the culmination of what Brookings economist Robert W. Crandall has called a "recurrent crisis" dating back to the late 1960s. Until the early 1960s, domestic steel producers were shielded from foreign competition by a combination of factors—not only relatively high tariffs, but also high transportation costs and relatively inefficient foreign industries. Unconcerned about competition, big oligopolistic firms such as U.S. Steel and Bethlehem Steel charged high prices to consumers, paid relatively high wages to unionized workers, and failed to adopt newly developed technologies.

All this changed dramatically starting in the 1960s, for three reasons. First, western European and Japanese steelmakers invested in new, more technologically up-to-date steelmaking facilities, which significantly reduced their costs of production. Second, the United States lowered its trade barriers as part of the multilateral tariff reductions negotiated under the GATT. Third, the invention of larger, more efficient cargo ships sharply reduced transportation costs, making it possible for Japan and other resource-poor countries to import iron ore and coking coal cheaply and to re-export finished steel at competitive prices.

As a result of these factors, European and Japanese steel producers significantly increased their sales in the U.S. market, starting in the mid-1960s. These countries were joined in the late 1970s and 1980s by newly industrializing countries, such as South Korea, Thailand, and Brazil, and in the 1990s by "transition economies," such as Russia, Ukraine, and China. Although these new entrants could not equal the Japanese or Europeans in technology or productivity, they all had relatively low labor costs and high excess capacity. Many countries allegedly also had significant government assistance and/or collusive business practices that enabled them to become low-priced steel exporters.

American steel producers responded to these successive waves of import penetration by repeatedly seeking protection under the U.S. trade laws. Whenever imports increased, the industry petitioned for relief under either the escape clause or the unfair trade (antidumping and countervailing duty) statutes. Several times, presidents offered the industry special forms of protection in return for abandoning these standard legal remedies. The industry was protected by voluntary export restraint agreements (VERs) with foreign exporters in 1969–1974 under President Nixon; the "trigger price mechanism," which used threats of antidumping investigations to effectively establish de facto minimum prices on steel imports under President Carter in 1978–1980; and a series of VERs that eventually covered most steel imports in 1982–1992 under the Reagan and Bush I administrations. Each time one of these special arrangements expired, the industry filed more petitions for import relief under the trade laws, but had varying degrees of success.

The domestic steel industry also made dramatic internal adjustments in the past four decades. Although often characterized by critics as technological dinosaurs, the large steel firms began to invest more in new technologies. Numerous old, obsolete mills were shut down. New domestic competitors called "minimills" mounted a serious challenge to the older, "integrated" firms. The minimills were small firms that used electric arc furnaces to produce basic steel products inexpensively from scrap metal, instead of the old integrated method that required costly blast furnaces for melting iron ore into steel. Many minimills were nonunion firms that had lower labor costs. In addition, foreign steel producers began to invest in U.S. facilities, sometimes in joint ventures with U.S. companies. Although steel employment fell from about 600,000 workers in the 1960s to barely 200,000 around 2000, labor productivity increased so much (more than *three times*) that the industry could still produce roughly the same amount of output.

The upshot of all this restructuring was that a more efficient, productive, and competitive steel industry emerged in the 1990s. Yet, in the latter part of that decade, in spite of robust growth in the rest of the U.S. economy, the steel industry entered a new crisis phase. Prices and profits plummeted, many companies went bankrupt (thirty-one by March 2002), and more workers lost their jobs. Thousands of retired steelworkers who were owed pensions by now-unprofitable or bankrupt companies feared the loss of their promised retirement benefits. The large "legacy costs" of these pensions helped push some of the major integrated firms (such as LTV and Bethlehem) into bankruptcy— and into requesting the government to assume their pension costs and allow them to merge with U.S. Steel. The steel producers blamed an import surge that began around 1996 for their troubles, first charging unfair trade practices in a long series of antidumping and countervailing duty cases involving specific products and countries, and then alleging "serious injury" from all steel imports in the escape clause case.

Unquestionably, the global steel industry developed a glut of excess capacity in the late 1990s, resulting in sharply falling prices. Most analysts attributed the overcapacity to depressed economic conditions among the world's leading steel exporters, including Japan, other East Asian countries, Argentina, Brazil, and Russia. Another factor was the significant appreciation of the U.S. dollar in the late 1990s (see Chapter 4), which made imported steel up to 30 percent cheaper by 2001 than it would have been otherwise. The domestic industry argued that foreign governments contributed to the global glut through a combination of protectionist policies, government subsidies, and tolerance for collusive business practices, which together restricted competition in their home markets, kept their domestic prices artificially high, and enabled their steel producers to dump their excess supplies at lower prices in the U.S. market. Critics of the U.S. industry (including both foreign producers and domestic steel consumers) responded that the problems of the domestic producers were largely domestic in origin. The critics cited cutthroat competition between the newer minimills and the older integrated mills, the large financial burden of the legacy costs, and the failure to eliminate obsolete capacity as a result of prior import relief. Once again, conflicting assessments of "reality" complicated the policymaking process.

President Bush's reasons for supporting the steel industry's demand for protection were largely political. Not wanting to be a one-term president like his father, Bush decided to appease concerned voters in key steel-producing states such as Pennsylvania, West Virginia, and Ohio. Bush also needed to be responsive to members of Congress from the steel states because their willingness to support fast-track renewal was seen as contingent on protection being extended to the steel interests in their districts. Although the president didn't give the steel industry everything it wanted (for example, the tariffs were lower than the 40 percent urged by the domestic industry and several countries were excluded, such as NAFTA members Canada and Mexico), his decision was seen as mainly favorable to the industry.

Defenders of Bush's decision argued that he used the escape clause for exactly its intended purpose: to give limited, temporary protection to a particular industry, in order to maintain a broad political coalition in favor of generally liberal trade policies. Supporters also claimed that steel companies and their workers and communities should not suffer for reasons beyond their control, such as the economic troubles in our trading partners and the overvaluation of the dollar. Industry advocates argued that protection would give the industry some "breathing room" in which to restructure and improve its competitiveness, while lessening the painful plant shutdowns and job losses that all agreed were unavoidable to some extent. Finally, defenders of Bush's action argued that the U.S. should not stick to free-trade principles in a sector in which many of its trading partners routinely flout those principles.

Critics of Bush's decision disputed all these points. They argued that the necessary and inevitable restructuring of the industry would be better promoted by *less* protection, not more, and that three years of protection would only delay the necessary capacity reductions and corporate mergers. Opponents claimed that the tariffs would be costly to domestic steel consumers and did not address the underlying causes of the steel crisis, especially global excess capacity and high "legacy costs." The critics argued that the decision was politically motivated and legally unjustified (e.g., because imports peaked earlier than 2001), and would not stand up to appeal at the WTO. Finally, some opponents charged that it was not worth antagonizing major U.S. trading partners in order to try to save a moribund domestic industry, and that protecting it would undermine rather than enhance U.S. trade liberalization efforts.

President Bush's decision was not the end of the issue. As soon as he announced the tariffs, many leading steel exporting nations announced their intention to file a complaint at the WTO (see Chapters 8 and 13) seeking to have the tariffs judged to be a violation of international trading rules. The EU began threatening retaliation against specific U.S. exports, the exact dimensions of which would depend on the outcome of their complaint at the WTO. Thus, no end is in sight yet for the nearly forty-year debate about the propriety of import relief for the American steel industry.

## Legislated Relief from Unfairly Priced Imports

Although the president has considerable discretion in deciding whether to provide relief from injury judged to have been induced by fair foreign competition, he has very little flexibility if a final determination of an *unfair* foreign trade practice is made. The three main forms of unfair foreign competition are dumping (imports priced at less than fair value), certain kinds of foreign government subsidies designed to lower the production costs of exporters, and imports involving violations of intellectual property rights. International agreements and U.S. trade law unambiguously permit an importing country to impose penalty duties when foreign producers are found to be using these legally unacceptable practices to lower the prices of their exports artificially, and when domestic producers are found to be injured by imports selling at less than fair value. Although the legal right to respond to these price distortions is not in question, disputes frequently arise about how governments enforce their laws dealing with unfair foreign trade practices. Some economists suggest eliminating unfair trade practice laws, mainly because of their argument that most people (consumers) receive economic benefits when foreigners choose to ship them underpriced goods.

Congress views statutes to address unfairly priced imports as a political necessity. These laws have the irresistible allure of providing members with a win-win position: The peoples' elected representatives can assert that they are in favor of a free flow of trade, but only as long as it is conducted in a "fair" manner. The broad private sector coalition that has provided essential support for a liberal trade policy in the United States would likely be undermined if American companies and unions felt they had no legal redress against unfair, or nonmarket, practices by foreign competitors. As with any major issue on trade policy, there is an opposite viewpoint. Free traders and foreign interests argue that a new form of "procedural protectionism" has been created by the proliferation of petitions for imposing antidumping and countervailing duties, the relatively high percentage of success by U.S. companies filing such petitions, and the relatively low level of proof required to demonstrate import-induced injury in these cases. In this view, the result is an American market made less accessible by an increasing array of alleged "self-defense" measures against illegal foreign trade practices.

## The Antidumping Law

When imports enter a country either at a price less than that normally charged for the same goods in their home market or at a price below production costs and a "normal" profit margin, an unfair trade practice—dumping—is presumed to have occurred. Goods in the international marketplace are supposed to compete on the basis of market prices that reflect the producer's true costs of production. Although consumers in the importing country benefit from below-market prices for foreign-made goods, governments have been unwilling to allow injury to domestic producers and workers by reason of such unfair competition. When dumping occurs *and* it inflicts economic injury on domestic producers of "like" products,[5] international trade law clearly empowers the importing country to impose duties (tariffs) by the margin necessary to establish a "fair price" for the imports in question.

In economic terms, dumping is conceptualized as a form of price discrimination; that is, a situation in which different prices are charged in different markets.[6] The validity of calling such price discrimination "unfair" is a judgment call. Low-priced imports can be a problem for domestic producers of similar products in the importing country who face the unenviable choice either of cutting their own prices and profit margins to meet the competition or of losing sales to the dumped imports. Feelings that the price discrimination is "unfair" are intensified when higher retail prices in the exporting country are facilitated by trade barriers imposed by that country's government to reduce competition in its home market or by official toleration of restrictive business practices within the country's industrial or agricultural sectors. On the other hand, some American companies have complained openly when the imposition of dumping duties on components they were importing meant that they could no longer buy these cheap inputs from abroad. The possibility of reduced market share or lower profit margins resulting from increased duties on imported inputs is part of the reason that U.S. industry does not speak with one voice on import policy (see Chapter 6).

On occasion, companies knowingly dump their goods in foreign markets; several reasons encourage such tactics. They may want to eliminate a temporary surplus of goods and thereby avoid the costs of holding excessive inventories, especially if the goods are perishable or might become obsolete. Dumping is also encouraged by a recession in the home market, which increases pressure on a company to maintain sales by shifting to faster-growing overseas markets. Industries that have high fixed costs, such as integrated steel mills, are especially susceptible to pressures to make sales below production costs when demand is low because their factories have to produce large volumes of output if they are to operate efficiently. Companies may dump as part of a business strategy for increasing market share in other countries. In extreme cases, a company may engage in "predatory" dumping that is deliberately designed to drive its overseas competition out of business and gain control of foreign markets for its own goods. Presumably, predatory dumping is a medium-term strategy that eventually will be followed by large increases in export prices when the domestic industry in an importing country has been decimated or eliminated.

Dumping is not always deliberate. Foreign producers may sometimes inadvertently price certain of their exports too low because of inadequate or inaccurate accounting practices or ignorance of U.S. definitions of a "fair" price. Rapid fluctuations in exchange rates can also lead to charges of dumping, because, for example, the depreciation of an exporting country's currency can lead to lower dollar prices in the U.S. market.

Consideration of import relief under U.S. antidumping laws begins when American producers, wholesalers, an association representing a domestic industry, or a union submits a petition to the Commerce Department and the ITC alleging injury from goods being imported into the United States at *less than fair value.* Alternatively, the Commerce Department can initiate an investigation on its own initiative, although it does so only rarely. The U.S. antidumping statute outlines a complex set of procedures whereby these two government agencies act in a presumably objective, nonpartisan manner to determine within a few months whether the goods mentioned in the petitions meet the statutory criteria for being declared to have been sold at less than fair value and to have injured the domestic industry.[7] First, the ITC initiates a preliminary investigation. The purpose is to determine as definitively as possible whether there is a "reasonable indication" that an industry in the United States is "materially injured" or threatened with material injury. Although it seldom happens, an investigation may also be made to determine whether a petitioner's complaint is valid in claiming that the establishment of an industry in the United States is being "materially retarded" by reason of imports of the merchandise named in the petition, whose volume must be "not negligible."

The majority of preliminary determinations are affirmative, a logical result in view of the relatively pro forma standards for demonstrating a "reasonable indication" of injury or threat of injury by reason of dumped imports. The odds of an affirmative action at this stage also reflect the propensity of experienced trade attorneys representing domestic producers to assess the economic environment carefully and advise their clients to delay filing an antidumping petition until conditions seem favorable for winning (e.g., the domestic industry is suffering an accelerated decline in sales). If the commission's preliminary determination is negative on all countries named in the petition, that is, the ITC finds no reasonable indication that injury or threat has occurred, as a result of the imports, the investigation is terminated.

If the ITC's preliminary finding is affirmative, and if the Commerce Department finds that the petition accurately and adequately makes a case for relief, the latter initiates a preliminary investigation to determine whether there is reason to believe that dumping—sales at less than fair value—has occurred.[8] At this point, the ITC begins a final investigation of import-induced injury, in which the legal standard for an affirmative finding is higher than for a preliminary determination. In a final determination, the ITC must find that the dumped imports were a "cause of material injury" (or threat of material injury or retardation of the establishment of an industry), and the injury (or threat) must be "by reason of" the unfairly traded imports. The ITC's investigation includes obtaining information through questionnaires sent to producers, importers, and purchasers, and holding public hearings at which representatives of all interested parties can appear and testify.

While the ITC is conducting its final investigation of injury and causation, the Commerce Department begins the review process that will make a final determination of whether dumping occurred, and if so, by what amount. If either agency's final determination is negative, the proceedings are terminated. If the ITC makes an affirmative determination that material injury (or a threat of material injury) was caused by the imports in question, and if the Commerce Department makes a final determination that these goods were sold at less than fair value, then duties (paid by the importer) are imposed. The antidumping duty (in effect, a tariff) imposed on each unit of merchandise from each foreign producer equals the percentage difference between the estimated "fair value" and the price at which the good has been imported into the United States. By way of example, if the fair value was found to be 25 percent higher than the import price, the dumping duty applied would be 25 percent of the invoice price. Imposition of an appropriate penalty duty offsets the margin of dumping and thereby raises the import price to fair value. No presidential discretion is allowed in terms of not responding to this unfair trade practice. The one exception is that the administration can opt to negotiate "suspension agreements" with the accused exporting countries. These agreements provide either higher export prices or limitations on imports of the goods designated as being dumped into the United States. In either case, antidumping duties are suspended.

Quantification of a dumping margin involves an unusually complex series of computations performed by the Department of Commerce's International Trade

Administration (ITA). The ITA first sends out a lengthy questionnaire to all interested parties, domestic and foreign, to collect information concerning production costs and the prices and volume of sales of the allegedly dumped goods, both in the foreign and the U.S. markets, over a period of at least six months. Many foreign companies, especially relatively small ones, have bitterly complained of onerous, if not impossible burdens imposed by the Commerce Department's demands for voluminous material to be submitted in accordance with detailed instructions and in a relatively short time (a few weeks). Some foreign companies do not want to provide proprietary information to a U.S. government agency, perhaps because it will substantiate charges of dumping. When foreign producers cannot or will not submit their responses to the Department of Commerce, the latter follows rules that allow it to estimate the dumping margin based on other information, as discussed below.

There is also little precision in the methods used by the ITC to determine if a U.S. industry is materially injured or threatened with material injury by reason of the dumped imports. "Material injury" is defined as harm that is not inconsequential, immaterial, or unimportant. This term has been interpreted as being less rigorous than the standard for demonstrating "serious injury" under the escape clause (Section 201) law. The legal definition of "material injury" is general enough that a relatively low degree of injury might be found to satisfy the standard, depending on the discretion of the commissioners. In addition to finding that the domestic producers of the like product have been injured, the ITC must determine that the imports found to have been dumped were "a cause" of the injury. In antidumping investigations, the imports do not have to be at least as important as any other cause, as in escape clause cases, and imports can be found to be "a cause" of material injury or threat even if other factors, say, a decrease in domestic demand, have caused even more injury. In making these determinations about both injury and causation in dumping cases, the ITC is not bound by its own precedents, and different commissioners may use different standards. If the commission's determination is negative, that is, it finds that no injury has occurred to the company or industry, by reason of the imports, the investigation is terminated.

Dumping investigations can be exceptionally complicated. Many companies in different countries may be named in the suit, and each of these companies may charge different prices and have different production costs for the same product. Dumping accusations may be made against many different styles or models of a product, and each might have different production costs and prices. When a variety of imported goods are being investigated, it can be difficult to determine exactly which U.S. goods to compare them to. Furthermore, each of the exporting companies may have changed their prices for the same commodity during the period (several months) of alleged dumping, and their costs might have changed as well.[9] The "fair value" of an import is usually defined as the wholesale price paid in the ordinary course of trade for consumption in the foreign market, otherwise referred to as the "home market price."

If the imported product is not sold in the home market, the ITA may calculate the fair value by determining the price at which the good is sold when exported to another large industrialized export market similar to the U.S. market. Alternatively, the ITA may use its own in-house methodology to construct a fair value by estimating the cost of production and adding a "fair" profit margin (which may be greater than the profit margin typical in the domestic market of the exporting country). The ITA will use a "constructed value" if it determines that the home market price is less than the actual cost of production or if not enough information is available to determine the home market price. When dumping cases involve nonmarket economies such as China and Russia, the ITA constructs a "fair value" of the exported goods based on the estimated cost of comparable labor and materials in a surrogate market economy at roughly the same level of development as the nonmarket economy. For example, India has been used as a surrogate for the Chinese economy.

To assure that the government receives all dumping duties owed to it in connection with an antidumping determination, importers are required to post cash bonds for each entry of these imports in an amount equal to the Commerce Department's preliminary estimate of the margin of dumping. Liabilities for dumping duties and the posting of bonds usually begin at the conclusion of the Commerce Department's preliminary investigation. Importers then face a difficult choice: They can continue to bring in the potentially dutiable goods and pay money into an escrow account; or they can suspend further shipments for six months or more until the process formally concludes, either with the imposition of final antidumping duties (which might be higher than the preliminary duties) or with the termination of the case and the return of all security deposits. Rather than placing itself at risk from the possibility of unexpectedly big liabilities for paying retroactive dumping duties, a cautious importer might seek alternative suppliers, perhaps domestic, of the affected product. A foreign exporter could then lose several months of sales in the American market even if it is ultimately found innocent of dumping. Thus domestic producers can sometimes win in economic terms from filing a case that they lose.

From 1980 through 2000, an average of about forty new antidumping petitions were filed annually. Of all the cases concluded during these years, slightly less than one-half eventually resulted in the imposition of duties after determinations were made that sales at less than fair value caused material injury (or threat of injury) to domestic producers.[10] Under the 1994 Uruguay Round GATT agreement, the Commerce Department and the ITC are now required to hold "sunset reviews" no later than five years after imposing an antidumping duty to determine whether it could be revoked without a continuation (or threat of recurrence) of the injury caused by less-than-fair-value imports. Many old antidumping duties have been eliminated through these sunset reviews, but others have been kept in place after an investigation similar to that for an initial complaint. Even if antidumping orders are retained, the amount of the penalty duty can be revised as a result of periodic reviews conducted by the Commerce Department.

## The Controversies Surrounding Antidumping Laws

The antidumping statutes have become, for domestic supporters of liberal trade and foreign exporters, the single most disparaged aspect of U.S. trade policy. This criticism is part of a larger charge that U.S. trade remedy laws are being administered in a way that makes them inconsistent with U.S. market-opening commitments agreed to in international trade agreements. As seen by an economist at a think tank oriented to free trade, the United States "more than any other country" is the subject of complaints to the WTO dispute settlement mechanism that it is violating the multilateral rules that govern national use of antidumping, countervailing duty, and safeguards provisions. U.S. trade remedy laws, especially antidumping, "have become a flash point of tension in the international trading system."[11]

Except for predatory pricing, most of the low prices that are considered to be "unfair" competition under international trade law would be *perfectly legal* in domestic business. Domestic firms are free to compete with each other by lowering prices, even if the prices fall below costs. Furthermore, domestic firms are not required to charge the same prices in all markets as long as they are not attempting to monopolize a market by driving their competitors out of business (which is illegal under U.S. antitrust laws). For example, domestic companies and stores that put certain products on sale are not generally engaging in an illegal anticompetitive practice unless it can be shown that they are trying to drive their rivals out of business. Supporters of these laws counter that other countries have business practices, financial systems, and government regulations that can effectively allow their producers to charge artificially low prices in the relatively open and less-regulated U.S. market.

The U.S. antidumping laws are criticized by foreign governments and corporations and by pro-import domestic groups as arbitrary, capricious, and protectionist. Calculating the dumping margin is highly complex and involves many judgment calls. Reasonable people will not agree on which prices to include in the weighted average, what constitutes differences in the circumstances of sale, which prices are reasonable in constructing a fair value, how much of a normal profit margin should be assumed, how to identify a surrogate country, or which adjustments may be appropriate. Foreign countries complain that the U.S. approach to antidumping protection is excessively burdened with paperwork, legal costs, and procedural complexity. They also claim that U.S. antidumping administrative procedures are biased in favor of U.S. domestic producers for reasons that include the Commerce Department's method of calculating dumping margins; the ITC's rule of favoring domestic producers in cases of a 3–3 tie; and the weak legal standards for proving "material injury" or threat of injury caused by allegedly dumped imports.

The unpredictability, complexity, and discretionary nature of the antidumping laws allegedly makes it difficult for foreign exporters, especially if they are relatively small or inexperienced, to know exactly how to price their shipments to the U.S. market. If the producer sets the price too high, it will not be able to compete in the market; if the price is too low, the producer risks being subjected to a costly administrative proceeding that could end in imposition of antidumping duties. Importers complain that they can be intimidated into raising prices merely by a threat from their U.S. competitors to file an antidumping action. Even a minor producer in a small developing country may be subject to a dumping duty because a U.S. industry can ask the ITC to "cumulate" the adverse effects of competition from many different producers in many countries for purposes of determining material injury. In rebuttal, domestic producers argue that many dumped imports would not be competitive in the U.S. market if they were sold at fair prices that truly reflected the costs of production in their countries of origin.

Both importers located in the United States and foreign companies can accrue legal bills that may amount to several millions of dollars. In addition, importers (not exporters) are subject to the major uncertainties that go along with open-ended liabilities, namely, antidumping duties of unknown amounts. They face the possibility of current and retroactive dumping duties high enough to result in serious losses on transactions involving goods found to have been exported at prices less than fair value. It is conceivable that if high enough dumping duties on a large enough volume of imports are imposed, a relatively small-scale importer could be forced into bankruptcy. Antidumping liabilities are open-ended because a final determination of dumping margins can result in penalties that are significantly higher than 100 percent of the value of the imports. For example, if the fair market value of widgets that were imported at $10 apiece is pegged at $30, a dumping duty of 200 percent ($20) would be necessary to offset the declared margin of dumping.

According to many economists who advocate free trade, dumped imports are like a gift from foreign suppliers because they benefit domestic consumers. From this perspective, antidumping duties are economically irrational: They force consumers to pay higher prices for goods that otherwise could be had more cheaply. Supporters of the antidumping laws counter that producers' interests are important too, and that it is in the national interest to protect against artificially cheap imports, especially when the domestic producers are more efficient than the foreign producers. Defenders of these laws also argue that traditional economic calculations of the cost effectiveness of antidumping protection wrongly omit the potential long-term harm to the U.S. economy of having manufacturing industries, which may contribute to increased productivity and higher living standards for the economy as a whole, driven out of business by foreign companies willing to price below their production costs. Critics assert that the antidumping law does not take into account efficiency and, as a result, antidumping relief often ends up protecting relatively inefficient domestic producers.

All laws addressing unfair foreign trade practices can be defended in part by suggesting that without them, the fear factor would quickly erode political support for liberal trade if producers and workers had no legal remedy to defend themselves in such situations. They would not accept being deprived of a safety valve and effectively being at the mercy of foreign competitors possessed of the resources and determination to make inroads into the American market.

The opposite school of thought avers that American companies are using these statutes to create protected home markets in which they are insulated from the legitimate foreign competition that is the hallmark of an open trading system. In this view, the legal standards for proving both the existence of dumping and the causation of injury or the threat of injury from dumped imports are too lax. Allegedly, the antidumping laws are being used as a substitute for the escape clause, because the latter involves more stringent legal conditions that are harder to satisfy (as discussed in the previous section). Some domestic producers presumably perceive a greater chance of winning import relief by filing an antidumping petition. As noted economist Joseph E. Stiglitz has written, "Because positive dumping margins are almost always found and because any significant fall in sales is sufficient for a positive injury finding (even if most of the fall in sales is caused by other factors), the antidumping laws are now effectively acting like market surge statutes, especially for moribund industries."[12]

Supporters of the antidumping laws counter that dumping is a genuine problem and not a legal fiction. As they see it, foreign producers can take advantage of protected home markets or domestic monopoly positions to engage in price discrimination in export markets; when this happens, U.S. producers have no other effective remedy but to seek protection under these laws. In this view, the antidumping laws are characterized as counterweights to foreign countries' alleged mercantilist practices (see Chapter 3). Greg Mastel has argued that "repeated dumping is a predatory practice inevitably directly associated with mercantilist practices such as a sanctuary home market, subsidies, and cartels," and concludes that the antidumping laws are "the only viable tool for countering trade unfairness and establishing a level playing field."[13]

The steady stream of foreign accusations that the United States is making excessive use of antidumping actions tends to overshadow the rapid growth in the use of this provision in many other countries. During the 1990s, 2,483 antidumping actions were taken worldwide, a more than 50 percent increase in similar actions taken in the 1980s. The countries imposing antidumping duties went from twelve to twenty-eight between 1993 and 1999. The United States is now one of the most frequent targets of overseas antidumping investigations.[14] The countries that still don't use these provisions, especially the Asian countries and countries in transition, are often accused of employing other methods to close their markets (e.g., government industrial policies or corporate buying practices that favor national enterprises) so that they don't need antidumping laws to keep out undesired imports.

Although U.S. procedures can be criticized for being legalistic and complex, they can also be defended as being relatively transparent. Foreign producers and domestic importers are fully informed of the complaints against them, and have the opportunity to refute the charges at the Commerce Department and the ITC. The losing party in a dumping investigation may appeal to the U.S. Court of International Trade and, if necessary, to the U.S. Court of Appeals for the Federal Circuit in Washington, D.C., and the Supreme Court. Foreign governments also can request hearings from WTO dispute resolution panels (and are increasingly doing so). Ironically, some American industry advocates also object to the legalistic nature of U.S. antidumping procedures, in which an industry usually has to suffer substantial injury before it can file a winnable petition for relief.[15] Other countries allegedly protect their producers in advance of actual injury from imports.

Those who think that the antidumping laws are frequently abused would prefer that the U.S. negotiate international agreements about competition policies—essentially, the international equivalent of the domestic antitrust laws—to prevent companies from monopolizing global markets and establish uniform standards for permissible competitive activities. In theory, such policies could prevent predatory pricing in the international arena while allowing more benign forms of competitive pricing to proceed uninhibited. In addition, liberalizing foreign trade barriers can discourage dumping because depriving foreign producers of protected home markets can help prevent price discrimination in exports. Supporters of the antidumping laws do not necessarily object in principle to these alternatives; they argue they that international competition policies and foreign-market opening initiatives are hard to negotiate and even more difficult to enforce. Therefore, they feel that American producers need a more reliable mechanism to counteract foreign unfair trade practices when they occur.

Some foreign governments are firmly committed to adding "reform" of the antidumping and countervailing duty (discussed below) laws, especially those of the United States, to the agenda of the next round of multilateral trade negotiations. Led by the EU, they have already filed several complaints with the WTO asking that a dispute settlement panel declare various parts of the U.S. antidumping laws incompatible with WTO agreements. The U.S. government's professed opposition to weakening what it regards as politically necessary and internationally legal trade remedy laws suggests that this issue will be one of the most contentious points in upcoming trade talks.

A good insight into the politics and decisionmaking dynamics of U.S. trade policy was the very public advice that members of Congress gave in 2001 to the Bush administration not to agree to weaken U.S. import-remedy laws. For example, a letter was sent to the president by sixty-three senators explaining their strong feelings on this issue. On another occasion, senators predicted a hostile congressional reception to any new trade agreements requiring revisions in U.S. laws that would limit the government's ability to restrict imports linked to unfair foreign trade practices. Angered by what they saw as an assault on these laws by other countries in WTO dispute settlement panels, members of Congress urged the Bush administration to prevent discussions of these laws from being added to the agenda of the upcoming round of multilateral trade negotiations.[16] In November 2001, the House of Representatives passed a nonbinding resolution exhorting the administration in all forthcoming trade negotiations to preserve the ability of the U.S. government to "enforce vigorously" its trade remedy laws, especially antidumping and countervailing duty statutes. When the U.S. delegation could not thwart an overseas consensus that reform of trade remedy laws must be included as an agenda item in the upcoming negotiations, several members of Congress publicly voiced displeasure. The result is that the USTR is facing a classic "two-level" negotiation with Congress and with foreign governments on legal standards for dealing with unfair trade practices.

It is probably unrealistic to expect that a society as litigious and legalistic as the United States will abandon a legally and administratively complex system of trade laws, or that the antidumping laws will cease to "provide substantial and growing income to a small army of trade lawyers and their consultants who are hired to represent both petitioner firms and respondent importers and exporters."[17] It is also probably unrealistic to expect foreign governments and producers to accept a system in which fairness and accuracy are unusually ambiguous or to approve of the increased U.S. use of its antidumping statutes.

## Countervailing Duties and Foreign Subsidies

Another form of unfair import pricing is presumed to occur when foreign exporting companies receive subsidies from their governments that result in reduced production costs and export prices below those that market forces would dictate. Public sector subsidies to producers are considered an unfair trade practice because privately owned domestic companies are expected to compete with private foreign companies, but are not expected to compete with the combination of foreign companies and foreign governments. If subsidized goods are exported to the United States, consumers benefit from lower prices, but American workers and producers may be "unfairly" injured by them. To offset the effect of the subsidy, the U.S. countervailing duty law, the origins of which go back to 1897, provides for the imposition of a duty equal to the estimated impact of the subsidy on the price of each unit of the import in question. The bottom line is that a countervailing duty is designed to neutralize the financial benefits received by the foreign company that allowed them to charge below-market prices for exports to the United States.

Consideration of import relief under the countervailing duty statute begins when American producers, unions, wholesalers, or an association representing a domestic industry submit a petition to the Commerce Department and the ITC alleging injury from a foreign government subsidy on a specific product. The Commerce Department can also begin an investigation on its own initiative, although this rarely happens. The government then follows the same two-track procedure used in antidumping cases. American companies often file simultaneous complaints of both types of unfair practices against the same foreign companies; when this happens, the U.S. government conducts the two investigations concurrently.

The ITC initiates a preliminary investigation to determine whether there is a "reasonable indication" that the imports being investigated are in fact inflicting "material injury" on or threatening material injury to, domestic producers of like products. The Commerce Department conducts a preliminary investigation to determine whether there is a reasonable probability that a countervailable subsidy has been provided. A final investigation is begun if the ITC's preliminary injury determination is affirmative. Unless *both* agencies make final determinations, respectively, that material injury and an unfair trade practice have occurred, the process is terminated and no import relief action is taken. (The injury test is waived if the offending country is not a WTO member.) If they both make an affirmative determination, the Commerce Department imposes a countervailing duty (literally, a tariff) on each unit of the applicable merchandise from the country in which the subsidy has been found. The amount of the duty is what is necessary to negate the estimated effect of the subsidy on import prices on an item-by-item basis.[18] The duty is applied retroactively if the Commerce Department's preliminary determination found probable cause that a countervailable subsidy existed.

Before 1979, the U.S. countervailing duty statute, unlike those in most other countries, made no provision for an injury test as a prerequisite for imposing these penalty duties. In an example of the international regime constraints model of decision-making, Congress and the executive branch in 1979 responded to intensifying foreign pressure to remedy this omission. They brought the U.S. statute closer to international norms by requiring an injury test for imports, at least from countries that had at that time accepted the standards of the GATT code on subsidies.

The law defines a subsidy as a payment, or any form of income or price support, by a government or public body that confers an economic benefit on specified enterprises, industries, or groups of enterprises. Subsidies can be in the form of a direct transfer of funds (grants or loans on more favorable terms than market rates, for example), a potential direct transfer (loan guarantees at below-market interest rates, for example), foregone government revenue (tax credits or preferential tax rates for exporters), or artificially cheap input prices (discounted energy from a government-owned utility, for example). A domestic subsidy must be judged "specific" to be considered an unfair trade practice; that is, it must benefit an *individual* firm, industry, or group of enterprises. A government program that benefits *all* industries, such as public education or road construction, is not a countervailable subsidy. The key test is whether the subsidy is generally available. The appellate opportunities for the losing party in a U.S. countervailing duty case are exactly the same as those for antidumping cases, discussed above.

An average of twenty petitions were filed annually between 1980 and 2000 under the countervailing duty law (the number fluctuated considerably each year). During these same two decades, approximately 23 percent of all investigations resulted in an affirmative finding leading to the imposition of countervailing duties.[19] Of the forty-four countervailing duty orders still in effect at yearend 2000, the majority applied to steel products. The Commerce Department and the ITC are required to hold a "sunset review" no later than five years after imposition of a countervailing duty in order to determine whether it could be revoked without a continuation or recurrence of the injury caused by the offending subsidy.

With the enactment of the Uruguay Round Agreements Act in 1994 and the implementation of the WTO Subsidies Agreement, new legal strictures were introduced to U.S. government efforts to combat foreign subsidies. First, decisions by the Commerce Department about whether a countervailable subsidy exists must now be weighed according to established standards determining which actions constitute acceptable and unacceptable governmental assistance. The Subsidies Agreement unconditionally prohibits certain economic practices; these so-called *red-light subsidies* are those that are contingent upon export performance or substitution of domestic goods for imports by companies. Some domestic subsidies are unacceptable only when they are specific to certain companies or industries. Finally, *green-light subsidies* are considered acceptable and not grounds for retaliation; for example, certain research subsidies, aid to depressed regions, and subsidies that assist existing business facilities to meet new environmental protection requirements.[20] A second important change associated with the WTO agreement is that the United States (and other member countries) can ask that a dispute settlement panel rule that foreign subsidies hurt its exports in third markets and thereby violated international trade rules. A WTO complaint, if successful, might persuade a country to end a subsidy program across-the-board. A duty applied under the U.S. countervailing duty law imposes import fees only on a specific product. It has no direct impact on the source of the subsidy, that is, the action taken by a foreign government to provide financial help to private sector exporters.[21]

### Violation of Intellectual Property Rights

Section 337 of the Tariff Act of 1930 declares it unlawful to engage in unfair acts or unfair methods of competition in the importation or sale of imported goods. Most investigations under this section deal with allegations of the infringement of intellectual property rights, usually U.S. patents (investigations involving copyrights and trademarks occur less often). Section 337 can also be applied to imports linked to such unlawful practices as price fixing and false labeling or advertising. The ITC conducts Section 337 investigations through adjudicatory proceedings conforming to the Administrative Procedure Act. An administrative law judge issues an initial determination that is subject to review by the full commission. If a violation is found, the ITC may issue an exclusion order and/or issue a cease and desist order that is subject to presidential disapproval within sixty days (an action that virtually never occurs). Imports found to be in violation of Section 337s can be barred entirely from entry into the United States. Furthermore, because importation has been found unlawful, injury to domestic producers need not be established. When finding a violation of Section 337, the ITC must decide whether certain public interest factors (the public health and welfare, consumer interests, etc.) suggest the advisability of waiving the otherwise automatic exclusion of the imports.

In deciding whether an article has infringed upon a valid U.S. patent, the ITC applies the same law as a district court would when hearing a patent infringement case brought by one U.S. company against another. A violator of a cease and desist order under Section 337 is subject to a civil penalty of up to the greater of $100,000 per day or twice the domestic value of the articles concerned for each day they enter the country in violation of the order. All legal determinations under this section are subject to judicial review the U.S. Court of Appeals for the Federal Circuit and possible appeal to the U.S. Supreme Court. In 1988, a GATT expert panel found that Section 337 violated GATT national treatment rules by treating imports that violated intellectual property rights differently from the federal district court rules that applied to domestic products accused of having violated the same intellectual property rights. Section 337 was amended by the Uruguay Round Agreements Act of 1994 to conform to the GATT panel report.[22] Seventeen new Section 337 investigations were initiated during 2000, all dealing with allegations of patent infringement. The fifty-one exclusion orders based on violations of this statute that were in place at yearend 2000 covered products ranging from plastic bags to semiconductors.

## Export Promotion and Market-Opening Laws

The impact of export policy is no less important than the impact of import policy on domestic production, employment, and corporate profits. Yet laws governing exports are often overlooked in discussions of U.S. trade policy. Possible explanations include the relatively high profile accorded to import-induced injury and the frequency with which export control policy is subordinated to concerns of national security and human rights. Another explanation is that its unique ability to use its own currency to pay for all its imports rather than having to earn foreign exchange means that the United States has relegated export maximization to a second-tier issue. Whereas the antidumping and countervailing duty provisions, for example, are fairly technical and provide relatively objective criteria for determining when to impose tariffs, the statutes governing exports give the executive branch broad discretion in deciding how to regulate exports in a given situation.

There are two distinct categories of export laws to correspond to two opposite policy objectives. The first category seeks to increase exports through promotion and market-opening efforts; the second delegates authority to the president to impose restrictions on U.S. exports in retaliation for certain actions by foreign governments.

The U.S. government has a variety of legislatively-based programs for promoting U.S. exports. The Export-Import Bank supports about 2 percent of total U.S. exports through three programs that provide financing on terms better than those available from commercial banks and insurers, or not available at all. In dollar terms, the two largest programs extend export credit guarantees and export credit insurance to commercial banks providing trade credits for U.S. exports to countries where commercial and political uncertainties might discourage such lending. A third program offers direct financing to American exporters, primarily to match subsidized export credits offered to foreign competitors by their governments. Concessional credits are a form of export subsidy, but all major industrial countries maintain such programs in a "live and let live" environment that seeks to minimize the extent of below-market lending.

The Export-Import Bank operates under a fixed year, renewable charter under the Export-Import Bank Act of 1945 and has a budget that in recent years has averaged about $800 million annually. Various administrations have tried to make large reductions in its annual appropriation on the grounds that the bank's programs could be pared back with no significant damage to overall U.S. exports. Inevitably, business lobbying pressures on Congress resulted in its restoring some or all of the president's proposed budget cutbacks. (A description of export promotion programs run by the departments of Commerce and Agriculture can be found in Chapter 9).

The Foreign Sales Corporations (FSC) statute reduces the tax burden on U.S.-based companies that establish FSCs by exempting between 15 and 30 percent of taxable income received overseas from goods and services exported from the United States. This measure combines a limited incentive to export with an effort to replicate comparable tax benefits in other countries, some of which have different tax systems than the United States. FSCs have been mired in a prolonged trade dispute with the EU, which believes that they are a prohibited export subsidy under the WTO Subsidies Agreement (see Chapter 8). The FSC provision was enacted in 1984, three years after the EU successfully argued before a GATT dispute settlement panel that the operations of its predecessor, the Domestic International Sales Corporation, represented an illegal subsidy. In 1999, a WTO dispute settlement panel agreed with the EU's complaint that the revised FSC formula was insufficient to bring this tax provision into conformity with international rules. The U.S. government did not want to terminate the FSC tax benefit, nor did it want to face the economic costs associated with the EU's threat to impose retaliatory barriers of an unprecedented $4 billion, the estimated amount of tax exemptions provided by FSCs. The compromise strategy selected was for Congress to pass new legislation[23] designed specifically to comply with the WTO panel's ruling and meet the EU's objections. The Europeans were still not satisfied with the result, and history repeated itself. Once again, the EU filed a complaint with the WTO alleging that the remodeled FSC was still an illegal export subsidy, and in mid-2001 a dispute settlement panel once again ruled that the new U.S. law was still not WTO-compliant.

Sections 301 through 309 of the Trade Act of 1974 (as amended), collectively known as Section 301, comprise the major piece of U.S. trade legislation addressing foreign barriers and distortions harming U.S. export performance. Section 301 investigations into "unfair" foreign trade barriers and practices are conducted by the USTR office. An investigation is initiated if the USTR finds credibility in a petition filed by a company or group of companies; the agency may also self-initiate an investigation. After confirming that an action discriminating against U.S. exports exists, the USTR requests consultations with the relevant foreign government to discuss modification or elimination of the alleged infraction. Foreign practices that can be targeted by Section 301 include traditional trade barriers, denial to foreign companies of rights given to local companies ("national treatment"), allowing domestic firms to engage in anticompetitive behavior (that may or may not involve collusion against imports), and export subsidies on goods shipped to third countries. If the other government fails to respond in a manner deemed acceptable, the USTR has authority under U.S. law to retaliate in kind (see below).

Conditions for invoking Section 301 differ according to which of two situations exist. At the insistence of Congress, language was inserted into this provision making it "mandatory" for the USTR to take retaliatory action if it determines that a policy or action of a foreign country violates or is inconsistent with a trade agreement involving the United States, that is, it impinges on U.S. trade rights. Action is also technically required if the other country's trade action is "unjustifiable and burdens or restricts" U.S. commerce. At the insistence of the executive branch, additional language is included to provide enough backdoor escape devices that retaliatory action is never an absolute requirement. For example, the USTR is not required to act if the foreign country is taking steps to remedy the problem or is providing compensation to the United States for lost exports. The USTR can also waive retaliation if such action would have a disproportionately adverse effect on the U.S. economy or if it could cause serious harm to U.S. national security.

The second situation involves a determination that a foreign act, policy, or practice is "unreasonable or discriminatory and burdens or restricts" U.S. commerce. The USTR has discretionary authority in such cases to determine whether retaliation should be invoked if the other country refuses to act. Whether it is mandatory or discretionary, U.S. retaliation can consist of suspending a trade agreement or withdrawing from it, imposing tariffs or quotas on imports from the foreign country, or negotiating a new agreement to eliminate the offending policy. In principle, retaliation is supposed to approximate the value of lost U.S. exports. The USTR has broad discretion to decide which goods to target and the form of retaliation.

Although the establishment of an effective and widely used dispute settlement mechanism in the WTO did not change the letter or intent of the Section 301 statute, it did change how it is applied. Usually, a Section 301 investigation that identifies an action discriminating against U.S. exports now means that a complaint will be filed in the WTO (see Chapter 8). The multilateral venue would not be used when the other country preferred bilateral talks or was not a member of the WTO, or if the action that was the source of the U.S. complaint was outside of the WTO's jurisdiction.

In 1988, Congress lost patience and decided it was time to do something to alleviate its concern with the persistent U.S. trade deficit and remedy its perception that the administration was not sufficiently aggressive in seeking the removal of foreign trade barriers. Ignoring entreaties from the White House, Congress transferred Section 301 retaliation authority from the president to the USTR and added two enhancements to Section 301's jurisdiction. *Super 301* required that in 1989 and 1990, the USTR publicly identify "priority foreign countries" and unfair "priority practices" that were major impediments to U.S. exports (see Chapter 9). Having done so, the USTR was required to initiate a Section 301–style negotiation with each of the offending countries and aggressively press for relaxation of their designated barriers. Retaliation was authorized if the other government was not forthcoming.

Super 301 led to several market opening agreements with Japan (the main target of the provision), limited success with Brazil, and no response from India, the third country named in the initial "priority" list. The original two-year authority for Super 301 actions lapsed in 1990, but it has been periodically renewed by executive orders. The first renewal, in 1994, was largely inspired by the Clinton administration's mounting frustration with unsuccessful efforts to gain increased access to the Japanese market. By 2001, the Super 301 process had evolved into an annual statement containing the administration's overall trade expansion priorities for the forthcoming year, rather than the designation of specific countries that would be the subject of unilateral U.S. market-opening demands.

The purpose of yet another provision, Special 301, is to protect U.S. intellectual property rights (IPRs) in foreign markets and thereby minimize the displacement of overseas sales of American goods and services by counterfeits. (The Section 337 provision discussed above only addresses intellectual property violations of goods exported *to* the United States.) American producers of software, movies, CDs, digital video disks, and pharmaceuticals have been the hardest-hit victims of patent and copyright infringements in other countries. In administering this provision, the USTR annually issues a three-tier list of countries judged to have inadequate procedures in place to protect intellectual property or to be restricting imports of IPR-related products. "Priority foreign countries" are those judged the worst violators of U.S. IPRs. This designation means they will be the subject of a Section 301 investigation (unless the USTR determines that an investigation would be harmful to U.S. economic interests and explains why to Congress) and face possible retaliation if they fail to address the practices identified by the U.S. government. "Priority watch list countries" have been judged to have serious deficiencies in their IPR protection regime, but do not warrant bilateral consultations. "Watch list countries" indulge in practices that are the lowest level of concern. Disputes with China alleging piracy of software, CDs, and so on have been the most significant (in dollar terms) use of this statutory authority (see Chapter 10).

## Export Controls and Sanctions

The United States did not invoke peacetime controls on exports until the onset of the Cold War in the late 1940s created the perception of a new kind of strategic threat. The Export Control Act of 1949 established the ground rules of the new U.S. approach to export controls that persists to this day. The executive branch was delegated broad power to restrict exports for any of three reasons. The first is to protect national security by preventing foreign adversaries from obtaining weapons and technology that could contribute to their military capabilities. The second reason is to promote foreign policy objectives; this has been a frequently used provision that serves as the basis for various trade sanctions. It was used, for example, in 1979 by President Carter to reduce grain sales to the Soviet Union as punishment for its invasion of Afghanistan. The third stipulated reason to restrict exports is to minimize shortages and price increases; in this case, export controls are applied to commodities that are in short supply in the United States. The most important application of this authority is the near-total ban on exporting oil that has been pumped from wells in the United States.

The Export Control Act was renewed several times before being transformed in 1969 into the Export Administration Act (EAA), which, in turn, has been repeatedly extended and amended. The provisions of the EAA require exporters of goods and technical information to obtain licenses from the Commerce Department's Office of Export Administration. The export of most commercial goods is permitted by a general license, except for goods destined for certain countries subject to almost total embargoes (e.g., Cuba and North Korea). Some sensitive goods and technical data require special licenses to export. These goods are identified on a commodity control list containing some two hundred categories of goods and technologies and seven country groups ranked by perceived threat to U.S. national security. The Commerce Department issues licenses for listed goods and data only if it is satisfied that the items shipped abroad to friendly countries will not be diverted for potential military uses to a country deemed unfriendly to the United States.

Exporters whose economic interests have been adversely affected by the imposition of export controls and some members of Congress have been instrumental in having the EAA amended over the years to make these controls at least marginally less onerous and bring them slightly more into conformity with the relatively lenient standards of the other industrialized countries. In the pursuit of a policy of fewer controls and stricter enforcement, Congress has amended the act several times to reduce the number of goods on the control list. Efforts to this end include eliminating export license requirements for certain relatively low-technology items and introducing the principle of "foreign availability," which seeks to discourage the executive branch from restricting the export of goods available from foreign producers. Congress also has tried to reduce the overall regulatory burden to the business community by discouraging the imposition of export controls on goods under existing contracts and by shortening deadlines for the government to approve export licenses. Despite these efforts at restricting the president's discretion to control exports, the executive branch has been able to continue implementing export controls with relative autonomy.

The EAA also authorized U.S. participation in the informal multilateral export control forum known as the Coordinating Committee on Multilateral Export Controls (COCOM). For more than four decades, COCOM coordinated export control efforts among the NATO countries and Japan that sought to prevent the Communist countries from obtaining sensitive goods and technology. Gradually, other countries adopted more relaxed export control standards than the United States. This gap continued after the dissolution of COCOM in 1994 and the subsequent entry into force in 1997 of its even more informal replacement, the Wassenaar Arrangement.

Since 1989, Congress has tried unsuccessfully to make major revisions in U.S. export control legislation. The unusually perplexing question of exactly how to do this in a post–Cold War era characterized by globalized, fast-changing technology and the emergence of "rogue states" has prevented (at least through early 2002) passage of the numerous legislative proposals introduced for major reform of the EAA. The resulting combination of temporary extensions and extended periods during which the legislation lapsed entirely (export control authority in these years derived from executive orders issued under the International Emergency Economic Powers Act, discussed below) became a metaphor for the long-running policy split between hawks and doves on the issue of export controls and sanctions.

In response to the Arab boycott of Israel and efforts by Arab governments to punish foreign companies that do business with Israel, Congress amended the EAA in 1977 to prohibit U.S. firms or individuals from participating in boycotts organized by a foreign government against a friendly country. The antiboycott provisions prohibit U.S. companies either from refusing to do business with an Israeli, U.S., or other firm or individual in compliance with the Arab boycott or from providing information requested by Arab governments to assist the boycott. A U.S. person or firm that knowingly or willfully violates provisions of the EAA may be subject to substantial criminal and civil fines or imprisonment of up to ten years.

Several other statutes are part of the legal framework allowing the president to invoke export controls. The Nuclear Regulatory Commission is responsible for the licensing of nuclear materials and technology under the Atomic Energy Act. The Department of State has the responsibility to license exports of weapons and military-related services and maintains the Munitions Control List created by the Arms Export Control Act. The Narcotics Control Trade Act of 1986 delegates authority to the president to impose certain trade restrictions against countries that refuse to cooperate with U.S. efforts to control illegal narcotics trade. (Two country-specific sanctions acts, the Cuban Liberty and Democratic Solidarity Act, which is more commonly known as Helms-Burton, and the Iran and Libya Sanctions Act are discussed in Chapter 9.)

The president has special authority delegated from Congress to respond to an "unusual and extraordinary" threat to the national security, economy, or foreign policy of the United States under the International Emergency Economic Powers Act (IEEPA) of 1977. When the president declares a national emergency, the IEEPA grants him broad authority to regulate virtually any international trade or financial transaction relating directly to the declared emergency. The act urges the president to consult Congress before declaring an emergency and, once one is declared, requires him to submit a detailed report to Congress explaining and justifying the action. The IEEPA was used as the legal basis for continuing the U.S. export control regime whenever extensions of the EAA lapsed, and it has been used to impose trade sanctions on South Africa, Iran, Iraq, and other countries.

The Trading with the Enemy Act of 1917 (TWEA), originally designed to prohibit trade with an enemy during wartime, was gradually expanded to give the president broad authority to control domestic and international economic actions during periods of declared "national emergencies" in peacetime. Congress rescinded this power when it enacted the IEEPA in 1977.

Before that year, the TWEA was often invoked in circumstances that seemed far removed from its original purposes. For example, the Nixon administration's threat in 1971 to unilaterally impose barriers on imports of textiles from Japan if that country did not agree to a "voluntary" export restraint arrangement was based on the broad authority of this statute. The TWEA was also cited as legal authority for the administration's imposition of a tariff surcharge in that same year.

Another statute that indirectly regulates exports is the Foreign Corrupt Practices Act of 1977 (FCPA), as amended by the Omnibus Trade and Competitiveness Act of 1988. The FCPA resulted from a congressional investigation into the payment of bribes by U.S. companies to foreign governments and agents to obtain sales contracts. The statute prohibits a U.S. firm or its employees, agents, officers, or directors from obtaining or retaining business by improperly giving something of value directly or indirectly to a foreign official, foreign political party, or foreign party official or candidate. The act does not apply to "grease payments" intended to obtain a routine government service from a clerical employee, such as a customs official. Violations of the FCPA may result in substantial civil or criminal fines against the individuals and firms involved and imprisonment of up to five years. Many U.S. exporters have criticized the FCPA, claiming that it disproportionately disadvantages U.S. exports because many foreign companies continue to bribe foreign officials because other governments have fewer legal prohibitions on such practices.

A slight thaw in the relatively hard-line U.S. sanctions policy was suggested by passage of the Trade Sanctions Reform and Export Enhancement Act of 2000. In a nod to humanitarian concerns, it authorized (with conditions) commercial sales of food, medicine, and medical equipment to Cuba, Iran, Libya, North Korea, and Sudan. The hotly contested policy debates about whether the United States imposes excessive handicaps on its exporters through overusing sanctions and how well sanctions achieve their goals will be discussed in Chapter 9.

## Conclusions and Outlook

The trade statutes of the United States are uncommonly numerous and detailed. The complex and comprehensive nature of these laws is an inevitable outgrowth of a policymaking process that has emerged from a unique sharing of power by two branches of government. U.S. trade laws are the link between the complex political and economic pressures that shape the formulation of trade policy and the policies and programs that are ultimately adopted. An evaluation of the effectiveness of these statutes at any given time will be heavily influenced by the extent to which the evaluator likes or dislikes their output: the substance of trade policy.

U.S. laws regulating imports can never be fully consistent as long as they are assigned the task of helping attain two mutually exclusive policy goals. On the one hand, the preference of large, internationally active corporations for a world economic order relatively unfettered by government controls, together with the repeated expressions of faith by economists in the benefits of free trade, have led to laws liberalizing the flow of imports to the United States. On the other hand, the periodic political need to be responsive to domestic producers and workers claiming to have been injured by foreign competition has led to laws restricting the flow of imports. Besides addressing instances of social and economic disruption, import-restrictive laws serve a practical political purpose. Relief from intensifying foreign competition must be provided to at least some uncompetitive industries and workers as a way of softening the opposition of industry and organized labor to liberal trade policies. The underlying philosophy here is that a little bit of protection is better than a lot of protection.

U.S. laws regulating exports also have been shaped by two contradictory impulses, in this case simultaneous pressures for expansion and restrictions. A lack of consistency is the result. Export policy has been influenced by repeated efforts by many members of Congress, acting on behalf of their constituents, to force a relaxation in the executive branch's use of export restrictions and an intensification in the executive branch's efforts to reduce barriers to U.S. exports. In deference to the president's foreign policy prerogatives, Congress for the most part has recognized the need to resist severely limiting his discretion to restrict trade with countries acting in a manner offensive to U.S. interests and values. However, even this guideline is breached when Congress is particularly angry with a foreign government or receives intense constituent pressures, as seen in legislation directly imposing sanctions on Cuba, Iran, and Libya (see Chapter 9).

The writing of new trade laws and the revising of existing ones will continue indefinitely. Trade legislation will probably never stop having to catch up with the inevitable growth and change inherent in something as dynamic as international trade. New economic and political as well as new domestic and external contingencies will never stop materializing; this means that trade policymakers will constantly need additional legal authority and guidance to manage their enlarged responsibilities. No permanent set of laws will suffice as long as economies are becoming more sophisticated and more integrated.

## For Further Reading

Bhala, Raj. *International Trade Law: Theory and Practice.* New York: Lexis Publishing, 2001.

Boltuck, Richard, and Robert E. Litan, eds. *Down in the Dumps: Administration of the Unfair Trade Laws.* Washington, D.C.: Brookings Institution, 1991.

Hudec, Robert. *Enforcing International Trade Law.* Salem, N.H.: Butterworth Legal Publishing, 1993.

Jackson, John H. *The World Trading System: Law and Policy of International Economic Relations.* 2d ed. Cambridge, Mass.: MIT Press, 1997.

Long, William J. *U.S. Export Control Policy: Executive Autonomy vs. Congressional Reform.* New York: Columbia University Press, 1989.

Mastel, Greg. *Antidumping Laws and the U.S. Economy.* Armonk, N.Y.: M. E. Sharpe, 1998.

Stiglitz, Joseph. "Dumping on Free Trade: The U.S. Import Trade Laws." *Southern Economic Journal* 64, no. 2 (1997): 402–424.

U.S. Department of Commerce, Bureau of Export Administration. *Annual Report.* Available at www.bxa.doc.gov/publications/ann99toc.htm/.

U.S. House of Representatives, Committee on Ways and Means. *Overview and Compilation of U.S. Trade Statutes.* Available at www.frwebgate.access.GPO.gov/.

U.S. International Trade Commission. "Summary of Statutory Provisions Related to Import Relief." Available at www.usitc.gov/.

## Notes

1. U.S. International Trade Commission, *The Year in Trade, 2000,* June 2000, 5–18, 5–20, and A–50.

2. Two products may perform somewhat the same function and compete for customers—such as a passenger car and a motorcycle—but they are not necessarily alike or directly competitive.

3. J. F. Hornbeck, *Trade Adjustment Assistance for Firms: Economic, Program, and Policy Issues,* Congressional Research Service Report dated 1 February 2000, 2–3.

4. See, for example, Robert W. Crandall, "Import Quotas and the Automobile Industry: The Costs of Protectionism," *The Brookings Review* (summer 1984): 8–15.

5. See the discussion of like product issues in the section on the escape clause, above.

6. See Thomas A. Pugel, Peter H. Lindert, *International Economics,* 11th ed. (Boston: Irwin McGraw-Hill, 2000), 184–189, for an economic analysis of dumping and antidumping policies.

7. The procedures described for antidumping and countervailing duty investigations are based on U.S. International Trade Commission, "Summary of Statutory Provisions Related to Import Relief," accessed at www.usitc.gov.

8. If the Commerce Department makes a preliminary finding of dumping, it immediately "suspends liquidation" (i.e., it delays the formal completion of goods passing through customs) of the subject imports.

9. There may be many different prices paid by different importers for different volumes of the import. For example, producers may offer seasonal discounts, and many offer high-volume discounts. The ITA calculates a weighted average price from the many individual transactions over the six months prior to the filing of the petition.

10. U.S. International Trade Commission, "Antidumping and Countervailing Duty Handbook," November 1999, accessed at www.usitc.gov; and *The Year in Trade, 2000.*

11. Lewis Leibowitz, *Safety Valve or Flash Point? The Worsening Conflict Between U.S. Trade Laws and WTO Rules,* Cato Institute report, 6 November 2001, 2–3.

12. Joseph E. Stiglitz, "Dumping on Free Trade: The U.S. Import Trade Laws," *Southern Economic Journal* 64, no. 2 (1997): 410–11.

13. Greg Mastel, *Antidumping Laws and the U.S. Economy* (Armonk, N.Y.: M. E. Sharpe, Inc., 1998), 137, 141.

14. See: Cato Institute press release, 30 July 30 2001, announcing publication of a study called *Coming Home to Roost: Proliferating Antidumping Laws and the Growing Threat to U.S. Exports.*

15. Legally, a domestic industry can win antidumping relief demonstrating a threat of material injury, or by proving that the establishment of an industry is being retarded. In reality, however, final determinations in antidumping cases are usually based on actual injury rather than threat, and decisions based on retardation have been extremely rare.

16. See, for example, the letter dated 1 October 2001 to Ambassador Robert Zoellick signed by Senators Baucus, Rockefeller, and Bingaman. The text was posted in December 2001, accessed at www.usinfo.state.gov/wto/0110203/html/.

17. Richard Boltuck and Robert E. Litan, eds., *Down in the Dumps: Administration of the Unfair Trade Laws* (Washington, D.C.: Brookings Institution, 1991), 4.

18. Once the Commerce Department's ITA determines that a subsidy exists, valuing the net amount of the subsidy is more complicated than merely dividing the nominal amount of a

grant by the number of imports. For example, if a producer receives $1 million from the government for new equipment, what is the life of the subsidy? Generally, the ITA assumes that the subsidy continues to benefit the producer for the life of the equipment, but not necessarily in the same amount each year. Arguably, the amount of the subsidy may diminish over time as the equipment ages and depreciates, or it may increase as the producer has additional cost savings to reinvest each year. Another consideration is the time value of money. If a producer receives $1 million annually for ten years, it is not the same as receiving $10 million the first year; the producer would prefer to have the money sooner so that it can be invested. Therefore, it may be necessary to calculate the present discounted value of the stream of future payments.

19. U.S. International Trade Commission, "Antidumping and Countervailing Duty Handbook"; accessed at www.usitc.gov.

20. The formal agreement on what constitutes "green light" subsidies expired, and, in early 2002, no effort had been made to renew it.

21. Section 406 of the Trade Act of 1974 was enacted to provide a special procedure to deal with potential market disruption in the United States from a surge in imports from Communist countries where all industry received direct government funding. The transition of nearly all Communist countries from command economies to market-based economies has effectively rendered this provision a casualty of the Cold War's end.

22. House Ways and Means Committee, *Overview and Compilation of U.S. Trade Statutes;* accessed at the U.S. Government Printing Office: www.gpo.gov.

23. The FSC Repeal and Extraterritorial Income Exclusion Act of 2000 was the first U.S. legislation enacted specifically to comply with a ruling of a WTO dispute settlement panel.

# 8 The World Trade Organization: International Trade Law and Trade Liberalization

Given the multilateral nature of the international trading system, neither the United States nor any other country can unilaterally determine the rules that will guide its commercial relations with other countries. The domestic statutes discussed in the previous chapter do not exist in a legal vacuum; they seek to conform with international trade rules accepted and sometimes proposed by the United States. These rules are much like international laws because countries agree to follow them or to accept the right of trading partners injured by violations to retaliate in kind. This chapter reviews the history of multilateral negotiations that have progressively reduced barriers to trade and expanded the rules governing trade, explores the nature of the rules (the key principles in the GATT), examines the institutional framework for creating and enforcing international trade law (the GATT and WTO), and comments on the prospects for future reductions in trade barriers in the new trade round by a steadily increasing number of participating nations.

From 1947 to 1994, eight multilateral negotiations were held to reduce barriers to trade. In the first trade round, 23 countries, roughly half of them developed countries and half developing countries, agreed to reduce tariffs and to facilitate trade and rebuild their economies after World War II. They created the GATT to provide a set of principles and guidelines under which trade could be gradually liberalized. In the last completed trade round, the Uruguay Round concluded in 1994, 123 nations agreed to reduce a long list of tariff and nontariff barriers and to create the WTO with, for the first time, significant enforcement powers. In the half century following the initial 1947 GATT agreement, the eight trade rounds succeeded in reducing average tariffs on industrial products from roughly 40 percent to 3.8 percent and in lowering many other barriers; world trade grew fourteen fold. In November 2001, in Doha, Qatar, 140 nations agreed to an ambitious agenda for reductions in barriers to trade and investment in a ninth trade round.

## Why the GATT, and More Recently the WTO, Came Into Being

The Great Depression of 1929–1933 and the continuing economic malaise that lasted until World War II played an important part in changing attitudes toward the role of governments in economic affairs. The severity of the depression was due to various factors, including the action of the Federal Reserve System in contracting the money supply and raising interest rates when it should have done the opposite. It was worsened by an epidemic of protectionism that began in the United States and spread to other countries.

After the 1929 stock market crash, investment slowed, unemployment rose, foreign loans became increasing difficult to collect, and political support for keeping out imports reached a peak. In 1930, to "protect the American workers' standard of living," high tariffs were enacted (Smoot-Hawley law). Critics commented that the United States was "trying to collect debts from abroad and at the same time shutting out the import goods that could alone have provided the payment for those debts."[1]

Many nations followed the same policies as the United States. Each country, as it raised tariffs, imposed quotas and devalued its currency, acted as if it could improve its trade balance and its employment at the expense of others. As economists have often noted, "the fallacy of composition" was at work, the often erroneous belief that what is true of a part is therefore true of the whole. The results of the "beggar-thy-neighbor" policy were drastic declines in world trade, production, growth and jobs. World trade of about $3 trillion in 1929 fell to roughly $1 trillion by 1933; some countries resorted to barter, such as Latin American countries when they traded food staples to Germany in return for aspirin.

As a result, as World War II appeared to be drawing to a close, the leading nations of the world came together at Bretton Woods, New Hampshire; the conference was an attempt to create institutions that might help prevent another economic depression and reduce the likelihood of economic conditions in which another Hitler might flourish. At Bretton Woods, blueprints were developed for the IMF, to provide balance of payments loans to help countries avoid competitive devaluations; the World Bank (International Bank for Reconstruction and Development [IBRD]), to provide loans for economic development; and the ITO, to administer agreed-upon rules for trade.

In 1947, at the United Nations Conference on Trade and Employment in Havana, the Havana Charter for the International Trade Organization (ITO) was negotiated and the GATT was concluded as an annex to the charter. The Charter was signed in early 1948, but ratification by some national legislatures proved impossible. Many members of the United States Congress thought the ITO charter went too far in addressing the interests of other countries and in inviting discrimination against the United States. In 1950, the Truman administration announced that it would not seek congressional ratification of the Havana Charter. With no prospect of establishing the ITO, nations that wanted to liberalize trade decided to work with the GATT trade rules as a foundation. Although the GATT remained "provisional" from 1947 until 1994, its rules were gradually amplified and membership expanded. By the 1980s, the system needed an overhaul. Because many new kinds of trade agreements were added in the Uruguay Round, 1986–1994, support grew for creating an organization to administer these new rules and the idea for an ITO was revisited. The WTO was created as a part of the Uruguay Round.

## Trade Barrier Reduction Negotiations under the GATT

Although the GATT lacked the authority to enforce rules, it nonetheless brought about an impressive series of reductions of tariffs and other trade barriers. Table 8.1

TABLE 8.1   Summary of Rounds of Multilateral Trade Negotiations

| Year | Where Negotiated (Name of Round) | Subjects Covered | Number of Countries Negotiating |
|---|---|---|---|
| 1947 | Geneva | Tariffs | 23 |
| 1949 | Annecy, France | Tariffs | 13 |
| 1951 | Torquay, U.K. | Tariffs | 38 |
| 1956 | Geneva | Tariffs | 26 |
| 1960–1961 | Geneva (Dillon) | Tariffs | 26 |
| 1964–1967 | Geneva (Kennedy) | Tariffs and antidumping measures | 62 |
| 1973–1979 | Geneva (Tokyo) | Tariffs, non-tariff measures, "framework" agreements, *"codes" not accepted by all GATT members, called GATT à la carte"* Geneva/Uruguay Tariffs, non-tariff measures, rules, services, intellectual property dispute settlement, textiles, agriculture creation of WTO, et cetera, *"single-package"* all members accept | 123 |

tells quite a story. It illustrates how the world has gradually moved toward freer trade in the eight trade rounds since the first in Geneva 1947 until the Uruguay Round began in Punta del Este, Uruguay, in 1986, and was signed in Marrakesh, Morocco, in 1994. The first few rounds covered tariff reductions among 20 to 30 countries. As the tide of high tariffs receded through successive rounds, the shoals of nontariff barriers were exposed; as a consequence, beginning with the Kennedy Round of 1964–1967, there has been a steady increase in trade issues and participants.

When the first round of GATT negotiations was completed in 1947, 23 nations signed on and the amount of trade covered by the agreement was roughly $8 billion. When the Uruguay Round establishing the World Trade Organization was concluded in 1994, 123 countries were signatories and the amount of trade affected was nearly $7 trillion.[2] At the opening of the Doha WTO ministerial meeting in November 2001 (described later in the chapter), there were 140 members. The applications of China and Taiwan for accession were accepted in Doha and some 20 other countries were in various stages of applying for membership.

### The Tokyo Round

In the Tokyo Round, 1973–1979, a round that greatly expanded trade liberalization, participants achieved a one-third cut in tariffs. At the end of the round, the average import duty on industrial products had fallen to 4.7 percent. The large tariff cuts were encouraged by member agreement on the concept of "harmonization," the idea that there should be larger cuts in the higher tariffs and that the members should move toward more uniform tariff rates. In making "harmonization" a goal for the tariff negotiations, the participants were voicing support for two basic elements of trade policy theory. First, a tariff almost always lowers the well-being of each nation of the world, including the nation imposing the tariff. Second, the larger the range of tariffs, the greater the range of market distortion and the greater the economic welfare loss.[3]

The Tokyo Round also represented the first attempt to reform the international trade rules that had existed since 1947 by including many more issues and policies that could affect trade. On nontariff barriers, the Tokyo Round added "codes." Codes were agreements that were not accepted by the full GATT membership in contrast to all previously GATT agreed-upon measures. This was also called "GATT à la carte." Five of these codes provided rules governing Subsidies and Countervailing Measures, Technical Barriers to Trade, the "Standards Code," Import Licensing Procedures, Customs Valuation, and Antidumping (replacing the Kennedy Round code). In general, these codes specified practices that functioned as barriers to trade, noted those that were to be discontinued, and cited procedures that were in accord with GATT. Some practices that could act as barriers were not included because participants could not agree; some of these have become subjects in subsequent negotiations. The five codes became integral parts of the GATT in the Uruguay Round, which, in contrast to the Tokyo "à la carte" approach, was termed the "single package." An additional four codes were negotiated at Tokyo but not accepted by all the membership; they remained plurilateral agreements in the Uruguay Round. These are the Agreement on Government Procurement (aimed at limiting governments from favoring domestic suppliers and opening competition to the widest possible market), the International Bovine Meat Agreement, the International Dairy Arrangement, and the Agreement on Trade in Civil Aircraft.

In its large reductions in tariff barriers, mainly on manufactured goods, and in adding new subjects for trade rules, the Tokyo Round represented a major breakthrough in multilateral trade negotiation and paved the way for the Uruguay Round, in which the WTO was created.

## The Uruguay Round

The Uruguay Round took eight years to negotiate, 1986–1994, and broke more new ground than all the previous multilateral negotiations put together. The dispute settlement mechanism was radically restructured. Important new subjects and revisions of earlier topics were incorporated into the GATT rule system. With the exception of four plurilateral agreements noted in the previous paragraph, the 558 page "Legal Texts"[4] and some 25,000 pages listing individual tariff and other concessions were accepted as a *single package* by a membership that had doubled since the Kennedy Round. The texts of GATT 1947, as amended various times over the years, including in the Uruguay Round, are incorporated and remain as core rules for trade.

***The Creation of the WTO.*** The most significant innovation of the Uruguay Round was the creation of the WTO. The Legal Texts, called "GATT 1994," established the

**TABLE 8.2    Comparison of Dispute Settlement in the Original GATT and the WTO**

| | *GATT*<br>*GATT 1947* | *WTO*<br>*GATT 1994* |
|---|---|---|
| | Agreement | Organization |
| Dispute settlement | *Ambiguous* = decision-making, waiver authority, and legal status subject to consensus. Tokyo—3 paragraph "understanding"—if GATT Council (general membership) approves the decision it is binding, but *if a country loses in panel, it could block consensus in council.* | Generally *rule oriented.* Generally *automatic* = panel and appellate reports almost always binding. Dispute Settlement Understanding is 40 pages. *It eliminates "blocking" of final panel report unless there is a consensus against the decision.* |
| Procedure | Fragmented—8 to 10 steps | Unified and continuous (see Table 8.3) |
| Continuity | Jurisprudence of GATT 1947 for "consensus" in favor of a GATT finding. Consensus was not defined and one country was able to block consensus. | "Consensus" was defined as no formal objection by member present and is required to start a new trade round; BUT in dispute settlement, only a "consensus" against can block a decision. |

WTO as a legal organization to administer the new mechanism for dispute settlement and the many new trade agreements and rules adopted during the eight years of negotiations. The texts also gave the WTO the ability to enforce its decisions, which the original GATT never had. As noted in Table 8.2, in the original 1947 GATT, if a member lost in a review of a particular trade dispute, it could block consensus; in other words, it had a veto. In the WTO dispute settlement, a review can be overturned only if all members agree that it should be reversed; but this is highly unlikely because the winner in the dispute will probably not agree. Table 8.2 highlights key differences in dispute settlement between the original GATT ("GATT 1947") and the WTO ("GATT 1994").

In addition to creating an enforcement mechanism that could not be easily blocked, the Uruguay Round incorporated a broad reduction in farm subsidies, textile quotas, and industrial tariffs.

Four significant trade agreements were added in the Uruguay Round. Three covered new subjects, the General Agreement on Trade in Services (GATS), Trade-Related Aspects of Intellectual Property Rights (TRIPS), and Trade-Related Aspects of

Investment Measures (TRIMS). The fourth, Agreement on Agriculture, addressed a subject of previous GATT negotiations, but one that had been particularly intractable. The Uruguay Round texts also include agreements that updated and broadened earlier GATT rules, including agreements on Sanitary and Phytosanitary Measures, Textiles and Clothing, Technical Barriers to Trade, Implementation of Article VI of the GATT 1994 (on dumping), Pre-shipment Inspection, Rules of Origin, Import Licensing Procedures, Subsidies and Countervailing Measures and Safeguards, and a series of "Ministerial Decisions" and declarations on specifics in the overall Uruguay Round Agreement. The texts of GATT 1947, as amended at various times over the years, including in the Uruguay Round, are incorporated and remain as core rules for trade. The broad new scope of the WTO is well illustrated by the SPS (see below) and TRIPS agreements.

The *Sanitary and Phytosanitary Agreement (SPS)* elaborates on Article XX of the GATT, which allows governments to restrict trade when *necessary* to protect the life and health of humans, animals, and plants. These measures are permitted as long as they do not create different limits for different countries (the principle of nondiscrimination) and as long as they are not a disguised means of protecting domestic interests. For example, if a WTO member wishes to ban the import of beef that has been treated with hormones, the ban must be based on scientific principles, evidence, and assessment.

The *intellectual property agreement, the TRIPS,* covers copyrights, trademarks, patents, geographical product labeling, industrial designs, integrated circuit design, and other proprietary information. In each area, WTO members must change laws or regulations to put them in accordance with the standards agreed upon in TRIPS. For example, in the area of patents, members must defend standards regarding what is patentable, what exceptions are permissible, the rights of the patent holder, and the length of the patent protection.

The Uruguay Round agreements are complex, and the interpretation of the many rules and agreements is evolving in the common law of dispute settlements (discussed later in this chapter).

# The Trade Principles of the GATT and WTO

The core principles of the original GATT ("GATT 1947") are carried over in the WTO ("GATT 1994"). In general, these principles are the pillars of the two transcendent concepts of multilateral trade rules: nondiscrimination, and the view that protectionism weakens the world economy and liberalization strengthens it. These international trade rules, as amended somewhat in several trade rounds since 1947, and notably in the Uruguay Round, explain the success of the GATT and the WTO in expanding trade.

### 1. The principle of nondiscrimination

A. *Most-favored-nation (MFN), now called Normal Trading Relations (NTR) by the United States.*   MFN prevents countries from discriminating between trading partners who are members of the GATT/WTO. With MFN, if you grant a trade benefit to one country (such as a lower tariff on one of its products) that would make it temporarily the "most-favored-nation," you must do the same for all members of the WTO. MFN acts as a firewall between the possible political desire of a nation to favor another nation and the economic goal of lowering barriers equally among a group of nations that are members of the WTO and GATT. This parity is so important that it is enshrined in Article I of the General Agreement on Tariffs and Trade. To illustrate, consider the following hypothetical example: suppose the United States and Switzerland were negotiating tariffs concessions, as each member does with each other member during each trade round. The U.S. tariff on watches is 10 percent and the Swiss tariff on hard winter wheat is 12 percent. The United States wants lower Swiss tariffs on a series of products, including hard winter wheat. Switzerland wants lower U.S. tariffs on various products, including watches. Suppose that, as a part of the respective lists of bilateral tariff reductions, the United States reduces its tariff on watches to 5 percent and Switzerland lowers its tariff on hard winter wheat to 6 percent. At that instant they are each other's "most-favored-nation" for those products. Under Article I of the GATT, however, the U.S. tariff on watches is now 5 percent, not just for Switzerland but for all GATT members, and Switzerland's tariff on hard winter wheat is 6 percent for all GATT members. So each set of tariff negotiations on a bilateral basis led to massive tariff reductions on a multilateral basis.

MFN is also important in the GATS and in TRIPS, discussed later in the chapter. Few exceptions to MFN are allowed. One is for free trade areas such as NAFTA or for customs unions such as the European Union if they facilitate trade between the constituent territories and do not raise barriers to other WTO members (see Chapter 12).[5] Another exception involves raising barriers on goods that are traded unfairly, which is discussed below under core trade principle number 4.

**B.** *National treatment.*    National treatment, covered in Article III of the GATT, gives foreign goods the same treatment, legal and regulatory, in the domestic market as locally produced goods. This covers nondiscrimination between equivalent imported and nationally produced products for taxation, regulation, or requirements that affect the sale, use, purchase, and distribution of the products. The few exceptions mostly apply to certain government purchases.

## 2. Freer trade gradually through negotiation
Barriers to trade are gradually reduced through successive rounds of trade negotiation and application of the most-favored-nation principle.

## 3. Predictability through binding
When countries reduce trade barriers, they "bind" them; that is, they commit not to raise them. If a country wants to change its bindings it must negotiate with its trading partners and compensate them for the estimated loss of trade. The result is that bindings seldom change. This stability and predictably can be as important as lowering barriers because it gives producers and traders a clearer idea of business opportunities over the longer term. Investment is encouraged, jobs are created, and consumers can enjoy the benefits of competition—choice and lower prices. The Uruguay Round, completed in 1994, greatly increased bindings, as shown in Table 8.3.

TABLE 8.3   The Large Jump in Tariff Bindings During the Uruguay Round

| Percent of Tariffs Bound | Before (%) | In Uruguay Round (%) |
|---|---|---|
| Developed countries | 78 | 99 |
| Developing countries | 21 | 73 |
| "Transition" (former communist) economies | 73 | 98 |

### 4. Promoting fair competition

The WTO is often described as a "free trade" institution. More accurately, the WTO is the administrative arm for a system of rules that have been negotiated by its members. In general, the rules are concerned with open, fair, and undistorted competition. Most-favored-nation and national treatment—the rules on nondiscrimination—are clearly designed to secure fair trade (see Chapter 7). However, if rules are violated, such as when a producer in one country exports to another country at below cost to gain market share, or receives a subsidy for exporting, fair trade allows retaliation in the form of antidumping or countervailing duties.

### 5. Resolution of disputes through the rule of law

The WTO's singular and most controversial contribution to the world trading system is its new mechanism for settling disputes. If one member country believes that the trade rules of the WTO are being violated by another member country, it can call for consultations with the alleged violator(s). If the dispute can not be resolved by consultation or negotiation, the dispute is reviewed by a panel of three to five people. If either the plaintiff or defendant is not satisfied with the decision of the panel, that party can subsequently take the dispute to an appeals panel. Consultations and negotiations between the interested parties are the preferred means of resolving a dispute. Throughout the dispute settlement, including the meetings of the panel and the appeals panel, consultations are encouraged. A little more than half the disputes presented have gone to panel; the others have been settled by consultations or negotiations between the interested parties. The panels are chosen from a list of candidates selected by the member states for their professional or academic credentials and reputation for impartiality and competence. The appeals panels are chosen in a similar fashion from a list of specially qualified jurists or specialists having knowledge of the issue in dispute. Typically, the panelists are from nations perceived to be neutral in the dispute. Parties can block the selection of panelists, as in the jury selection process; if an impasse develops, the Director General names the panelists. The key points of the new dispute settlement are:

- *Decisions by the panels cannot be blocked by a single country,* as was possible in the previous GATT. This reinforces the commitment a country makes when it signs onto the WTO.
- *The procedure is based on the rule of law.* The Uruguay Round treaty and its component agreements are the law. One hundred and forty member nations had agreed to it by the opening of the Doha conference in November 2001. A panel decision can be appealed to an appeals panel based on points of law.

**TABLE 8.4   The Dispute Settlement Timetable**

| *First Stage* | *Consultation Before Any Other Action* |
|---|---|
| 60 days | Countries consult and can ask the Director General to mediate. |

| *Second Stage* | *The Panel and, if Necessary, the Appeals Panel* |
|---|---|
| 45 days | Panel is set up and panelists appointed. |
| 6 months | Panel issues report to the parties to the dispute. |
| 3 weeks | Panel circulates the report to WTO members. |
| 60 days | Dispute Settlement Body (DSB), the WTO members, adopt the report. |

| **Total: 1 year** | **From initiation to adoption of the Panel Report. If a party wishes to appeal the panel report, it goes to an Appeals Panel.** |
|---|---|
| 30–90 days | Appeals Panel is selected and appeals report is prepared. |
| 30 days | Dispute Settlement Body adopts any changes to the panel report made in the appellate report. |

| **Total: 3 months** | **General amount of time for an appeal.** |
|---|---|
| *Last Stage* | *Implementation, Negotiation Between the Disputants, or Retaliation* |
| "reasonable period of time" | Implementation: losing party reports its proposed implementation within a "reasonable period of time." Proposed actions to implement and amount of time are approved by the parties in dispute. If not, an arbitrator is appointed and member has approximately 15 months to comply. In cases of non-implementation, (a) the parties to the dispute can negotiate compensation pending full implementation or (b) DSB authorizes retaliation by the winning party to the dispute pending full implementation. |
| 30 days | DSB authorizes retaliation (on the same or other sectors or other agreements) until implemented OR parties negotiate agreement or "compensation." |

| **Maximum Time** | **1 year + 3 months + 16 months = 2 years and 7 months** |
|---|---|

- *Timetables are clearly set out,* and they allow several avenues to reach a settlement. Table 8.4 summarizes the key steps in resolving a dispute.

In one of the first cases decided in the WTO, Venezuela, and, later, Brazil, petitioned for WTO action against the United States because of its pollution control rules on reformulated gasoline. Venezuela claimed that the United States applied stricter rules on gasoline additives in imports than it did on domestically refined gasoline and thus violated the key WTO principle of "national treatment." The case is interesting because developing countries challenged a developed country and because it involved environmental regulations. The environmental controversy over the WTO and details of this case are discussed later in the chapter. Table 8.5 illustrates how an actual case often follows the dispute settlement timetable.

## Overview of the Dispute Settlement Mechanism

Is it a perfect system? No. Will it be amended at some time? Yes. (See the agenda agreed to at the Doha, Qatar, trade conference later in this chapter.) Although the dispute settlement procedure is transparent, it could be made more so. Official parties to a dispute (i.e., the governments), can present their viewpoints, but some argue for allowing amicus briefs.[6] The panel selection process is spelled out and parties can reject panelists they do not want, although some advocate the creation of a larger panel corps from which to select. Other critics claim that the WTO Secretariat (see the section on the structure and evolution of the WTO) has too much power and may suffer from conflicts of interest and that the panels and appellate bodies make law that is not in the WTO. Most of these criticisms derive from decisions in the most controversial cases. Whatever one's point of view, the WTO dispute settlement process is a type of judicial review of cases presented by plaintiffs and defendants based on the WTO/GATT texts. In contrast to courts in individual countries, oversight of WTO judicial decisions is delayed for years until a new trade round begins and the members of the organization can clarify, improve, and add to the GATT texts. Some argue that this might be improved by creating some form of interim review of WTO decisions and establishing a full-time group of judges to serve on the appellate panels.[7]

*The question of sovereignty.* Because decisions can*not* be blocked by one country, a country found in violation of a WTO/GATT trade rule must either end the violation, compensate the plaintiff in a manner satisfactory to the plaintiff, or be faced with trade barrier retaliation, usually high tariffs on an amount of trade equal to the estimated amount of trade affected by the violation. So, in joining the WTO, a country cedes some sovereignty for making trade policy in that it might receive what it considers undue pressure from an international organization, the WTO, to change its trade policy. This was a point of contention in various countries as they negotiated in Uruguay and later sought ratification of the Uruguay agreements.

In the debate in the U.S. Congress over ratification, some representatives and senators raised the sovereignty issue implicit in the WTO Dispute Settlement Mechanism (DSM). Concerns were expressed that the WTO might make decisions overriding U.S. trade laws or be otherwise objectionable. However, since the WTO's inception, the United States has been the most frequent plaintiff in the dispute settlement process and, with few exceptions (see discussion of the beef hormones and Foreign Sales Corporation cases below), the United States has generally been satisfied with the WTO DSM through at least 2001. The sovereignty issue has faded in other countries, too, as they have used the DSM. The number of disputes filed in the DSM—nearly 250 since the WTO began operating in 1995 through early 2002—suggest that the WTO members believe in it. During the life of "GATT 1947," from

TABLE 8.5    Reformulated Gas Case: Venezuela-U.S. (time to resolve: 2 years and 7 months)

| Target | Date | | Action |
|---|---|---|---|
| | 1990 | | U.S. Clean Air Act amended. |
| | Sep | 1994 | U.S. restricts imports under the act. |
| | Jan | 1995 | Venezuela complains to the DSB. |
| 60 days | Feb | 1995 | Consultations fail (30 days). |
| | Mar | 1995 | Venezuela requests a panel. |
| 45 days | Apr | 1995 | DSB agrees, U.S. says it won't try to block panels, Brazil joins and supports Venezuela during the process. |
| 6 months | Dec | 1995 | Panel gives report to Venezuela, Brazil and U.S. |
| | Jan | 1996 | Panel circulates final report to DSB. |
| | Feb | 1996 | U.S. appeals. |
| 60 days | Apr | 1996 | Appellate Panel submits its report. |
| 30 days | May | 1996 | DSB adopts panel and appellate reports. |
| | Dec | 1996 | U.S. and Venezuela reach agreement on implementation. |
| | Jan | 1997 | U.S. sends its first report to DSB on implementation. |
| | Aug | 1997 | New U.S. regulations equalize treatment of imports and domestic production. Implementation period ends with U.S. compliance. |

1947–1994, 195 GATT panels were convened.[8] The comparatively small number is due to there being many fewer members of the GATT in the early years and the fact that, although some of these panels resulted in recommendations that were adopted, others were thwarted by the ease of blocking consensus under the GATT 1947.

Also, evaluations of the WTO dispute settlement process[9] suggest that most of the panel decisions have been thought consistent with the trade rules the members negotiated. Usually, the decision has been accepted and the trade violation has ended. An evaluation of WTO dispute settlement from the U.S. perspective was submitted to Congress by the U.S. General Accounting Office (GAO) in June 2000. Through April 2000, 187 complaints had been filed. Of these, 42 involved the United States and had been resolved either by the parties or with a WTO ruling. The United States was plaintiff in 25 cases and defendant in 17. Overall, the GAO concluded that the United States had gained more than it had lost. Three-fourths of the cases filed by the United States led other WTO members to change their practices, and some of these changes benefited U.S. exports. When the United States was obliged to amend its laws or regulations, the GAO concluded that the changes were minimal and technical.[10]

This analysis is useful, but it was completed before the Foreign Sales Corporation case involving roughly $4 billion of trade. The FSC case is related to two other acrimonious cases, one on bananas (resolved in 2001) and another on beef hormones, that concern the two largest members of the WTO, the United States and the EU (see

Chapter 11). In another important case involving the United States and the EU, the Section 301 case, a reasonable solution was found.

## Is Section 301 of the U.S. Trade Act of 1974 Consistent with U.S. Obligations in the WTO?

The EU questioned whether fundamental U.S. trade law is consistent with the WTO, particularly in reference to Section 301 of the Trade Act of 1974, as amended, the principal U.S. statute for addressing foreign unfair practices affecting U.S. exports and enforcing U.S. rights under bilateral and multilateral trade agreements (see Chapter 7).[11] In 1998, the EU alleged that Section 301 was incompatible with the WTO because it obliges the United States to act unilaterally in disregard of the multilateral nature of the WTO dispute settlement.[12] The EU charged that Section 301 set time limits for determinations and trade sanctions that could take place before a WTO dispute settlement was concluded. The WTO panel reviewed the case in 1999 and upheld the consistency of Section 301 with the WTO. Both the United States and the EU claimed vindication. The United States emphasized that it had and would continue to act "in accordance with its WTO obligations in every Section 301 determination involving an alleged violation of U.S. WTO rights."[13] The EU stressed that Section 301 was in conformity only because the United States told the panel that "in each and every case it would use its discretionary powers . . . in compliance with WTO rules and procedures."[14]

## The Beef Hormone Case[15]

At issue is the ban by the EU of six growth-promoting hormones in beef, including imports of beef products in which the hormones have been employed. The U.S. Food and Drug Administration and its equivalents in approximately twenty other countries have approved the use of the hormones in beef production. The only hormone of the six that is a known carcinogen in large amounts is oestradiol–17ß, natural estrogen, which all animals produce internally. For promoting faster growth and leaner meat, a pellet containing hormones is inserted in the cow's ear. 1.9 ng (nanogram = 1 billionth of a gram) of estrogen is found in three ounces of implanted steer. There are 34 ng in 8 oz of milk; 993 ng in an egg; 2,700 ng in 4 oz of cabbage; and 35,000 ng in a low-dosage birth control pill.

Prior to 1981 in Europe, some countries permitted the use of hormones, others did not. To determine a common policy in 1984, the European Commission set up a scientific group of twenty-two notable European scientists to study the matter. The scientists concluded that the hormones were safe as growth-promoting agents when used according to good veterinary practices and proposed that the European Parliament not ban the hormones. But the Parliament rejected the proposal, claimed the scientific information was not complete, added that "there is overproduction of meat and meat products in the European Community which adds considerably to the cost of the CAP [EC's Common Agricultural Policy]",[16] and insisted on a ban.

In 1987, the United States invoked dispute settlement under the Tokyo Round on Technical Barriers to Trade. The EC blocked the formation of the technical experts' group, effectively ending the review. In 1996, armed with subsequent studies approving the use of hormones, including one from the Codex Alimentarius Commission, which is recognized by the WTO as the source of international standards for food safety purposes, the United States and Canada sought a WTO ruling. In 1997, the panel found the EU ban violates EU obligations under the SPS because it is not based on scientific evidence, on risk assessment, or on relevant international standards. The appeals panel noted that a WTO member has the right to choose the level of health protection it deems appropriate, but said the ban was not reasonably supported by available scientific evidence and thus did not satisfy the SPS agreement. After the EU failed to implement the WTO recommendation to bring its practices into conformity with the SPS, the United States and Canada were allowed by the WTO to invoke sanctions of 100 percent duties on EU exports (on $116.8 million for the United States and Can$11.3 million for Canada).

## The Foreign Sales Corporation Case[17]

The EU was unhappy with these sanctions and with those following a ruling against the EU on the bananas case (since resolved). Some argue that as a result of these two cases the EU decided to challenge the foreign sales corporation ("FSC") provisions of the U.S. tax law, claiming that they constitute prohibited export subsidies under the Subsidies Agreement, and that they violate the export subsidy provisions of the Agreement on Agriculture. Approximately $4 billion in U.S. exports is involved.

The dispute is rooted in long-standing differences between EU and U.S. corporate income tax structure: EU corporations are taxed on a "territorial" basis (i.e., only on income in the jurisdiction in which it is earned), whereas U.S. companies are traditionally taxed on a "worldwide" basis (i.e., on income earned anywhere in the world when the income is repatriated to the United States).[18] In addition, EU countries have long relied on an *indirect* tax system using value-added taxes, which may be rebated upon export without triggering a subsidies finding, whereas the United States relies mainly on a *direct* tax system—the corporate income tax. Rebates of *direct* taxes upon exportation were prohibited in the 1947 GATT.[19] Accordingly, the United States has enacted laws over the years to equalize, in some fashion, the grievances which U.S. corporations have expressed against the more advantageous tax scheme from which EU companies benefit when they export. One law had allowed U.S. companies (and EU and other foreign companies with operations in the United States) to shelter a portion of their export earnings from U.S. income tax by recording export sales through FSC subsidiaries.

In October 1999, a WTO panel found that the FSC tax exemption constituted a prohibited export subsidy under the Subsidies Agreement and also violated U.S. obligations under the Agriculture Agreement. The United States appealed. In February 2000, the Appellate Body said, "A Member of the WTO may choose any kind of tax system it wishes—so long as, in choosing, that Member applies that system in a way that is consistent with its WTO obligations. . . . Subsidies contingent upon export performance . . . are not permitted under the covered agreements."[20] The United States repealed the FSC law in November 2000 (FSC Repeal and Extraterritorial Income Exclusion Act of 2000—ETI), and excluded taxes on profits of any goods outside the United States but required that 50 percent of the value be produced in the United States. The EU then filed a new complaint, which was decided against the United States. Although the EU has spoken of levying 100 percent duties on lists of U.S. imports worth $4 billion, Pascal Lamy, the European Union Commissioner for Trade, and Robert Zoellick, the U.S. Trade Representative, have pledged to work together on a new trade round and on resolving pending disputes.[21] In January 2002, the WTO Appellate Body found that the November 2000 U.S. act repealing the FSC (the aforementioned Extraterritorial Income Exclusion Act) was inconsistent with U.S. obligations under the WTO. U.S. Trade Representative Zoellick expressed disappointment with the decision and said that it "raises questions of a level playing field with regard to tax policy"; but he pledged to cooperate with the EU in managing and resolving the dispute and to work with Congress on the next steps.[22] The amount of trade involved and the threat of a trade war between the two largest economies in the WTO if sanctions were invoked have led to hope and expectations that a compromise solution can be achieved.

## Criticisms of the WTO from Environmental and Labor Activists

The principles of the WTO—nondiscrimination, predictable commitments, fairness in rules and dispute settlements, and recognition of a nation's right to protect its environment—seem reasonable and fair, yet advocates for environmental and labor causes have been extremely vocal in their criticisms of the WTO. Why?

Two reasons are the changing *context* of trade liberalization and the new *scope* of the WTO. From 1947 until the 1990s, trade issues involved mostly tariffs and quotas and negotiations took place in the context of the Cold War; this meant that open trade among non-Communist countries generally received bipartisan support. Now formerly Communist countries are joining the WTO, and the WTO treaty has far wider scope than the first GATT; for this reason, some see the WTO as an organization with a large mandate, one they might use to promote their specific interests. Another set of critics, such as some of those who appeared at the Seattle meeting in 1999 (see discussion below), oppose the very existence of the WTO. They see WTO success in resolving trade issues as aiding multinational corporations and capitalism, which they denounce.

### Environment

Critics, such as members of Public Citizen, assert that "the WTO has been a disaster for the environment."[23] To back up their claims, they and other environmental activists often cite the Reformulated Gas Case, the Shrimp-Turtles Case, and the Tuna-Dolphin Case. These cases are discussed below, and a careful review of them shows that none of them resulted in lower environmental standards. Rather, the cases highlighted environmental concerns and the right of countries to choose environmental standards as long as they did so in a way that did not discriminate between nations. Although the agreement establishing the WTO is competent only to deal with trade, its preamble states that WTO goals include sustainable development and environmental protection (see Chapter 13). In addition, various WTO agreements include "green" provisions, which recognize and support environmental objectives as long as the principles of nondiscrimination and transparency are observed. In so doing, the WTO and some two hundred Multilateral Environmental Agreements (MEAs), which exist to protect the environment, avoid conflict. Some of the MEAs allow trade bans and trade restrictions in certain instances. Among these MEAs are the Montreal Protocol for protection of the ozone layer; the Basel Convention regarding trade or transportation of hazardous waste; and the Convention on International Trade in Endangered Species (CITES).

In the *Reformulated Gas Case,* (see dispute settlement timetable outlined earlier in this chapter) Venezuela and Brazil claimed that the United States had discriminated against foreigners in its implementation of the Clean Air Act. Under this act, the Environmental Protection Agency sets standards for gasoline to reduce pollution. Both the WTO panel and Appellate Body found that the standards applied to gasoline exports from Venezuela and Brazil were more burdensome than those applied to domestic U.S. refineries. In certain circumstances, even though a domestic refiner and a foreign refiner refined gasoline having identical chemical composition, the foreign refiner did not meet the standard and the U.S. refiner did.[24] The WTO Appellate Body notably upheld the right of the United States to adopt the highest possible standard to protect its air quality, provided that it did so in a way that was not discriminatory.

The *Shrimp-Turtle Case* involved restrictions by the United States on the import of shrimp from India, Malaysia, Pakistan, and Thailand because these countries did not require commercial shrimp trawlers to use Turtle Excluder Devices (TEDs), which protect endangered sea turtles. In April 1998, a WTO panel found the U.S. measure inconsistent with Article XI proscriptions on import restrictions. When the United States appealed in October 1998, the panel's finding was reversed by the Appellate Body. The Appellate Body found that the U.S. law is covered by the exception in GATT Article XX (g) for measures relating to the conservation of exhaustible natural resources and that all WTO agreements must be read in light of the preamble to the WTO agreement, which endorses sustainable development and environmental protection. However, the Appellate Body ruled that the United States had unjustly discriminated among exporting countries in applying the law and instructed it to amend the law accordingly. The United States did so and offered technical assistance to shrimp fishing nations in the use of TEDs.

Nonetheless, in October 2000, Malaysia, alone, challenged the U.S. administration of the ruling. A WTO panel, in June 2001, and an appeals panel, in October 2001, found that U.S. implementation of its sea turtle protection law is fully consistent with WTO rules and complies with the earlier recommendation.

*The Tuna-Dolphin Case* was brought by Mexico and others against the United States under GATT in 1991. It stemmed from an embargo the United States had imposed on the imports of tuna that had been caught in "purse seine" nets[25] because such nets resulted in the deaths of many dolphins. Because the U.S. embargo was based on the Marine Mammal Protection Act, the case involved two interesting issues:

- whether one country can tell another what its environmental regulations should be and
- whether GATT rules allow a country to take action against the *method* another country used to produce the goods (i.e., versus the *process,* not the *product*).[26]

A panel found that if the U.S. arguments were accepted, any country could ban imports because the exporting country had different environmental, health, and social policies from its own. This GATT review preceded the existence of the WTO. The panel report was never adopted, and the problem was eventually resolved by cooperation between the United States and Mexico to improve fishing methods.

## Labor

The issues involved are whether the WTO should be used to pressure countries to honor "core labor standards"; whether a country employing lower labor standards gains an export advantage; and whether it is proper to discuss labor questions in the WTO. Core labor standards refer to the treatment of workers and include a wide range of issues from child labor and forced labor to the right to organize trade unions and strike (see Chapter 13).

*Labor critics of the WTO argue that the WTO should include labor as part of its mandate.* For example, in testimony before the House Ways and Means Committee in May 2000, representatives of the United Auto Workers said: "As long as the WTO rules fail to contain protections for the rights of workers . . . the WTO . . . just advances the interests of corporations and economic elites and not the well being of working men and women."[27] Defenders of the WTO say this type of argument concerns workers in certain industries or unions rather than workers in general, who, they believe, benefit from freer trade.

*Economists argue that labor issues should not be part of the WTO.* Many economists fear that including labor in the WTO could lead to trade barriers based on labor issues and believe this would seriously impede the WTO's work to sponsor trade liberalization. They defend the ability of trade to lead to net job creation, lower costs, greater choices, and increased wages in the export sector. They employ theoretical arguments, beginning with David Ricardo's theory of comparative advantage, and empirical arguments, including the great increases in trade and growth during the 1890 to WWI era of globalization, the great decreases in trade and growth following the Smoot-Hawley tariff and retaliatory measures by other countries, and the striking contrast in recent decades of high growth in countries that opened their economies and slow growth in countries that practiced import substitution.[28]

*Job losses as trade is liberalized.* Undeniably, however, as trade liberalization proceeds, some producers and their workers lose their jobs to new competition. Some adapt quickly and find other employment either by moving to another area or through education and training. Some countries are better than others at easing the transition; they have more efficient markets and more effective adjustment policies, education, retraining and social safety nets. To the extent that trade boosts the economy as a whole, there are potentially more resources that can be used in the adjustment process.

*What do the WTO* texts *say in regard to these arguments?* First, tariff and other trade barrier reductions are made gradually to provide countries time to adjust. Second, WTO rules permit the use of certain safeguard or contingency measures if imports are particularly damaging. Third, members may adopt measures to block the products of prison labor.

*What do the WTO* members *say in regard to these arguments?* As for including workers' rights in the WTO, a large majority of WTO members are opposed. At the 1996 Singapore ministerial, labor standards were discussed and it became clear that most developing countries and some developed nations believed that although workers' rights are important and deserve international attention, the WTO was not the right organization. A ministerial declaration was issued in which participants said they "renew our commitment to the observance of core labor standards"[29] and affirmed that the International Labor Organization (ILO), which was established in 1919 and which has formulated approximately 170 labor standards conventions,[30] was the competent body to deal with these standards. The WTO ministerial declaration rejected the use of labor standards for protectionist purposes and noted that "comparative advantage of countries, particularly low-wage developing countries, must in no way be put into question."[31] The declaration affirmed that the Secretariats of the WTO and the ILO would continue to collaborate. In 1998, the ILO members, generally the same as those in the WTO, adopted a declaration endorsing freedom of association, the right to collective bargaining, the elimination of forced labor, and the effective abolition of child labor. In 1999, the ILO members agreed further to prohibit the worst forms of child labor while recognizing that child labor is largely a function of poverty and that sustained growth is the key to eliminating its abuses. In the 1999 WTO ministerial in Seattle, a new proposal to use WTO mechanisms to enforce labor rights led many developing countries to announce their withdrawal from the negotiations (see discussion of the Seattle conference later in this chapter and in Chapter 13).

## The Structure and Evolution of the WTO

In contrast to the World Bank and the IMF, where power is delegated to a board of directors and the staff contributes to decisionmaking, the WTO is run by its member governments; they make the decisions and the Secretariat plays a support role. Major decisions are made by the membership as a whole, either by ministers who meet every two years or by officials who meet regularly at the Geneva headquarters of the WTO. Generally, decisions are made by consensus. One variant is that panel and appellate reports in the trade dispute settlement process, which are submitted to the members for approval, can be overturned only if is there is a consensus *against* the panel or appellate rulings.

The highest authority is the Ministerial Conference; four have been held since the WTO came into existence in 1995: Singapore, Dec. 9–13, 1996; Geneva, May 20, 1998; Seattle, Nov. 30–Dec. 3, 1999 and Doha, Nov. 10–14, 2001. At these meetings, members negotiate and make decisions affecting the fundamental GATT rules and WTO procedures they can also establish an agenda for a new round of trade negotiations, as was done in Doha.

The day-to-day work of the WTO is handled by the General Council, which can meet in three forms: as the General Council itself; as the Dispute Settlement Body (DSB); and as the General Trade Policy Review Body. Each consists of all WTO members and reports to the Ministerial Conference.

Reporting to the General Council are three more councils: the Goods Council, the Services Council, and the Trade-Related Aspects of Intellectual Property (TRIPS) Council, responsible for WTO agreements dealing with their respective areas of trade; and five committees: Trade and Environment, Trade and Development, Regional Trade Agreements, Balance of Payments Restrictions, and Budget, Finance, and Administration. Reporting to these councils and committees are subsidiary committees, working groups, and working parties. Important breakthroughs are often developed in working groups composed of Heads of Delegation, who thrash out certain issues and submit their ideas to the formal structures for consideration.

The Secretariat consists of about five hundred staff headquartered in Geneva and is headed by a director-general. Its main duties are to provide technical support for the various councils and committees, to provide technical assistance for developing country members, to analyze world trade, to explain the WTO to the public, and to provide some forms of legal assistance during dispute settlement. The latter can include providing conciliation or mediation to the parties to a dispute; in certain cases appointing panel members (see section on the Dispute Settlement Mechanism); when necessary, appointing an arbitrator to determine the reasonable time for carrying out a decision; supplying administrative support; and assisting the panels on the legal, historical, and procedural aspects of matters before the panels.[32]

## Trade Barrier Reductions Between Trade Rounds

The principal reductions in trade barriers historically have occurred in formal multilateral trade rounds. However, the councils, committees, and working groups just mentioned continue work between rounds and are often able to complete trade agreements that then become a part of the WTO mandate. Since the Uruguay Round, three new market-opening agreements have been negotiated on information technology, communications, and financial services. The Information Technology Agreement entered into force in 1997 and provided for phased-in reductions of tariffs to zero by January 2000, or no later than 2005 for certain developing countries. In early 2001, fifty-five countries, representing 93 percent of trade in information technology products, had put the agreement into effect. The agreement covers a long list of products in the areas of computers, telecommunications, software, semiconductors, and printed circuit boards. The Agreement on Basic Communications Services came into force in 1998 and opened more than 95 percent of the world telecommunications market (by revenue) to competition. The majority of WTO members signed on and agreed to improved regulatory and market access commitments on a vast range of services and technologies, including submarine cables, satellite systems, broadband data, cellular services, business networks on the Internet, and technologies to bring low-cost access to rural communities. The Financial Services Agreement entered into force in 1999. Seventy-one countries, accounting for over 95 percent of the world's trade in financial services, signed the agreement in 1997. The agreement provides for market-opening commitments in banking, securities, and financial data services; and life, casualty, reinsurance, brokerage, and auxiliary insurance services.

## Ministerial Meetings in Seattle and Doha, Qatar, and a New Trade Round

*Seattle, Nov. 30–Dec. 3, 1999.* To the casual observer following television news or the press headlines, it appeared that the protestors succeeded in dismantling the conference. The press reported the presence in the Seattle of groups ranging from the Ruckus Society from Berkeley, California, to Zapatistas from Mexico and supporters of the man who torched a McDonalds in France. Although the protestors were violent and the Seattle government failed to provide adequate security, the collapse was as much due to events *inside* the meetings as *outside*. One knowledgeable observer describes it as "self inflicted."[33] A particular stumbling block was the U.S. effort to create a Working Group on Trade and Labor that was strongly opposed by developing countries. Reflecting U.S. labor demands, on arriving in Seattle, President Clinton told the *Seattle Post-Intelligencer* that core labor standards should figure in the new agreements; he added, "Ultimately I would favor a system in which sanctions would come for violating [such provisions]."[34] As the statement came over the wires, India and other developing countries announced their withdrawal from the conference. A press statement was issued the next morning softening the call for sanctions. However, USTR and State Department representatives, who were in the negotiating sessions at the time, reported that talks never seriously resumed.

Even without labor rights, there were other difficult issues. Although progress was made in the negotiation sessions, even if the conference had not come to a sudden end, agreement was not certain on some items. Certain developed countries resisted increasing market access for agriculture or apparel. Some developing countries argued for holding back their concessions until the developed countries made certain trade reforms. Some members wanted to expand the agenda on controversial issues, the United States to include labor and environmental issues, the EU to add investment and competition policy, and Japan to add antidumping rules.[35]

*Doha, Qatar, November 9–14, 2001.*[36] Not surprisingly, most of these issues and others discussed in Seattle resurfaced at the Ministerial Conference in the Persian Gulf state of Qatar, November 9–14, 2001. These were tremendously difficult negotiations. Many believed they were crucial given the fiasco in Seattle and the slowdown in the world economy that began in mid-2000 and turned sharply downward in the aftermath of the attacks on the World Trade Center and the Pentagon on September 11, 2001. After marathon sessions for the first few days, the negotiations were extended twenty-four hours; a tired group of delegates eventually agreed on an agenda embodying significant and difficult concessions by many parties. This agenda becomes the game plan for negotiating the next multilateral trade round and can suggest some of the outcomes.

Table 8.6 summarizes some of the key breakthroughs and the key source of resistance to each. Although these items in the declarations at Doha are political and not legally binding, a new trade round is unlikely to succeed unless progress is made on these items.

## Brief Guidebook to a New Round and the Surprising Influence of Developing Countries

In Doha, 140 signatories agreed to negotiate various subjects under different timetables. One of the most significant developments at Doha was the strong influence of the LDCs and the responsiveness of the industrialized countries to LDC demands and requests. In a *separate ministerial declaration on implementation* addressed to LDC concerns, and in various agenda items, support is expressed for LDC wishes such as reviewing agreements on antidumping and countervailing duties (see below); for committing to a goal of duty-free, quota-free market access for products from LDCs; and for "special and differential treatment" for LDCs. In general, the latter means that developing countries will be given more time to apply the liberalized trade rules that have already been negotiated or that may be negotiated under the Doha agenda; for example, six months for the Agreement on the Application of Sanitary and Phytosanitary Measures, five years for the Agreement on Trade-Related Investment Measures, and even more time for the "least developed" of the developing countries. The Doha parties agreed to help LDCs participate more fully in the WTO, which is likely to include training and funds to support the expenses of some delegations in Geneva.

Following are some key agenda items that members are called upon to negotiate:

*Agriculture*
- "Substantial improvements in market access; reductions of, with a view to *phasing out* [the EU fought hard to see that the text did not commit WTO members to *eliminate*], all forms of export subsidies; and substantial reductions in trade-distorting domestic support";[37] submission of draft commitments to reduce barriers by the next Ministerial Conference.

*Services*
- Services already under discussion, requests and offers due in two years.

*Market access for nonagricultural products*
- The reduction or elimination of tariffs and nontariff barriers, particularly for LDC products.

TABLE 8.6   Brief Overview of Doha Agreements for the Next Trade Round

| *New Agenda Item* | *Major Source of Resistance* |
| --- | --- |
| Cutting tariffs on industrial goods | Resistance mostly from developing countries. |
| Phasing out farm subsidies | EU farmers, particularly the French, dependent on generous subsidies and protection in the EU Common Agriculture Policy (CAP) and Japan and Korea. |
| Reducing barriers to foreign investment | India led opposition and won concession to delay start of talks on the most significant issues until at least 2003. |
| Limiting use of antidumping (AD) laws | U.S. steel industry which uses AD to combat imports from low-cost producers. Many in U.S. Congress oppose agreeeing to renegotiate U.S. AD laws. |
| Giving LDCs rights to obtain low-cost version of drugs still under patent | U.S. and EU wanted to limit such rights to pandemics such as HIV/AIDS. Instead, Doha agreement reopened the TRIPS agreement to allow great "flexibility" to members to decide when public health required violation of patents. |
| Bringing WTO rules closer to environmental treaties, possibly giving tariff preferences to environmentally sound products. | LDCs are the primary resisters. This rule change was a concession to EU to win "green" votes for a possible new trade agreement. |

- Comprehensive product coverage so that no sectors or products can be excluded at the outset.

*Trade-Related Aspects of Intellectual Property Rights (TRIPS)—*
*the subject of a separate declaration*
- Support for public health, access to existing medicines, and R&D into new medicines.
- Increased "flexibility" of LDCs to ignore patents if the government declares a "national emergency" or situation of "extreme urgency" (see discussion below).

*Trade and Investment*
- Stable conditions for long-term foreign direct investment and clarification on issues such as transparency (whether investment rules are clear and administered in an open fashion), nondiscrimination, exceptions and dispute settlement by the next Ministerial.

*Trade and Competition Policy*
- The clarification of issues, principally antitrust laws that can block trade and investment, by the next Ministerial. (See the discussion of competition policy at the end of this section.)

*Transparency in Government Procurement*
- Transparency in government procurement to combat corruption, after the next Ministerial.

*Trade Facilitation*
- The improved transparency and efficiency of cross-border shipments, after the next Ministerial.

*WTO Rules*
- Improved procedures for antidumping and countervailing measures (see below, on antidumping); and other matters, including "on trade distorting practices." (Could include taxation of trade—see FSC case above and conclusions below.)

*Dispute Settlement Understanding*
- Improvements and clarifications for WTO dispute settlement by the next Ministerial. (Issues may include greater transparency and allowing more participants into the process; making it faster and more effective; walling off of the WTO Secretariat, which some accuse of having conflicts of interest; creating a more permanent judiciary than the list of people usually contracted for the Appellate Body; and allowing more frequent oversight of WTO interpretation of GATT texts than only when a new round is being negotiated.)

*Trade and the Environment*
- Improved coordination between existing WTO rules and specific trade obligations of members who are parties to specific MEAs.
- The reduction or elimination of environmentally harmful subsidies in fisheries (requested by World Wildlife Fund and other nongovernmental organizations [NGOs]) and of export subsidies in agriculture.
- A stronger role for the Committee on Trade and the Environment in the WTO.

*E-commerce*
- Agreements to extend the moratorium on customs duties on e-commerce for two years.

*Trade, Debt and Finance*
- The improved coordination of the WTO with the World Bank and IMF on trade, debt, and finance to aid LDCs (done at the urging of African WTO members).

Some trade issues not agreed upon for the agenda which are likely to be raised in the future:

- **Agriculture**   Rules for trade in genetically modified food (i.e., that contains genetically modified organisms, GMOs).
- **Textiles**   Although the Uruguay Round phased out quotas on textile imports by 2005, developing countries wanted to advance this date and significantly reduce textile tariffs.
- **Investment**   Rules beyond the limited scope of the TRIMS to eliminate other barriers to investment. Obstacles to investment often serve as barriers to trade because a vast amount of trade takes place within corporations. Many LDCs opposed.
- **Competition policy**   Rules regarding trade-distorting policies of government-encouraged or -tolerated cartels and other anticompetitive arrangements beyond antitrust (see below).
- **E-commerce**   Agenda to prevent new barriers other than customs duties to a technology that is extending the reach of small and medium-sized enterprises across borders.
- **Taxation of trade**   The ministers did not deal with WTO tax rules that *allow* the EU to rebate *indirect* taxes on exports but does *not* allow the United States to rebate *direct* taxes on exports. This is crucial to the FSC case, and the United States could raise this issue in negotiations.
- **Customs**   A future reform might deal with how to upgrade customs processing, invoicing, and valuation, and to reduce the corruption that exists in some customs' facilities.
- **Labor clause**   A nonstarter given what happened in Seattle; some in the U.S. Congress may push for a labor clause in the Free Trade Area of the Americas (FTAA) or bilateral trade agreements.

### *Contentious Issues: Antidumping, TRIPS, and Competition Policy*

*Antidumping.*   Commenting on Doha's reopening discussion on antidumping and antisubsidy measures that were difficult to negotiate in the Uruguay Round, Senate Finance Committee Chairman Max Baucus says, "Our trading partners have only one goal here: to weaken our trade laws."[38] He and others holding similar views in the Congress argue that dumping, and not antidumping, is the trade distortion (see Chapter 7). They have tried to block giving the president "Fast-Track," or Trade Promotion Authority (TPA), to negotiate a new round and vow to oppose agreements that, in their view, go too far. They cite countries that have encouraged certain industries such as steel to develop great excess capacity and then wind up dumping (i.e., selling at less than fair value or the cost of production) in the U.S. market. Other members of Congress believe that some methods employed in calculating "less than fair value" are discretionary and capricious and that as more countries adopt antidumping (AD) measures against the United States, it stands to gain from improving antidumping disciplines. USTR notes that the United States can advance an agenda, including transparency and due process, that would help U.S. exporters. As the largest trading nation in the world, and one that has run large trade deficits for many years, it is not surprising that the United States has been the largest initiator of anitdumping actions.

In recent years, other countries, especially developing countries, are making increasing use of antidumping measures to protect their domestic industries. While there are anecdotal claims that some countries are singling out the United States for antidumping enforcement in retaliation against the United States for its antidumping claims, the Congressional Budget Office (CBO) did not see such a pattern in its 1998 and 2001 studies. In these analyses of the complex and confusing data on antidumping, the CBO notes that the ratio of case initiation the U. S. to case initiation against all countries is less than the ratio of imports from the United States to imports from all countries.*

Nonetheless, as the number of cases against the United States continues to rise, it is adding to the controversy on antidumping and to the arguments of those in the United States opposed to the WTO.

*TRIPS.* The TRIPS agreement concluded in the Uruguay Round was the subject of a separate "Declaration on the TRIPS Agreement and Public Health."[39] In reinterpreting the Uruguay Round agreement, some are concerned that a Pandora's box of trade confrontations might have been opened. Largely in response to LDC demands, the declaration states' members should have "flexibility" to determine what constitutes a "national emergency" or circumstance of "extreme urgency" and freedom to decide the grounds on which compulsory licenses[40] can be granted and existing patents ignored. The United States and several European countries, where most of the expensive[41] research related to discoveries of new medicines is done, agreed in the context of TRIPS and Doha that patents could be suspended for pandemics of such diseases as HIV/AIDS, tuberculosis, and malaria. The declaration allows for great discretion by local authorities; some conclude that the declaration could allow the suspension of patents even for illnesses for which remedies exist, including relatively low-cost generics. Also, the least developed of the LDCs are given an extension to 2016 (from 2005) to comply with TRIPS. One concern is that these measures could limit the amount of spending on R&D for certain tropical diseases if there were no way to recoup the costs through the market.

Another concern is that the declaration might discourage some governments from modernizing their intellectual property laws as they react to pressure from local companies that profit greatly by manufacturing drugs developed elsewhere that are still under patent. Although local "pirates" benefit, economists note that this tends to stifle the development of research in those countries, leads to a so-called brain drain as scientists move to countries where their discoveries will be protected by patents, and hurts a country's reputation regarding respect for intellectual property.

*Competition Policy.* This mainly concerns antitrust policy. A brief review of the European Commission's (EC) decision to block the GE-Honeywell merger illustrates the complexity of the issues. Although both the United States and the EU share precepts and goals and signed an agreement on competition law,[42] they have differences

---

*Congressional Budget Office, *Antidumping in the United States and Around the World: An Analysis of International Data,* June 1998, and *Antidumping Action in the United States and Around the World: An Update,* June 2001.

on the scope of evidence, theories of harm, and interpretation. The U.S. Department of Justice approved the GE-Honeywell merger and noted that the products of the two were complementary, not overlapping, and that GE and Honeywell rivals were large, financially healthy, and had a large share of the relevant markets.[43] The U.S. review focused more on consumers and saw the merger benefiting consumers with lower prices. The EC focused more on competitors and expressed concern over the merged firm's ability to bundle GE engines with Honeywell avionics and that GE's aircraft leasing affiliate would be anticompetitive. The U.S. view is that this was not a problem because the leasing affiliate controlled no more than 10 percent of the commercial aircraft purchases.[44] According to former GE CEO Jack Welch, during the second and last day of a crucial hearing before the commissioners, competitors testified all day and GE was allowed only fifteen minutes to rebut the charges and claims. Welch comments that at the hearing the prosecutor also served as judge, and that in the United States antitrust authorities have to get a court order to stop a deal.[45] So the issue is contentious and complex, and negotiations to achieve an agreement by the EU, the United States, and other WTO members are likely to take a few years before they are reasonably settled. Another competition policy issue that some would like to see covered in the WTO concerns the cartel behavior among firms, as in Japan, that discriminates against imports.

### Doha in Perspective

The GATT requires a consensus of its members to obtain agreement on an agenda for a new round of multilateral trade negotiations. As a result, although there are many issues on the Work Program agenda, not all issues of interest to members were included. Also, the wording in some sections is "squishy,"[46] allowing enough loopholes to permit differing interpretations. Without such language, many international agreements or negotiations would never get off the ground. This is especially so for the WTO with its requirement for consensus before a new trade round can be launched. The phrase inserted at French insistence in the paragraph dealing with agriculture, "without prejudging the outcome of negotiations," refers to the phase-out of export subsidies for agricultural goods, but it could be said to apply to the rest of the agenda as well. On the other hand, some of the wording allows individual members to bring up issues in the negotiation that are not apparent from the text. The phrase in the section on WTO rules referring to "disciplines on trade distorting practices" enables the United States to open negotiations on taxes and trade—including the FSC case—if it wishes.[47]

## Conclusions and Outlook

The role and power of the WTO are twofold:

1. It provides a regular and useful forum in its Ministerial Conference in which its members can negotiate to set an agenda for a new trade round or negotiate changes in the rules for trade in a trade round that is already underway.

2. It offers an arbitration mechanism having real power of enforcement to aid members in obtaining a decision on a dispute involving the allegation that one member has violated one of the agreed-upon trade rules. This Dispute Settlement Mechanism has been reasonably successful. In nearly all cases either the mechanism provided a setting or an incentive for the disputant parties to settle the dispute (a) by themselves through consultations or (b) through recommendations by the panels or the appeals panels that led to an end of the trade rule violation or a suitable agreement between the disputants.

Effective use of these powers, the large increase in the number of trade issues covered by international trade rules agreed to in the Uruguay Round, and the steadily increasing membership, which reached 140 countries at the beginning of the Doha Ministerial, have made the WTO an important force in globalization. They have also made the WTO controversial. The WTO is admired for the successes that have been achieved in liberalizing trade since its inception in 1995. It is also criticized for decisions that go against individual country or sectoral interests and it is criticized, or envied, by advocates for other causes, such as the environment or labor, who would like to see the WTO use its enforcement mechanisms to advance their interests.

Although serious disputes between the WTO's largest members, the United States and the EU, remain unresolved in early 2002, it appears that the WTO will continue its role in aiding the expansion of trade and continue to evolve in the trade issues covered by its rules and in its methods of resolving disputes. The agreement at Doha, Qatar, in November 2001 to launch a new trade round is a most significant achievement. The consequences of failure—either stagnation in trade liberalization or a possible relapse into protectionism—were avoided; now many important issues are on the table and there is a consensus on making progress.

## For Further Reading

Hudec, Robert E. "The New WTO Dispute Settlement Procedure: An Overview of the First Three Years," *Minnesota Journal of Global Trade* 8, no. 1 (winter 1999).

Jackson, John H. *The World Trading System: Law and Policy of International Economic Relations.* 2d ed. Cambridge, Mass.: MIT Press, 1999.

"Office of the United States Trade Representative." Available at <http://www.ustr.gov>.

*The Results of the Uruguay Round of Multilateral Trade Negotiations: The Legal Texts.* Geneva: GATT Secretariat, 1994.

Schott, Jeffrey J., ed. *The WTO After Seattle.* Washington, D.C.: Institute for International Economics, 2000.

Thomas, Jeffrey S., and Michael A. Meyer. *The New Rules of Global Trade: A Guide to the World Organization.* Scarborough, Ontario: Carswell, 1997.

"World Trade Organization." Available at <http://www.wto.org>.

## Notes

1. Paul A. Samuelson, *Economics,* 9th ed. (New York: McGraw-Hill, 1973), 706.

2. Thomas C. Fischer, *The United States, the European Union, and the "Globalization" of World Trade* (Westport, Conn.: Quorum Books 2000), 202.

3. Many economics texts analyze the economic welfare aspects of tariffs; for example, see chapter 7 in Peter H. Lindert and Thomas A. Pugel, *International Economics,* 10th ed. (Chicago: Irwin, 1996).

4. World Trade Organization, *The Results of the Uruguay Round of Multilateral Trade Negotiations: The Legal Texts* (Geneva: GATT Secretariat), 558 pages.

5. According to Article XXIV of the GATT, an exception to MFN for regional trading associations such as customs unions or free trade areas is granted if the regional trading association facilitates trade between the constituent territories and does not raise barriers to the trade of other contracting parties. In reviewing the regional associations, the discussions often focus on whether the estimated amount of trade *created* by a regional trading group is larger than the estimated amount of trade *diverted* by the group; that is, if the associations are truly trade-creating on a net basis. John Jackson, *The World Trading System: Law and Policy of International Economic Relations,* 2d ed. (Cambridge, Mass.: MIT Press), 165–167.

6. Amicus briefs are statements to the court; in this case it would be to the WTO panel, by a party that is not involved in a particular litigation but that is allowed by the court to advise it on a matter of law directly affecting the litigation. Those in favor of allowing amicus briefs into WTO dispute settlement argue they would add important information and viewpoints to the proceedings. Those opposed note that the parties are seldom shy about contacting outside sources so they can present every possible argument to the panel, and that the panel reports now routinely exceed two hundred pages and contain great amounts of unnecessary detail.

7. The author of this chapter has heard these ideas expressed by officials from the Department of State and USTR over the past three years. Some of these ideas were also a subject of discussion in the Brookings Institution Roundtable on Trade and Investment Policy, in which Alan. W. Wolff, Managing Partner of Dewey Ballantine, LLP; Gary C. Hufbauer, Reginald Jones Senior Fellow, Institute of International Economics; and Bernard M. Hoekman, Research Manager, International Trade, the World Bank; and others from the State Department, the World Bank, the International Monetary Fund (IMF), and various universities analyzed the Doha declarations; 20 November 2001.

8. Susan A. Aaronson, "What About Trade," *The International Economy* (Sept./Oct., 1996): 47.

9. See citations under further reading at the end of the chapter and reference to the GAO report later in these endnotes.

10. GAO, *World Trade Organization, U.S. Experience to Date in Dispute Settlement System,* GAO/NSIAD/OGC–00–196BR, June 2000.

11. USTR, *2002 Trade Policy Agenda and 2000 Annual Report,* 207–209.

12. "EU requests WTO panel against US section 301 legislation," press release from the European Union, Brussels, 17 February 1999.

13. USTR, "WTO Panel Upholds Section 301," press release 99–012, December 22, 1999.

14. "WTO report on U.S. section 301 law: a good result for the EU and the multilateral system," press release IP/99/1051, Brussels, 23 December 1999; accessed at www.europa.eu.int/comm/external_relations/news/12_99/ip_99_1051.htm.

15. Leonard W. Condon, "The WTO Dispute Between the United States and the European Union Involving Growth-Promoting Hormones: An Abbreviated History." Condon is Vice President International Trade, American Meat Institute, Arlington, VA, 24 June 1998, 1–6;

"The 'Hormone' Case: Background and History, MEMO/00/27, European Commission, Brussels, 24 May 2000.

16. Condon, 3.

17. Elizabeth C. Seastrom and Robert E. Nielsen, "U.S. Countervailing Duty Law and WTO Subsidies Agreement." Seastrum is Senior Counsel, and Nielsen is Senior Attorney, Office of Chief Counsel for Import Administration, U. S. Department of Commerce ITA Seminar, Basic Trade Law Course, 2–5 May 2000, 10–11; Gary Hufbauer, "A Critical Assessment of the WTO Panel Report on Tax Treatment for 'Foreign Sales Corporations' and an Appeal for Fundamental Tax Reform," (Washington, D.C.: Institute for International Economics, March 2000), 1–9.

18. To illustrate, a French pharmaceutical firm would be liable to France for corporate tax on earnings from its plant in France but not on earnings from a plant in the United States. A similar U.S. firm would be liable to the United States for corporate tax on its pharmaceutical plant in the United States *and* in France. Because of this inequity, which is based on the different approaches in the "territorial" and "worldwide" tax liabilities, the U.S. Congress has repeatedly toyed with the U.S. tax code to begin to address the problem. Some of the changes allow certain tax credits for corporate taxes paid in another country and for a discount for earnings from exports first via the Domestic International Sales Corporations (DISCs) and then the Foreign Sales Corporations (FSCs). Full discussions of the issue can be found in Hufbauer, "A Critical Assessment," and in the WTO cases, for example, "United States: Tax Treatment for 'Foreign Sales Corporations,' Oral Statement of the United States of America," AB–1999–9, 19 January 2000 before the World Trade Organization Appellate Body.

19. Alan Wm. Wolff, Partner, Dewey Ballantine, LLP, "What Did Doha Do? An Initial Assessment," the Brookings Institution Roundtable on Trade and Investment Policy, Washington, D.C., 20 November 2001, 7. Wolff is a partner at Dewey Ballantine, LLP, Washington, D.C.

20. World Trade Organization, *United States: Tax Treatment for Foreign Sales Corporations, AB–1999–9, Report of the Appellate Body,* WT/DS108/AB/R, 24 February 2000, paragraph 179.

21. Pascal Lamy and Robert B. Zoellick, "In the Next Round," *Washington Post,* 17 July 2001, A17.

22. U.S. Mission to the EU, Brussels, Belgium, "U.S. Disappointed with WTO Ruling on Foreign Sales Corporation Tax," press release, 12 January 2002; accessed at www.useu.be/Categories/FCS/Jan1402FSCWTORuling.html.

23. Lori Wallach and Michelle Sforza, with an introduction by Ralph Nader, *The WTO: Five Years of Reasons to Resist Corporate Globalization* (New York: Seven Stories Press, 1999).

24. Specifically, "domestic refiners were held to an individualized standard based on their own contaminant level, foreign refiners were held to a statutory standard equal to the average 1990 contaminant level of all refiners. In other words, half of the domestic oil refiners—by definition—were held to a lower standard than foreign refiners." (Testimony of Gary Horlick of O'Melveny & Myers before the House Foreign Affairs Committee on 20 June 2000.)

25. A purse seine is a fishing seine that is drawn into the shape of a bag to enclose the catch. A seine is a large fishing net made to hang vertically in the water by weights at the lower edge and floats at the top.

26. The panel also found that the trade embargo differentiated products (tuna) at the border according to their nonproduct processes and production methods (PPMs), which is not a

legitimate GATT basis for distinguishing between otherwise "like products"; report accessed at www.wto.org/english/thewto_e/whatis_e/eol/e/wto09_10.htm.

27. Statement of Alan Reuther, Legislative Director, UAW, before House Ways & Means Committee, 3 May 2000, 5.

28. The author observed this first hand in countries he lived in or visited during periods in which they followed import substitution policies (Brazil, southern cone countries, Venezuela, and Mexico in the 1960s and 1970s) as well as in countries that had opened their economies and were enjoying increasing trade and growth (Chile and Mexico in the 1980s and Argentina in the early and mid-1990s). Many studies have shown how much faster countries have grown when they liberalized their trade regimes in comparison with countries relatively closed to trade. These studies include *Towards Renewed Growth* by the Council of Americas and research by Jeffrey Sachs and Andrew Warner of Harvard.

29. WTO, "Trading Into the Future: The Introduction to the WTO, Labor Standards: not on the Agenda," accessed at www.wto.org/english/thewto_e/whatis_e/tif_e/bey7_e.htm.

30. John Jackson, *The World Trading System, Law and Policy of International Economic Relations,* 2d ed. (Cambridge, Mass.: MIT Press, 1999), 245.

31. WTO, "Trading Into the Future."

32. WTO, "Transparency and the Rules of Law, Section: Dispute Settlement Mechanism, Unit: DS: The players, Slide No. 23," accessed at www.wto.org/english/thewto_e/whatis_e/eol/e/wto08/wto8_30.htm.

33. Jeffrey J. Scott, *The WTO After Seattle* (Washington, D.C.: Institute for International Economics, 2000), 5.

34. Scott, 6.

35. Scott, 3–40.

36. This review of the Doha results is drawn from (1) conversations with United States government officials; (2) various WTO documents (including the "Ministerial Declaration," WT/MIN(01)DEC/W/1, 14 November 2001; "Declaration on the Trips Agreement and Public Health," WT/MIN(01)DEC/W/2, 14 November 2001; "Implementation-Related Issues and Concerns," WT/MIN(01)/W/10, 14 November 2001; and "Proposed Procedures for Extensions Under Article 27.4 for Certain Developing Country Members," G/SCM/W/471/Rev. 1, 14 November 2001 and (3) various press reports including Helene Cooper and Geoff Winestock's "Poor Nations Win Gains in Global Trade Deal As U.S. Compromises," *Wall Street Journal,* 15 November 2001, 1, 12.

37. "Ministerial Declaration," WT/MIN(01)DEC/W1, 14 November 2001, 3.

38. *Congressional Record* (15 November 2001), pt. S11899.

39. WTO, Ministerial Conference, Fourth Session, WT/MIN(01)DEC/W/2, 14 November, 2001.

40. A compulsory license is issued by a government without patent owner agreement, usually at an artificial price so that a company other than the patent holder can sell the product. Think tanks involved in the issue of reasonable protection of intellectual property rights argue that compulsory licensing or local working requirements (forcing the patent holder to manufacture in a certain country) is legitimate *only* if (a) the patent holder has violated competition laws or (b) in an emergency; for example, if a cure for the Ebola virus were found for countries where this disease is a threat.

41. Most reports on pharmaceutical patents note that $200–300 million are required to bring a new drug to market. This includes the costs, often over ten years, of discovery, assaying, and rounds of trials to test efficacy, side effects, and the action of additional ingredients crucial to delivering the drug to the organ or area to be treated. The cost includes "dry holes," drugs found wanting at some point during the process.

42. *Agreement Between the European Communities and the Government of the United States of America Regarding the Application of Their Competition Laws,* 23 September 1991; accessed at www.usdoj.gov/atr/public/international/docs/ec.htm.

43. Timothy J. Muris, Chairman, Federal Trade Commission, in remarks before the Brookings Institution Roundtable on Trade and Investment Policy, 21 December 2001, Washington, D.C., 2–9.

44. Muris, and "Commission Decision of 03/07/2001 declaring a concentration to be incompatible with the common market and the EEA Agreement, Case No COMP/M.2220 General Electric/Honeywell," accessed at www.europa.eu.int/comm/competition/mergers/cases/decisions/m2220_en.pdf; and "The Economics of GE/Honeywell—Part 1: Mixed Bundling," accessed at www.lexecon.co.uk/publications/memoslist.html.

45. Jack Welch, *Straight from the Gut* (New York: Warner Books, 2001), 368, 375.

46. Al Larson, Under Secretary of State, "The WTO: Doha and Beyond," remarks to the European Institute, 28 November 2001, 2.

47. Gary Hufbauer, Senior Fellow, Institute for International Economics, "The Doha Declaration," the Brookings Institution Roundtable on Trade and Investment Policy, Washington, D.C., 20 November 2001, 2.

# Part Four

# Major Contemporary Issues

# 9 Trade Sanctions Versus Export Expansion

In analyses of the intricacies of trade policy, export strategy normally generates far less attention than import strategy. Export policy tends to be relatively less intellectualized in part because in every country but one it has an unequivocal, simply defined mission: to do whatever is necessary to maximize exports. Domestic politicians and businesspeople revere exports for the jobs, profits, and foreign exchange they generate, whereas at best, they tolerate imports that compete with domestic production. Economists tend not to focus on exports because they are viewed merely as the means to pay for imports. Because scholars stress that the benefits of trade to a country accrue mainly from importing goods made more cheaply and efficiently overseas, it is not unusual for books dealing with foreign trade (especially those written by Americans) to lack a separate discussion of, or even index entry for, "export policy."

The U.S. government is in a class by itself in dealing with the core inconsistency of the export policy of all industrialized countries. Despite a common overriding wish to encourage strong export growth of technologically sophisticated goods, these governments occasionally feel compelled to block overseas shipments of some goods to countries whose policies are considered threatening or especially odious. Since World War II, the U.S. government has been uniquely aggressive in imposing export restraints in the pursuit of noncommercial objectives. It pays lip service to the principle of export expansion and then proceeds to impose more impediments to exporting than any other government, a pattern that incites little opposition among the general public. Also since World War II, the United States has been unique in its reluctance to appropriate official funds to assist would-be exporters. After placing the distinctive contemporary American situation in context, this chapter examines the two "poles" of U.S. export policy, the "discouraging" one based on sanctions and controls and the "encouraging" one composed of various enhancement programs.

## The Political Economy of U.S. Export Policy

The export policy of the United States is similar to its import policy to the degree that it often has been inconsistent and occasionally hypocritical. Differences, though, outweigh the similarities. U.S. export policy has been—without apologies—much more interventionist. To be sure, efforts have long been made to conclude multilateral agreements to limit direct and indirect amounts of concessional (i.e., government subsidized) financing for exports. But like every other country, the United States has overtly refused to allow the invisible hand of the marketplace to allocate the volume and product composition of its exports of goods and services. Unlike its record in import policy, the United States government has not sought to shrink intervention in export policy because it remains committed to official measures to restrict exports. Senior U.S. foreign policy officials have had a special interest in export policy since the 1950s. They have deemed export controls and sanctions as two integral means to achieve a broad range of objectives in national security and foreign policy that outweigh commercial considerations. These views have prevailed, and export expansion has been relegated to a secondary priority.

The United States has good reasons for not according export maximization the uppermost priority as other governments do. Exports of goods and services are only about 10 percent of total U.S. GDP (merchandise exports represent only 7 percent), the lowest share for any major economy. In addition, the United States is unique in its ability to pay for all its imports with its own currency, that is, by drawing on its domestic money supply. The continuing role of the dollar as the world's major reserve and transactions currency absolves the United States from having to do what every other country must do: earn foreign exchange to pay for most, if not all its imports. As long as foreigners accept payments in dollars for their exports to the United States, Americans will not share the rest of the world's urgency for export success. Furthermore, as long as the dollar stays stable-to-strong despite an escalating trade deficit (as it did in the early 1980s and again at the turn of the century), export enhancement will not be a vital U.S. need that trumps other policy goals.

A third factor contributing to unique export attitudes among U.S. policymakers in the executive and legislative branches is the absence of a proactive, comprehensive industrial policy seeking to enlarge and strengthen targeted industries. Unlike the situation in many countries, there is no direct linkage in the United States between domestic economic planning (it does not exist) and trade strategy. The result is an economic policy vacuum that eases the way for the dominant superpower status of the United States to shape an export policy uniquely more concerned with attaining qualitative foreign policy goals than a quantitative increase in corporate sales overseas.

Finally, philosophical beliefs have been a contributing factor in several respects to an extraordinary U.S. export mentality. Funding for export promotion programs is relatively low because most Americans disapprove of government largesse that transfers taxpayers' money to politically favored companies or sectors, a practice derisively dubbed corporate welfare. In addition, most Americans are not comfortable with maintaining a business-as-usual relationship with countries that challenge American security interests or that are run by dictators who show contempt for rule of law and human rights. American policymakers, more than their foreign counterparts, link the conduct of unfettered trade relations to the willingness of foreign governments to adhere to minimum standards of conduct considered acceptable by the United States. U.S. export policy is distinctive in its preference to impose immediate economic penalties on offensive foreign behavior rather than the alternative preferred by its allies, namely, the long-term strategy of building bridges through engagement. Congress in a few cases has gone as far as imposing strictures on the behavior of domestic business people engaged in overseas marketing activities (see, for example, the discussion of the Foreign Corrupt Practices Act in Chapter 7). For better or worse, the U.S. government has discouraged and prohibited exports to a degree unknown anywhere else in a world where an "export or die" mentality is palpable.

A superb case study of the uniquely nonchalant U.S. attitude towards exports was the Reagan administration's posture in the early 1980s when the U.S. trade deficit swelled to what were then record highs. The upward spiral was due mainly to the over-valued exchange rate of the dollar, which made U.S. goods more expensive to foreign buyers and foreign-made goods cheaper to U.S. consumers. The administration displayed little sympathy for the cries of American business about its being adversely affected by an import boom and by stagnant exports, the results of continued appreciation of the dollar. Instead, it told the private sector to live or die by the market mechanism and bragged that the strength of the dollar was a welcome reflection of growing American economic strength. Congress eventually applied sufficiently intense pressure—in the form of inching closer to passing protectionist trade legislation—that the administration eventually was forced to shift policy gears and respond in 1985 with initiatives in remedial trade and international monetary policy.[1]

It is not hyperbole to argue that no parliamentary government in the world would have been able to survive the inflexible policy stance toward the economic consequences of an overvalued currency that the Reagan administration maintained with respect to the dollar from 1981 through 1984. European and Japanese prime ministers would not have had the political gall or the ideological disposition to respond in the same way to a deteriorating trade balance of comparable magnitude. It would have been politically disastrous for them to display the same prolonged outpouring of free market rhetoric and overt indifference to legitimate concerns in the private sector about international competitiveness. The ability of Congress to prod the Reagan administration to take the foreign trade situation more seriously was a dramatic example of the counterbalancing forces inherent in a separation of powers between branches of government.

Despite the aforementioned factors explaining the singular lack of urgency in U.S. government circles toward export maximization, several counterarguments can be advanced in support of the thesis that a strong, thriving export sector is very much in the interests of the United States. First, given the government-private sector consensus on both the dangers of an unchecked increase in the currently large U.S. trade deficit and the prohibitive costs of reducing it through reductions in imports, the optimal path of adjustment is clearly a much higher rate of export growth than import growth.[2] Second, exports of goods and services do make a significant contribution to the overall American economy. A disaggregation of U.S. GDP data reveals that exports of American merchandise represent a surprisingly large 40 percent-plus of U.S. output of manufacturing, agricultural, and mining goods.[3] Many individual companies and farms are heavily dependent on exporting to generate profits and economies of scale through increased sales volume. During most of the early years of the 1990s, increases in U.S. exports accounted for at least 20 percent of annual GDP growth. Although exports still represent a relatively small percentage of total GDP, by 2001 their share was almost three times greater than their minimal contribution in 1960. Finally, jobs in the export sector are especially desirable. The ability of a product to compete successfully on a price basis in the world marketplace presupposes higher-than-average levels of labor productivity. Wages for jobs in the export sector are estimated to be somewhere from 15 to 18 percent above the average level for all production jobs.

# Controls and Sanctions

The embrace of trade sanctions and export controls by the U.S. government began as a noncontroversial component of Cold War strategy to deny military goods and advanced technologies to adversaries in the Communist bloc. The Export Control Act of 1949 provided the first legislative authority for the executive branch to impose comprehensive export controls in peacetime. For the first time, the president was delegated authority to restrict exports for the broad purposes of protecting the national security as well as enhancing foreign policy goals—powers far more explicit than all comparable authority to limit imports. "Short supply" was (and still is) the third legislated rationale for applying U.S. export controls, the goal being to limit price increases associated with domestic shortages by limiting foreign sales of the scarce commodity.

Over time, a growing number of observers came to view the multiple forms of export impediments imposed by the U.S. government as being increasingly out of synch with global economic and political trends. Critical scrutiny was encouraged when these impediments increased rather than diminished after the end of the Cold War. Intensifying doubts about their relative costs and benefits, relative successes and failures, and possible overuse have generated some of the most vexing political and economic issues in all of U.S. trade policy. Congress, receiving no clear signals from the public at large, has spent years unsuccessfully trying to determine where the right dividing line is between hard-line and flexibility in the wording of U.S. trade sanctions legislation. The inordinate difficulty of devising optimal language is demonstrated by the inability of Congress, despite repeated efforts, to pass (by early 2002) permanent sanctions-authorizing legislation to replace the Export Administration Act that expired in 1994 (see Chapter 7 ). Even the effort to catalogue the exact number of sanctions imposed is mired in a debate over definition. For example, there are different interpretations about whether such limited actions as suspending U.S. foreign aid commitments, withholding exports of certain military and crowd control equipment, or denying Export-Import Bank financing constitute a "sanction."

Controversies associated with the relatively frequent U.S. use of export controls and trade sanctions exist on the domestic and international levels. Domestically, there is a fundamental disagreement between those with a direct financial interest in exporting and those with a political interest in pressuring foreign governments to modify their behavior. The business community leads the campaign for fewer restraints, while foreign policy hard-liners and human rights groups believe it is in the national interest to impose additional trade restraints as needed (e.g., China).

Other industrialized countries have long displayed a far greater skepticism about export sanctions and controls as an effective method to halt state actions thought hostile or repugnant. They do agree with the need to restrict the proliferation of major weapons systems. On limited occasions they have taken the lead in opting for economic sanctions, as they did with Serbia. The reluctance of Western Europe and Japan to adopt export sanctions partly reflects a mercantilist's abhorrence of shackling domestic exporters. Their posture is also driven by skepticism about what can be achieved. They tend to assume that a target country will eventually circumvent sanctions by finding some means, legal or otherwise, of obtaining the goods it most needs. Policymakers outside the United States tend to believe that pursuing closer economic ties, rather than isolating and excluding offending countries, will produce a vested interest in cooperation and more positive behavioral changes in the long term. They prefer engagement, not provocation, which allegedly encourages defiance in targeted governments that wish to demonstrate that they cannot be intimidated. These attitudes collectively explain the overt desire of many countries in Western Europe to relax sanctions and resume a lucrative commercial export business with Iraq, its interest in developing weapons of mass destruction and its brutal dictatorship notwithstanding. Publicly, foreign government officials deride U.S. export impediments; privately, most of them take delight in what they probably perceive as a quixotic and economically costly U.S. effort to emphasize ethics in the cutthroat atmosphere of the international marketplace.

Application of *export controls* began as a Cold War measure based on a straightforward and, to this day, noncontroversial premise: It makes sense to deny, or at least delay, the ability of potential adversaries to import weapons and state-of-the-art dual-use commercial technologies, such as computers and machine tools, that can contribute directly to their increased military strength. U.S. Cold War military strategy (successfully pursued, as it turned out) was based on a "force multiplier" concept: offsetting the Soviet bloc's numerical superiority in manpower and weapons with superior Western technology. The United States initially had few problems convincing its compliant Western European and Asian allies to go along with a rigid regime of economic denial through comprehensive export controls. In the years immediately after World War II, other countries' fears of Soviet intentions were intense, the United States was the undisputed leader in most advanced technologies, and its leadership of the free world bloc was at its peak.

Despite continuing harangues by U.S. officials committed to erring on the side of caution, Western Europe, Japan, and Canada by the 1960s were relaxing their definition of what kinds of goods directly enhanced the military might of the Soviet Union and its allies. Their export control regimes became increasingly less rigid as they sought to increase trade and political engagement with the Eastern bloc countries. By standing still, the U.S. system became progressively more extensive and invasive than that of any other country. It retained a far more lengthy list of restricted goods and technologies (requiring the government's specific approval of export licenses) than the multilateral list maintained by the other industrialized countries.

The United States also found itself being criticized for applying extraterritorial export controls. U.S. export controls statutes are applicable to American-owned overseas subsidiaries, to foreign-owned companies re-exporting U.S.-made products, to U.S.-made components incorporated into foreign-made goods, and even to products manufactured by foreign companies with U.S.-licensed technology.[4] Anecdotal evidence has long existed regarding efforts by foreign manufacturing companies to shun U.S.-based suppliers of components to avoid the need to comply with externally imposed constraints for which they had no sympathy.[5]

A dilemma that has never changed for industrialized countries is where to prudently draw the line in controlling the export of merchandise and technology that would directly assist potential adversaries in becoming a bigger military threat. The accelerated pace of technological change in the information processing and telecommunications sectors has further compounded the problem. The constant increases in the speed and power of commercially available computers, for example, has necessitated repeated relaxation of U.S. export control standards on computing power lest foreign customers buy state-of-the art computers in Europe or Japan (or off the shelf in an American retail store). Concern in the U.S. intelligence community about diminished capacity to intercept foreign communications signals has generated considerable controversy from its efforts to restrict exports of U.S.-made encryption devices because this technology is available elsewhere.

There is no ambiguity in the repeated laments of American companies that the breadth and depth of their government's export control system has the unintended effect of boosting the export sales of their European and Japanese competitors. No one can deny the relative complexity of U.S. export controls. The Commerce Department's Export Administration Regulations fill more than 1,000 pages and list some 2,400 dual-use items requiring issuance of an export license. U.S. industrial companies have complained for decades about a relatively slow approval process that, given the clout of the Defense Department, allegedly tilts too far in the direction of enhancing national security and entails more administrative delays and uncertainties than the export control system of any other major industrialized country. A specially convened congressional study group reported in 2001 that the existing U.S. system to control the export of militarily sensitive goods and technologies "is increasingly at odds with a world characterized by rapid technological innovation, the globalization of business, and the internationalization of the industrial base."[6]

*Economic sanctions* are also closely linked to foreign policy, but they differ from export controls as a policy instrument in several respects. They are country-oriented rather than product-specific; in other words, they usually involve a formal cessation of all or most trade relations.* Sanctions are imposed for the primary purpose of pressuring a foreign government to change policies considered dangerous or objectionable by others. On a second-best basis, sanctions seek to punish or burden a government that refuses to modify the actions in question and to create enough discomfort in the population that it will force a change in government. On a third-best basis, imposing a sanction can make the initiating country feel good about itself because it has at least symbolically demonstrated moral outrage at the target country's policies. Whether it is appropriate or misguided to use trade sanctions in support of values such as human rights is part of the larger, highly subjective question of the role of ethics in foreign relations.

For the past six decades, the United States has imposed more trade sanctions against more countries than anyone else. Depending on how narrow or broad a definition one uses, the U.S. government at the start of the millennium maintained some form of economic "sanctions" against twenty-nine countries at a minimum and sev-

---

*Economic sanctions can consist of retribution other than halting trade, for example, seizing financial assets, prohibiting private capital flows to the target country, and suspending foreign aid loans and grants. Retaliation against unfair trade practices such as violations of intellectual property rights is excluded from this discussion.

enty-five countries (including multilaterally mandated sanctions) at a maximum. Assuming that one includes China, India, and Pakistan in the list of targets, the United States at this time was applying sanctions against countries accounting for more than one-half of the world's population and about one-fifth of world trade. Some even advocated sanctions against a staunch American ally, Germany, because of concerns in 2000 about reported religious discrimination in that country.

The use of sanctions accelerated sharply in the 1990s. The U.S. government applied sanctions for foreign policy purposes an estimated 104 times between 1945 and early 1998, of which 61—more than 50 percent of the total—were applied in just the last five years of that period.[7] Despite the misgivings of some, trade sanctions became so popular in the United States at the end of the twentieth century that many state and city governments imposed their own trade restrictions as a personalized expression of pique against certain foreign governments. (A Supreme Court decision in 2000 declaring Massachusetts's sanctions against Burma an unconstitutional intrusion into federal prerogatives may discourage local sanctions in the future).

Several reasons explain why sanctions have struck a special resonance in the American psyche. The U.S. economy has a low dependence on export earnings, and Americans have a high propensity to inject moral principles into their foreign policy (especially when the costs are not prohibitive). Sanctions provide an appealing middle ground to the usually less desirable extremes of military intervention or of doing nothing in the face of provocation by an aggressive or ruthless foreign government. They are a policy instrument that offers what usually appears to be a proportional response to a challenge in which the interests at stake are less than vital, for example, expressing commitment to behavioral norms like supporting human rights and opposing the proliferation of weapons of mass destruction. The so-called CNN effect, in which the media graphically depict human suffering and other problems in far away lands, has enhanced support for some kind of action after verbal entreaties have been ignored. The increased influence of single-issue constituencies in American politics is also a factor. Small, well-organized interest groups—often acting through Congress—can have an impact that far exceeds their numerical strength.[8]

Sanctions have been imposed in connection with more than forty separate laws. There is a long list of U.S. policy objectives inspiring sanctions: to contain former Cold War adversaries (the former Soviet Union, China, Cuba, etc.); to retaliate against military aggression (Iraq, Serbia, North Vietnam, etc.); to protest violations of human rights (South Africa, China, etc.); to respond to alleged state-sponsored terrorism (Libya, Iran, Syria, Sudan, etc.); to demand that a democratically elected government be restored (Haiti); to try toppling regimes deemed odious (Panama, Cuba, Burma, etc.); to promote nuclear nonproliferation (India, Pakistan, North Korea, etc.); to demand better antinarcotics efforts (Columbia, Afghanistan, etc.); and to promote workers' rights (China, Saudi Arabia, etc.).

Inconsistencies and anomalies are the main recurring themes in an objective analysis of contemporary U.S. trade sanctions policy. On the one hand, the imposition of every major trade sanction thus far has had some justification because each has been provoked by a foreign action that is offensive to American values. On the other hand, a review of history shows that, by a wide margin, sanctions have failed to achieve their primary objective of inducing changes in the behavior of targeted governments. (By the authors' measure, achieving the incidental, feel-good objective of symbolically aligning the United States with righteous causes is not a "success.") According to one expert, the success rate for unilateral and multilateral sanctions involving the United States has declined markedly from the already unimpressive 34 percent rate for the period between World War I and 1990. Sanctions in the 1990s contributed to the achievement of American foreign policy goals in less than 20 percent of the cases.[9] A major American business lobby observed that the business community is often asked whether it supports human rights, opposes nuclear proliferation, and so on. The more appropriate question, the National Association of Manufacurers argues, "is whether or not denying American manufacturers the ability to export is an appropriate and effective response" to such violations abroad. Its answer is no: "The evidence indicates that U.S. sanctions outside a multilateral framework lead to lost American exports and jobs, with little or no impact on the targeted government."[10]

Unilaterally imposed sanctions stand the least chance of success because they can do relatively little to impose damage or deprivation. Even multilateral sanctions can fail to the extent that the targeted government is strong, resolute, and resourceful. Iraq is a classic example. By historical standards, there were few loopholes in the universally applied, U.N.-administered sanctions imposed after that country invaded Kuwait. However, they failed to convince the Iraqi government to withdraw. Having subsequently been linked to Iraq's acceptance of UN weapons inspections, these seemingly devastating measures are now in their second decade. The heads of government in the countries that defeated Iraq militarily come and go, but Saddam has remained firmly in power. While containing the country's military capabilities, the sanctions maintained by the international community have failed in their post-Kuwait objective of softening the militancy of Saddam Hussein's government. Ironically, the United States imports significant quantities of oil from Iraq, its implacable foe.

No definitive assessment of the net cost-effectiveness of U.S. sanctions is possible. The benefits are qualitative. The exact loss of potential American exports and national income can only be guessed at because it is not possible to know for certain how much would have been exported in the absence of confrontation. Uncertainty about economic losses is also a function of disagreement about exactly which actions conform to the definition of a sanction. Furthermore, as noted in Chapter 4, economic theory holds that macroeconomic factors and the difference between a country's saving and investment ultimately determine the overall balance between its exports and imports. The most widely cited guesstimate of costs is a study done by scholars at the Institute for International Economics; they calculated that in 1995, U.S. exports to twenty-six countries subject to major sanctions were $15 to $19 billion lower than they would otherwise have been. Unless these lost exports were offset by increased shipments to other markets, an estimated 200,000 relatively high-paying jobs could have been lost.[11] Another estimate calculated that the total value of lost exports from all U.S. sanctions, controls, and impediments in the mid-1990s might have been as much as $40 billion annually.[12] The cost to U.S. exports might be even higher if we could calculate the extent to which countries that worry about future U.S. sanctions reduce their dependence on American suppliers by deliberately buying manufactures and agricultural goods from other countries.

One of the more striking anomalies of U.S. sanctions policy is the frequency with which domestic lobbying power rather than meticulous analysis and consistent criteria determines which countries are hit with sanctions and which are merely verbally censured. A united business lobby prevailed in the decision to reject major trade retaliation to protest the many U.S. political, military, and human rights grievances against the Chinese government. Washington has decided not to risk a trade war and terminate MFN treatment lest American business lose access to one of the world's largest, most promising markets. The Cuban-American community has prevailed on how to deal with the dictatorship of Fidel Castro. The strategy chosen here is to retain across-the-board sanctions even though Cuban efforts to incite political revolution in other Latin American countries have ended, no other country sanctions Cuba, and the Cuban government is publicly able to blame U.S. intransigence for Cuba's decades of economic failures. Secretary of State Colin Powell has written that sanctions against China are not advisable because expanding economic relations gives the United States "an opportunity to promote rule of law, transparency and accountability . . . and thus promote change in China. . . . Trade with China is not only good economic policy, it is good human rights policy and good national security policy."[13] Inexplicably, the exact opposite formula is judged appropriate to alter Cuban policies.

Contradictory congressional behavior is another anomaly in export policy. As stated in the last chapter, members of Congress have been perennial allies of the business community in seeking to subject fewer goods to U.S. export controls and to lessen the waiting time for obtaining approval of export license applications. Yet the situation with respect to sanctions is radically different. Congress frequently passes new legislation ordering the executive branch to cut trade relations, as it did with South Africa in the 1980s. Congressional ire was responsible for two of the most controversial sanctions laws, the Iran and Libya Sanctions Act and the Cuban Liberty and Democratic Solidarity Act (popularly known as the Helms-Burton bill) dealing with Cuba. These bills have thus far inflicted more political tension on U.S. relations with friendly countries than damage to the economies of Cuba, Libya, or Iran. Although they have the laudable aims of increasing human rights in three dictatorships and discouraging Libya and Iran from supporting international terrorism, these statutes go beyond the traditional boundaries of U.S. sanctions to include the legally questionable acts of extraterritorial application and secondary boycotts. (They are also unusual because they target private companies and people, not governments.)

The Iran-Libya statute subjects foreign individuals and businesses that invest $40 million or more in any one year in the oil sectors of Iran or Libya to a variety of retaliatory U.S. trade sanctions. Section III of the Helms-Burton bill makes any foreign person, company, or government that "traffics" in (i.e., receives financial benefit from the use of) confiscated American property in Cuba liable for monetary damages in U.S. federal courts. Another of the bill's provisions contains a section mandating denial of entry visas to the United States for foreign nationals who individually or through their employers are financially tied to confiscated American property in Cuba. Unambiguous threats of counter-retaliation from the European Union and Canada have resulted in the use of presidential waiver authority (without which the bill probably would have been vetoed) to suspend implementation of these sections. The U.S. and EU governments concluded an "understanding" that sanctions would not be taken against Western European companies under the Helms-Burton and Iran-Libya acts; in return, the EU suspended its complaint in the WTO that the extraterritorial aspects of these statutes violate world trade law.

Another case study of export policy inconsistency in Congress began with its taking the initiative in passing legislation that requires the president to impose sanctions on countries testing nuclear weapons. In accordance with the Arms Control Act, the president applied export-related sanctions on India and Pakistan following their nuclear tests in 1998. However, this homage to nonproliferation wilted under intense lobbying pressure by the agricultural community, led by wheat growers in the Northwest. Not wanting to be blamed for a loss of several hundred million dollars in wheat exports to Pakistan, Congress passed the Agriculture Export Relief Act later in 1998. The act authorized the president to exempt Department of Agriculture concessional export credits and guarantees (essential for facilitating wheat sales to Pakistan) from sanctions imposed for nonproliferation reasons—authority that President Clinton immediately used. Foreign policy considerations induced another easing of pressure against Pakistan in the fall of 2001, when that country's importance to the U.S. military effort in Afghanistan resulted in President Bush's signing a waiver that suspended all significant bilateral economic sanctions against it.

A final anomaly of sanctions is that they inflict their greatest harm on everyday citizens who have nothing to do with determining the policies of their government. Elites everywhere have relatively easy access to the black market. In any event, the limited number of successes attributable to past sanctions efforts has not been an observable factor in dissuading U.S. policymakers from imposing new unilateral or multilateral sanctions.

## Official Efforts to Promote Exports

U.S. government efforts to promote exports are similar to the array of programs maintained by all large industrial economies for the benefit of their private sectors. Governments engage in this activity partly because they believe they can be genuinely useful and partly because of competitive pressure to match the efforts of other governments. Large American companies selling expensive high-tech products are the major beneficiaries of the Export-Import Bank's loans and loan guarantees for U.S. exports that are extended on more favorable terms than could be obtained from commercial banks. When very large procurement contracts are at stake, presidents have occasionally communicated directly with their foreign counterparts to make a pitch on behalf of the American bidder.

Agribusiness has access to concessional export financing facilities such as the Commodity Credit Corporation in the Department of Agriculture. The latter's share of the total export promotion budget remains disproportionately high relative to agriculture's 7 to 8 percent share of total U.S. exports. Agricultural exports also get a boost from Public Law 480, a segment of the U.S. foreign aid program that provides agricultural commodities to LDCs on a concessional loan or grant basis. Small and medium-sized companies are the principal users of government-funded services such as overseas trade fairs, market research on foreign countries, business development missions, advice to first time exporters, and so on.

Administrations since the 1970s have announced countless export promotion packages in connection with their professed commitment to assisting export expansion. None of the announcements have had a dramatic, across-the-board impact, nor have any of them permanently changed the policy culture in Washington that treats export expansion as a secondary priority. One critic complained that export expansion packages have been announced with a regularity that "by itself suggests something less than total commitment by the government to these initiatives."[14] The 1993 comprehensive review of government efficiency led by then Vice President Al Gore determined that the United States, unlike its major foreign competitors, "does not possess an export strategy or an export infrastructure capable of assisting U.S. businesses interested in pursuing global opportunities."[15] Congress's General Accounting Office criticized the export promotion system in the mid-1990s for being fragmented among ten departments and agencies, lacking integrated strategy or priorities, and suffering from a degree of "inefficiency, overlap, and duplication" that often confused the business community it was created to serve.[16]

No empirical data have been produced thus far that unequivocally demonstrate a direct link between the extent of official export promotion efforts and the value of a country's exports. Once again, there are two contending schools of thought about U.S. export policy. Critics of export promotion programs decry the misallocation of financial resources and waste of taxpayers' money. Supporters point to market imperfections that need to be overcome and warn that "unilateral U.S. disarmament" would allow foreign governments' concessional financing and other support measures to annually displace hundreds of millions of dollars of American exports. They also point out that the United States spends less on concessional financing in proportion to its total exports than the large West European economies, Japan, or Canada, and advocate increased budget allocations. While this debate continues inconclusively, the policy status quo is sustained by the self-interest inherent in the "iron triangle" of executive branch bureaucracies, business lobbyists, and supportive members of Congress.[17]

Seeking improved overseas market access for American goods is a second, distinct track of U.S. government efforts to assist exporters. Presidential authority to press foreign governments to reduce, if not eliminate, actions that have been found to discriminate against U.S. exports is provided under the provisions of Section 301 of the Trade Act of 1974, one of the trade remedy provisions discussed in Chapter 7. Approximately 120 Section 301 cases were initiated between 1975 and the end of 2001. The protectionist aspects of the EU's Common Agricultural Policy have been one of the principal targets of this measure for many years. Energetic, often aggressive assaults by U.S. trade officials on foreign barriers and distortions judged harmful to American commerce have created a major backlash against an export policy unique to the United States. Market-opening demands made under the 301 provision rank alongside the antidumping law as the largest source of foreign anger with U.S. trade policy since 1975.

Despite this resentment, the implicit threat of U.S. retaliation if other governments refuse to respond adequately had a reasonably good success rate in reducing foreign trade barriers. A good argument can be made that Section 301 has been the most cost-effective U.S. export promotion program (expenditures are minimal since the conduct of investigations and negotiations represent a negligible fraction of the USTR office's relatively modest personnel budget). The best-known independent assessment of the use of this authority determined that in the seventy-two cases it studied, U.S. negotiating objectives were at least partially successful about half the time (a far better percentage, it was noted, than the use of economic sanctions to achieve objectives in foreign policy). Section 301, the study concluded, had been a "reasonably effective" trade policy tool, was "generally market-opening rather than market-closing," did not result in frequent retaliation by the United States, and infrequently provoked counter-retaliation.[18]

Congress has been dissatisfied on a number of occasions with what it regarded as a lack of commitment by the executive branch in vigorously pursuing demands for improved foreign market access. The result was a series of amendments to the Section 301 provisions (see Chapter 7) that increased the number of foreign trade practices covered and reduced the administration's discretion in deferring retaliation when foreign governments spurn demands to reduce specified trade barriers. Mounting frustration on Capitol Hill regarding the growing U.S. trade deficit in general and the perceived refusal of Japan to engage in genuine market-opening measures caused Congress to insert the so-called Super 301 provision in the 1988 trade bill. It was a watered-down version of an earlier, quite draconian legislative proposal that would have required sanctions against countries that did not reduce "excessive and unwarranted" bilateral trade surpluses. The Super 301 provision instructed a reluctant Bush administration in 1989 and 1990 to review the international trade landscape and designate "priority" practices in "priority" countries that were especially damaging to U.S. export potential. The provision then required the executive branch to self-initiate Section 301 investigations that presumably would lead to bilateral negotiations to reduce the specially designated barriers. Although these negotiations operated under the same legal framework as "regular" 301, Super 301 attracted harsh criticism about the legitimacy and propriety of the United States to unilaterally and proactively label other countries as unfair traders.

The heated debate surrounding Section 301 is an excellent example of perceptions being more important in trade policy than elusive truths. On one side of the argument, successive generations of trade policymakers in Washington have felt fully justified in attacking foreign trade barriers under threat of retaliation if the other country refused to liberalize. U.S. public opinion believes the American market has long been well above average in its openness to imports, and that it is necessary to seek a "level playing field" that minimizes the "victimization" of American economic interests. This mind-set feels that "fair trade" requires trading partners, notably Japan, to reciprocate this openness rather than employ trade barriers to serve domestic development policies. Removing foreign trade barriers is defended as an integral part of the larger, "economically correct" U.S. strategy of correcting its large, potentially destabilizing merchandise trade deficit through export expansion rather than import contraction. Furthermore, inducing foreign countries to reduce their trade barriers is seen as being fully compatible with the virtuous pursuit of a more liberal multilateral trading system. Image conscious Democratic and Republican administrations have welcomed the availability of Section 301 initiatives to demonstrate an activist, sympathetic trade policy to aggrieved U.S. companies and farmers.

Critics offer a different perspective on the virtues of Section 301. They label it as "aggressive unilateralism" that violates the spirit, if not the letter of international trade law. U.S. trade policymakers are condemned for appointing themselves prosecutor, judge, jury, and executioner in determining acceptable behavior by other countries while exempting U.S. trade actions from an external review process.Critics categorize Section 301 as protectionist. They dismiss the U.S. government's argument that it is not intended to restrict access to the American market because retaliation is supposed to be a threat meant to enhance negotiating leverage, not something to be invoked. One European pointed out that when Section 301 was utilized, other countries had to negotiate on the basis of an agenda set by the United States to suit its judgments and timetables—"all of which is a departure from the rule of international law."[19]

The controversy has been muted by the creation in the WTO of a Dispute Settlement Body to administer a dispute settlement mechanism (see Chapter 8) that is now the preferred venue for resolving trade disputes. The diminished role of Section 301 was first demonstrated in 1995 when Japan refused American pressures for bilateral negotiations to resolve the Section 301–originated dispute regarding the extent of the former's market-opening measures for automobiles. Japan's suggestion that the U.S. government should file a complaint in the WTO was supported by all other major trading countries. They were united in the belief that refusal by the United States to use the newly strengthened multilateral dispute settlement mechanism would undermine its chances of growing into the facility that all member countries wanted to succeed.

The bottom line is that a Section 301 investigation determining that a discriminatory foreign action exists now usually prompts the U.S. government to file a complaint in the WTO (assuming the other party does not want to talk bilaterally). Thus, the likelihood of unilateral U.S. retaliation in the absence of a favorable WTO decision has become remote. The determination of whether or not this change is "progress" depends on the extent to which one prefers that the United States prove the legal validity of its complaint before a formal group of neutral jurists from third countries. Most American trade policymakers and companies prefer the old technique of head-to-head political pressure on countries that knew refusal to accommodate at least some of the American demands—even those they considered unjustified—ran the risk of reduced access to the lucrative U.S. market.

## Conclusions and Outlook

U.S. export policy inevitably moves in opposite directions. There are compelling economic reasons to increase exports. This is the optimal means of reducing the structural U.S. trade deficit (as opposed to reducing imports), and it is an efficient means of allowing U.S. companies to increase profits and reduce per unit production costs. Increasing the number of workers employed in export-related jobs with above average levels of pay and productivity is inherently desirable. Such employment is also the ideal means of accommodating workers who have lost their jobs through imports of relatively less sophisticated, more labor intensive goods.

For many people, there are equally compelling reasons to restrict trade with countries that persist in objectionable behavior. The responsibilities that go along with being the world's only superpower, the American propensity to insert ethics into trade policy, and the ability of the domestic economy to afford the luxury of pursuing goals in foreign policy and human rights at the expense of foreign sales suggest that a major diminution in the "negative" pole of U.S. export policy will not occur in the foreseeable future.

Although neither U.S. export controls nor sanctions will dramatically diminish, a committed opposition against their allegedly excessive use exists in the corporate world and among some members of Congress. It is likely that their efforts will cause the administration of U.S. export restraints to undergo evolutionary changes. The campaign to prevent excesses will apply pressure on future presidents to keep new sanctions to a minimum and to move the relatively restrictive U.S. export control regime gradually into harmony with other major trading countries. The logic of restricting goods and technologies readily available from other countries will be increasingly contested. Sanctions will probably be subject to periodic public review to determine whether they should continue or be terminated. Another likely change is enhanced efforts to design sanctions that inflict maximum punishment on ruling elites and minimum harm on the populace at large ("smart sanctions"). If most or all of these changes materialize, exports for some American companies will increase, but no dramatic increase in U.S. exports as a whole should be expected.

The relative U.S. success in pursuing complaints through the WTO dispute settlement mechanism (see Chapter 8) suggests that the government's premiere export expansion effort will be the use of this multilateral forum to challenge discriminatory foreign trade barriers. A radical change that elevates export promotion to a top-tier policy priority will not occur short of a dramatic, prolonged crisis in the dollars exchange rate that causes foreign exporters to the United States to demand payment in other currencies that will have to be earned through increased American exports.

## For Further Reading

Bayard, Thomas O., and Kimberly Ann Elliot. *Reciprocity and Retaliation in U.S. Trade Policy.* Washington, D.C.: Institute for International Economics, 1994.

Bhagwati, Jagdish, and Hugh T. Patrick, eds. *Aggressive Unilateralism: America's 301 Trade Policy and the World Trading System.* Ann Arbor, Mich.: University of Michigan Press, 1990.

Carter, Barry. *International Economic Sanctions: Improving the Haphazard U.S. Legal Regime.* Cambridge: Cambridge University Press, 1988.

Haass, Richard N. *Economic Sanctions and American Diplomacy.* New York: Council on Foreign Relations, 1998.

Haass, Richard N., and Meghan O'Sullivan. *Honey and Vinegar: Incentives, Sanctions, and Foreign Policy.* Washington, D.C.: Brookings Institution Press, 2000.

Hufbauer, Gary Clyde, Jeffrey J. Schott, and Kimberly Ann Elliott. *Economic Sanctions Reconsidered.* Washington, D.C.: Institute for International Economics, 1990.

Long, William, *U.S. Export Control Policy, Executive Autonomy vs. Congressional Reform.* New York: Columbia University Press, 1989.

National Academy of Sciences, *Finding Common Ground: U.S. Export Controls in a Changed Global Environment.* Washington, D.C.: National Academy Press, 1991.

## Notes

1. For details of this process, see chapter 10 of Stephen D. Cohen, *The Making of U.S. International Economic Policy,* 5th ed. (New York: Praeger, 2000).

2. The U.S. trade deficit in the early years of the twenty-first century was so large that arithmetically only a very large relative growth in exports would allow for a meaningful contraction of the deficit.

3. Calculated from data in Table B–12 of the *Economic Report of the President* (Washington, D.C.: U.S. Government Printing Office, January 2001), 290.

4. Arvind Parkhe, "U.S. National Security Export Controls: Implications for Global Competitiveness of U.S. High-Tech Firms," *Strategic Management Journal* (January 1992): 54.

5. See, for example, National Association of Manufacturers, *A Catalog of New U.S. Unilateral Economic Sanctions for Foreign Policy Purposes 1993–96* (Washington, D.C.: National Association of Manufacturers, March 1997), 10.

6. The report was accessed at www.stimson.org/tech/sgemec/index.html/.

7. Testimony of Under Secretary of State Stuart Eizenstat, *Economic Sanctions and U.S. Policy Interests,* hearing of the House Committee on International Relations, 3 June 1998, 75.

8. Richard N. Haass, "Economic Sanctions: Too Much of a Bad Thing," Brookings Institution Policy Brief Number 34, accessed at www.brook.edu/es/policy/policy/.htm/.

9. Testimony of Jeffrey Schott, *Economic Sanctions and U.S. Policy Interests,* hearing of the House Committee on International Relations, 3 June 1998, 149.

10. National Association of Manufacturers, *Catalog of New U.S. Unilateral Economic Sanctions,* 8.

11. Gary Clyde Hufbauer et al., *U.S. Economic Sanctions: Their Impact on Trade, Jobs, and Wages,* working paper, Institute for International Economics 1997; accessed at www.iie.com/sanctnwp.htm/.

12. J. David Richardson, *Sizing Up U.S. Export Disincentives* (Washington, D.C.: Institute for International Economics, 1993), 2.

13. Colin L. Powell, "The Promise of China Trade," *Washington Post,* 1 June 2001, A31.

14. Penelope Hartland-Thunberg, *The Political and Strategic Importance of Exports,* Center for Strategic and International Studies, 1979, 17.

15. *Department of Commerce,* accompanying report of the National Performance Review; accessed at www.ibiblio.org/pub/academic/polit. . . /doc.txt.

16. Press release of the testimony of Allan Mendelowitz, U.S. General Accounting Office, to the House Committee on Small Business, 26 October 1993, 2.

17. For a detailed examination of the pros and cons of U.S. export promotion efforts, see *Federal Export Promotion Programs: An Academic Perspective,* hearing of the Subcommittee on Procurement, Exports, and Business Opportunities, House Committee on Small Business, 23 May 1995.

18. Thomas Bayard and Kimberly Ann Elliott, *Reciprocity and Retaliation in U.S. Trade Policy* (Washington, D.C.: Institute for International Economics, 1994), 64, 331, 334.

19. Corrado Pirzio-Biroli, "A European View of the 1988 Trade Act and Section 301," in *Aggressive Unilateralism,* Jagdish Bhagwati and Hugh Patrick, eds. (Ann Arbor, Mich.: University of Michigan Press, 1990), 261.

# 10 Trade Relations with Japan and China: The New "Twin Deficits"

This chapter discusses the two stormiest bilateral relationships in contemporary U.S. trade policy. If a public opinion poll was taken in the United States inquiring which country was most in violation of international trade protocols, Japan and China would surely be the top contenders for the dubious distinction of being ranked number one. The approach of U.S. trade policymakers toward these two countries has been long on demands and criticism and short on warmth. Japan and China are the most illuminating examples of how the economic, political, and legal dynamics of American trade policy react to important trading partners that embrace economic philosophies and institutions differing in many important respects from those of the United States.

Neither country believes in the degree of market freedom found in the United States, and both accept the need for a more active and extensive role for government in the economy than do the large majority of Americans. Both countries are widely perceived to have harmed U.S. economic interests through import barriers and aggressive export programs that encourage unfair trade practices. China's government is also viewed by many Americans as a potential threat to their national security and as a serial violator of human rights. When judged by American standards, both countries embrace protectionist, if not outright mercantilist, policies designed to maximize exports and inhibit imports. Rightly or wrongly, the main justification for accusations that these countries have not been playing the game fairly is their large trade surpluses, both on a multilateral basis and bilaterally with the United States.

Most economists are delighted that these countries willingly supply tens of billions of dollars annually (the equivalent of their bilateral trade surpluses) of net real economic resources to American consumers in return for paper money, most of which is sent back to the United States. For every contented economist, however, there are a thousand people who would prefer a more hard-line U.S. trade policy to encourage these countries to accelerate market-opening measures and induce corrections in the large U.S. trade deficits with them. Countless heated dialogues with U.S. trade officials conveying complaints, demands, and threats have turned the Japanese and Chinese governments into reluctant experts in the letter but not the spirit of U.S. trade laws.

# Japan

Most newcomers to the study of international trade relations will be surprised to learn that the industrial country suffering the lowest growth rates in the ten-year period beginning in 1991 had, for many years previously, generated more angst for U.S. industry and trade policy than any other three countries combined. Early in the new millennium, however, U.S. policymakers spent little time worrying about Japan's displacing the United States as the world's premier industrial economy. The new worry is how to find effective remedies for Japan's long-term economic stagnation and a dysfunctional banking system that could trigger a financial meltdown. This was the second stunning reversal of economic fortunes for these two countries in three decades. Although Japan had been physically devastated by World War II, by the early 1970s, it was being hailed as an "economic miracle." Its export success also was miraculous, and its big manufacturing companies began to overwhelm one U.S. industrial sector after another. Japan seemed to have perfected a flawless formula for sustained economic success and looked ready to dominate a large proportion of emerging technologies. Shortly after Japan's economic success had peaked at the end of the 1980s, the two economies again unexpectedly traded places.

No one foresaw that Japan's economic bubble was about to burst, even though that phenomenon repeatedly appears after great success leads to great economic excess (wildly inflated land and stock price increases in the case of Japan; later, excessive investment in information and telecommunications technology in the United States). What might have been a temporary setback in growth rates was extended indefinitely by the Japanese government's failure to revise long-standing domestic economic policies and regulations. The latter had been successful in the catch-up phase, but in the 1990s and beyond, the old economic formula did more to perpetuate inefficiency than promote growth and innovation. What worked superbly in the catch-up phase suddenly seemed ill-suited to a mature Japanese economy competing in an increasingly interdependent and faster moving world economy.

Meanwhile, in Silicon Valley, U.S.A., the information technology revolution was quietly gathering momentum. Along with effective monetary and fiscal policies, the subsequent investment boom in technology by American industry boosted U.S. productivity increases to a rate that allowed the "new" economy to achieve sustained increases in GDP and employment amidst price stability. Full employment and an industrial sector operating at near full capacity caused acute American distress over its large bilateral trade deficit to wither away. American anger about Japan's closed markets also abated as continuing liberalization measures and mounting corporate problems caused some once sacrosanct barriers to be lowered, such as the unwritten rule against foreign takeovers of major Japanese companies. More improbable, the U.S. government's economic focus on Japan shifted away from trade policy anxiety about that country's competitive strengths to macroeconomic anxiety about the global implications of prolonged malaise in the world's second largest national economy. Symbolically, Japan was replaced by Mexico in the late 1990s as the second largest trading partner of the United States.

A lack of urgency is the antithesis of any characterization of U.S. trade policy toward Japan in the thirty years after the late 1960s.

## The Domestic Foundations of Japan's Export Success

Japan's somewhat unusual export and import patterns are mainly the product of domestic economic phenomena. A strong domestic industrial base spawned a strong export sector, not vice versa. Japan's economic history is as different from that of the United States as its version of capitalism. It has always put the preservation of its culture and the minimization of foreign intrusion into the affairs of its homogeneous population ahead of satisfying consumer wants. It has faced a recurring need to catch up to the more advanced Western economies without the benefit of indigenous natural resources. Since the late nineteenth century, pursuit of a stronger economy to make Japan more self-sufficient came mainly through officially sponsored industrial policy. There has never been an ideological disposition to let the invisible hand of the marketplace—or foreigners—determine the fate of the country. Defeat in World War II caused Japan to abandon its effort to achieve international stature and security through military means and concentrate instead on achieving these goals through economic strength. A unanimous national consensus accepted the need to limit short-term gratification in order to channel maximum resources into developing a world-class industrial sector. Japan's entire economic system was deliberately tilted in favor of producers and away from consumers.

When the United States emerged from the war as an international colossus, much of American industry rested on its laurels, thinking its international competitive lead was insurmountable. The United States wound up playing the hare to Japan's tortoise. The speed and degree of Japan's successful effort to achieve industrial strength impressed all who observed it. But in the process, its economy came to be viewed by many foreigners as "a sort of perpetual-motion machine that generates trade surpluses, cranking out a surfeit of exports . . . while drawing in a relative paucity of imports."[1]

The long record of Japanese industrial successes from the early 1960s to the early 1990s does not so much reflect accident or conspiracy as it does a favorable mix of cultural values, management strategies, production know-how, and official policies that mutually reinforced one another in a favorable environment for industrial growth. An unusually positive synergy developed, and the Japanese did a lot of things correctly while making relatively few mistakes in addressing their economic priorities.[2] Still, foreigners whose knowledge of Japan comes mainly from a flood of imports develop an overly rosy view of what is actually a "dual" economy that excludes many sectors from the economic renaissance. Small farms keep the agricultural sector relatively inefficient. The services sector was and is a mixed bag. Japan's highly inefficient, multilayered distribution system is mainly designed, it seems, to maximize jobs. Several manufacturing sectors, including food processing, pharmaceuticals, commercial aircraft, and chemicals, never became global powerhouses.

The first and arguably most important explanation for Japan's domestic economic success has been the ability of an elite group of manufacturing companies to achieve world-class quality levels and reduce production costs. Though accounting for only a small percentage of the overall GDP, major companies in the electronics, automobile, optical equipment, business machines, steel, and machine tools sectors contributed disproportionately to the extraordinary growth and success of Japanese exports. These companies are also the main reason that, from the 1960s through the 1980s, Japan devoted a larger percentage of its GDP to investment in new plants and equipment than any other major industrial economy. Management stressed attention to detail, unceasing efforts at increased productivity, and long-term concerns with increased market share (thanks largely to the lack of shareholder power to demand short-term profits). As best exemplified by Toyota's revolutionary development of "lean manufacturing," many Japanese companies were able to increase their efficiency dramatically and over an extended period of time. They emerged in the 1970s as world leaders in process technology, the totality of the manufacturing process that begins with new product development and ends with its final assembly on a production line. As discussed below, many American manufacturing companies eventually studied and adapted Japanese manufacturing techniques to avoid a disastrous drop in their competitiveness. Once the student of American production methods, Japan was now the teacher.

There is also a dark side to the success of Japan's big industrial corporations: To minimize unit labor costs, they have consistently held workers' wage increases below their productivity increases. When they face business adversity, they demand price cuts from their highly dependent, intensely loyal suppliers and subcontractors.

Culture and history are the second source of Japan's industrial success. Relevant Japanese cultural values can be discerned on three different levels. The first is strong belief in hard work, frugality, honesty, and education. The intermediate level consists of group loyalty and collective goals (in lieu of self-aggrandizement), mutual trust and obligations, simultaneous competition and cooperation, social harmony, and respect for hierarchy. The third level is the intense desire to control, to the maximum extent possible, the terms upon which foreign ideas, goods, business practices, and technology penetrate their intense in-group bonding, which might be described as "Japaneseness." The related drive to minimize dependence on the rest of the world has provided an extraordinary incentive to do whatever its takes to build a strong industrial base.

Economic policies are the third and most controversial component of the Japanese economic miracle. The net impact of intensive government intrusion in the economy is hard to measure objectively. Not all successful Japanese companies directly benefited from the largesse of industrial policy, and not all companies receiving financial assistance from the government prospered. Where all companies did benefit was the government's unstinting efforts to create an environment conducive to corporate growth. On the macro level, saving was encouraged to keep the cost of corporate borrowing low, and banks were urged to lend to targeted industries. Disdainful of the notion that the market mechanism works best when left alone, the Japanese government employed a multifaceted industrial policy. This consisted of direct subsidies for research and development, tax incentives to invest in state-of-the-art capital equipment and to conduct research, buy-Japanese government procurement practices, and relaxed enforcement of antitrust laws that encouraged price collusion and market-sharing cartels. Another integral component of industrial policy was import protection to assure that targeted industries had little or no foreign competition to inhibit their growth into world-class competitors. Japan's economy was also the beneficiary of the military umbrella provided by the United States that allowed Japan to limit defense expenditures and devote more resources to relatively productive investments in the private sector.

Japan's economic planners were bright senior civil servants who did their homework in determining criteria for choosing which industries should be targeted for growth. Unlike government planners elsewhere, the bureaucrats intensively engaged in two-way communication with the private sector about what were the best future directions for the Japanese economy. As companies expanded and became financially more self-reliant, financial subsidies diminished, but to this day, business is still intensively regulated. By the late 1990s, the Japanese government was being criticized for causing economic stagnation; it no longer was being praised as an architect of economic success.

## The Unique Aspects of U.S.-Japanese Trade Relations

U.S.-Japanese trade relations are an integral component of what has been called—mostly by people involved in the process—the most important bilateral relationship in the world. In addition to being the most important U.S. ally in the western Pacific, Japan became a top priority of U.S. trade policy because of its exceptional economic accomplishments. It was the first non-Western society to become an international economic superpower. It was the fastest growing major economy from the 1960s through the 1980s. No other country in the post–World War II era has challenged U.S. industrial and technological leadership as much as Japan, and no other exporter of sophisticated manufactured goods has competed as successfully in the global marketplace. It has long generated the world's largest annual trade surplus and until 2000 long accounted for the largest U.S. bilateral deficit. No other country has generated as much anger among its trading partners for allegedly being an "underachiever" when it comes to importing manufactured goods. A final indicator of uniqueness is that only in Japan would a leading national political figure feel compelled to urge that it become a "normal" country.[3]

Japan was far and away at the top of the list of countries inspiring new themes in U.S. trade policy during the last three decades of the twentieth century. Anxiety over Japan's export dynamism and anger over its import barriers were the principle causes of U.S. trade policymakers introducing such new measures as voluntary export restraint agreements, demands for reciprocity of market access, enhanced government support for high-tech R&D, managed trade, results-oriented trade, voluntary import expansion efforts, and strategic trade theory.

Japan was also unique because in the 1980s it held a virtual monopoly on inspiring improved production processes among U.S. manufacturing companies: enhanced quality control; just-in-time delivery of components from a few carefully chosen, highly trusted suppliers; development of new products through joint efforts among R&D engineers, product designers, parts suppliers, and production line workers; reduced middle management; increased authority for production line workers, and so on.

Japan is second to none in exemplifying the subjective nature of U.S. trade policy. Formulating strategy toward that country was the most polarized, emotional segment of U.S. trade policy between 1970 and 1995. Determining the optimal action in dealing with Japan has been extraordinarily complicated because an unusually intense disagreement over the source of the problem (assuming an economic problem actually existed) precluded consensus on the remedies. Most American participants in the debate gravitated to one of two mutually exclusive extremes: blaming Japanese avarice or blaming American ineptitude. The debate became so heated that the two sides eventually coined disparaging (and somewhat exaggerated) nicknames for the other: "bashers" and "apologists."

Hard-liners perceive a naive United States as the victim of calculated, aggressive Japanese trade policies designed to enhance their industrial strength. The soft-liners look at the same situation and perceive a relatively hard-working Japan as the victim of a U.S. refusal to accept responsibility for its own economic and business shortcomings. One side is dismayed and alarmed that a vital political-military relationship could be put at risk because of inappropriately hard-line trade tactics. The other side is still dismayed and alarmed that the U.S. government stood idly by and let Japan inflict serious damage on U.S. economic strength. Further complicating the situation is the propensity of some advocates in both schools of thought to engage in hyperbole, be it claiming that the United States is a bully and should be ashamed of itself, or declaring that the Japanese market is "closed" to imports.

Depending on individual personal philosophy, one can focus on data suggesting that Japan is an arch-mercantilist that practices an inexcusable double standard regarding market access for manufactured goods. Alternatively, data can be selectively chosen to portray Japan as a victim of foreign jealousy and misunderstanding that does not need to apologize for its hard-won achievements and trade surpluses. Some see it as a country receiving inadequate respect not only for its excellent products but also for the high saving rate that provides needed capital to an outside world committed to over-consumption and dependent on imported capital. Defenders of Japan are correct in a literal sense when they assert that its levels of formal import barriers compare favorably with those of any other industrialized country (but that omits informal impediments such as collusive corporate discrimination against foreign goods). The noted economist Jagdish Bhagwati has argued that the "better-crafted" econometric studies "certainly do not support the thesis that Japan imports too little, nor do they indicate a special and extraordinary effect of informal trade barriers that make Japan a fit case for unusual treatment in the world trading system."[4] It also can be argued that, because Japan lacks raw materials, trade patterns consisting mainly of imports of primary products and exports of finished goods are normal and appropriate.

American companies as a group have been criticized for being too concerned with current profits and not spending the money, time, and energy necessary to succeed in an admittedly difficult-to-crack Japanese market that does not welcome newcomers, be they Japanese or foreigners. Prior to the U.S. industrial renaissance in the late 1990s, the Japanese were critical of American industry, citing factors ranging from its inadequate levels of investment and productivity to its lack of concern with the manufacturing process. Akio Morita, the founder of Sony, wrote in the 1980s that

"America no longer makes things, it only takes pleasure in making profits from moving money around."[5]

The pro-Japan brief points out that no one is holding a gun to the heads of consumers in foreign markets to buy its products. In other words, Japan's export success is a function of corporate excellence in reducing prices, increasing quality, producing goods that individuals and companies want to buy, providing attentive after-sales service, and meticulously studying consumer tastes in overseas markets. Another key argument in defense of Japan is the assertion that Americans use Japan as a scapegoat because it is easier to criticize alleged foreign misdeeds than to admit to their own shortcomings. The Japanese point out that on a per capita basis, they buy more U.S. goods than Americans buy Japanese goods, and that no other country has come close to matching their efforts since the late 1960s to reduce trade barriers unilaterally.

The critical school of thought that would "bash" Japan expounds a core premise that the pro-Japan faction angrily dismisses out of hand. It is the contention of the so-called revisionists that the Japanese economic order is significantly different from that of the United States and other market economies. The accommodating school of thought argues that all market economies are subject to certain basic disciplines, and cultural factors cannot dominate the underlying forces of the marketplace. The bashers counter that very distinctive Japanese values and traditions assure government policies, business procedures, and consumer behavior that are distinctly different from their American counterparts. This is a critical issue. If the Japanese economy works differently, its trade sector presumably works differently. In turn, the U.S. government would be fully justified in custom-crafting tough trade policies for a country that distrusts free markets and is well outside the international trade mainstream.

A 1989 report of the president's Advisory Committee for Trade Policy and Negotiations concluded that in "response to the question, 'Is there anything different about Japan's pattern of trade, especially manufactures trade?' . . . studies suggest the answer is an unqualified yes."[6] One example of unusual trade patterns is the remarkably steady 10 percent share of the Japanese market for semiconductors held by American producers during a thirteen year stretch beginning in 1973; it never varied, despite reduced Japanese tariffs, yen appreciation, and other changing conditions. Japan is the only industrial country accused of systematically seeking to undermine the effects of formal trade barriers by initiating informal, inside-the-border impediments (such as a discriminatory distribution system). As noted in Chapter 4, Japanese trade policymakers inflicted a self-imposed wound on their credibility in the 1980s when they imposed stringent new safety standards on imported skis on the grounds that Japanese snow was unique.

The argument on behalf of taking a hard-line stance against a maverick Japanese economic order cites numerous comparative studies that all reach a similar conclusion: Retail prices for most goods in Japan are well above American (and some European) levels. This has led economists to argue that if the Japanese market was really as accessible as soft-line advocates say it is, low-cost imports would flow in at a sufficient rate to make all or most differential price levels disappear.[7] Other special difficulties that have been faced by exporters to Japan include the propensity of member companies of the large industrial groups (keiretsu)[8] to buy from one another; the ingrained preference for preserving long-term business relations; and brazen pressures on retailers by large Japanese manufacturing companies to sell only their goods.

The more severe critics accuse Japan of being an "adversarial" trader that elevates foreign trade from a commercial consideration to a life-and-death struggle for national power and self-esteem. The result is seen to be an intensely nationalistic view of the international trading system, and an insatiable, state-inspired urge to maximize exports and minimize imports that would interfere with industrial targeting and traditional ways of doing business. Hard-liners note that most of Japan's trading partners, including highly successful exporters such as Korea and Singapore, have had the same problems with Japan's export success and have made the same criticisms of its relative paucity of manufactured imports. Global discontent with Japanese trade practices allegedly undermines the thesis that bilateral problems are caused by deficient U.S. exporting efforts and skills.

A close examination of Japan's trade statistics reveals import patterns for manufactured goods that deviate from the international norm. In 1990, manufactured goods were only 44 percent of Japan's total imports, compared to 73 and 71 percent for the United States and all high-income countries, respectively.[9] Japan's relative industrial strength and relatively high dependency on imports of raw materials can explain some, but not all, of the discrepancy. Imports of manufactured goods displayed higher rates of growth after 1990 because of the cumulative effects of reduced impediments to imports and outsourcing of production elsewhere in Asia by Japanese manufacturers. Japan also ranks at or near the bottom on measures of intra-industry trade, the extent to which a country imports and exports different versions of the same products, such as chemicals and automobiles. In addition to importing an unusually low volume of goods that it also exports, Japan is unusual in not recording increases in levels of intra-industry trade.[10]

## The Arithmetic and Significance of the Chronic U.S. Trade Deficit with Japan

Japan occupied the position as the largest bilateral U.S. trade deficit for more than three decades and by a large margin. (In 2000, China took title to the largest U.S. deficit because of continued rapid increases in U.S. imports from that country, not because of a decline in Japan's ability to export nor a spike in its import of American-made goods.) The importance and cause of the perennial U.S. trade deficit with Japan is a source of heated controversy. Economists discount the technical significance of a bilateral trade deficit because, to them, the total or multilateral trade balance is what really matters. For simple arithmetic reasons, a country's total trade is always composed of a mix of bilateral deficits and surpluses. Politically, the deficit is important because it has epitomized and sustained American discontent with Japanese trade practices. Multiple decades of persistent bilateral trade deficits (see Table 10.1) is

TABLE 10.1    U.S. Trade Deficits with Japan (in billions of U.S. dollars)

|      | U.S. Bilateral Deficit | U.S. Imports from Japan | U.S. Exports to Japan |
| ---- | ---------------------- | ----------------------- | --------------------- |
| 1970 | 1.2                    | 5.9                     | 4.7                   |
| 1980 | 9.9                    | 30.7                    | 20.8                  |
| 1990 | 41.1                   | 89.7                    | 48.6                  |
| 1995 | 59.3                   | 123.6                   | 64.3                  |
| 2000 | 81.3                   | 146.6                   | 65.3                  |
| 2001 | 69.0                   | 126.6                   | 57.6                  |

SOURCE: U.S. Department of Commerce trade statistics from various publications.

proof to many Americans that Japan systematically engages in unfair trade practices and gets away with it.

The long-standing bilateral disequilibrium is unique in its stubborn resistance to repeated efforts to reduce it on a long-term basis. Japan's bilateral surplus has endured since the late 1960s despite the application of every known adjustment measure, some being used on multiple occasions. These measures include yen appreciation relative to the dollar, stimulation of Japanese aggregate demand (to increase import demand), dozens of packages of market-opening measures, voluntary export restraints (in effect, Japanese export quotas), relaxation of regulations hampering foreign companies, increased selling in the American market through foreign direct investment rather than exports, and official import promotion programs. No other bilateral U.S. trade deficit has been so entrenched. Furthermore, the U.S. deficit at present would be larger but for the fact that many Japanese makers of mature technologies, such as televisions and recording devices, began exporting to the United States from subsidiaries in East Asia. Off-shore production became increasingly necessary for competitive reasons in the 1980s after the yen appreciated and Japanese labor costs became relatively expensive.

Another unique aspect of the U.S. bilateral deficit is its swift decline in importance in the collective mind of the U.S. trade community. U.S.-Japanese trade relations descended to secondary issue status beginning in the late 1990s despite a series of recordbreaking bilateral deficits. Americans differentiated between larger deficits and fewer dislocations in the American economy from these deficits. Near full employment was one reason. Another moderating factor was that imports from Japan for many years have not caused significant new corporate distress or job losses in the United States. One reason for this declining impact is that Japanese competition has largely stopped displacing U.S.-based manufacturing. Automobiles, the top U.S. import from Japan, have stabilized in volume because of heavy reliance on Japanese foreign direct investment to produce for the American market. The more benign impact of imports from Japan is also a reflection of the relatively stagnant product innovation since the 1990s that has prevented Japanese companies from taking significant market share in the United States away from domestic producers of new technologies such as computer servers and Internet routing equipment.

Some economists believe the saving-investment imbalances (see Chapter 4) in the two countries have caused the structural trade disequilibrium. It is true that Japan for many years has spent less than it produced and the United States has spent more than it produced, the result being the macroeconomic inevitability of a multilateral current account surplus in Japan and a multilateral deficit in the United States. However, there is nothing in this statistical rule of thumb that dictates one country must have a *bilateral* deficit with any other individual country, even one with a large surplus. During the 1980s, the "apologist" position made the mistake of blaming the U.S. saving-investment imbalance, specifically the growing federal budget deficits, for U.S. trade deficits. That this was an oversimplification was demonstrated by the sharp increase in U.S. multilateral and bilateral trade deficits after the budget deficit had turned into a surplus. By the year 2000, macroeconomic explanations of the bilateral disequilibrium correctly emphasized the growth differential between the two countries.

## Three Decades (and Counting) of Efforts to Resolve U.S.-Japanese Trade Frictions

Trade relations between the United States and Japan had an inauspicious beginning. The first partial opening of the Japanese market was made possible only after a determined show of military force in 1853 by Commodore Perry and his well-armed "black ships." Except in the years immediately following World War II, when the United States was dedicated to aiding Japanese economic recovery, bilateral trade relations have never enjoyed great cordiality. The contemporary era of bilateral trade began in the late 1960s when a progressively sophisticated chain of Japanese exports increased their share of the U.S. market. This trend caused many years of painful decreases in domestic production, increases in job losses and factory closings, and escalating U.S. trade deficits.

To some Americans, including U.S. trade policymakers, these changes were mainly the result of unacceptable avaricious trade practices and nonmarket forces. The result has been a nearly continuous series of bilateral negotiations since the late 1960s in which the United States makes demands and Japan responds in word if not in deed. Attributing its second-place finish in head-to-head industrial competition to pervasive and unfair Japanese trade practices, the U.S. government, encouraged by the private sector, embarked on a controversial crusade to achieve a level playing field. More than sixty bilateral agreements have been signed in which Japan promised either to open its markets or to restrain certain exports. Virtually all these commitments came only after the U.S. application of what the Japanese call *gaiatsu,* foreign pressure. The Japanese were content with bilateral trade relations and would have preferred to be left alone. U.S. government officials became the equivalent of the only effective opposition party in Japan, dragging reluctant Japanese politicians and bureaucrats kicking and screaming into altering what had been a winning formula: an import-discouraging, export-maximizing trade regime.

Perceptions of the success of the American effort to "open" Japan differ sharply. There is no denying that Japan effected more nonreciprocal, that is, unilateral, trade liberalization measures than any other country in modern history. The statistics show that Japanese import liberalization measures often led to increases in U.S. exports of goods previously denied entry.[11] On the other hand, Japan sometimes refused to respond to U.S. demands, and even deliberately undermined reductions in tariffs or nontariff barriers by quietly imposing new kinds of barriers. U.S. complaints about restricted market access for some goods, such as flat glass and soda ash, have dragged on for many years. In any event, after more than three decades of activity, U.S. demands for a more import-friendly Japan continue unabated, as does the bilateral trade disequilibrium.

Soft-liners emphasize how forthcoming and patient Japan has been in the face of endless U.S. demands, and how the United States should expect increased imports to the extent that its industrial sector cannot compete more effectively. The opposite viewpoint suggests that the Japanese domestic economic system is so intrinsically biased against most imports that traditional trade negotiations are inadequate for resolving more deeply rooted problems. Clyde Prestowitz, an alleged "basher," described the situation this way:

> Nothing in U.S. law or tradition . . . anticipated the possibility of trade and indus- try being organized as part of an effort to achieve specific national goals. . . . The United States understood military competition . . . but not national industrial com- petition. The result was a series of negotiations that never focused on the main issues and that dealt with symptoms instead of causes.[12]

Evaluations of results differ, but there is no denying that the chronology of bilater- al trade relations since the late 1960s consists of nonstop tensions ameliorated from time to time by a negotiating process that springs from an unending series of U.S. demands. Dozens of major negotiating events transpiring over some thirty-five years of ostensibly goodwill efforts are only partially summarized here.[13] The best means for making sense of them is to recognize two transcendent and permanent themes. The first is the sheer volume and repetition of two generic trade actions adopted by the Japanese to avoid retaliation by the United States: (1) market-opening measures designed to provide various degrees (from nothing to a lot) of greater market access for U.S.-made goods; and (2) voluntary export restraint agreements (through the 1980s) that gave the Japanese a voice in establishing the economic equivalent of American import quotas. The second theme is a constant expansion of the negotiat- ing agenda as U.S. officials tried one new gambit after another to secure the results that continued to elude them.

The common denominator of both themes is the cumulative failure of more than three decades of intense negotiations to resolve American grievances and secure a sus- tained bilateral trade balance equilibrium. The tendency to point fingers and simply fault one side or the other has contributed to a situation in which the communica- tions gap between the two perspectives on which country is mostly responsible for the trade frictions has closed either not at all or imperceptibly. More progress might have been made in narrowing disagreement if the problem had been defined as two sepa- rate, though related, issues. The first was a widespread inability of many American manufacturers to protect their domestic market share from stronger, more determined Japanese competitors—primarily the fault of Americans. The radical shift in bilateral economic relations that materialized in the late 1990s is perhaps best illustrated by the almost total abatement of American industrial companies' fear of crushing competition from imports of manufactured goods from Japan. The second issue is the singular difficulty of successfully exporting manufactured goods to Japan—the fault primarily of Japanese practices. In short, both sides share the ample blame that can be apportioned.

The ripple effect of spiraling imports from Japan displacing more and more domestic production led to U.S. trade policy's idea of negotiating voluntary export restraints (VERs), sometimes referred to as orderly marketing agreements. They are a middleground between the undesirable economic extreme of unilateral protectionism and the political extreme of doing nothing. More than any other country, Japan found itself on the receiving end of U.S. demands that it either choose self-imposed restrictions on the volume of sensitive exports or accept the more restrictive measures that would be unilaterally imposed. Demands for VERs were derided by Japan and American liberal trade advocates as being hypocritical and in conflict with the vigorous U.S. advocacy of freer trade.

The first major VER began in 1968 when Japan unilaterally implemented a program of "voluntary" restraints on steel exports to the United States.[14] These restraints have been informally retained through the present with only a few brief interruptions. The end of U.S. economic benevolence to its ally was clearly delineated by the beginning of a bitter three-year dispute in 1969 in which the Japanese initially refused to accept the U.S. demand that they restrict shipments of synthetic textile products. Japanese shipments were increasing rapidly, yet still accounted for less than 4 percent of the rapidly growing U.S. market for those goods. The United States would later pressure the ever-successful Japanese into restraining exports of color televisions,[15] automobiles, and machine tools.

The first phase of Japan's import liberalization began in the late 1960s. Initial targets were the country's most expendable import barriers and its increasingly superfluous export incentives. A steady stream of unilateral liberalization measures was adopted over the next two decades, with results, as noted above, that fell well short of American expectations. These frustrations translated into even more market-opening demands relayed from the private sector by the executive branch to the Japanese government. An increasingly impatient Congress began signaling Tokyo that at least one branch of the U.S. government was fed up and ready to retaliate. Numerous legislative proposals were introduced—but never enacted—that would have imposed discriminatory trade restrictions on Japanese goods. Nonbinding resolutions were passed calling on the administration to treat Japan as an unfair trader. In addition, Japan was the inspiration for the Super 301 market-opening provision that originated in Congress (see Chapter 9) and the measures designed to enhance U.S. competitiveness contained in the Omnibus Trade and Competitiveness Act of 1988.

The 1986 semiconductor agreement introduced three novel approaches to bilateral trade relations: a comprehensive set of minimum prices imposed on U.S. imports of Japanese semiconductors to prevent dumping; an agreement by Japanese producers not to dump in third-country markets; and a loosely defined goal of a 20 percent market share in Japan for foreign semiconductor producers. The last provision was the first formal U.S. foray into managed trade whereby a numerical increase in Japanese purchases of foreign semiconductors would be the U.S. criterion for measuring Japanese compliance. A fourth new wrinkle followed shortly after: The United States for the first time in the post–World War II period hit Japan with unilateral sanctions—as retaliation for alleged violations of the agreement.

The perceived inefficiency of making demands on a product-by-product basis eventually prompted a shift in U.S. trade strategy to seek more comprehensive adjustment measures. The market-oriented sector-selective (MOSS) talks begun in 1985 were designed to address all identifiable trade barriers in several sectors in which the United States was internationally competitive but relatively unsuccessful in exporting to Japan: electronics and computers, telecommunications equipment, medical equipment and pharmaceuticals, and forest products; automobile parts were added later. Also in 1985, the two countries figured prominently in the Plaza Agreement by the Group of Seven industrial countries to coax the foreign exchange markets into significant dollar depreciation relative to the yen and other major currencies.

The Bush I administration was the first to engage the Japanese government in dialogue about the underlying domestic causes of the bilateral competitiveness and trade disequilibria. The Structural Impediments Initiative (SII) was established in 1989 and immediately broke new ground as one sovereign country scrutinized the internal affairs of another, a reflection of just how far economic interdependence between the two countries had progressed. The Japanese heard U.S. proposals for changes in their business structure, goods-pricing mechanism, working hours, land use policy, and distribution system. The U.S. side, among other things, heard Japanese recommendations on the need for increased U.S. rates of saving and investment, reductions in the federal budget deficit, longer time horizons for business executives, and a more effective educational system. In the end, only a few modest changes were adopted, none of which seriously addressed the structural phenomena affecting the two countries' divergent performances in foreign trade. Simultaneous with the SII, the administration pursued product-specific agreements in which the Japanese committed themselves to new import liberalization actions that included computers, supercomputers, government procurement procedures, automobiles and auto parts, glass, legal services, cellular telephones, and paper.

The Clinton administration's initial trade team was dominated by people who viewed the Japanese economic system as fundamentally different and therefore deserving of special trade policies. Believing that the traditional approach to the "Japan problem" had yielded woefully inadequate results, this administration initially adopted a results-oriented trade strategy toward that country. The Clinton trade team pressured the Japanese to agree to specific numerical targets for a reduction in their current account surplus and increases in imports of certain manufactured goods to designated levels. Japan balked at these requests because it did not want to be stigmatized as having a government that could command specified quantitative changes in business transactions. Nor did it want to be seen as a country where the traditional liberalization of formal trade barriers did not really matter. Eventually, an ambiguously worded "framework" agreement in 1993 called upon Japan to work toward a "highly significant" decrease in its trade surplus. The agreement also stipulated that there would be an emphasis on "objective criteria, either qualitative or quantitative or both," to measure future Japanese progress in opening its markets. The U.S. interpretation of the agreement was that tangible increases in U.S. exports would be a more important means of evaluating the outcomes of future negotiations than the degree to which Japan relaxed its regulations. Japan's interpretation was that it would be responsive to American requests but would not and could not commit itself to specific numerical targets.

The determination of the Clinton administration to impose retaliatory trade sanctions if the Japanese did not further open their market for U.S.-made automobiles and auto parts led the two countries to the brink of what up to that time was arguably the most widely discussed and most widely feared near-trade war in history. The United States declared its intention to retaliate after unsuccessful efforts to achieve its minimum demands for regulatory changes in Japan's automobile retail system and a renewal by Japanese auto makers of their pledge to buy a minimum amount of U.S.-made auto parts. Having declared the existence of discriminatory trade barriers under the Section 301 provision, the administration announced that, in the absence of an agreement by June 28, 1995, it would unilaterally retaliate by imposing prohibitive 100 percent tariffs on imports of Japanese luxury cars valued at nearly $6 billion annually.[16] The Japanese promptly announced that they would file a grievance against the United States in the newly established WTO dispute settlement mechanism because they rejected the accuracy of the U.S. complaint and the legality of unilateral U.S. retaliation. Thanks mainly to another ambiguously worded agreement that the two governments publicly interpreted in different ways, a last-minute resolution of the dispute was reached.

The automobile settlement marked the end of "bilateralism," in which the two countries demonstrated their special relationship by dealing directly with one another to resolve trade disputes rather than using a larger forum. The U.S. government is still making trade demands in telecommunications, insurance, glass, general business deregulation, and so forth directly to the Japanese government. The difference is that now Japan decides whether it wants to respond to a specific demand. If Japan decides that a U.S. complaint is groundless, it balks at bilateral talks and suggests the two sides use the WTO dispute settlement facility where the U.S. case must be presented before a panel of neutral judges from third countries. This is what happened when the USTR wanted to discuss the Eastman Kodak Corporation's allegation that collusion in Japan's wholesale film distribution system discriminated against imports. When a WTO panel surprised the United States and ruled against this complaint, some cheered the end of "aggressive unilateralism." Others fretted that Japan had been given a free pass to retain collusive domestic business practices that discriminated against imports.

At the beginning of the new century, the tone of once shrill U.S. demands for greater market access had noticeably softened. The most important reason for this change was the poor state of the Japanese economy: It remained mired in a prolonged recession that in turn kept the banking system in a precarious position due to the continued dangerously high levels of bad loans. The U.S. economic priority in relation to Japan shifted from fighting trade barriers to the revival of its moribund economy. The new atmosphere prompted the two countries in 2001 to establish a new forum for dialogue, the Economic Partnership for Growth. This agreement served as the platform for the U.S. government's new, nonconfrontational approach that focused on further deregulation of what many in both countries viewed as an economy burdened by excessive and often outdated regulation. Administration officials felt that presenting a long series of proposed deregulation measures to the Japanese government would encourage sustainable growth and increase business competition within Japan, provide a more open, hospitable environment for U.S. exports, and complement the Bush administration's market-oriented economic philosophy.[17]

# China

The modern era of U.S.-Chinese trade relations is relatively young, having begun only in the late 1970s. Political and economic contact between the two countries had been virtually nonexistent since China entered the Korean War at the end of 1950 and engaged in undeclared war with American and UN troops. The United States quickly imposed comprehensive economic sanctions, and bilateral trade flows ceased for more than two decades. Even without sanctions, trade would have been hampered by a backward Chinese economy that produced little that Americans would have wanted to buy. The first phase of restoring trade relations began in the 1970s when the Nixon administration radically altered course and pursued a gradual process of normalization with a country that had long been designated for isolation and containment by U.S. foreign policy. The second phase commenced with two major events in 1979: China's domestic economic reforms got fully underway, and a bilateral trade agreement was signed (political normalization cannot get very far in the absence of improved economic relations). The United States extended year-to-year MFN tariff treatment to China and began easing trade sanctions.

China has become what is arguably the most vivid demonstration of the internal and external economic successes that can result when a country moves away from a government controlled command economy and gradually adopts market-oriented reforms compatible with domestic capabilities. Few anticipated the subsequent boom in bilateral trade flows. Unfortunately, the tranquil bilateral trade relations that commenced in 1979 ended literally with a bang ten years later when Chinese troops opened fire on demonstrators in Tiananmen Square. From 1989 on, U.S.-Chinese trade relations became contentious, and the appropriate U.S. trade policy stance became the subject of heated debate among an unusually large number of constituencies.

## *Unique Aspects of U.S.-Chinese Trade Relations*
China is by far the biggest trading partner of the United States that is neither a democracy nor primarily a market-based economy. It is by far the biggest trading part-

ner that openly dislikes and seeks to counter the magnitude of U.S. international political, economic, and military power. Although not an enemy, neither is it a friend. (President Bush [II] has referred to China as a "strategic competitor" of the United States.) It wants to be an acknowledged regional power and to reduce U.S. influence in Asia. It is sensitive to past foreign intervention and leery of a world economic order that it had no role in creating. China's trade policy is administered by an unelected ruling party that represents one-fifth of the world's population and that unapologetically puts staying in power ahead of respecting personal freedoms. The country lacks the rule of law as defined in Western democracies. Concerns about national security and human rights violations have resulted in limited and relatively brief U.S. trade sanctions (see Chapter 9). In addition, China now frequently surpasses Japan as the largest U.S. bilateral trade deficit.[18] Like most developing countries, China has extensive import barriers in place.

If an economically and politically less significant country had rebuffed the same large number of demands for policy changes as has China, the United States almost surely would have been provoked into imposing aggressive retaliatory sanctions to slow the growth in, freeze, or shrink the volume of bilateral trade. Similarly, more sanctions may have been forthcoming if other countries had felt intensely about China's actions and announced their willingness to act in concert with the United States if the Chinese government refused to moderate its behavior. However, other governments had little desire to be in the vanguard of threatening trade sanctions against China because they lacked superpower status, were fearful of retaliatory import barriers, and were under intense pressure from domestic companies to maintain cordial economic relations with China. Instead, they have been content to let the United States retain its near monopoly in annoying and threatening China.

The intensity of U.S. concerns about China's import barriers and violations of international trade standards has varied over time. They peaked in importance in the mid-1990s and became progressively less relevant to the larger American dissatisfaction with that country's political and military policies. The most powerful Communist Party leaders believe that economic modernization is crucial to prevent challenges to its monopoly political power and that a controlled transition to a market-based, private sector economy is critical to an increasing standard of living and the eradication of poverty. The ascendant economic reform faction has chosen the standard formula of decontrol, privatization, and increased competition from imports. It sought WTO membership to make it difficult, if not impossible, for reactionaries to reverse the move toward a market-based economy (the same basic reason that Mexico sought a free trade agreement with the United States). China's trade policy since the mid-1990s has become more compatible with U.S. trade demands mainly because of Beijing's calculation that a more liberal trade policy was in its own self-interest and partly in recognition of the need to retain full access to the large, relatively accessible American market.

If trade issues were all that mattered in trade policy, U.S. trade relations with China would have assumed a much more harmonious tone by the beginning of the millennium. By that time, the Chinese government had agreed to reduce trade barriers in general and to grant greater access to specific goods of interest to the United States.

Furthermore, no evidence had appeared showing that the geometric increase in imports from that country was inflicting injury on American companies and workers. Few U.S. trade officials still believed that China was going to be the "next Japan," that is, an adversarial trader that would hide behind a thicket of informal trade barriers and not respect international trade rules. During President Clinton's second term, the questions of granting permanent MFN status to China and supporting its WTO membership were not about doing that country a favor. They were about squeezing as many market-opening concessions as possible from an emerging economic superpower.

China and Japan have inspired intense American resentment for their large trade surpluses with the United States. Both countries have engendered U.S. government demands to modify discriminatory trade policies. The similarities end there. Since the mid-1990s, most of the criticism leveled at China has no longer dealt with trade issues. Demands for sanctions have been mainly related to the desire to punish China for refusing to moderate specific foreign policies and human rights abuses. This change in focus was diametrically opposite from the unchanging, one-dimensional rationale of U.S. advocates of hard-line policies toward Japan: the purely economic need to force open the allegedly closed markets of a friendly, allied, and democratic country.

The upsurge of U.S. imports from Japan, which began in the late 1960s, caused widespread dislocations, including the near disappearance of entire industrial sectors, such as consumer electronics. U.S. imports from China (at least through the early years of the millennium) have been overwhelmingly low-tech, labor-intensive goods, the production of which long ago moved off-shore in search of cheap labor. A considerable proportion of U.S. imports from China consists of apparel, shoes, and toys; these goods had previously been produced in and exported from the so-called newly industrialized countries. By the late 1980s, South Korea, Singapore, Taiwan, and Hong Kong were moving upmarket to higher-value-added goods such as steel, electronics, and semiconductors. Many producers of labor-intensive goods in these countries moved some or most of their production to China. Furthermore, China's low production costs and nearly limitless supply of cheap semiskilled labor also allowed it to grab the lion's share of incremental U.S. demand for labor-intensive goods that might otherwise have been supplied by other low-wage countries, such as India or Pakistan. A significant proportion of increased U.S. purchases from China merely represented a different geographic source of imports and did not result in closed factories and unemployed workers at home.

The U.S. trade experience with booming imports from China is also distinct from the Japanese case in that innovative Japanese companies account for that country's export success. Nearly all Chinese exports to the United States to date have been either shipments by companies with some degree of foreign ownership or goods specifically contracted for by American producers and retailers of consumer goods.

There was and is no real controversy within the United States about the desirability of pressing for changes in those political, military, and economic policies of China that are widely considered incompatible with U.S. national security interests and social values. The real question is the appropriate means to the agreed-upon end.

When a "friendly" country is the target, interest group agitation about trade matters is almost always limited to business, labor, and agricultural complaints about unfair trade practices. The U.S. debate concerning trade policy toward China attracts a much larger and more diverse political community.

U.S. trade policy toward China in the post-normalization era first transcended commercial issues in response to the 1989 Tiananmen Square massacre, where lethal force shut down a massive pro-democracy demonstration. From that point on, the dichotomy between China's shift to economic liberalization and retention of its political iron fist attracted the interest of advocacy groups in the United States from outside the mainstream foreign trade lobby. Activists having no direct stake in economic relations with China trade recognized the potential of using the threat of trade sanctions as leverage to achieve their noneconomic agendas for change in China. In a word, they resurrected the old Cold War concept of linkage: Good trade relations with another country should be contingent on the latter not engaging in acts that seriously endanger American interests or violate international norms of behavior.

The government of China provided ample ammunition subsequent to Tiananmen Square to the growing numbers of Americans demanding that China pay an economic price for its objectionable actions. In the national security area, fears grew that Chinese military threats against Taiwan might escalate into an invasion and possible armed conflict with U.S. forces sent to defend the island. Chinese exports of weapons and missile technology to the Middle East, Libya, and Pakistan generated U.S. anger, as did China's efforts to improve Iraq's air defense systems. China's image in the United States has suffered from repeated media reports about the absence of legal due process for persons arrested on criminal charges or for challenging the absolute authority of the government. Other human rights violations involved religious persecution, mainly of Chinese Christians and the Falun Gong, and repression of the independence movement in Tibet. The dubious arrests, detention, and trials of Chinese-American scholars on spying charges brought new controversy. Beijing generated even more hostility in the United States in its handling of the emergency landing of a U.S. surveillance plane on Chinese territory after it had collided with a Chinese fighter plane that was shadowing it. Keeping the crew under house arrest and demanding a U.S. government apology suggested a Chinese government that was far from being a friend of Americans. More than simple trade issues are inserted into a policy debate in which some Americans metaphorically suggest that doing business with China is like dealing with the devil.

There are two directions for U.S. trade policy to go when dealing with the world's most populous country and fastest-growing economy whose government is operating under a value system overwhelmingly dissimilar to that of the United States. The first-best policy cannot be determined on the basis of incontrovertible scientific method. A political choice must be is inevitable, and it must be based on personal values and priorities. To repeat a recurring theme of this book, perceptions define reality.

One option in dealing with China is to maximize economic engagement. This is the preferred strategy of those who claim that a progressively stronger Chinese economy will foster a growing middle class that, in turn, will inevitably demand a more democratic, law-based political system and a more market-based economy. This is a plausible scenario, but one that Chinese society and history does not make inevitable. Advocates of the "carrot" approach suggest that China's growing appetite for imports will easily be fed by buying the goods of other countries, thereby assuring that U.S. sanctions would hurt domestic economic interests far more than the foreign target.

Advocates of the "stick" approach believe that the United States must draw the line somewhere to demonstrate that it stands for something besides monetary gain. The U.S. government therefore should be prepared to impose costs on egregious Chinese behavior. This school of thought, also based on assumptions rather than hard evidence, believes that credible threats to close the U.S. market to most Chinese goods through highly discriminatory tariffs are the tactic most likely to evoke a China more accommodating to U.S. desires. Their position is that in an eyeball-to-eyeball confrontation, the Chinese leadership would blink first, not wanting to risk the economic disruption that would ensue from the potential loss of one of its largest export markets. U.S. trade statistics show that imports from China totaled $100 billion in 2000. The importance of the U.S. market for China is suggested by the fact that $100 billion was equal to 10 percent of China's total GDP (calculated at the equivalent of $1 trillion) and was approximately 23 percent of its estimated manufacturing output in that year.[19] These hardliners suggest that even if threats are ignored and sanctions are imposed, the United States would occupy the moral high ground by having acted on behalf of personal freedom and respect for law and international agreements.

### Trade Tensions in the Early 1990s

The unexpected surge in U.S.-Chinese trade that occurred in the 1980s pleased China, but created a long series of U.S. objections, demands, and threats. In retrospect, at least some trade disagreements between two dissimilar economic systems were inevitable. One was a hybrid part-market, mainly government-owned economic order displaying a distinct lack of transparency in its often unpublished foreign trade regulations. The other economic system was the self-styled champion of free market economics and trade liberalization. China was intent on protecting a noncompetitive economy. It simultaneously was embarking on a long learning process to master the intricacies of an international trading order developed and managed by capitalist democracies who were not above demanding that China violate market principles by "voluntarily" restricting export shipments. The ability of China's factories to increase exports seemed to far outpace the ability of China's undemocratically elected government to comprehend that the U.S. government's desire for "strategic engagement" and the American business community's desire for commercial engagement did not give China a green light to ignore those international trade laws that it found inconvenient. Hindsight also suggests the inevitability of a growing U.S. irritation with Chinese trade practices that tracked the unusually rapid growth in its bilateral trade deficit (see Figure 10.1).

Following its imposition of mostly financial sanctions to protest the 1989 Tiananmen Square massacre, the U.S. government has threatened or physically imposed trade sanctions for a number of perceived Chinese political and economic transgressions. Unlike any other country, the United States on several occasions nearly got into a trade war with

**Figure 10.1 U.S.–China Trade (in billions of U.S. dollars)**

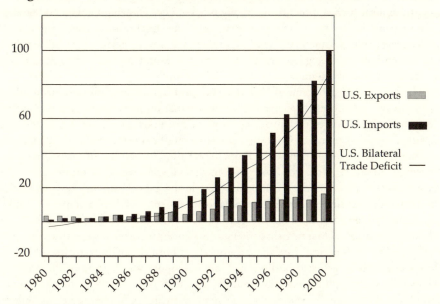

SOURCE: U.S. Department of Commerce data.

the world's most populous country and fastest-growing market. The possibility of ter-
minating MFN treatment to China and that country's equally serious threat to retaliate
in kind against U.S. goods overshadowed the less publicized disputes, which fall into
two broad categories. The first consists of political actions taken by China and considered unacceptable by the U.S. government and a high percentage of American public
opinion. These included further allegations of continued human rights abuses, use of
prison labor to make exported goods, and shipments of missiles and offensive weapons
in violation of international treaty obligations. When the Clinton administration determined in 1993 that China was violating the Missile Technology Control Regime (by
allegedly selling missile parts to Pakistan), it was bound by domestic law to retaliate by
imposing export sanctions. The result was restraints on exports of several categories of
high-tech goods to that country.

The second category of Chinese behavior angering the United States consisted of
commercial practices that were judged to be inconsistent with U.S. trade laws and
standards. The U.S. government accused the Chinese government of fraud in its
efforts to circumvent export quotas on textile and apparel shipments to the United
States that had been negotiated under the Multifiber Arrangement. (Illegal transshipments occur when textile products pass through third countries where country-of-
origin documentation is altered to disguise their true source.) Seeking to discourage
this practice, the U.S. government unilaterally reduced China's 1991 textile and
apparel export allotment to the United States. At the beginning of 1994, the Clinton
administration was on the verge of a 25 percent unilateral cutback in textile imports
from China because of an estimated $2 billion in illegal transshipments. U.S. retaliation

was averted at the last minute when the two governments signed a new agreement that sought to limit such shipments by, among other things, allowing the United States to impose penalties against China's textile export quota equal to three times the value of every illegal transshipment that was identified. The several relatively small penalties subsequently invoked suggest that the Chinese textile and apparel sector reduced this practice, but did not eliminate it.

The Special 301 provision of U.S. trade law requires the executive branch to identify "priority" countries that violate U.S. intellectual property rights and then either to secure agreements to end such violations or to impose economic retaliation (see Chapter 7). Designation of China as a priority country was the result of data collected by the International Intellectual Property Alliance, a coalition of major American copyright-intensive industries (software, movies, books, recorded music, etc). The group asserted that American companies were losing export sales in excess of $2 billion annually because of systematic violations in China of U.S. companies' trademarks, copyrights, and (to a lesser extent) patents.[20] As directed by the law, the Bush (I) administration demanded that the Chinese government take steps to curb large-scale pirating of American intellectual property at both the manufacturing and retail levels. After prolonged stonewalling by China, temporary resolution of the problem was achieved through a bilateral agreement signed in January 1992—just in time to avoid an announced $1 billion U.S. retaliation against Chinese goods, as well as threatened Chinese counterretaliation. In 1994, the U.S. Trade Representative's office rejected as insufficient China's enforcement of its newly enacted laws and regulations to halt production of counterfeit goods.

The events that followed were viewed as harassment by the Chinese and an ongoing law enforcement exercise by American officials. At issue was how effective the Chinese government could be in stopping what is probably still the world's largest output of counterfeit goods. The Clinton administration invoked Special 301 in both 1995 and 1996 to threaten discriminatory tariffs against more than $1 billion in imports from China if more effective measures to halt intellectual property violations were not taken. To avoid these sanctions, the government of China agreed to reduce barriers to imports of intellectual property-related U.S. goods and to be more aggressive in targeting high-volume domestic factories producing counterfeit goods. American companies and trade officials remain dissatisfied with continuing high levels of intellectual property rights violations. In apparent acceptance of the inability of the Chinese government to end all commercial piracy, recent U.S. policy has been to apply informal pressure for incremental improvement rather than overt threats of retaliation.

A third case of bilateral trade friction is associated with ongoing demands by the United States for unilateral market-opening measures. In 1991, for example, the administration initiated what is arguably still the most sweeping investigation of discriminatory foreign import practices ever conducted under the Section 301 statute (discussed in Chapter 7). Rather than targeting discrimination against a specific product, U.S. trade negotiators demanded a sweeping liberalization of China's import control regime. Beijing's unsurprising reluctance to comply produced a U.S. threat to impose prohibitive tariffs on $3.9 billion worth of imports, which would have been the largest retaliatory action ever taken under Section 301. China promised retaliation against a comparable level of U.S. exports. But on the day in October 1992 that the U.S. sanctions were due to take effect, the Chinese government agreed to a memorandum of understanding in which it pledged to reduce tariff and nontariff barriers on more than 1,000 products, make its trade regime more transparent by publishing key laws and regulations, eliminate most import substitution laws, and adopt other measures demanded by the United States. The decision to liberalize was also influenced by the Bush (I) administration's linking support for China's GATT membership bid (the WTO had not yet been created) to further import liberalization. The United States insisted that China achieve reasonable compatibility with the market-oriented, liberal trade policies characteristic of most member countries of that organization.

### The Long March to Full Trade Normalization

The most recent chapter in U.S. trade policy toward the People's Republic of China comprises the long, impassioned debate about what economic and political conditions—if any—should be attached to the extension of most-favored-nation tariff treatment and what reservations—if any—should be attached to the approval of its membership in the WTO. The twists and turns of this debate provide a classic case study of how economics, politics, and law interact to produce U.S. trade policy. Completion of the final stage (in legal terms) of trade normalization with China required a delicate and subjective balance between international economic and foreign policies, and domestic economic and political factors. Americans again perceived different priorities, dangers, and strategies when contemplating how best to deal with China. No theory, precedent, or econometric equation was available to define the U.S. national interest in a way that all policymakers could agree was correct. Instead, conflicting value judgments needed to be reconciled, first by the collective judgments and political calculations of the George Bush (I) and Bill Clinton administrations, and second, by the broad barometer of public opinion that presumably resonates in the two houses of Congress.

The MFN issue was so sensitive that it brought a change in U.S. trade policy terminology. Nontrade specialists were inclined to interpret *"most favored nation"* tariff status as something that would give China privileged or especially favorable treatment. In fact, a country receiving MFN from the United States is merely receiving the same relatively low tariff rates on their exported goods as those being applied to nearly every other country in the world. To assuage potential opponents to unconditional MFN treatment, the Clinton administration repackaged the long-standing term *MFN* as "normal trade relations." If MFN* status were withdrawn, it would be legally necessary for the United States to apply a highly discriminatory tariff schedule (dating back to the Smoot-Hawley tariff of 1930) on imports from China. As a result, import duties on Chinese goods would increase about ten-fold, a change that would put a majority of that country's exports to the United States at risk.

---

*For the purposes of continuity, the phrase most favored nation (MFN) is used throughout this book in lieu of "normal trade relations." MFN has deep historical roots, and it is still universally used by other countries and international organizations.

China had first expressed interest in joining the GATT in 1986 and by the late 1990s was becoming impatient. It wanted to be in the GATT/WTO to receive nondiscriminatory treatment from other member countries, to use the dispute settlement mechanism in resolving trade problems, to influence the agenda of future trade negotiations, and to gain prestige. Because China was not a "model citizen," a case could be made that designated changes in its official policies should be the quid pro quo for agreeing to China's request that it be fully integrated into the international trading system. Recommendations for "improved" behavior ranged from liberalizing technical trade regulations to the formal protection of human rights.

The task of senior U.S. policymakers was to choose between two contradictory perceptions. Different parts of the American body politic view trade relations with China through an intellectual filter composed of different values and different self-interests. United by a sincere belief that their view most equates with what is best for the United States, they are separated by different prescriptions for doing the right thing.

The utility of minimal conditions was championed by those who see intensified engagement with China as the optimal means of serving U.S. national interests. As noted above, the "engagers" view increased economic integration into the world economy and domestic economic progress as the most subversive forces for what Americans would categorize as positive change in China. A related argument is that once China became one of the ten largest trading countries (measured by dollar value of trade flows), its absence from the WTO threatened to undermine the credibility and effectiveness of the organization.

Advocates of a "maximum conditions" strategy saw completion of the final stage of trade normalization as a golden opportunity for demanding numerous changes in Chinese behavior. Their viewpoint was that the industrialized countries' leverage would quickly dissipate once China joined the WTO and received permanent MFN status. They insisted that China should be made to move closer to Western economic and political norms *before* being admitted to the WTO. If China chose to reject the conditions imposed for integration into the world trading system, it should be excluded. If China was not ready for trade "primetime," the hardliners argued, the price of keeping it on the periphery was justified and would assure that it did not flaunt WTO rules.

When producers of goods and services look at China, they see what has for many years been the world's fastest-growing major market that is on course to be no less than the world's second largest national economy. China offers phenomenal potential for a high volume of sales to manufacturers the world over. If shut out of this market, a company faces the prospect of lost profits and the lost opportunity to reduce per unit cost through high sales volumes. With rare unanimity, American companies and farmers are afraid that if their government goes too far in provoking the anger of China's leadership, their ability to export and make additional direct investments in the equivalent of a commercial "promised land" will be severely curtailed. Besides wanting to protect their own financial interests, some business people were genuinely skeptical that threatening to terminate MFN status would induce changes in Chinese behavior.

Economists also support policies conducive to increased bilateral trade. This is consistent with their larger desire to allocate global resources in the most efficient manner possible (see Chapter 3). Most economists also are sympathetic with the somewhat self-serving arguments of American importers of Chinese goods that low-income Americans would be disproportionately penalized by higher prices for consumer goods no longer imported from China at low tariff duties.

The foreign policy "establishment" views the China trade debate through a national security lens. For most foreign policy officials and scholars, the first priority is fostering positive relations with a growing Asian power possessing nuclear weapons. An acrimonious trade relationship would complicate U.S. efforts to secure China's cooperation on issues of foreign policy, such as having it act as a moderating influence on North Korea.

Hawkish U.S. foreign policy pundits view China as a potential enemy that does not deserve to profit from growing sales to the United States until they act more "responsibly." A similar conclusion was reached at the opposite end of the spectrum by human rights activists, who observe China through yet another prism. Their definition of good policy is maximum pressure on China to respect the rule of law and due process, and to inflict a costly economic price to the extent that the leadership in Beijing refuses to respect human rights and personal freedom. Economic and foreign policy goals in this case are subordinated to moral issues. For a different reason, much of organized labor in the United States agrees with the strategy of imposing strong demands on China (even to the point that Beijing would refuse to comply) as the quid pro quo for guaranteed access to the American market and membership in the WTO. Many union officials fear that an open market to Chinese goods will eventually produce a flood of increasingly sophisticated imported goods made by low-wage Chinese workers that will exert downward pressure on the U.S. wage level and a widespread loss of American manufacturing jobs.

In the late 1990s, the U.S. trade community needed to reevaluate MFN policy towards China for two reasons. The first was a growing consensus in Washington that because the outcome of the annual MFN renewal exercise was no longer in doubt, it had become a shallow, time-wasting endeavor that Beijing was ignoring in its policy calculations. The second reason related to international trade law. A growing global consensus suggested the inevitability of China's becoming a member of the WTO. Once it joined, all other members would be expected to grant it permanent and unconditional MFN treatment, something only the United States was not already doing.[21]

The so-called Jackson-Vanik Amendment to the Trade Act of 1974 was responsible for an annual ritual exclusive to Washington in which opposing factions publicly clashed over the merits of unconditional renewal of MFN status for China. It was the legal basis for restoration of MFN trade status for China in 1980 (and to other previously Communist countries stripped of this status during the Cold War). In keeping with its tradition of delegating only limited, circumscribed trade policy authority to the president, Congress dictated that a grant of MFN treatment made under this statute is valid for only one year at a time. The president must make an annual determination that there is no compelling reason not to extend it and inform Congress of his intention to renew. Congress holds hearings to review this decision and can overrule it by voting against renewal. Proponents of unconditional MFN felt this procedure was inimical to a deeper trade relationship with China. Opponents of permanent or unconditional renewal welcomed an annual platform on which to air grievances publicly against that country's trade, human rights, weapons proliferation, prison labor, and military policies and to demand that MFN renewal and WTO membership be conditional on changes in at least some of these policies.

The most intense conflict between the differing perceptions on the proper U.S. trade policy towards China occurs when each tries to influence legislation. U.S. MFN policy in a literal sense consists of statutory language; the ultimate issue is whose political viewpoint determines that language. As long as China's MFN status was temporary and had to be renewed annually, the executive branch could not disregard congressional sentiment. President Bush in 1991 and 1992 had to contend with legislation passed by Congress requiring that MFN renewal be absolutely contingent on improved human rights conditions in China. Those actions reflected congressional sentiment that Mr. Bush was appeasing China. Conversely, the president viewed his emphasis on engagement as a realistic calculation that the confrontational approach would backfire by alienating the Chinese leadership. The bills failed to become law only because the Senate could not muster the votes to override either of Mr. Bush's vetoes.

In May 1994, President Clinton reversed the China MFN stance that he had advocated while running for office. He dropped his support of conditionality and announced that henceforth extension would be decoupled from demands for an improved human rights record in China. The president argued that the policy linking MFN and human rights progress had reached the end of its usefulness and it was time to take a new path to achieving U.S. objectives. This decision symbolically demonstrated the political reality that defenders of commercial interests and engagement had achieved the upper hand. This group included not only the business sector but many key parts of the executive branch, including the Treasury and Commerce departments as well as the office of the USTR. The Clinton policy turnaround also reflected the Chinese government's clearly communicated messages that it was not about to change internal political policies to please the United States and would not hesitate to retaliate if hit with discriminatory tariff treatment.

The struggle between the hard-line and soft-line trade strategies took on additional complexity when the Clinton administration concluded a pivotal trade agreement with China in November 1999. Because its purpose was to clear the way for U.S. support of that country's membership in the WTO, the agreement consisted mostly of unilateral Chinese market-opening measures that would benefit American exports of goods and services. Among the liberalizing provisions were reductions in tariffs, a phase out or easing of many quotas, extension to U.S. firms in China of previously denied rights to import and distribute imports directly, and relaxed regulations on foreign subsidiaries in that country. Furthermore, China accepted interim discrimination in the form of temporary modifications of U.S. trade remedy laws that will make it more likely that American interests win their petitions for import relief. For several years, the wording of the escape clause statute is to be relaxed so that it can restrain "surges" of imports from China. In addition, the antidumping and countervailing duty statutes can use provisions designating China as a nonmarket economy.[22] By mutual consent, the terms of the agreement did not go into effect until China officially became a member of the WTO, which happened in December 2001.

Once again, the clash of values centered on legislation sent by the administration to Capitol Hill that would authorize "permanent normal trade relations" (PNTR) status for China. Passage of this bill was far from certain. It was an election year, numerous groups opposed it, some expressed fear of a surge in U.S. imports, and the Republican-controlled Congress at the time was showing miniscule desire to accommodate any of President Clinton's legislative requests. Nevertheless, final approval of H.R. 4444 came in September 2000 with surprisingly comfortable margins.[23]

Various factors can be cited to explain why most members of Congress supported permanent MFN status for China. The first was the unanimous and intense lobbying efforts by the U.S. industrial and agricultural sectors on behalf of a bilateral trade policy based on minimum conditionality and no direct linkage to foreign policy and concerns about human rights. They had no doubt that China would make good on its threats of retaliation if it was ever deprived of MFN. Unlike the industrial sector's frequent endorsement for retaliation against entrenched Japanese trade barriers, American business saw unparalleled opportunities for sales and profits in a huge, rapidly growing market that seemed genuinely committed to liberalizing its regulation of imports and foreign direct investment. Second, defeat of the bill would not block China's entry into the WTO. However, failure of the United States to extend permanent MFN to a fellow WTO member would give China the legal option of denying U.S. goods the MFN treatment it was extending to other countries.

The syndrome of Congress's assuring itself an oversight role after passing trade legislation (see Chapter 6) was manifested in the form of amendments to the bill establishing a joint congressional-executive branch commission to monitor human rights abuses in China and requiring an annual report from the USTR on that country's compliance with its WTO obligations. Both subjects will be regularly reviewed in future committee hearings on Capitol Hill.

## Conclusions and Outlook

Whether Americans should punish Japan and China for their mercantilist trade philosophy or thank them is a value judgement. The American economy as a whole has been enriched by the real economic resources imported from them. Ironically, but for its own trace of mercantilist philosophy, U.S. trade policy would not have expended so many resources to repeatedly press these two countries to reduce import barriers and stop the use of unfair practices to increase their exports. The Japanese and Chinese societies may not be grateful for repeated hectoring by the United States, but in theory their economies will be made more efficient by increased foreign competition and their consumers will benefit from lower prices and a wider choice of goods. Without U.S. intervention, the move by these two countries to a more liberal trade policy would not have happened at all or they would have happened at a much slower pace.

Neither the Japanese nor the Chinese government philosophically believes in the greater virtue of imports over exports or the more rational allocation of resources that devolves from allowing relatively inefficient domestic producers to be put out of business by stronger foreign competition. Neither government wants or absolutely needs trade policies that replicate those of the United States. However, no country can become a major exporter to the United States and expect to violate its core trade values without triggering an angry, persistent response. A central tenet of American trade politics is that preservation of the liberal trade coalition is critically important. And preservation requires the U.S. government to be responsive to private sector complaints about injury from foreign trade barriers that stifle their exports and injury from increased foreign competition, both fair and unfair. It is therefore a foregone conclusion that the U.S. government would feel obliged to nudge Japanese and Chinese trade policies closer to the spirit and letter of the liberal trade-oriented rules and philosophy embodied in the WTO. The problem is that the line between appropriate and excessive U.S. pressure on these countries, or any others, cannot be objectively identified. The big question is why the United States has had no identifiable allies in publicly applying pressure on these two countries.

The medium to long-term outlook for U.S. trade strategies toward Japan and China is uncertain. U.S. policy toward Japan will be heavily influenced by the latter's ability (or inability) to shake off the serious structural problems that have weighed down its economy for over a decade. The current lack of concern among most Americans about Japan's competitive edge could revert to the near hysteria of the 1980s if U.S. economic fortunes sharply decline and Japan regains its dynamism. The outlook for U.S. policy toward China is similarly clouded by several uncertainties. How well and how far can the move toward a more market-based economy be reconciled with an authoritarian political regime? Will China begin exporting goods that directly compete with U.S. domestic production? What will be the impact of WTO membership on China's economy and trade policy? Only time will tell.

The least likely scenario is that U.S. bilateral trade problems with these countries will disappear because someone finally figures out the optimal means of solving the "Japan problem" and the "China problem."

## For Further Reading

Bergsten, C. Fred, and Marcus Noland. *Reconcilable Differences? United States-Japan Economic Conflict*. Washington, D.C.: Institute for International Economics, 1993.

Cohen, Stephen D. *An Ocean Apart: Explaining Three Decades of U.S.-Japanese Trade Frictions*. Westport, Conn.: Praeger, 1998.

Johnson, Chalmers. *Japan: Who Governs? The Rise of the Developmental State*. New York: W. W. Norton, 1995.

Katz, Richard. *Japan: The System that Soured*. Armonk, N.Y.: M. E. Sharpe, 1998.

Lardy, Nicholas R. *Integrating China into the Global Economy*. Washington, D.C.: Brookings Institution, 2002.

Lincoln, Edward J. *Japan's Unequal Trade*. Washington, D.C.: Brookings Institution, 1990.

Porter, Michael, Hirotaka Takeuchi, and Mariko Sakaibara. *Can Japan Compete?* Cambridge, Mass.: Perseus Publishing, 2000.

Prestowitz, Clyde, Jr. *Trading Places: How We Allowed Japan to Take the Lead.* New York: Basic Books, 1988.

Pyle, Kenneth B. *The Japanese Question: Power and Purpose in a New Era.* 2d ed. Washington, D.C.: The AEI Press, 1996.

## Notes

1. "Reform May Reshape Japan's Edge in Trade," *Washington Post,* 27 June, 1993, H1.

2. For a more detailed analysis of these multiple sources of domestic economic strength, see chapter 6 of Stephen D. Cohen, *An Ocean Apart: Explaining Three Decades of U.S.-Japanese Trade Frictions* (Westport, Conn.: Praeger, 1998).

3. This phrase originated with Ichiro Ozawa, who became the leader of one of Japan's new reform parties that set out to challenge the long rule of the Liberal Democratic Party. See, for example, Richard P. Cronin, *Japan's Ongoing Political Instability: Implications for U.S. Interests,* Congressional Research Service report, 8 July 1994, 2.

4. Jagdish Bhagwati, "Samurais No More," *Foreign Affairs* 73 (May–June 1994): 11.

5. As quoted in *Fortune,* 25 September 1989, 52.

6. President's Advisory Committee for Trade Policy and Negotiations, *Analysis of the U.S.-Japan Trade Problem* (Washington, D.C.: Government Printing Office, February 1989), 77.

7. See, for example, Robert Z. Lawrence, "How Open Is Japan?" in Paul Krugman, ed., *Trade with Japan: Has the Door Opened Wider?* (Chicago: University of Chicago Press, 1991), 25–28.

8. The major keiretsu, such as Mitsui and Mitsubishi, are descendants of the giant conglomerates broken up after World War II by U.S. occupation forces. The various companies composing the modern Japanese business group are still closely bonded to one another through the extensive holdings of each other's stock (i.e., partial ownership), interlocking directorates, regular meetings among senior company officers, tradition, and so on.

9. Imports of manufactured goods as a percent of total Japanese imports rose to 58 percent in 1999, but were still far below comparable figures for the United States and all high-income countries. World Bank, *2001 World Development Indicators,* 215–216; accessed at www.worldbank.org/.

10. See Edward J. Lincoln, *Japan's Unequal Trade* (Washington, D.C.: Brookings Institution, 1990), 39–47.

11. See, for example, the report of the President's Advisory Committee for Trade Policy and Negotiations, *Analysis of the U.S.-Japan Trade Problem* (Washington, D.C.: Government Printing Office, February 1989), 92–98.

12. Clyde Prestowitz, *Trading Places* (New York: Basic Books, 1988), 47.

13. For a more complete review of the history of bilateral trade relations, see chapter 2 of Cohen, *An Ocean Apart.*

14. Sporadic U.S. demands for export restraints by Japan began in the 1950s, when restraint agreements were negotiated on cotton textiles and several lower-volume goods, such as bicycles and baseball gloves.

15. It was later revealed that one reason for the upsurge in imports of Japanese televisions was a surreptitious effort among major Japanese producers to engage in market rigging and

dumping to aggressively displace domestic production. See Prestowitz, *Trading Places,* 202–205.

16. The choice of expensive luxury cars purchased by the affluent as targets of retaliatory tariffs was probably made with the idea—correct as was later proved by opinion polls—that this move would minimize a backlash by middle-income American consumers opposed to price increases in lower-priced, widely used goods.

17. The new emphasis on cooperation in lieu of confrontation is clearly seen in the USTR press release dated October 14, 2001, announcing forty-seven pages of U.S. government proposals advanced in connection with the bilateral Regulatory Reform and Competition Policy Initiative. It stated that the United States "has made a concerted effort to focus on issues that Prime Minister Koizumi and his Administration have identified as important areas for reform, such as information technologies, telecommunications, . . . and competition policy." The full text of the U.S. proposals was accessed at www.ustr.gov/.

18. Some China scholars have argued that U.S. statistics exaggerate its deficit with China because they undercount the value of American exports to Hong Kong that are re-exported to the mainland and include most or all of the middleman markups on U.S. imports arriving from China via Hong Kong.

19. Data source for the calculation of Chinese manufacturing as being 43 percent of GDP: *China Statistical Yearbook 2000* (Beijing: China Statistics Press, 2000).

20. Wayne M. Morrison, *China-U.S. Trade Issues,* Congressional Research Service report, 13 April 2001; accessed at www.cnie.org/nle/econ–35.html/.

21. If China (or any other country) joined the WTO before the United States had granted it MFN, the U.S. government would presumably invoke the obscure, seldom-used "nonapplication" provision in the WTO agreement. Under such circumstances, WTO obligations would not automatically apply to U.S.-Chinese trade relations.

22. U.S. International Trade Commission, *The Year in Trade 1999* (Washington, D.C.: U.S. International Trade Commission, 2000), 66–69.

23. The president could not extend permanent MFN status until China became a WTO member and only if it did not renege on any of the liberalization measures agreed to in the bilateral trade agreement of 1999.

# 11 European Union–United States Trade Relations

The European Union (EU)* is an unprecedented political and economic phenomenon in the international community. Its past, present, and projected future make it an extraordinary regional institution that has changed the political and economic contours of Europe and altered the international trading system. The EU's emergence as the world's most important trading bloc marked the end of the historical pattern of trade policy being the exclusive preserve of sovereign nation-states.

The ongoing need to deal with a constant procession of new institutions and policies created explicitly to advance European economic integration has produced a major new chapter in U.S. trade policy. The EU's size and scope have created commercial problems and opportunities alike. On the one hand, American national security objectives and many economic interests have been advanced by the rising affluence and political harmony resulting from economic integration in Western Europe. On the other hand, some commercial interests have been hurt from discrimination by the world's largest customs union (an internal free trade area having common institutions and a common external tariff) that has not hesitated to demand modifications in U.S. trade practices that it thinks are improper. This chapter examines the transatlantic relationship by explaining the unique inner workings of the EU, analyzing the "ties that bind" Western Europe and North America, and examining the repeated eruption of bilateral trade frictions since the 1960s. The integrating theme here is that the failure of harsh words and periodic threats of trade wars to cause serious or permanent damage to U.S.-European relations (at least through 2001) is indicative of a mutually beneficial but less than perfect economic relationship. The so-called Atlantic Community is comprised of people who share many of the same basic economic and political values, a strong self-interest in the economic well-being of the other, and a few differences in what makes for good economic policy.

## The EU's Goals and Institutional Framework

The EU is the result of historical events and the contemporary need for size to maximize industrial efficiency. In 1945, the economies of continental Europe again lay in ruins, ravaged by the unprecedented devastation of World War II. War-weary

---

*The European Union has had more than one name in the course of its evolution. For the sake of clarity and consistency, this term is used in this chapter and throughout the book, even when discussing past events that occurred when the institution was known as the European Economic Community and, later, as the European Community.

Europeans cast a jaundiced eye toward a once-hallowed institution, the nation-state. They thought it guilty of aiding and abetting the unrestrained growth of national-ism—the primary cause of three major wars among western European countries since 1870. The concept of seeking European economic union and political confederation was a radical idea whose time had arrived. European "visionaries" found an increas-ingly receptive audience. "The intensification of efforts toward European unification after the Second World War sprang from the realization that there was no other sure way to put an end to Europe's sorry history of conflict, bloodshed, suffering and destruction."[1]

Beginning with the Roman Empire, dictators have attempted to unify Europe forcefully by military conquest. Whereas all these efforts failed, there is every indica-tion that the positive-sum game of voluntary economic integration may be the first formula to successfully bring about European confederation if not unification. The imperative of regional economic cooperation has created an unprecedented, still-evolving supranational institution—its ultimate power, configuration, mandate, impact, and membership being impossible to predict. In the meantime, the EU has become the world's largest trading bloc when measured by the value of total trade flows.[2] The EU has a population of about 370 million people; it is one-third larger than the United States and almost three times more populous than Japan. Its GDP is nearly as large as that of the United States and almost twice the size of Japan's (exact GDP relationships vary according to the exchange rates at which euros and yen are converted into dollars).

The EU is best described as a supranational organization because it has been given jurisdiction over many economic policies and regulations that previously had been the jealously guarded prerogatives of nation-states. Although not depriving its members of their sovereignty, the EU institutions have diminished much of their autonomy. The ultimate purpose of the organization is to provide the framework for an eco-nomically and politically integrated Europe. It is constructing this framework by designing and administering harmonized economic policies outside the jurisdiction of national governments. More specifically, the EU formulates and conducts external trade relations on the collective behalf of its member countries, making them excep-tions to the rule that sovereign nations control their own foreign trade policies. From the time that the Treaty of Rome took effect at the beginning of 1958, there has been a steady transfer of national economic autonomy to regional institutions. Optimists assume that EU law will continue to expand and that member countries will accept increased supranational control over their economic policies because regional cooper-ation is perceived to provide more economic benefits than could be generated unilat-erally at the national level. Believers in a united Europe anticipate that continued eco-nomic integration eventually will trigger de facto political confederation. Ultimately, a federally administered "United States of Europe" (or perhaps a "Europe of united states") may emerge. In the meantime, the European Union is still a work in progress.

It is still too early to predict the ultimate breadth and depth of European regional uni-fication. The momentum behind integration most likely will continue indefinitely, but it will not necessarily move forward quickly or in a straight line. Failure to move per-manently beyond a discriminatory trade bloc is theoretically possible, as is dismemberment in a worst-case scenario should it become so top-heavy that benefits to member countries are no longer perceived as outweighing the costs. In any event, the EU at present is the world's clearest symbol of "non-nationalism": individual nation-states recognizing that they have achieved a far greater economic reward for their citizens and a louder political voice at the international level in a collective effort than they could have accomplished by going it alone. Given the enduring political will to create some form of united Europe, uncountable compromises in uncountable negotiating sessions have reconciled countless differences in national interests and desires.

Encouraged by their success in creating the European Coal and Steel Community (ECSC) in 1951, Belgium, France, the Federal Republic of Germany, Italy, Luxembourg, and the Netherlands signed the Treaty of Rome six years later and created what was originally called the European Economic Community. Through common institutions and a harmonization of national economic policies, the EEC was designed to move to an "ever closer union" in Europe by pursuing four economic freedoms: the free movement of goods, services, capital, and workers. Implicit in the aspiration to forge regional economic integration was the desire to replace historically costly European nationalism with positive mutual cooperation. More specifically, regionalism was viewed as essential, first, to channel German energies away from nationalism and in a positive direction; and second, to avoid repeating the disastrous mistakes made after World War I when the defeated Germany was isolated and financially punished. In July 1967, the EEC, the ECSC, and a third institution, the European Atomic Energy Community (popularly known as Euratom), were merged to create what was known for the next twenty-five years as the European Community (which then became the European Union).

The overall goal of converting individual European economies into an integrated common market is embodied in some 80,000 pages of treaties, regulations, agreements, case law, and joint resolutions. In addition to continuous passage of binding commitments and changes in national laws to bring member states into conformity with EU rules, European integration has been advanced by new treaties amending the original Treaty of Rome. The most important of these amendments were the Single European Act of 1986 and the 1992 Treaty on European Union, usually called the Maastricht Treaty. The latter formally placed Western Europe on a path to political, economic, and monetary union. The clearly defined effort to go beyond economic integration and seek common European foreign and security policies generated the loftier term *European Union* as the umbrella designation for the European unification movement. A third amendment, the 1997 Treaty of Amsterdam, increased the kinds of decisions that can be taken by a qualified majority rather than unanimity, and strengthened cooperation in pursuing common foreign and security policies.

The European Union has grown physically as well as administratively and legislatively. Neighboring countries took notice of its early successes. Growth rates accelerated, and intra-EU trade increased 168 percent between 1958 and 1964, while total world trade grew only by 58 percent.[3] Because government leaders decided that their countries literally could not afford to be left outside looking in, the United Kingdom, Denmark, and Ireland successfully negotiated full membership at the beginning of 1973. Membership later expanded to twelve with the accessions of Greece (in 1981) and Spain and Portugal (in 1986). Freed from Cold War political constraints, the formerly "neutral" states of Austria, Finland, and Sweden joined the EU in 1995. There was a further expansion of people and land in 1990 when the five Laender (states) of the former East Germany were reunited with West Germany.

The addition of new members is far from complete. All European countries are eligible for consideration providing they meet established criteria that include a democratic government, the rule of law, and the protection of human rights. Thirteen countries were in various stages of negotiating full membership in mid-2002. The closest to completing the arduous (in part because all thirteen candidates have less-developed economies and lower wages than the EU average) process were Hungary, the Czech Republic, Poland, Cyprus, Estonia, and Slovenia. Negotiations were also being held with Romania, the Slovak Republic, Bulgaria, Latvia, Lithuania, and Malta. Turkey long ago applied for membership, but opposition from Greece and other concerns have delayed Turkey's accession. Looking further into the future, a dozen other countries in Eastern and Southern Europe and three relatively wealthy Western European countries (Norway, Switzerland, and Iceland) may be the next wave to realize that staying outside the "club" is prohibitively expensive. The dramatic possibility that Russia will someday seek membership in the EU cannot be dismissed; if it joins, the EU will stretch from the Atlantic to the Pacific.

The EU already has a global presence through an "extended family." The Europeans have used preferential access to their regional market as a geopolitical tool for creating closer ties with some 150 countries. Beginning in the 1970s, the EU initiated a Mediterranean policy built around association agreements with Turkey, Cyprus, Algeria, Morocco, Libya, Tunisia, Israel, Egypt, Jordan, Lebanon, and Syria.[4] Economic ties with other LDCs have been enhanced by the Cotonou Agreement (successor to the Lome Agreements that began in 1975), which provides foreign assistance and reduces (on a nonreciprocal basis) EU barriers on most exports from 77 African, Caribbean, and Pacific countries that were former colonies of European countries. The EU's generalized system of tariff preferences in 2001 provided duty-free access to a broad range of nonagricultural goods from 142 developing countries and former Communist countries in transition to market economies (including China). The "Everything But Arms" initiative announced in 2000 will provide, over a phased period, complete duty-free access (except, of course, for arms) for goods from countries designated as the least developed.

The "Europe Agreements" provide limited preferential access to the EU for the major economies of Central and Eastern Europe (Hungary, Poland, the Czech Republic, and so on). Comprehensive free trade agreements established near-membership status for the European Free Trade Association countries: Norway, Switzerland, Iceland, and Liechtenstein. A free trade agreement has been signed with Mexico, and others are pending.[5] The net result is that the United States is one of no more than ten countries subject to MFN tariff treatment for all its exports to the EU; this means that none of its goods have any preferential tariff access.

Like all nonmember governments, U.S. trade officials deal not with individual European governments but with the EU Commission, which speaks on the collective behalf of member countries and represents them in all international trade negotiations. The commission alone proposes new actions and programs to advance the development of EU objectives and policies. It is solely responsible for carrying out and administering these initiatives. Administratively, it is headed by twenty commissioners, one of whom is appointed (by consensus) as the president. Although each member country selects a predetermined number of commissioners, once in office they are charged with acting solely on behalf of the EU's needs and goals, independent of instructions or requests from their national governments. (France, Germany, Italy, Spain, and the U.K. select two of their nationals as commissioners, and the other ten members select one; in 2005, the policy will change and each country will choose only one commissioner.) The nineteen commissioners working under the president have assigned portfolios, not unlike those of traditional cabinet ministers. The commissioners are supported by some 16,000 "Eurocrats," a large transnational civil service and translator corps based mostly in Brussels (hence the use of "Brussels" as a shorthand reference for the EU institutions). As part of its overall responsibility to ensure that the principles of the EU treaties and laws are respected and properly maintained, the commission possesses investigative powers and controls spending.

The Council of Ministers, composed of ministers representing the governments of member countries, is the body that approves new EU policies. The council's ministerial composition varies according to the issues (e.g., trade, environment, or finance) discussed at each meeting. Decisions on matters considered to be of major importance (e.g., admitting new members and changes in taxation) require unanimous approval to pass. For more routine issues, a qualified majority is sufficient for approval. The council is the residual link between national sovereignty and regional government. As such, it is the key decisionmaking institution in approving (but not conducting) the EU's negotiating position in trade relations with the United States in both multilateral and bilateral forums. Procedurally, this means that EU trade negotiators cannot go beyond the limits imposed by the council even if additional accommodation of U.S. demands is essential to reach a trade agreement. (To make such an accommodation, commission officials would need to request and receive a more flexible brief from the council.)[6]

A third institution directly affecting U.S. economic interests is the European Central Bank (ECB), the institutional center of the European monetary union. The ECB has assumed the functions previously performed by the central banks of the twelve (at yearend 2001) EU countries participating in the Eurosystem. These are the countries that have replaced their currency with the new European currency, the euro, and permanently adhere to the common monetary policy. Operational since the beginning of 1999, the ECB sets short-term interest rates and initiates changes in the money supply. It also controls the monetary reserves of the Eurosystem countries and conducts foreign exchange operations that seek to stabilize the euro's exchange rate. The bank's influence on both macroeconomic conditions in the euro-zone and the euro's exchange rate will be one of the underlying factors determining future trade flows between the United States and the EU.

Four other major EU institutions, the European Parliament, the Court of Justice, the European Council (a meeting held at least twice a year by the member countries' heads of government), and the development funds for less developed regions within the EU are important in European affairs, but they do not have a direct, day-to-day impact on U.S. trade interests.

If the institutions are the hardware of the EU, the "software" consists of the common policies and regulations that contribute to achieving a single European market. Uniformity and harmonization are the transcendent goals in the effort to make national borders in the EU as irrelevant to planning and conducting business as state borders are to economic transactions within the United States. Economic heterogeneity at the nation-state level is incompatible with a genuine regional common market. In a literal sense, European economic integration is about transferring control over a wide range of economic decisions from individual national capitals to one EU institution.

One of the core common policies covers foreign trade. Control of national trade policy is surrendered when a country becomes a full EU member. All member states allow free movement of goods, services, capital, and labor among themselves. Decisions on reducing or imposing import barriers to nonmembers are made by the EU Commission (with the approval of the Council of Ministers). Protectionist measures, such as the common external tariff, are applied uniformly on behalf of all member countries by the commission. This authority also applies to decisions on the increase or decrease of export promotion programs and export controls. The commission, as previously noted, negotiates trade policy (under a mandate defined by the council) with other countries in bilateral and multilateral meetings.

The first tangible indicator that the EU would be a success was the lack of major dislocations during the initial phasing out of tariffs on intra-EU trade. This led to the decision to eliminate all internal tariffs in 1968, many months ahead of schedule. Well into the 1980s, however, so many nontariff barriers remained that a genuinely single market still had not been created. Escalating worries about flagging European economic vigor and competitiveness relative to the United States and Japan led to the "Europe 1992" exercise. Based on a growing consensus in Europe that its greatest economic asset was its market size, the Single European Act of 1986 initiated efforts to remove nearly three hundred identified obstacles to completely free internal trade and maximum economic efficiency. Most of these obstacles consisted of physical barriers such as border and customs controls, and technical barriers such as different product standards, restrictions on capital and labor flows, and restrictive government procurement practices. As the result of the success of this effort, manufacturers found it much easier to make a uniform product for sale in all member countries rather than needing to produce specialized models to meet disparate local regulations.

Because the EU from the outset has had ambitions to break new ground and move beyond internal free trade, a series of other common policies have been adopted in direct pursuit of full economic integration and indirect pursuit of political confederation. What follows is a sampling of other common policies, not a definitive list.

As part of the effort to create a single market, member countries have harmonized the basic structure of their tax systems. All have adopted value-added sales taxes, but product-by-product tax rates are not yet uniform. Countries participating in the monetary union follow the terms of the Stability and Growth Pact, which affects national fiscal policy decisions by allowing financial penalties to be imposed on governments having budget deficits that go beyond agreed-upon ranges. There is a common transport policy. The common competition policy sets uniform standards for antitrust enforcement and gives the commission supervisory powers over national subsidies to local industries and authority to approve major corporate mergers and acquisitions.

Arguably, the most dramatic surrender of national sovereignty is the EU's common monetary policy. Historically, control over money supply, interest rates, and exchange rates has been one of the most jealously guarded powers of national governments. These factors are critically important in determining growth rates and price stability—and therefore the fate of incumbent national political leaders and those who aspire to office. Leaving aside technical details, the historic agreement to create a regional currency, the euro, a regional central bank, and a single interest rate stems from a familiar calculation by member countries. Achievement of a true single market in Western Europe was not possible as long as exchange rates among the different national currencies of EU member countries were subject to constant change. (Try to imagine what would happen to the cohesiveness of the U.S. economy if each state had its own currency and fluctuating exchange rate.)

The adoption of a common currency in the EU eliminates the possibility of exchange rate changes among member countries, and it eliminates the need to do business in Europe in multiple currencies. This immediately facilitates trade and enhances economic efficiency. The euro saves tens of millions of dollars a year in conversion fees for exchanging one EU currency into another. It also effectively eliminates the bank fees for foreign exchange hedging operations previously needed by European importers and exporters to remove the financial risk of fluctuations in the rates between European currencies. In the long run, the euro may become a major international transactions and reserve currency. If this occurs, the Euro will challenge the global dominance of the U.S. dollar. A major global role for the euro would likely limit the ability of the United States to run large trade deficits indefinitely; thus far, its chronic deficits have been facilitated by the willingness of foreigners to continue accumulating large amounts of dollar assets.

The last but far from least significant regional economic policy is the Common Agricultural Policy (CAP). Often called the "political glue" holding the EU together, the CAP—allegedly the "single largest sectoral impediment to free trade in the world"[7]—has been the single biggest irritant in U.S.-EU trade relations. It is also the biggest component of the EU budget (before being slightly scaled back in the 1990s, it had accounted for well over half of annual spending). The genesis of the CAP was a political and economic bargain between France and West Germany. French farmers received a continental market for their produce as well as subsidies that are still largely paid for by Germany's contribution to the EU budget.[8] As stated in Articles 39 and 40 of the Treaty of Rome, the major objectives of the CAP are ensuring adequate incomes for farmers, raising agricultural productivity, stabilizing agricultural markets and providing for food security, and providing reasonable prices for consumers. On a more practical level, EU farmers have long possessed political clout disproportionately greater than their numbers. European politicians have perceived that they would reap great political benefits from meeting the economic demands of this vociferous swing vote for relatively high prices for farm goods. The major means to the end of relatively high farm prices was to give the CAP the responsibility for keeping out cheaper imports of commodities that compete with European production. Urban consumers in EU countries have never objected strongly to the resulting high food prices. Farmers' benefits have been cut back on occasion only because runaway budgetary outlays were becoming prohibitively expensive.

The mechanics of the CAP, first set in motion in 1962, are built on the notion of uniform prices throughout the EU for all major crops produced in member countries. The uniform prices are set at levels high enough to please European farmers and to provide strong financial incentives to produce. To oversimplify slightly, a target price is established for each product. Until the reforms of 1992, farmers received a guaranteed minimum price for an unlimited amount of any commodity covered by the CAP. This commitment had the domestic effect of dramatically increasing the EU's agricultural production, changing the region from being a net importer of most commodities in the 1960s to a self-sufficient-to-surplus producer of many commodities by the 1980s.

The internal market distortions unleashed by the CAP have had two important implications for international agricultural trade in general and U.S. trade flows in particular. First, because politically selected EU target prices normally are well above world prices for agricultural goods, a "variable levy" is employed to impose whatever degree of tariff protection is necessary to discourage competitive imports by raising their prices above domestic target prices (again, this is a slight oversimplification of the formula). To the extent that lower-priced imports are allowed into regions or countries guaranteeing farm prices higher than world prices, unrestrained import flows would cause massive transfers of cash from official coffers to farmers. In such a scenario, the government would be forced to purchase vast unsold amounts of overpriced domestic production that could not compete with cheaper imports. Even with the import-retarding effect of the variable levy, the EU still commits the equivalent of about $50 billion annually, almost 50 percent of its total budget, to agricultural support programs.

The second international implication of the CAP has been the periodic use of export subsidies by the EU to reduce growing stockpiles of surplus agricultural production, colorfully referred to in such terms as "butter mountains" and "wine lakes." Because the CAP for many years set lucrative minimum prices for most crops without effectively limiting production, overproduction became a constant problem, one that was at least partially relieved by exporting at "discount" prices (i.e., dumping). The EU's export subsidy would pay farmers the difference between their relatively high support prices and world prices, thereby making international price competitiveness irrelevant. The Tokyo Round of GATT trade negotiations in the 1970s permitted agricultural export subsidies so long as they were not used by countries to earn more than an "equitable" share of world markets. Throughout the 1980s, the United States objected strenuously to EU export subsidies, arguing that they constituted an unfair trade practice and reduced U.S. world market share beyond a reasonable amount. After failing to persuade the EU to restrain its agricultural export subsidies, the U.S. government responded in kind by introducing its own export subsidy program in 1985.

# Unique Aspects of U.S.–European Union Commercial Relations

The United States and Western Europe designed the post–World War II international trading and monetary systems, and until the 1970s they had free rein to determine international trade and monetary policies. Virtually every major multilateral agreement affecting import liberalization and export controls since the late 1950s can be traced to a convergence of interests and joint efforts by the United States and the EU. Even after the economic boom in East Asia, the EU and the United States currently account for about 55 percent of world GDP. In the early 2000s, they together account for just over one-half of total world trade (the EU represents 36 percent when trade among member countries is included, and the U.S. share is slightly more than 15 percent). By virtue of market forces and official policies, the United States and Western Europe developed an extraordinary degree of economic interdependence. By necessity, they created what quickly became one of history's most successful and enduring military alliances. The countries comprising the so-called Atlantic Community were linked by similar cultural, political, and economic traditions as well as mutual fear of Soviet expansionism. It was no exaggeration (at least at the time) when Robert D. Hormats, then a senior U.S. State Department official, declared in 1981 that the U.S.–Western European relationship "remains at the heart of our foreign policy and our international economic policy."[9]

When measured by trade and foreign direct investment flows, the two-way commercial flow between the EU and United States approached $1 trillion in 2000. They are each others' largest trading partners when goods and services transactions are combined. In 2000, merchandise exports to the EU of $164 billion accounted for 21 percent of total American overseas shipments. U.S. imports from the EU of $220 billion represented 18 percent of total U.S. merchandise imports in the same year. U.S. exports of services to the EU in 2000 of $95 billion accounted for 32 percent of the total; U.S. imports of services from the EU in that year, $79 billion, were 37 percent of all its services imports.

Nowhere is the trend of foreign direct investment's being a complement to exporting as a means of selling goods in foreign markets (see Chapters 3 and 4) so clearly displayed as it is in the United States and Western Europe. U.S. direct investment flows to EU countries were about $83 billion in 2000. This brought the value of U.S. direct investment there to an estimated $573 billion (measured on the historical cost basis), or 46 percent of the global U.S. investment total of $1.24 trillion. EU foreign direct investment flows into the United States exceeded $200 billion in 2000, raising the total (historical cost) value of its investment to about $803 billion, or 65 percent of direct investment in the United States from all countries (also $1.24 trillion on the historical cost basis). The two-way flow of income receipts from foreign direct investments in each others' territory was almost $100 billion in 2000.[10] Majority-owned U.S. affiliates in Western Europe and European-owned affiliates in the United States each generated annual sales of about $1 trillion annually, and each employed approximately 3 million workers in the late 1990s.[11]

The continued integration of the manufacturing, services, and financial sectors of the EU and American economies has led to informal brainstorming about the possibility of creating a Trans-Atlantic Free Trade Area (presumably excluding agriculture). Although this idea is at a minimum decades away from materializing, a series of ongoing government and private sector dialogues (the Transatlantic Economic Partnership and the Transatlantic Business Dialogue, for example) have been building on the trade liberalization measures previously agreed upon in multilateral negotiations. The most tangible result of these dialogues has been the easing of regulatory standards that both sides have agreed is one of the biggest impediments to bilateral trade in manufactured goods. "Mutual recognition" agreements have streamlined product testing and inspection. When an agreement has been signed for a particular product sector, the importing country accepts tests conducted in the exporting country that certify the product standards of the importing country have been met. This arrangement does away with the need for duplicate testing and eliminates the possibility that goods will fail their safety and performance tests after arriving in the importing country.

The classic question involving U.S. exports to the very important EU market is whether their impressive growth (U.S. exports tripled in value between 1986 and 2000)[12] has been either due to the creation of the European customs union or despite it (or perhaps a combination of the two). On the one hand, as the world's preeminent trading bloc, the EU provides the greatest empirical proof of the economic theory describing the dynamic, or follow-on, benefits of trade liberalization. When trade barriers are eliminated among countries, efficient companies tend to thrive in their expanded sales market; inefficient companies either adjust, specialize, or disappear. The result is a "virtuous" cycle of increases in efficiency, economic growth, and trade. The well-above-average growth rates in GDP and intra-EU trade experienced by EU countries for many years after the removal of internal tariff barriers were not a coincidence.

On the other hand, the absence of internal trade barriers in a customs union is inherently discriminatory against goods produced in nonmember countries and is likely to result in some degree of trade diversion, that is, growth in intrabloc trade at the expense of nonmembers facing import barriers (see Chapter 12). Subsidies given by the EU to some domestic companies and agricultural exports can also give a competitive edge to domestic producers and thus affect trade flows outside of Western Europe. For all these reasons, once it became clear in the late 1950s that the EU would become a reality, U.S. trade policy took on a new mission. Assurance of continued access to the biggest trading partner, Western Europe, quickly became the top priority of U.S. trade policy. In operational terms, this meant an effort to limit the negative impact on American goods of common external tariffs and nontariff barriers imposed on non-EU members. It would be a relatively smooth, successful effort, with one big exception: agriculture.

A strong argument can be made that the leadership exerted by the United States beginning in the 1950s for progressive multilateral trade liberalization has been the most important force shaping the contemporary international trading system (see Chapter 2). In turn, a strong argument can be made that the most important inspiration for this U.S. initiative, at least into the 1980s, was concern about economic conditions in Western Europe. The exact nature of this concern has differed over time. In the years following World War II, the foreign policy imperative of reviving fragile European economies meant granting them easy access to the U.S. market without making demands for reciprocity. By 1960, U.S. concerns were transformed into the perceived need for a defensive response to an economically resurgent EU. Specifically, efforts were made to ensure that the EU's common external trade barriers were not high enough to create a "Fortress Europe" that would diminish American exports to the Continent. The subsequent U.S. effort to negotiate reductions in the common external tariff was successful because members of a customs union by definition recognize the benefits of free trade. EU countries dedicated to elimination of regional trade barriers would logically be amenable to moving towards a less protectionist international trade order, again with the exception of agriculture.

The successes of the Kennedy, Tokyo, and Uruguay Rounds of multilateral trade liberalization negotiations meant that for the most part, the common external tariff and NTBs were lowered sufficiently that the EU market has remained relatively accessible to virtually all American *manufactured* goods. In bilateral negotiations, the EU complied with its obligations under the WTO to compensate the United States (through unilateral tariff cuts) for exports lost to new EU members because of higher rates of import protection after these countries adopted EU tariffs and agricultural policies. Many of the remaining EU trade barriers were made irrelevant by the profusion of U.S. foreign direct investment inside of Europe. The bottom line is that following establishment of internal free trade in the EU, trade diversion affecting U.S. goods has been insignificant, except in agriculture.

The U.S. market for EU imports has also remained relatively open to EU goods. Two significant exceptions are when U.S. retaliation against EU agricultural trade practices and recurring U.S. restraints on imports of steel products are in effect. Otherwise, the EU has had relatively few complaints that insurmountable U.S. tariff and nontariff barriers confront their potential exports. The comfort level of the EU with U.S. export and sanctions policies has been much lower. The EU has long been vociferous in its criticism of the unilateralist nature of the Section 301 provisions and the extraterritorial aspects of the Helms-Burton Act and the Iran and Libya Sanctions Act that can trigger U.S. reprisals against even friendly foreign governments and corporations for specified commercial activities in Cuba, Iran, or Libya (these statutes are discussed in Chapter 9).

## Family Feuds

The propensity for periodic U.S.-EU trade disputes and threats to attract extensive media coverage tends to overshadow the fact that these colorful blowups deal with relatively few commodities. As a European official suggested in May 2001, "Over 98 percent of trade between the EU and the U.S. is dispute-free."[13] Thanks to the close overlap in economic, political, and cultural values, as well as a stoical tolerance for each others' most offensive hyperbole, the vast majority of disputes has been resolved. An effective, albeit amorphous, system of conflict resolution has minimized interruptions of trade flows and allowed transatlantic economic cooperation and interdependence to grow steadily. The glaring exception is agriculture, specifically the brick wall around the EU market that since the 1960s has prevented imports of many American agricultural products. The claim that 98 percent of bilateral trade was free of dispute in 2001 is literally correct only because U.S. trade policymakers have put their public criticism of, and demands for, changes in the CAP on hiatus.

The United States provided enthusiastic, unqualified support to the European unification movement from the beginning of the planning process. National security policymakers anticipated great political benefits from an increasingly prosperous, cohesive, and self-confident Western Europe. Regional economic cooperation was viewed as a means of promoting peace in Western Europe and of assuring the economic strength and political stability needed to counter the military threat from the Soviet bloc. During the ten years following the creation of the EU in 1958, the benefits from attaining U.S. geopolitical objectives heavily outweighed the moderate commercial costs of trade discrimination against U.S. goods. The upsurge in West European economic growth was a visible triumph over the dismal economic conditions in Communist-controlled Eastern Europe. Furthermore, the virtual overnight economic success of the EU was a boon to American industry. Exports of nonagricultural goods accelerated, and the prospect of selling in a prosperous European regional market caused a geometric increase in the value of U.S. foreign direct investment from $6 billion in 1960 to $201 billion in 1992.[14]

The end of the U.S.-EU trade relations honeymoon coincided with the fading of the so-called golden age of international economic prosperity and the relative declines in U.S. domestic economic and foreign trade fortunes, all of which materialized in the late 1960s. The 1970s brought a global upsurge in inflation, international monetary instability, two energy crises, and an increase by Western Europe and the United States in protectionist policies, mainly towards Asia. Changing American priorities caused a fundamental shift in the U.S. government's calculation of its national interests concerning Western Europe: The United States now felt the need to actively promote its own domestic economic interests.

The thrust of U.S. trade policy toward the EU in the 1970s therefore shifted from general acceptance and approval to demands for reforms in the CAP and a legalistic determination to have the customs union conform fully with its obligations under the GATT and later the WTO. Because Europe disagreed with the changing U.S. trade priorities, tensions escalated and an only slightly exaggerated appearance of diverging economic interests resulted. A quantitative measure of the new strain in bilateral relations was the frequency with which the EU and the United States used the GATT dispute settlement process in an attempt to resolve bilateral disagreements. They squared off as the "defendants" and "plaintiffs" in almost one-third (twenty-six of eighty) of what were in effect international lawsuits heard by GATT tribunals between 1960 and 1985.[15] As discussed below, this pattern continued after the creation of the enhanced WTO dispute settlement mechanism.

The series of trade frictions that have dominated bilateral U.S.-EU trade relations since the early 1970s have a few similarities with U.S.-Japanese trade relations (e.g., vociferous U.S. concerns about market access), but for the most part they have differed in substance. In the first place, U.S. trade policy initiatives and complaints toward the EU have been more heterogeneous in that they frequently deal with issues outside the range of traditional protectionism. Transatlantic trade relations have lacked the relatively neat, long-running symmetry of U.S. demands for a genuine opening of allegedly closed Japanese markets .

A second distinction is the overwhelming preponderance of disputes involving sectors other than advanced, state-of-the-art technologies. Unlike in the Japanese-U.S. relationship, EU-U.S. trade frictions have mostly involved agriculture and mature industries, such as steel; the dispute over Airbus (discussed later) is the main exception. A third basic difference from the Japanese issue is the relative absence of disputes involving U.S. perceptions of excessive export zeal and unacceptably large bilateral trade balance disequilibria. Until the U.S. trade deficit began to balloon in the 1990s, the United States in most years registered a trade surplus with the EU. Finally, neither the United States nor the EU has accused the other of practicing a different brand of capitalism or behaving like an "adversarial trader."

The high-level 1981–1983 disagreement over appropriate economic strategy toward the Soviet Union is an excellent example of the endless variety of bilateral trade disputes that arise and the propensity for one or both sides to defuse a lingering standoff. Specifically, the Reagan administration opposed the assistance given by several countries in Western Europe to the Soviet effort to build a natural gas pipeline from Siberia to feed into Western Europe's gas network. EU countries strongly opposed President Reagan's year-end 1981 extension of existing U.S. export controls toward the Soviet Union to include energy-related equipment and technology.

Western Europeans were livid when, shortly after the June 1982 Versailles summit meeting, the administration without warning expanded the U.S. export ban on oil and gas equipment to include sales to the Soviets by overseas subsidiaries of U.S. companies and foreign firms producing such equipment under U.S. licenses. This decision didn't just involve the issue of extraterritoriality; it also applied retroactively to goods already under contract, thereby precipitating "an almost unprecedented clash of legal, economic, and political interests across the Atlantic."[16] U.S. companies operating in Europe were placed in a classic "damned if they do, damned if they don't" situation. They were threatened with legal sanctions both by the U.S. government if they defied U.S. export controls and by European governments if they reneged on preexisting sales contracts to export energy equipment to the Soviets. The Reagan administration eventually backed down in the face of united European opposition that threatened to cause a major schism in the Atlantic Alliance. However, the EU and the United States never resolved this philosophical dispute on larger issues of political economy. They disagreed about whether the Europeans were setting themselves up for a dangerous degree of vulnerability to a Soviet cutoff of natural gas supplies and whether Soviet export sales of gas would significantly strengthen the economy by increasing the USSR's ability to pay for imports of Western technology.

Steel is the longest-running bilateral bone of contention in the manufactured goods sector. It is an unusually clear example of how the policies of both parties to a trade dispute can look bad. On the one hand, the U.S. government has been providing various forms of import protection to the domestic steel industry on a nearly continuous basis for four decades. On the other hand, the EU has created its own version of market distortions by adopting interventionist programs to cope with excess domestic capacity and declining competitiveness in steel. Consider this partial chronology of steel-related frictions:

- Stung by the first significant inroads of foreign competition, the U.S. steel industry in 1968 convinces the government to negotiate "voluntary" export restraints by Western European and Japanese producers that last through 1974.
- Faced with the impending imposition of severe U.S. penalty duties on imports of European steel found to be sold below fair value or benefiting from governmental subsidies, the EU agrees in 1982 to limit shipments of specified steel products through the end of 1985 to an average of 5.44 percent of total U.S. consumption.
- Unable to convince the EU countries to voluntarily restrict exports of specialty steel products not included in the 1982 agreement, the United States unilaterally imposes higher tariffs and quotas on European specialty steel as part of its efforts to reduce injury to the domestic industry. The EU retaliates by imposing import barriers on a comparable amount of U.S. manufactured goods.
- In September 1984, President Reagan announces that he will reject the import relief recommended by the International Trade Commission under the escape clause statute; but he states that the prevalence of unfair trade practices by foreign steel companies must be addressed through voluntary export restraints by all countries that are major steel exporters to the United States. A new bilateral steel pact broadens product coverage of the 1982 agreement and sets new limits for the market share of EU member countries in the United States; the arrangement expires in 1992.
- An early 1986 agreement ends a unilateral U.S. quota imposed on imports of semifinished steel from the EU as well as the latter's retaliatory barriers.
- In the late 1990s, the combination of the end of voluntary steel export restraints and the advent of slow economic growth that starts in East Asia and then becomes global results in a surge of relatively cheap imports of steel into the United States. Presumed injury to domestic steel producers results in the greater use of U.S. trade remedy laws. The EU objects and files several complaints in the WTO alleging that U.S. procedural actions (mainly involving antidumping) violate international rules.
- In the spring of 2002, the EU lambasts President Bush's decision to increase U.S. tariffs on most imported steel, announces its intent to file a complaint in the WTO, and warns of retaliation.

The major exception to the rule that U.S.-EU trade frictions do not involve advanced high-tech industries is the dispute surrounding Airbus jumbo jets. The United States has long asserted that the Airbus Industrie consortium became and remains a successful competitor in a lucrative but high-cost sector thanks to substantial subsidies given to it by four governments (France, Germany, the U.K., and Spain) committed to European production of large commercial aircraft. The Europeans downplay the impact (and amount) of the subsidies and assert that Boeing has received equivalent levels of assistance from U.S. government research support for defense and space programs.

U.S. ire peaked in 1988 when the German government agreed to provide a unique subsidy in the form of guarantees against adverse exchange rate swings to the private German participant in the Airbus consortium.[17] After a GATT panel found this arrangement a violation of the GATT subsidies code and the United States threatened additional complaints, a bilateral agreement on allowable government support for civil aircraft was signed in 1992. The main provisions restrict direct governmental support to 33 percent of total aircraft development costs, eliminate production subsidies, limit indirect subsidies (this mainly refers to U.S. Defense Department and NASA contracts), and establish procedures to increase the transparency of Airbus's finances.[18] This agreement partially defused this issue, but American concerns continue to resurface. In addition to Boeing's periodic discomfort with its competitor's rising world-wide market share, the U.S. government is closely watching evolving plans for governmental support to Airbus for a record $10 billion-plus cost of designing its planned super-jumbo jet, the A380. Of special concern was the suggestion that the aircraft agreement might be circumvented by channeling government financial support to subcontractors chosen to work on the A380. Should a disagreement on this issue reach a flashpoint, the United States would likely reopen the Airbus subsidy question by filing a complaint with the WTO.

Another unresolved bilateral friction involves the services sector and the sensitive issue of protecting national culture. Since 1989, the U.S. government has unsuccessfully sought to eliminate the EU "Broadcast Directive" that seeks to limit the number of U.S.-produced television programs that are telecast in member countries.

To examine the most serious, enduring, and acrimonious EU–U.S. trade dispute, it is necessary to look beyond the industrial sector.

## Food Fights

The EU has always strongly defended the CAP because it believes it is an essential component of postwar European cooperation. Spokespersons point out that even with the variable levy, the EU has remained a large and growing overall market for exports of American agricultural products, such as soybeans, not covered by the CAP. Between 1960 and 1980, the U.S. agricultural surplus with the nine countries that were EU members after 1973 rose from $1.4 billion to $7 billion.[19] Although it moved from being a net importer to a net exporter of some agricultural goods, the EU contends that this occurred in part because of increased productivity among its farmers. The EU also argues that U.S. farmers receive comparable levels of subsidies and that their economic problems should not be blamed on the EU. American farm problems are said to stem mainly from various non-European causes such as high U.S. interest rates, the strong dollar, and increasing competition for export markets from developing countries.

The U.S. government accepts none of this. Although it has never formally challenged the legality of the CAP in the GATT or the WTO, the United States has long harbored two major grievances against it. First, the CAP has caused a multibillion-dollar loss of U.S. agricultural exports to Western Europe; and second, it has spurred the rapid ascent of the EU as a major agricultural competitor in world markets. The

U.S. government has never publicly released official estimates of cumulative lost agricultural exports to Europe. The total net cost of the CAP to U.S. farmers is impossible to quantify precisely because it has not closed the European market to all U.S. agricultural products (just to those directly competing with European production) and not all American agricultural crops are uniformly price-competitive overseas.

The U.S. Agriculture Department's disdain for the international effects of the CAP was evident in 1986 congressional testimony by the administrator of the Foreign Agricultural Service. He said that after generating large agricultural surpluses in a period of sagging world demand, the European Union "has then used export subsidies to dump its surpluses, causing serious damage to U.S. export earnings in third country markets." It was also asserted that EU "export subsidies have significantly depressed world grain prices."[20]

One of the most consistent themes of U.S. trade policy since the early 1960s has been the long, usually frustrating, effort to shrink the import-retarding effects and export subsidy tendencies of the CAP. The first major skirmish in the U.S.-EU agricultural trade conflict, the so-called Chicken War, served notice that future disagreements could easily escalate beyond words into action. In 1962 the initiation of the CAP's variable levy raised a "bound" (not-to-be-increased) tariff on frozen poultry, thereby causing U.S. exports to fall rapidly. When the EU refused to meet U.S. demands for compensation owed under GATT rules, the United States retaliated in 1963 by raising tariffs (on an MFN basis as required by GATT) on various goods of export interest to EU countries. These higher duties were still in effect in the new millennium. One of them, on light trucks, was hurting Japanese companies the 1980s more than it was hurting the Europeans.

The frequency and relatively similar patterns of subsequent U.S. trade offensives against lost agricultural export potential to EU countries are suggested through the use, once again, of a partial chronology:

- A citrus-pasta dispute begins in the 1970s when the U.S. government cites EU tariff preferences extended to citrus fruits imported from some "associated" Mediterranean countries as discriminatory against U.S. citrus exports. When the EU blocks adoption of a GATT dispute settlement report supporting the U.S. complaint and recommending that the United States receive compensation, the U.S. government retaliates in 1985 by increasing tariffs on imports of EU pasta. After a failed cooling-off period and EU counter-retaliation against U.S. lemons and walnuts, a comprehensive resolution is reached in August 1986.

- When Spain and Portugal enter the EU on January 1, 1986, a near trade war erupts over the amount of compensation due the United States for lost agricultural exports, mainly corn and sorghum, resulting from those countries replacing national tariffs with the more protectionist CAP variable levy. The U.S. government announces a timetable for imposing 200 percent tariffs on an assortment of processed foods carefully selected to assure an adverse impact on the exports of all EU members. Undaunted, the EU responds by threatening to counter-retaliate with increased duties on U.S. corn gluten feed and rice. The mutual desire to deescalate trade tensions leads to an interim agreement on a compensation formula on January 30, 1987, just hours before U.S. sanctions are scheduled to be imposed.

• U.S. trade officials in 1988 demand an end to EU subsidization of oilseeds on the grounds that the subsidies are causing excess European production, which, in turn, impairs the trade benefits due American soybean producers from the EU's 1961 agreement to reduce to zero its duties on imports of soybeans and soybean meal. In their efforts to reverse the steady drop in the U.S. share of the EU oilseeds market, U.S. trade officials twice receive favorable rulings on their grievance against the Europeans from GATT dispute settlement panels but cannot secure a satisfactory response from the EU. The United States loses patience and announces a firm deadline of December 5, 1992, for the first installment of prohibitive 200 percent tariffs on EU countries' agricultural goods equivalent to U.S. imports valued at $1 billion annually, an amount equal to the alleged damage to U.S. soybean exports by the EU's domestic subsidies.[21] Two weeks before the U.S. retaliation deadline, the two sides reach a settlement, the main thrust of which cuts back European production of oilseeds by a sufficient amount to assure that an increase in imports (presumably from the United States) would be necessary to maintain existing domestic consumption levels.

Part of the long U.S. campaign to limit CAP-inflicted damage on U.S. agricultural exports has been efforts to secure a liberalization of barriers to agricultural trade in multilateral negotiations. This tactic was a failure for the better part of thirty years as the EU adamantly refused to agree to any meaningful liberalization of agricultural trade barriers in the Kennedy Round of multilateral trade negotiations (1963–1967) and the Tokyo Round (1973–1979). The United States and the EU finally took a step in the Uruguay Round of multilateral trade negotiations toward resolving their deeply entrenched disagreement on agricultural trade liberalization. One reason for this breakthrough was that the U.S. government, having long been rebuffed in its previous efforts to force reforms in the CAP, made an agreement on meaningful agricultural liberalization a nonnegotiable demand in the talks. EU concerns about the soaring budgetary costs of the CAP were the other important reason for the long-delayed compromise. The bilateral agreement on a formula for partially rationalizing trade in agricultural goods removed the last major obstacle to the successful conclusion of the Uruguay Round in December, 1993. (The EU-U.S. consensus on this issue brought overwhelming pressure on other reluctant countries, mainly Japan and Korea, to agree to relax their stringent agricultural import barriers.) The agreement, among other things, required signatory countries to convert import quotas on agricultural goods to tariffs that would be progressively reduced in the future. It also mandated reductions in the value of domestic farm subsidies and in the quantities of subsidized agricultural goods that could be exported.

U.S.-EU trade frictions entered a new phase after the Uruguay Round. Although EU agricultural practices remained the biggest source of American complaints, they now centered on nontraditional EU import barriers. A second difference was the frequency with which the two sides began filing complaints against each other after the dispute settlement mechanism of the WTO was up and running (see Chapter 8).

The two most significant complaints filed by the United States (through 2001) against the EU concerned agricultural commodities. The banana dispute is one of the more improbable international trade disputes ever recorded. Never before had two trading partners become embroiled in eight years of bitter argument about market access for a product that neither side produced. The bottom line was how the $5 billion annual EU market would be divided between American- and European-owned distributors. The banana split began in 1993 when a new EU-wide banana import system gave preferential entry to imports of fruit from EU overseas territories and former colonies in the Caribbean and Africa. Chiquita Brands International, an American-owned company whose chairman was widely reported to be a major donor to both political parties, complained to the U.S. Trade Representative that it was losing tens of millions of dollars annually in exports because of the new EU policy.

The U.S. government (and some Central American countries) subsequently requested the establishment of a WTO dispute settlement panel that in 1997 ruled that the new EU system violated international rules by discriminating against traditional Central American exporters. The EU lost its appeal of the ruling, and lost again when another WTO panel ruled that modifications that had been made in the banana import regime were insufficient to put it in compliance with international rules. After the EU refused to make further changes, thereby implicitly accepting U.S. retaliation, a WTO panel authorized the United States to do just that. The result was the imposition of 100 percent tariffs on imports from the EU (mainly from countries favoring the discriminatory banana policy) valued at $191 million annually, the estimated damage to U.S. economic interests. Two years of intensive negotiations culminated in a compromise in early 2001 that would facilitate increased exports by U.S.-owned banana distributors. U.S. sanctions were lifted, and the rift ended.

A different set of circumstances surrounded the U.S. argument (supported by Canada, Australia, and New Zealand) before a WTO dispute settlement panel that the 1989 EU ban on imports of meat derived from animals treated with growth hormones was illegal. There was unusual sensitivity associated with this issue because it touched on authority that was formerly the unquestioned, exclusive preserve of national governments: the right to draft internal regulations reflecting public concerns about food safety. The United States contended, and the WTO review panel agreed, that the EU's meat ban violated the 1994 multilateral Agreement on Sanitary and Phytosanitary Measures. The focus was on the provision requiring that a scientific basis exist for restricting imports on the grounds of health or safety concerns. The WTO panel and the Appellate Body found that the EU had not conducted a scientific risk assessment. As it did in the banana dispute, the EU refused to comply with the rulings. Its defense centered on the claim that a governmental authority had the right to take "precautionary" measures because there was at least a possibility of long-term health hazards from eating hormone-treated meat (i.e., there was no proof that it was safe). Again, the outcome was WTO-sanctioned retaliation. It took the form of imposition in 1999 of 100 percent U.S. tariffs on imports from EU countries valued at $117 million (and still in place three years later in the absence of a resolution). Whereas the amount of trade affected in this case is only about one-tenth of 1 percent of total bilateral trade, many American food companies have pressured the government to maintain a hard line because of the fear that the EU ban might be extended in the future to processed food made with chemical additives and to genetically engineered crops.[22]

Mounting congressional frustration with EU refusal to accept the WTO verdicts in these two cases resulted in the passage of a new, congressionally inspired trade statute in the spring of 2000. It mandated a periodic rotation of the products subject to U.S. retaliation when another WTO member has refused to change a trade policy to conform to a WTO dispute decision against it. The intent of "carousel retaliation" is to apply maximum pressure by increasing the number of foreign exporters lobbying their government for a settlement that would terminate U.S. sanctions hurting them.

Irritated by these U.S. complaints and retaliations against trade policies that were important to the commission, the EU took an especially hard look at U.S. trade practices. The apparent effort to send a message that the United States, too, was vulnerable to accusations of trade wrongdoings took the form of a wide-ranging series of complaints filed by the EU in the WTO beginning in the late 1990s. Many involved allegations that the U.S. government had violated international rules when deciding cases involving domestic antidumping, countervailing duty, and escape clause (safeguard mechanism) statutes. For example, the EU, joined by eight other countries, requested a WTO dispute settlement panel to consider their allegation that the so-called Byrd amendment (directing that antidumping and countervailing duties collected by the government be distributed to the injured companies; see Chapter 7) violates international trade law. EU-instigated panels also reviewed certain U.S. export expansion programs, the most important being the two WTO panel decisions ruling that U.S. Foreign Sales Corporations, a "paper" subsidiary created to reduce corporate taxes on export-generated revenue (see Chapters 8 and 9), violated multilateral agreements. A complaint also was filed about the legality of the previously mentioned "carousel retaliation." A congressional analyst concluded that this activism represented a tit-for-tat response to U.S. initiatives against European practices because, in most of its complaints, the EU had alleged little demonstrable harm to European producers. Rather, their complaints "reflect an effort by the Commission, backed with varying degrees of enthusiasm by the member states, to use the WTO dispute resolution mechanism to place the United States on the defensive and to gain leverage in more substantive cases that the EU has lost."[23]

## Conclusions and Outlook

European and American trade officials have become fond of using the metaphor of the two biggest elephants in the global economy when referring to their constituencies. This is no exaggeration. They no longer dictate the international trade agenda as they once did, but they still exert an influence disproportionate to their number. Consensus between the two trade powers is still a necessary though not sufficient factor to initiate negotiations and conclude agreements leading to multilateral trade liberalization.

The European Union and the United States have an extensive but not complete overlap in their self-interests, policies, regulations, and economic priorities. Perfect tranquility in bilateral trade relations is unlikely. New and unforeseen contingencies, such as the EU's disapproval in 2001 of the proposed General Electric–Honeywell merger, will inevitably cause strains in what is a fundamentally harmonious economic relationship. In the absence of rampant irrationality, political and business leaders on both sides of the Atlantic will almost certainly continue finding ways to contain disagreements before pro forma squabbling escalates into a spiral of counter-retaliations that inflict prohibitive or irreversible economic damage.

If there is a threat to positive cooperation and continued growth in economic interdependence between the EU and United States, it is that a steady procession of intractable disagreements might gradually push both sides to sour on one another and downgrade the importance of promoting continued growth in transatlantic trade. The disputes involving Foreign Sales Corporations and steel could escalate. The so-called agricultural "peace clause" contained in the Uruguay Round agreement expires in 2003. In the absence of new agreements, the EU and the United States will be entitled to begin filing WTO complaints and countervailing duty investigations against each others' exports of subsidized agricultural goods. Under a worse-case scenario, U.S. frustration could turn its trade policy energies towards regional free trade agreements in the Pacific and the Western Hemisphere (see Chapter 12). The United States implied just such a scenario when warning the EU in the early 1990s that if it continued holding out on an agreement to reduce agricultural import barriers and subsidies, the U.S. government would hold it responsible for the failure of the Uruguay Round negotiations.

For its part, the EU could become far more "Eurocentric" if it should experience an unexpectedly sharp drop in international competitiveness or if some, or all, of the potential internal strains it faces prove to be unexpectedly difficult to manage. The EU must confront the complications inherent in two huge changes in its institutional structure. The first is digesting what eventually will be the biggest ever increase in member countries and population. The second is the full onset of monetary union and all the attending economic uncertainties associated with applying one interest rate and one exchange rate to a large group of countries having different levels of industrial strength and experiencing diverse trends in growth, inflation, and unemployment.

## For Further Reading

Archer, Clive, and Fiona Butler. *The European Community: Structure and Process*. New York: St. Martin's Press, 1992.

Eichengreen, Barry, ed. *Transatlantic Economic Relations in the Post–Cold War Era*. New York: Council on Foreign Relations, 1998.

Gianaris, Nicholas V. *The European Community and the United States: Economic Relations*. New York: Praeger, 1991.

Neal, Larry, and Daniel Barbezat. *The Economics of the European Union and the Economies of Europe*. New York: Oxford University Press, 1998.

Pinder, John. *The European Community: The Building of a Union*. New York: Oxford University Press, 1991.

Pollack, Mark, and Gregory Shaffer, eds. *Transatlantic Governance in the Global Economy.* Lanham, Md.: Rowman and Littlefield, 2001.

Swann, Dennis. *The Economics of Europe: From Common Market to European Union.* London: Penguin Books, 2000.

Tsoukalis, Loukas. *The New European Economy Revisited.* New York: Oxford University Press, 1997.

U.S. House Committee on International Relations. *The Future of Our Economic Partnership with Europe.* Washington, D.C.: U.S. Government Printing Office, June 1999.

## Notes

1. European Union, *European Unification: The Origins and Growth of the European Community,* 3d ed. (European Union, 1990), 21.

2. When trade among member states is included in the total, EU exports in 2000 of $2.2 billion exceeded those of the three NAFTA countries. Data source: the World Trade Organization's 2000 Annual Report.

3. Data source: Delegation of the European Union Information Office, Washington, D.C.

4. The EU had twenty-nine bilateral free trade and special customs agreements in force with nonmembers in early 2002 and was negotiating with twelve more countries. Data source: U.S. Trade Representative Robert B. Zoellick, "Falling Behind on Free Trade," *New York Times,* 14 April 2002, sec. IV, 13.

5. Talks about possible free trade agreements were being conducted in 2002 with Russia and the four member countries of Mercosur (Brazil, Argentina, Uruguay, and Paraguay).

6. One of the most dramatic examples of this dynamic occurred in 1992, when the French government objected to the so-called Blair House Accords with the United States on agriculture and forced them to be reopened. France threatened to veto the agreement when it came before the Council of Ministers on the grounds that the commission had exceeded its negotiating mandate by conceding too much to the Americans.

7. John Hulsman, "How to Improve U.S.-EU Trade Relations," Heritage Foundation Backgrounder (31 October 2001): 3.

8. The German government was favorably disposed to the CAP from the beginning because the higher agricultural prices it generated were popular with German farmers, an important voting bloc. The Germans did not mind that the larger French agricultural sector would receive relatively more financial benefits from the CAP because it was assumed that German industry would derive the greatest benefit from a single European market.

9. "U.S.-European Economic Relations," U.S. Department of State press release, 16 December 1981, 5.

10. Data sources: U.S. Department of Commerce, *Survey of Current Business* (April and July, 2001). Data for calculating the EU share of U.S. foreign direct investment abroad and within the United States in 2000 were available only on the historical cost basis of measuring such investment.

11. These figures are for 1998, the latest data available. U.S. Commerce Department, *Survey of Current Business* (April 2001).

12. Data source: U.S. Commerce Department, *U.S. Foreign Trade Highlights,* various issues; the 1986 export number was adjusted to include the three countries that did not join the EU until 1995.

13. Speech by Dr. Gunter Burghardt, 7 May 2001, accessed at www.euruinion.org/news/speeches/2001/010507gb.htm/.

14. Data from U.S. Department of Commerce, *Survey of Current Business,* various issues.

15. Robert E. Hudec, "Legal Issues in US-EC Trade Policy: GATT Litigation 1960–1985," in R. Baldwin, C. Hamilton, and A. Sapir, eds., *Issues in US-EC Trade Relations* (Chicago: University of Chicago Press, 1988), 18.

16. Stephen Woolcock, "US-European Trade Relations," *International Affairs* 60 (autumn 1982): 611.

17. International sales of aircraft are denominated in dollars, and in 1988 the dollar was depreciating relative to European currencies, thus forcing profit-shaving price cuts by Airbus to stay competitive with Boeing.

18. John W. Fischer, *Boeing/Airbus—Aviation Subsidies and Related Competition Issues,* Congressional Research Service report, 14 June 2000, 2–3.

19. Data source: U.S. Department of State, *U.S. Trade with the European Community, 1958–1980,* special report no. 84, 28 June 1981, 4.

20. As quoted in Donna Vogt and Jasper Womach, *The Common Agricultural Policy of the European Community and Implications for U.S. Agricultural Trade,* Congressional Research Service report, May 1986, 16.

21. Charles Hanrahan, *The U.S.–European Community Oilseeds Dispute,* Congressional Research Service report, 13 November 1992, 1–3.

22. Raymond J. Ahearn, *Trade Conflict and the U.S.-European Union Economic Relationship,* Congressional Research Service report, 10 January 2001, 23.

23. John Van Oudenaren, "E Pluribus Confusio: Living with the EU's Structural Incoherence," *The National Interest* 65 (fall 2001): 29.

# 12 Regional Free Trade Blocs and the United States

The two most important changes in the international trade regime since the beginning of the 1990s have been the creation of the World Trade Organization and the increased numbers and size of new and proposed regional trade blocs. Exceptions to the traditional rule that trade liberalization efforts should be negotiated on a nondiscriminatory, multilateral basis are becoming so common that a structural change in the architecture of the international trading system appears to be in the offing. When a limited number of countries eliminate most or all the trade barriers among themselves, they create a preferential group that is premised on the virtue of trade expansion—presumably a good thing. Yet creation of a regional trade bloc produces discrimination against most exports of nonmembers that, by definition, are excluded from preferential trade status. As a result of the proliferation of regional trade agreements in recent years, their "two-edge sword" nature has triggered an animated, still inconclusive discussion about their net benefits to a more efficient, open global economy.

Adopting a policy of "parallel" trade liberalization on the two tracks of regionalism and multilateralism represented a major departure from traditional U.S. trade policy. Until the 1980s, the centerpiece of U.S. trade strategy was pursuit of a multilateral, nondiscriminatory trading system governed by international rules embodied first in the GATT and now the WTO. The prospect of U.S. membership in the proposed Western Hemisphere and Asia-Pacific free trade blocs has important implications for international trade, domestic economic, and foreign policies. After analyzing the political economy of the existing North American Free Trade Agreement, this chapter will examine the rationale behind the U.S. desire to join the two major regional trade groups currently under negotiation. To provide context for the newfound American interest in regionalism, it is appropriate first to address two larger questions: (1) are multilateralism and regionalism conflicting or complementary arrangements, or something in between? and (2) what are the reasons for the relatively sudden popularity of regional free trade groups?

## Why the Growing Popularity of Regional Trade Blocs? Is This a Good Thing?

Regional trade blocs are inherently contradictory. By reducing barriers to trade, they encourage competition, specialization of labor, and a better allocation of resources among member countries. They are also discriminatory in that preferential treatment is accorded the goods (and sometimes the services) of other member countries; this in turn means that nonmembers face higher barriers to their exports. Regional trade blocs simultaneously embody the principles of free trade and protectionism, the exact balance between the two being determined on a case by case basis according to the rules of each bloc.

Whatever its net merits, regional free trade has belatedly, but enthusiastically been embraced by governments around the world. Prior to the 1990s, the only economically significant regional free trade group was the European Union. Today, virtually every economically significant country either belongs to such a group (several belong to more than one) or is negotiating to be part of a bilateral free trade agreement or a regional trade group. Over 150 regional agreements were in force at yearend 2001, and the majority had come into existence after 1990.[1] More than one-third of world trade takes place within such agreements.[2] This figure will more than double if the vast free trade areas under consideration for the Western Hemisphere and the Asia-Pacific region are implemented.

Regional trade groups are an additional means for governments to pursue further trade liberalization, not a replacement for multilateral negotiations. Free trade areas and customs unions do not violate the rules of the WTO if they meet three stipulations contained in the original Article XXIV of the GATT. First, barriers must be removed on "substantially all trade"; partial liberalization is not acceptable. Second, the levels of tariffs and nontariff barriers imposed on nonmembers by participants in a free trade agreement cannot be higher than the barriers in effect before the agreement was implemented; in a customs union, barriers such as the common external tariff cannot be higher or more restrictive "on the whole" than the average of the external restraints imposed by individual member countries before they formed the customs union. In other words, a regional trade bloc may not create a higher incidence of protectionism against nonmember countries than that which existed before the group came into being. Third, trade liberalization among the signatories must be completed within a "reasonable" period of time. To legally ignore the all-important commitment to a nondiscriminatory (MFN-based) trade policy, member countries of a newly agreed-upon regional free trade agreement that are also members of the WTO must receive formal approval and pass periodic WTO reviews of the bloc's rules and operations.

Various reasons can be cited to explain the relatively recent surge in popularity of regional trade agreements. The relative importance of any of these factors differs according to time period and the countries involved. A desire to replicate some of the economic and political benefits accruing to European countries that joined the EU was one of the earliest stimuli to creating other regional trade blocs (simply stated, this is a demonstration of the old axiom that imitation is the sincerest form of flattery). A second factor was the fatigue and frustration associated with the record-setting eight years of hard negotiations required to successfully complete the Uruguay Round. Given the inexorable increase in the complexity of new trade problems and the growth in WTO membership, there is no reason to assume that future multilateral trade negotiations will be completed in a more expeditious manner. Not surprisingly, trade negotiators began looking for a simpler mode of negotiating trade liberalization, which they found in the regional approach. Such negotiations involve a limited number of usually like-minded

---

**BOX 12.1   The Terminology of Regional Trade Blocs**

The overlapping terminology of regional trade groups consisting of two or more countries can be confusing. The literature refers to them variously as trade blocs, free trade agreements, free trade areas, regional trade agreements, regional integration agreements, and preferential trade arrangements. Frequently, the term used is indicative of whether the writer has a positive or negative view of a particular group. Using "free trade" conveys a positive image of a trade bloc, but "preferential" has a more pejorative connotation. For consistency, this chapter will use the relatively value-free term *regional trade blocs*. These groups can take any of four forms, depending on the degree to which the member countries desire economic integration—a political decision.

1. A free trade area eliminates all tariff and most or all nontariff barriers among its members.
2. A customs union is a free trade area whose member countries adopt and impose a common external tariff on imports from nonmembers.
3. A common market is a customs union that also removes barriers to capital and labor flows among members.
4. An economic union is a common market whose members adopt additional common economic institutions such as common monetary and fiscal policies and a single currency.

At the end of 2001, only the European Union fully transcended the status of free trade area; hence the latter expression is widely used in referring to all other regional trade blocs.

---

countries. In addition, regional groups are mostly composed of countries that are geographically close to one another, a variable associated with deeply evolved trading relationships, best exemplified by the United States and Canada.

Most of the negotiations that have produced regional trade blocs were completed relatively quickly, even as they achieved deeper and broader trade liberalization actions than the multilateral trade negotiations (MTNs) conducted under the auspices of the GATT. Regional agreements have phased out all tariffs as opposed to the partial reductions on a limited number of goods that have marked multilateral efforts. NAFTA demonstrated that a regional agreement can go farther (and take less time in agreeing to do so) in reducing nontariff barriers on goods and barriers to trade in services as well as reducing restrictions on the local subsidiaries of foreign companies. Some trade analysts believe that the agreements on environmental and labor standards included in NAFTA involve issues that are too sensitive and complicated to be resolved in global negotiations. Regional trade agreements eliminate "free rider" countries that contribute little or nothing in a multilateral setting. This can be an additional incentive for a limited number of governments to agree to deeper and broader liberalization measures than they otherwise might.

Another economic reason for the growing interest in being part of a free trade bloc is the increasing need by corporations for larger markets to attain and retain price competitiveness in the production of relatively sophisticated manufactured goods. Maximizing sales volume is a prerequisite for a company to achieve economies of scale so that a company can spread high fixed costs (research and development, for example) over a larger sales base and reduce prices on each computer, semiconductor chip, airplane, etc. that it sells. Some less-developed countries see a regional trade bloc as a means of fostering "infant industries" that might become globally competitive after first succeeding in a regional market.

Political factors have sometimes been responsible for interest in a regional approach to free trade. The EU is the most important example of a group of countries seeking to end centuries of recurring military hostilities by irrevocably integrating their economies. Governments of smaller countries often see membership in a regional bloc as a means of enhancing their influence and stature on the world stage. Foreign policy considerations, not economics, were the driving force behind the U.S. decision to enter into a free trade agreement with Israel. Finally, a defensive reason is looming increasingly large as a spur to join regional trade blocs: the fear of being left out. As these groups proliferate, exclusion is becoming progressively more costly for the "outs." The Caribbean countries, for example, cannot be indifferent to Mexico's preferential access to the U.S. market, and no Central European country can be disinterested in the EU's eastward expansion.

All these attributes notwithstanding, some economists remain deeply skeptical about the long-term cost-effectiveness of regional trade blocs. Their reasoning starts with the premise that the world is the optimal free trade area because it maximizes global efficiency and trade. Regionalism, even under the best circumstances, is a second-best approach to maximization of global efficiency based on an international division of labor and a maximization of trade. Many economists and foreign policy specialists are deeply troubled by the scenario of three inward looking "mega-blocs" in Europe, the Americas, and East Asia. At some point, it is possible that critical mass might be hit and multilateralism would be subordinated permanently to the pursuit of regional interests and the open acceptance of discrimination against the goods and services of "outsiders."

A more immediate argument against regional trade blocs is the potential for inefficient, undesirable discrimination in the form of *trade diversion* (see Chapter 3). When "country A" eliminates trade barriers on the goods of a select few countries, it may effectively cause imports to lose price competitiveness if they are being shipped by the low-cost producer, "country B," that is not a member of the preferential trade group. "Country C" may now increase its exports to Country A, not because it is the low-cost producer, but because the removal of tariffs or nontariff barriers on its goods allows it to undersell all nonmembers of the regional group. By way of example, a low-cost clothing exporter in India may have lost its ability to be price competitive in the U.S. market when a relatively less efficient Mexican producer was relieved of paying U.S. tariffs after NAFTA went into force. Trade diversion can also deprive the government of the importing country of tariff revenues collected on imports from the original, low-cost producer.

An economically positive characteristic of trade blocs is that they inevitably result in at least some trade creation, a process that increases global efficiency through better allocations of resources. Eliminating trade barriers invariably causes countries to shift to lower-cost imports of some goods that had been previously produced in the home market. This occurs whenever the removal of trade barriers allows relatively efficient foreign producers to undersell previously protected domestic producers. The capacity of an individual regional trade bloc to provide economic benefits as well as harm was first articulated by Jacob Viner in his classic text *The Custom Union Issue,* published in 1950. Although he felt that there was a greater likelihood that these groups would actively seek to protect domestic production from outsiders, he wrote that due to varying circumstances, "Custom unions are, from the free-trade point of view, neither necessarily good nor necessarily bad."[3]

To use an often repeated phrase in this book, no definitive assessment has been produced on the net benefits of the growing popularity of regional free trade blocs. It is simply too early to tell whether these groups are "stumbling blocks" or "building blocks" to a more free-trade, market-based trading system and a more integrated world economy. No incontrovertible data have been published showing that any regional trade agreement has resulted in significantly more trade diversion than trade creation, the exception being agriculture in the EU. It is premature to predict the ultimate shape and impact of two major proposed trade blocs (in the Western Hemisphere and Asia-Pacific) that, once in operation, should have a significant impact on international trade flows.

Another unknown variable is the extent to which "open regionalism" will be accepted. Those devoted to multilateralism have proposed that regional trade groups allow any country, regardless of its geographic location, to become a full member so long as it agrees to follow all the rules established by the group it is seeking to join. If this becomes a standard practice, the likelihood increases that free trade areas will eventually overlap so extensively that they will effectively have achieved global free trade, a goal that has eluded multilateral negotiations. If open regionalism is not practiced, the scenario of inward-looking blocs becomes more plausible.

In any event, there is not yet incontrovertible evidence that regionalism has displaced multilateral trade liberalization efforts, or is about to do so. After completion of the Uruguay Round agreement, the newly created WTO served as the forum for three multilateral agreements on major reductions in trade barriers in the telecommunications services, information technology products, and financial services sectors. WTO members for several years have worked on constructing an agenda for a new round of MTNs. Perhaps the best medium-term indicator of the ability of traditional multilateralism to flourish alongside regionalism will be the ability of this new round of MTNs to produce meaningful results in further reducing trade barriers and distortions.

# NAFTA

The three-year effort to negotiate and implement the U.S.-Mexican axis of the North American Free Trade Agreement (NAFTA) was arguably the most controversial trade agreement and most hard-fought U.S. trade policy debate in the twentieth century. Reduced to bottom-line simplicity, the process involved a battle of perceptions on the question of whether such an agreement would be unacceptably costly to certain domestic constituencies. Those in favor of the agreement urged Congress to approve implementing legislation; those opposed urged Congress to reject the administration's proposed legislation. The events preceding the final passage of the NAFTA legislation in November 1993 embodied the political and economic crosscurrents repeatedly described in this book as the forces shaping U.S. import policy. Trade liberalization inevitably involves calculations of who will be winners and losers from reduced barriers and by how much; a Congress unsure of how to respond in the face of divided constituent sentiment; and a presidential commitment to further trade liberalization. Also present in the NAFTA debate was the larger reality that no matter how great the economic merits of this trade agreement, it could not enter into force unless Congress passed a statute authorizing U.S. participation in it. In the final analysis, this complex controversy boiled down to the simple arithmetic question of whether there were enough votes in Congress to pass the necessary legislation.

Despite the presence of the traditional issues associated with all major trade liberalization exercises, the struggle between NAFTA's supporters and opponents was imbued with a metaphysical importance seldom seen in the formulation of American trade policy. The unfolding debate on the cost-effectiveness of the proposed free trade agreement with Mexico produced extraordinary levels of public scrutiny and oratorical rhetoric. Some viewed the advent of free trade with a relatively low-wage country anxious to attract U.S. foreign direct investment as prohibitively costly. Others viewed it as nothing less than a critical indicator of American commitment to economic progress in, and improved relations with, a country with which it shares a border.

## *History, Content, and Controversy*

In the broadest sense, creating a free trade area in North America can be viewed as the logical culmination of market forces inexorably promoting commercial integration among the private sectors of the region's three countries. More specifically, the domestic economic problems that emerged in Canada and Mexico in the early 1980s were the catalysts for initiating the negotiations creating the free trade agreement. Although these problems were different, both governments concluded that their successful resolution required the same action: concluding a free trade agreement with the United States.

In the mid-1980s, Canada's political leaders were seriously worried about market access to what is by far its largest foreign market (exports of goods and services to the United States now account for about 30 percent of Canada's GDP). Specifically, there was the perception of a dangerous upsurge in U.S. measures to counter what U.S. government officials and affected industries alleged were unfair Canadian trade practices. The Canadian government was also increasingly concerned about the ability of the country's industries to achieve economies of scale—and thereby stay competitive—while producing for a market much smaller than any of the other major industrial markets: the United States, the EU, and Japan. Comforted because the vast majority of bilateral trade already had evolved to the status of zero or nominal tariff duties, the government of Prime Minister Brian Mulroney overcame generations of Canadian anxieties about economic domination by their larger neighbor to the south. The result was the request in late 1985 to the Reagan administration to initiate the negotiations that would lead to the U.S.-Canada Free Trade Agreement in 1989. Canada later decided to expand this agreement into a trilateral arrangement after the United States and Mexico commenced negotiations to create their own bilateral free trade agreement.

The Mexican government's similar decision to overcome generations of fear of economic domination by its larger neighbor to the north was an outgrowth of a 1990 decision by President Carlos Salinas de Gortari. He was convinced of the necessity of using free trade with the United States to reinforce and perpetuate the economic reforms that had been introduced in the late 1980s to rescue Mexico from its deteriorating domestic economic situation. By the early 1980s, Mexico's state-dominated economy was performing very poorly. A growing number of money-losing state-owned enterprises and import-substitution policies were important contributors to an economic policy syndrome that produced slow growth, high inflation, massive capital flight, and unproductive investments. The situation came to a climax when commercial banks began cutting back their lending activity after Mexico stunned the international financial community in 1982 by announcing that it could not service its external debt. The subsequent decline in world oil prices quickly produced a prolonged period of economic austerity in that country.

The remedy chosen was to move decisively toward a market-based economy. Prominent in the shock therapy applied by the Salinas administration immediately after its inauguration in late 1988 were accelerated reductions in trade barriers and the initiation of measures to encourage new foreign direct investment and enhance domestic efficiency. Within a few years, Mexico shifted from being "one of the world's most protected economies into one of the most open systems."[4]

President Salinas (like Canadian Prime Minister Mulroney) decided that Mexico needed assured, permanent access to its largest foreign market, and it needed to take steps that would make it impractical to return to the abandoned emphasis on state-interventionist policies. Establishment of a free trade area with the United States would accomplish both objectives. With no need to worry about opposition from another Mexican political party, all that remained was for the Salinas administration to convince the Bush (I) administration to open negotiations for a free trade agreement. It received a positive response from the United States by arguing that free trade between the two countries would reinforce Mexico's commitment to a market-based economy; this in turn would strengthen its economy and social fabric and gradually reduce the flow of illegal immigration to the United States.

On August 12, 1992, the United States, Mexico, and Canada concluded an agreement to establish the world's largest free trade zone as measured by economic output.[5] Unlike his Canadian and Mexican counterparts, President Bush could not assume that legislative ratification was a mere formality.

Specifically, the accord called for the gradual phase out—within a maximum of fifteen years—of all tariffs and traditional nontariff barriers to trade among the three countries in merchandise goods and most services. Eliminating trade barriers is simple in concept but incredibly complex in execution. The NAFTA accord consists of a five-volume, approximately 2,000-page text and three side agreements. It lays out detailed rules on the achievement and practice of hemispheric free trade; for example, rules of origin to qualify for free trade, emergency restraints in cases of import surges, protection of intellectual property rights, and procedures to settle disputes. The agreement also contains detailed provisions on how liberalization measures are to be applied to several economic sectors where American producers are relatively competitive; they include agriculture, automobiles and automotive parts, energy, financial services, telecommunications, and textiles and apparel.

The agreement moved beyond the usual parameters of a free trade area in several respects. A number of service sectors were liberalized, and national treatment (government regulation of domestic and foreign-owned corporations is identical) was extended to foreign-owned service companies. NAFTA provisions also liberalized the treatment of, and provided protection for, incoming foreign direct investment. All signatories are required to treat foreign investors from other member countries identically to domestic investors by providing guarantes of free transfers of funds, protection from unjust expropriation, elimination of export performance requirements, and so on.

In addition, the Clinton administration insisted on the addition of two side agreements to meet major complaints (above and beyond trade liberalization) about NAFTA voiced by U.S. environmental interest groups and organized labor. The first supplementary agreement encourages high environmental standards in principle, creates a cumbersome international bureaucracy to oversee enforcement of domestic environmental laws, and promises funding for environmental cleanup projects. Hence, supporters could praise the NAFTA as the first "green" free trade agreement. At the same time, opponents dismissed the enforcement power of these provisions as being completely inadequate. Environmental groups were divided on the merits of NAFTA. One side felt it was better than nothing and a first step to meaningful improvement in Mexico's enforcement of environmental protection laws; other groups thought that it would accelerate pollution as industrial production grew on the Mexican side of the border.

The second side agreement establishes forums—as opposed to binding enforcement mechanisms—for intergovernment cooperation to encourage the enforcement of most existing labor protection laws, to promote improved labor conditions, and to provide a system for resolving labor-related problems between member countries. Unlike the environmental NGOs, the U.S. labor movement was virtually unanimous in dismissing the adequacy of this agreement.

Negotiating NAFTA was the easy part of the U.S. decisionmaking process. Assuring congressional passage of the necessary implementing legislation under fast-track authority was a far more difficult endeavor. Problems arose on two levels. One was the traditional disagreement by potential winners and losers over the likely economic consequences of the agreement. The second level was an extraordinarily acrimonious dispute that raged among an unusually large number of interest groups in which emotional heat often overshadowed intellectual light. NAFTA was portrayed in extreme terms as either a necessary good or an avoidable evil. Either way, the expected good or evil was usually portrayed as materializing in amounts significantly greater than anything suggested by the relatively small size of the Mexican economy and the relatively limited reduction in existing bilateral trade barriers. So public and pervasive was the debate that it was the first trade policy issue to become grist for network talk shows, comedy monologues of late-night comedians on television, and even comic strips.

Very few Americans were distraught over the implications of concluding a free trade agreement with Canada. However, the prospects of free trade with the 85 million people living in Mexico, a country with a GDP at the time that was barely one-twentieth the size of that of the United States, generated deeply felt concerns and perceived economic threats to important interest groups. Much of this anxiety arose because previous successful free trade agreements had occurred between countries at comparable, advanced levels of economic development.[6] Mexico at this time did not practice multiparty democracy and was not committed to the rule of law to the same extent as the United States. Opponents of NAFTA were concerned about job security and viewed Mexico not as an equal trading partner but as a poorer country where officials were bent on luring numerous U.S. companies to move south of the border to exploit lax environmental standards and low-paid workers. In the words of Frederick W. Mayer:

> As apprehended by union members, grassroots environmentalists, [and] disaffected citizens . . . NAFTA had come to stand for stories of greedy corporations, corrupt politicians, and foreign interests in league against workers, family farmers, communities, and the environment. . . . Opposition to NAFTA wasn't a calculated choice to maximize one's interest, it was a matter of honor, a matter of moral imperative, and an affirmation of identity.[7]

Some in the pro-NAFTA faction favored the improved division of labor that follows reductions in trade barriers. In their view, the establishment of a free trade area in North America would be nothing more than a de jure recognition of de facto economic trends that clearly served the overall U.S. national interest. Other NAFTA proponents were motivated mainly by foreign policy concerns. In their view, NAFTA was fully consistent with the strong and abiding interest of the United States in promoting economic growth, political stability, and a move toward democracy in a country with which it shares a long border and that just a few years previously was in economic distress. As argued by one Latin American scholar,

> It is rather late in the game to debate whether the United States and Mexico should be closely connected, or to think that the United States unilaterally can stem the flow of capital and jobs across the border. . . . The central issue for the United States is whether the net benefits to this country of closer [bilateral] connections . . . are likely to be greater as a result of an unnegotiated and somewhat haphazard process of . . . accelerating functional integration . . . or whether the interest of the United States and of most of its citizens, on the whole, are more likely to be advanced within a thoughtfully negotiated framework.[8]

The pro-NAFTA side also argued that the larger, more technologically advanced United States had relatively little to fear from a free trade arrangement. Instead, it was Mexico and Canada, with much smaller, less powerful economies, that had legitimate concerns about becoming economic appendages of the much larger United States in a free trade area.

Proponents and opponents effectively converted the polemic into a grandiose plebiscite that had more to do with raw political power than hard economic data. President Bill Clinton said that at the core of the NAFTA debate was a fundamental question: Was the United States "going to face the future with confidence that we can create tomorrow's jobs, or are we going to try against all the evidence of the last 20 years to hold on to yesterday's?"[9] Conversely, one-time presidential candidate Ross Perot warned of economic disaster. Alluding to a "big sucking sound," he claimed that as many as 5.9 million U.S. jobs were at risk of being lost to Mexico.

The technical economic arguments in the NAFTA debate mainly revolved around four issues:

1. Net job changes: Would NAFTA have a positive or negative net effect on total jobs in the United States? Could those workers losing low-wage jobs to imports move to higher-skilled, higher-paying ones?
2. Wage impact: Would wages rise on balance as more capital-intensive goods were shipped to Mexico or drop as production was shifted south of the border?
3. Investment: Would NAFTA encourage significantly higher rates of new investment in Mexico that otherwise would have been made in the United States with its higher wages and tighter government regulations?
4. Trade: To what extent would NAFTA affect the volume, product composition, and net balance of U.S.-Mexican trade?

Despite the appearance of many elaborate economic models designed to generate answers to these critical questions, virtually no definitive, universally accepted answers materialized. The models exhibited substantial differences in their quantitative findings. In large part, this was because of fundamental differences in methodology and the assumptions made, often because analysts were predisposed to obtaining results either praising or condemning NAFTA. A Joint Economic Committee study spoke for many nonpartisan observers when it concluded that none of the economic impact studies it had examined represented "a thorough and comprehensive approach to [the] full range of economic questions."[10] The study also quoted the congressional testimony of one of this book's coauthors, who asserted that the "vast majority of existing studies are so strongly influenced by their authors' theoretical views and prior beliefs that they do little more than quantify those preconceptions."[11]

A majority of the economic forecasts conducted to guide U.S. policymakers on NAFTA's likely long-term impact concluded that it would provide a net plus—albeit a small one—for the overall U.S. economy. Typical of these findings was a report by the U.S. International Trade Commission (an independent governmental agency with no constituency to protect) concluding that it was "likely" that a United States–Mexico free trade agreement (FTA) "would provide net economic benefits to the United States, but the benefits would be small in relation to the size of the U.S. economy at least in the near to medium term. The benefits of an FTA would probably increase in time, but remain fairly small in the foreseeable future."[12]

The major source of opposition to NAFTA was based on the fear that waves of unemployment in the American manufacturing sector would be unleashed by removing trade barriers against goods made by relatively low-wage Mexican workers. U.S. wage rates in the industrial sector in 1992 were about seven times as high as those of Mexican workers, who also did not enjoy the same legal rights to form unions, strike, bargain collectively, or receive minimum safety standards. Ethical questions arose from the assumption that job losses in the United States would fall disproportionately on relatively unskilled and uneducated workers in the manufacturing sector—precisely those persons who would have the most difficulty finding comparable or better-paying jobs elsewhere. In some respects, a kind of class politics was at work: Big business as a whole could look forward to greater profits, but some workers faced the real prospect of losing their jobs in the abstract quest for greater economic efficiency. The Clinton administration sought to defuse this moral dilemma by promising increased funding for income maintenance, retraining, and job search assistance for workers who lost their jobs because of production shifts and increased imports. Groups supporting and opposing NAFTA produced a wide range of guesstimates on its impact on U.S. employment, from a gain of 1.5 million jobs to a loss of 900,000 jobs.[13]

Many U.S. labor unions opposed the agreement by drawing verbal pictures of exploited workers in Mexico. They told of abuses such as children being forced to work long hours, cited instances of unhealthy and unsafe factories, and accused the Mexican government of union-busting activities. U.S. workers, they argued, should not be asked to compete on such unequal terms. Given the weak enforcement mechanisms of the side agreement on labor, it was thought that these unequal terms would endure under NAFTA. The counterargument was that free trade would upgrade Mexican working conditions and salaries in the wake of an increase in Mexico's economic prosperity.

NAFTA proponents argued that the productivity of U.S. workers was higher than their Mexican counterparts by approximately the same multiple as the wage difference, thus virtually negating any effective differential in labor costs. The rejoinder to this assertion was that Mexican productivity in many key manufacturing sectors was rising more rapidly than wages, the result being reduced unit labor costs in those sectors.[14] According to this argument, the proper comparison was not relative productivity for the total economy, but rather sectors in which highly trained Mexican workers were joined with advanced state-of-the-art capital equipment and managerial know-how. In one study, the relatively low-paid Mexican workers at an automobile engine plant were found to be 75 percent as productive as their U.S. counterparts in a comparable U.S. factory.[15] Some proponents simply downplayed the importance of wages by claiming they were a small factor in decisions about where to make investments and much less relevant than the quality of a country's infrastructure, its proximity to suppliers, and the skill level of its labor force. That the preponderance of U.S. overseas investment in the manufacturing sector is located in other industrialized countries with high wages supports this thesis.

Another major source of contention went beyond trade and dealt with the prospects for a surge of new foreign direct investment in Mexico because American companies allegedly would want to take advantage of relatively cheap labor and loosely enforced environmental regulations. The anti-NAFTA faction warned that the already declining number of new U.S. manufacturing jobs were at risk because the Mexican government planned to use the agreement primarily as a magnet for new foreign direct investment rather than as an engine of free trade. A study by the Congressional Budget Office (CBO) suggested that the larger economic benefits accruing to Mexico would come not from increased trade but from increased foreign direct investment encouraged by the removal of most barriers and disincentives to inward investment. The key to Mexico's development strategy, said the CBO, was "to attract and productively absorb foreign capital." The study also concluded that NAFTA's investment provisions would reduce risks for foreign investors and therefore make Mexico "more attractive" for U.S. companies."[16] Another potential downside of NAFTA was fear that U.S. companies would repeatedly issue a new threat to their U.S. workers: If you do not accept wage and benefits restraints, we will be forced to shift production to lower-cost Mexico.

Pro-NAFTA forces saw the foreign direct investment issue quite differently. They suggested that because U.S. import barriers had long been relatively low, most U.S. companies interested in producing in Mexico had already established subsidiaries there. It also was likely, they said, that some existing U.S. subsidiaries would be closed down in Mexico and their production facilities brought back to the United States because they would no longer be needed to leapfrog Mexican import barriers. Another investment-related argument used by proponents was that, to a large extent, new U.S. corporate ventures in Mexico would come mainly at the expense of potential U.S. investments in the low-wage countries of Southeast Asia. This allegedly would be a positive step because manufacturing and assembly plants located in Mexico would more likely use U.S.-made parts and production equipment and hire American technicians and engineers.

As far as trade was concerned, a majority of U.S. industries stood to reap greater benefits from a mutual elimination of trade barriers than their Mexican counterparts. In the early 1990s, the average U.S. tariff level imposed on Mexican goods was low: approximately one-third of the average for tariffs imposed by Mexico on U.S. goods. In addition, a far greater share (45 percent) of Mexican goods entered the United States duty-free in 1990 than the 18 percent of U.S. goods that entered Mexico duty-free.[17] With Mexico buying about 70 percent of its imported goods from its northern neighbor, higher domestic growth rates in Mexico would provide a disproportionate stimulus to exports from the Unites States. Furthermore, in an exercise in which both countries phased out barriers to imports of services, Mexico would have to give up much more than the United States with its relatively low level of restrictions. Highly competitive U.S. service industries, such as financial services and telecommunications, would gain access to a market that effectively had been closed to them.

Foreign policy advocates looked beyond jobs and described what they saw as the global strategic implications of NAFTA. Henry Kissinger said, "About once in a generation, this country has an opportunity in foreign policy to do something defining, something that establishes the structure for decades to come."[18] Conversely, presidential candidate Patrick Buchanan spoke for isolationists and persons suspicious of the growing power of international economic organizations when he wrote that NAFTA was about much more than trade: "It is the chosen field upon which the defiant forces of a new patriotism have elected to fight America's foreign policy elite for control of the national destiny. . . . Contemptuous of states' rights, regional differences and national distinctions, NAFTA would supersede state laws and diminish U.S. sovereignty."[19]

NAFTA sometimes symbolized not an economic issue but a force for either increased or reduced levels of toxic waste accumulation and other forms of land, air, and water pollution. Some environmental groups concluded that NAFTA would cause grievous incremental damage to the already serious instances of industrial-based pollution along the border. Much of this pollution originated from the clustering near the border of hundreds of so-called maquiladora plants that import U.S. parts duty-free and then re-export them back to the United States, with duties being paid only on the value added in Mexico (usually assembly work by low-paid workers). The environmental groups opposed to NAFTA foresaw its creating a magnet whereby numerous U.S. factories would flock south of the border, attracted by the relatively lax Mexican enforcement of its sophisticated array of environmental protection laws. Instead of reduced trade barriers, these groups demanded reduced pollution. Other environmental groups accepted the rule of thumb that economic development leads to stronger popular demands for improved environmental standards as well as increased governmental resources to enforce them. They also believed that little or no cleanup of existing pollution would occur if NAFTA was not implemented and if Mexico continued to manage its environmental policy on an independent, unilateral basis.

Yet another viewpoint complained that the debate had lost sight of the issues at hand and had become a metaphor for political confrontation:

> The NAFTA debate is no longer about the agreement itself, or about Mexico, but about competing domestic political agendas and irreconcilable world views. Appeals are made not to economic interest but to nationalistic fears. On one side, there are scare-mongering claims about Mexican instability; on the other, crude appeals to the most xenophobic strains of American populism. Critics exaggerate the risks of more rapid economic integration while minimizing its rewards; advocates, no more responsibly, do just the opposite. On both sides, the agreement's true purpose—and its likely effects—have been distorted and obscured.[20]

## Marketing NAFTA

After NAFTA was signed by the three heads of state in December 1992, the preparations for congressional ratification triggered the most dramatic, expensive, and mass-marketed public debate in U.S. trade policy history. Three factors were mainly responsible. The first was that a value judgment, not a scientific determination, was mandated by the aforementioned lack of definitive economic proof about NAFTA's net long-term consequences. Proponents and opponents had diametrically different interpretations of the "national interest" and spoke completely different languages when articulating the rewards and hardships to be expected from adopting free trade with Mexico. What they shared was the belief that their opinion was correct and worthy of being transformed into policy. The second factor was the perception by dozens of important interest groups that they needed to wage an aggressive lobbying campaign because their collective welfare was about to be significantly affected. They viewed NAFTA's enactment or rejection as unleashing some very good or very bad political, economic, social, and environmental changes. The final cause of the long, anguished policy debate was the absence of a clear trend in public opinion. Polls repeatedly showed that the American public was about evenly divided on the overall desirability of NAFTA,[21] meaning that most members of Congress had no clear mandate on how to vote.

The only simple thing about efforts to sway Congress was that there were only two sides, each providing an unequivocal recommendation about which way members should vote to avoid an economic calamity. At every turn, opponents and proponents sharply disagreed on how to interpret available data and on forecasts of the economic changes that would follow enactment of the agreement. Governmental entities supported NAFTA; they included the Clinton administration, state and local U.S. governmental bodies, and the Mexican government. Dozens of interested American and Mexican private sector groups represented both sides of the issue; they included the business communities in both countries, U.S. labor unions, academic and think tank economists, environmentalists, consumer protection advocates, animal rights groups, lawyers, political pundits, and the media. Some skeptics denied that they were opposed to the principle of North American free trade and asserted they were merely demanding major changes in the text of the agreement. Their rallying cry became "Not This NAFTA." Supporters of free trade derided this idea as a ploy to kill the agreement by asking the U.S. government to make unacceptable demands on the Mexican government to renegotiate its terms.

To oversimplify slightly, the political debate about NAFTA was waged between "the establishment" and a variety of groups and individuals that mostly perceived themselves as politically disenfranchised and economically disadvantaged. The pro-NAFTA position was anchored by the White House, big business (the vast majority of executives in the manufacturing, service, and agricultural sectors were in favor),[22] all the living former U.S. presidents, and Nobel Prize–winning economists. Fearful of losing jobs on balance, several influential labor unions, such as the AFL-CIO confederation, joined with other single-interest advocates, mainly environmental groups, in urging a rejection of the legislation (see Chapter 13). A think piece in the *Washington Post* tried to put the opposition of the economically threatened in a broader context that closely foreshadowed the arguments mustered in the backlash against globalization: "NAFTA is the target, but the anger encompasses much more: the sense of betrayal by the Clinton administration; the frustration of steadily declining wages for workers; [and] a fury at what is seen as a new and arrogant corporate, political, media, and academic elite."[23]

One of the most striking elements of the debate was the extent to which NAFTA politics created strange bedfellows. Traditional alliances and political partisanship were replaced by a complex mosaic of disparate groups thrown together on the basis of whether they perceived their values to be net beneficiaries or net losers from free trade with Mexico. For example, right-wing isolationists found themselves aligned with radical environmentalists in opposition. A somewhat surreal scene of togetherness was played out by four ideologically dissimilar public figures. Ross Perot, Patrick Buchanan, Jesse Jackson, and Ralph Nader found themselves in agreement—for different, sometimes conflicting reasons—that NAFTA should be rejected. One side feared too much power would be given to governments to enforce NAFTA's side agreements; the other side felt that the proposed enforcement authority was inadequate to solve environmental and labor standards problems.

Groups in the environmental lobby were split in half, roughly according to the militancy of their philosophies. The textile lobby was torn between the labor-intensive apparel segment opposed to NAFTA and the capital-intensive makers of yarns and fabrics who saw a great export potential in Mexico. (The U.S. apparel industry had been successful in getting a tough country-of-origin provision inserted into NAFTA; the so-called triple transformation test essentially allows Mexican apparel to be imported duty-free into the United States only if the finished goods are made mostly of yarns and fabrics produced within the three signatory countries.)

Political alliances on Capitol Hill were mainly ad hoc. A majority of Republicans (including most of the party's leadership) were responsive to the views of the business community and supported President Clinton on NAFTA. At the same time, a majority of House Democrats (including two of its leaders, Majority Leader Richard Gephardt and Majority Whip David Bonior) were responsive to the views of organized labor and resolutely opposed the president on this issue. Political ideology was no better guide than party affiliation for predicting which members of Congress exhibited deep commitment in fighting or supporting NAFTA. The closest thing to an accurate predictor of legislators' leanings was which geographical region they represented. The Sun Belt states on or near the Mexican border anticipated that geographical proximity and a relatively large number of high-tech companies would allow them to account for a disproportionate share of the widely expected increase in U.S. exports of goods and services to Mexico following the dismantling of trade barriers. Most congressional representatives from the industrial states of the Midwest (often dubbed the Rust Belt) were ardently opposed to NAFTA. Their constituents had suffered more than most from import competition in the basic manufacturing sectors, such as steel and automobiles.

The lobbying effort was directed at the House of Representatives, where a large number of announced opponents and undecided members meant that passage was in real doubt. Passage seemed assured in the Senate. Many members of Congress were ambivalent about how to vote on NAFTA, but they had ample access to the pros and cons of the debate. From 1991 through the final vote in November 1993, at least fifty hearings were held by the many committees in the Senate and the House of Representatives, having their interests in various provisions of the agreement heard. Constituents' written and verbal communications bombarded Capitol Hill as part of having an extensive and intensive lobbying effort. Special economic studies were issued by all of Congress's support agencies (the Congressional Budget Office, the Congressional

Research Service, the General Accounting Office, and the Office of Technology Assessment).

Interest groups were active, and their campaigns were not cheap. U.S. companies and groups spent at least $10 million trying to influence the Congress; and Mexican interests in the three years beginning in 1991 spent an estimated $30–$45 million on no fewer than twenty-four lobbying, public relations, and law firms.[24] The elite of Washington lobbyists (some of them former trade policy officials) were retained to work Washington's corridors of power. Television and radio commercials collectively costing as much as $10 million appeared with increasing frequency as the critical House vote approached. Newspaper and magazine ads were equally plentiful. USA*NAFTA, the principal pro-NAFTA coalition established by the business sector, attracted over 1,400 members (some of whom did not provide any financial support) and spent an estimated $7 million to help guarantee passage of NAFTA.[25] Comparable amounts were spent by the major opponents: labor unions, coalitions (e.g., the Citizens Trade Campaign and the Alliance for Responsible Trade), and Ross Perot, who starred in self-sponsored television "infomercials."

As late as the month before the pivotal mid-November vote in the House, the votes for approval were not there. The message coming at the time from both sides was that "if the vote were held today, NAFTA would lose." The most critical force in assuring last-minute, come-from-behind victory for the NAFTA legislation was the late emergence of President Clinton as an indefatigable activist, fully committed to using the vast carrot-and-stick powers of the Oval Office. Pushing aside the effects of professional lobbyists and their sound bites, Clinton demonstrated the validity of the political maxim, "If you're 20 or 30 votes short, you can always win if you've got a president with the will to win."[26]

One part of the successful Clinton strategy took the form of plain hard work: The president and his cabinet initiated a long series of personal contacts with reluctant or undecided House members by phone or at White House meals, and they gave countless speeches and interviews to extol NAFTA's benefits.

The second, more controversial and arguably more effective component of the administration's policy was to offer a wide range of promises, some directly related to the agreement's provisions and some not, to representatives in exchange for yes votes. NAFTA proponents viewed the ensuing exercise as hardheaded political pragmatism, the kind often exhibited throughout U.S. history in times of close legislative votes. Opponents viewed it as an expensive, unseemly giveaway program whose total costs to the U.S. public could not be calculated, in part because some deals had not yet surfaced. The promises made public included establishment of a North American Development Bank to make loans to industries and workers affected by the agreement; special understandings made with Mexico that would limit increases in sugar and orange juice concentrate exports; and commitments to seek accelerated tariff reductions by Mexico on certain commodities.[27]

That dipping into the government "pork barrel" was a highly successful tactic is suggested by the unexpectedly large margin of victory in the House: thirty-four votes. Not only was this arithmetically a big change from the straw votes taken just a few weeks before, but it also upset the assumption that many undeclared representatives would vote against NAFTA (and thereby curry favor with constituents not tied to big business) once its passage was assured.

## The Impact of NAFTA on the U.S. Economy, 1994–2001

Eight years of experience with NAFTA has produced three dissimilar assessments of the impact that the transition to free trade with Mexico has had on the American economy. Because the phase-out of the relatively modest trade barriers between the United States and Canada was initiated well before the advent of NAFTA, efforts in the United States to evaluate the free trade area's cost-effectiveness have centered on changes in trade relations with Mexico. One of the very few unqualified conclusions that can be advanced is that after eight years of observing NAFTA, virtually no person or institution speaking publicly on the issue has changed their minds. The optimists who believed that free trade would provide mutually beneficial economic benefits and better political relations between Mexico and the United States cite overwhelmingly positive results, including estimates that on balance a few thousand new jobs were created. Those opposed to NAFTA's creation are nearly unanimous in denouncing its allegedly negative impact on the U.S. economy and the environment, as well as its having caused the net loss of several hundred thousand domestic jobs. The analysts who predicted that it would have a minimal impact on the United States as a whole continue to argue that the direct economic and employment effects on balance have been statistically insignificant.

All three viewpoints cite different data that purport to prove their mutually exclusive arguments. Once again, perceptions define "reality." This is mostly because ample opportunity exists to choose and massage data selectively in order to defend conflicting assessments. Different conclusions are forthcoming simply by selecting a macroeconomic analysis to show no significant harm to the overall American economy (through 2001, at least), or by using a microeconomic analysis to identify sectoral injury, lost jobs, and specific threats of layoffs.

A major factor contributing to ambiguous data is the near impossibility of empirically proving cause and effect (a commonplace problem in international economic analysis). No free trade area exists in an economic and policy vacuum. For example, trade data clearly show that U.S. trade with Canada and Mexico has grown dramatically since NAFTA's inception in 1994. U.S. exports to Canada increased from $100 billion in 1993 to $179 billion in 2000; U.S. exports to Mexico jumped from $42 billion to $112 billion during the same period. U.S. imports from Canada more than doubled, growing from $111 billion in 1993 to $229 billion in 2000; imports from Mexico during these years more than tripled, rising from $40 billion to $136 billion. Total U.S. trade with its two NAFTA partners in these years grew almost twice as fast as U.S. trade with the rest of the world.[28]

An objective analysis of NAFTA's economic impact must immediately emphasize the inability to calculate precisely how much of the increased U.S. trade with either Mexico or Canada can be *directly* attributed to reduced import barriers. Increased domestic economic growth would have generated some increase in trade flows even in the absence of trade liberalization. Furthermore, NAFTA is just one element of increased trade flows among the countries of North America. It was implemented *after* economic integration was well underway between the United States and its two immediate neighbors.

Efforts to produce a refined, objective analysis of NAFTA-induced changes in U.S.-Mexican trade flows are impaired by two additional statistical factors. First, traditional "competitiveness" is obscured because a significant portion—more than 25 percent—of bilateral trade consists of U.S. intermediate manufactures exported to Mexico for assembly and re-exported back to the United States. Given the boom in cross-border production, many U.S. exports to Mexico are not for consumption there, which in turn means that the value of U.S. manufactures imports from Mexico has a high U.S. content. Yet another methodological limitation is the impossibility of determining exactly how many of the incremental U.S. imports from Mexico (and Canada) would have been produced in the United States in the absence of NAFTA. To some extent, the incremental imports from Mexico (e.g., apparel) would otherwise have entered from third countries or could not have been produced domestically (e.g., petroleum) because of noncompetitive or nonexistent production facilities.

Indisputable cause and effect calculations for NAFTA-induced changes in trade flows are further limited by the importance of business cycles and exchange rate changes in determining trade flows (see Chapter 4). For example, the deep recession in Mexico triggered by the peso crisis that erupted in late 1994 caused a significant decline in that country's demand for imports, despite reduced tariffs. Given the relatively low average U.S. tariff rate of about 2 percent that was imposed on Mexican goods in 1993, the largest cause of the spurt in U.S. imports from that country was almost certainly the above average GDP growth rates enjoyed by the United States from the early 1990s to 2000.

Different interpretations are given to the significance of the traditional U.S. bilateral trade surplus with Mexico turning into a deficit by the mid-1990s. To those who deem trade deficits inherently bad, NAFTA is branded as the cause of a negative U.S. economic trend. Most economists would disagree and argue that the proper way to judge the success of a free trade agreement is whether trade increased overall and resources were used more efficiently in connection with an increased specialization of labor. By these criteria, NAFTA would be judged a success.

A definitive assessment of NAFTA's impact on the environment is even more difficult and less quantifiable than an assessment of changes in growth rates, trade, income, and jobs. Critics of NAFTA point to the limited enforcement power of the North American Agreement on Environmental Cooperation as proof of its shortcomings. Supporters point to the environmental protection projects that have been undertaken and note that NAFTA, at the time of its creation, was the "greenest" trade agreement in history and far preferable to having no framework for seeking Mexican cooperation in reducing pollution. The arguments and counterarguments are similar regarding the ability of the North American Agreement on Labor Cooperation to assure compliance with eleven labor principles, including the right to organize, that all three governments promised to uphold.

Not surprisingly, the three governments have led the chorus defending NAFTA and praising it as being mutually beneficial to all its members. A joint statement issued in 2001 by the three trade ministers asserted that

A principal effect of NAFTA has been to gradually shift capital and new job opportunities in all three countries toward more productive uses. NAFTA has contributed to raising standards of living. Trade has led to the development and dispersion of technology, greater productivity, and to the creation of more and better paying jobs in all three countries.[29]

The United States has benefited from NAFTA beyond export expansion, said U.S. Trade Representative Robert Zoellick. It has "boosted productivity and wages, reduced prices on everyday consumer goods, increased consumer choice, and stimulated economic growth. NAFTA has helped boost the competitiveness of the entire U.S. economy."[30] The pro-NAFTA argument also notes that when Mexico slid into economic crisis in 1995, it did not resort to the highly protectionist policies as it did in the past and exempted the United States and Canada from the limited tariff increases it did temporarily impose.

Supporters of NAFTA put a positive spin on the employment effects for U.S. workers. Clinton administration trade officials claimed that 1998 export data indicated that U.S. exports to Canada and Mexico had supported some 650,000 more jobs than in 1993, the year before free trade with Mexico began.[31] NAFTA supporters rebut allegations of large job losses (discussed below) by using the number of workers certified under the NAFTA-Transitional Adjustment Assistance Program as a rough approximation for jobs lost to increased imports from Mexico and Canada, or for plant relocations to these countries. Between January 1, 1994, and the end of September 2000, some 312,000 workers were certified as eligible for financial and retraining benefits under this program, of which about 64,000 were related to imports from Canada. (The Department of Labor cautions against specific interpretations of these numbers because not all affected workers apply for federal assistance, and in some years as few as 20 to 30 percent of certified workers collected benefits because either they were called back to work or they quickly found new jobs.) In fiscal year 2000, just over 47,000 workers were certified for adjustment assistance under the NAFTA program.[32] By way of comparison, the strong U.S. economy was creating on average more than 2 million new jobs annually during the mid-1990s; while an estimated 1 million workers—mostly in the manufacturing sector—lost their jobs in 2001 because of the economic slowdown.

A strikingly different assessment comes from U.S. critics of NAFTA who, from the beginning, have viewed it as benefiting a few big companies but harming hundreds of thousands of production workers. The United Automobile Workers has branded it a "disaster" and a "failed trade agreement."[33] Robert Scott of the Economic Policy Institute, a Washington, D.C., think tank that has ties to organized labor, argues that NAFTA has had a "devastating impact" on nearly all U.S. manufacturing sectors. Based on the value of increased imports of manufactured goods from Mexico and Canada between 1993 and 2000, he estimated that 766,000 actual and potential U.S. jobs were lost. Scott discounts the many new jobs created in the U.S. labor force during the boom years of the 1990s on the grounds that the majority of them appear to have been in low-wage service sectors, such as retail sales. "NAFTA—combined with large, growing trade deficits with Asia and Western Europe—has shifted domestic employment away from high-wage manufacturing jobs and into low-pay industries," he claims.[34]

Those who focus on the welfare of the U.S. labor force decry NAFTA's ability to impair the welfare of workers even if jobs are not physically lost to increased imports. It allegedly has contributed to rising income inequality, reduced real wages and fringe benefits, and weakened labor's collective bargaining power. Anecdotal evidence exists of threats by U.S. corporate executives to move production operations to Mexico if workers did not acquiesce to management's demands. One study found several instances in which employers warned workers, either directly or indirectly, that if they "ask for too much, or don't give concessions, or try to organize, strike, or fight for good jobs with good benefits, we will close, or move across the border, just like other plants have done before."[35]

A third evaluation of NAFTA denies that it has been either a disaster or a windfall for the United States. The "agnostics" argue that its impact has been too limited to be held responsible for any major economic changes, good or bad. The core ideas of this thesis are (1) that NAFTA is part of the larger process of regional economic integration, not the cause of it; and (2) the proper level of analysis is the U.S. macroeconomic situation. A study published in 1996 by the North American Integration and Development Center of UCLA concluded that

> there is not yet much difference between the pre- and post-NAFTA trade, investment and production trends. While NAFTA became operational only on January 1, 1994, trade relations within North America had already begun a dramatic transformation in the mid-1980s. Years before NAFTA was contemplated, Mexico underwent a dramatic opening to international trade and investment which ushered in a period of rapid trade growth . . . and large capital inflows.
>
> The most important structural transformation associated with this opening was a dramatic shift to a new . . . pattern of production based on [Mexico's] importing intermediate goods for use in manufactured exports. . . .
>
> A growing share of U.S. imports from Mexico in fact contain a very large proportion of U.S. intermediate goods that were exported to Mexico, processed there, and then re-exported to the United States. . . . By the same token, a significant part of U.S. exports to Mexico are in fact not really final exports, but are used as intermediates in production for re-export back to the United States.[36]

An assessment of the first three years of NAFTA by the U.S. International Trade Commission found "no effects" on U.S. GDP growth or domestic investment. The study also concluded that the aggregate domestic employment effects of NAFTA were "not discernible," which was "not an unexpected result." "The number of jobs existing in the economy is primarily a macroeconomic phenomenon; trade agreements such as NAFTA generally affect the composition, not the overall level, of U.S. employment," according to the ITC study. The volume of U.S. imports from and exports to Mexico were found to have increased in a statistically meaningful way only in a "modest number of industries."[37]

The propensity for people not to change their minds about NAFTA is also demonstrated by the failure to reach consensus on the net effects on the U.S. economy of increased foreign direct investment in Mexico. This was one of the most contentious disputes in the original debate on initiating bilateral free trade. One side points to data showing a steady increase in foreign direct investment in Mexico by multinational corporations based in the United States and other industrial countries. It then claims that these new subsidiaries are being established specifically to export to the United States, having been attracted by cheap labor and lax enforcement of environmental protection laws. The result, according to critics, is lost jobs and lower wages for U.S. workers. The pro-NAFTA faction denies the existence of a job drain on the grounds that the value of U.S. foreign direct investment in Mexico showed no dramatic increase from 1994 through the end of the century, and that such investment remains a minute fraction (less than one-half of 1 percent) of total private investment within the United States.

## Negotiating a Western Hemisphere Free Trade Area

NAFTA is but one of at least thirty different subregional free trade agreements operating in the Western Hemisphere in 2002.[38] Despite the political furor that the creation of NAFTA caused in the United States, there is a high probability that ultimately it will be viewed as having been only an intermediate step before the creation of a Western Hemisphere free trade area. Barring unexpected complications, five major subregional free trade areas will coalesce into one Free Trade Area of the Americas (FTAA) sometime after 2005. The thirty-four-country trade bloc would comprise the 800 million people living from Alaska to Tierra del Fuego and have a total GDP (in 2005) in excess of $13 trillion.

The goal of achieving free trade in the Americas was first officially articulated by President Bush in June, 1990, and enthusiastically pursued by the two succeeding administrations. U.S. trade officials have not needed to twist the arms of their hemispheric neighbors to endorse creation of an integrated free trade area. A mix of economic and political factors is responsible for what was a quick consensus that in principle the FTAA was a good idea. With every hemispheric country (except the Dominican Republic and Panama) a member of a bilateral or subregional trade bloc in the 1990s, the principle of free trade with neighboring countries was being widely practiced in Central America, the Caribbean, the Andean countries, and "southern" South America at the time of Mr. Bush's proposal. The spread of free trade groups was encouraged by the new emphasis on market forces that became widespread in Latin America in the 1990s. Reduced governmental control was evident both in domestic economic policies and in less protectionist foreign trade practices.

Latin American governments have believed that the benefits of the FTAA will exceed the costs, even though these countries have higher trade barriers to remove than the United States and Canada. The prevailing attitude throughout Latin America has been that faster GDP growth, greater economic efficiency, rising living standards, and increased trade will offset the dislocations caused by phasing out import restrictions. Central American, Caribbean, and South American countries also support the FTAA in principle because it would give them guaranteed access to the critically important U.S. market, including a phase out of barriers on goods of special interest, notably, apparel and agriculture. Furthermore, many Latin American countries viewed the obligations inherent in an FTAA agreement just as Mexico envisioned NAFTA: as a means of locking in economic reforms based on deregulation, privatization, and price stability. The prospect of attracting more foreign direct investment is an additional incentive for FTAA membership to Latin American countries, just as it was for Mexico with NAFTA.

Creation of an FTAA is consistent with U.S. economic philosophy, overall commercial interests, and foreign policy. Market-driven trade would presumably promote political cooperation and democracy throughout the hemisphere in general and closer political ties between the United States and its southern neighbors in particular.[39] An elimination of tariffs throughout the Western Hemisphere is appealing to U.S. companies because the average U.S. tariff rate is less than 40 percent of the average Latin American duty of about 10 percent. It is even more significant that every one of the thirty-three other countries negotiating the FTAA already has preferential access to the U.S. market for many or all products. Preferential access is provided through NAFTA, aid-related U.S. programs such as generalized tariff preferences and the Caribbean Basin Initiative, and the "NAFTA parity" provided in the U.S.-Caribbean Basin Trade Partnership Act.[40]

Growing concern about loss of markets in Latin America due to the proliferation of subregional trade agreements means that commercial self-interest is another reason for U.S. trade policy to support the creation of the FTAA. The world's largest national economy is a potential victim of "being left out" as bilateral and multilateral free trade agreements proliferate in its own backyard. As a nonmember of these trade blocs, the United States faces increased discrimination against its exports. Concerns about trade diversion are increasing. U.S. exporters are increasingly disadvantaged by having to compete with foreign companies that have duty-free access to one or more Latin American markets. Anecdotal evidence exists of lost exports because Canadian companies now have duty-free access to the Chilean market and because of internal free trade in Mercosur, a free trade area (with some common external tariffs) comprised of Brazil, Argentina, Uruguay, and Paraguay. More U.S. exports will be at risk owing to the free trade agreement signed in 2000 between Mexico and the EU and, eventually, to the free trade agreement being discussed between Mercosur and the EU. U.S. trade negotiators cannot help but be uncomfortable as the EU continues to sign free trade and special customs agreements throughout the world with nonmembers (twenty-nine of those agreements were in force in 2002 and more are pending). Presumed economic and foreign policy benefits aside, the willingness of Congress to pass appropriate legislation will ultimately determine U.S. membership in the FTAA and thus the fate of a final agreement.

At the Summit of the Americas held in December 1994, the thirty-four democratically elected governments (Cuba has been excluded from the negotiations) of the Western Hemisphere committed themselves to completing the negotiations on a free trade area by 2005. Progress in reaching final agreement on the FTAA has been steady, but does not exemplify the relatively quick pace of most regional free trade negotiations. An above average number of countries participating in the negotiations as well as the above average diversity in the size and sophistication of their economies are not compatible with rapid deployment of free trade. Furthermore, the FTAA will go

beyond reduced tariff and nontariff barriers on goods and include agreements on services, foreign direct investment, agriculture, government procurement procedures,
intellectual property rights protection, subsidy and antidumping duties, and competition policy.

That the political will necessary to create a hemispheric free area exists was suggested when the heads of government reaffirmed at the third Summit of the Americas
in April 2001 their desire to meet an early 2005 deadline for finalizing an agreement.
They also released for public scrutiny the nine chapters of a draft agreement replete
with alternative language for controversial passages.

Although these events bode well for the FTAA and success is probable, it is far from
guaranteed. Any of several complications could delay or, at worst, derail an agreement. Some of the most serious potential roadblocks are associated with the nuances
of U.S. trade policymaking. The first is the absence (at least through early 2002) of
fast-track negotiating authority for the president (see Chapter 7). Until and unless
Congress responds to repeated presidential requests for renewal of this authority,
chances decrease precipitously for passage of a "clean" (amendment-free) trade bill
approving U.S. membership in the FTAA under the terms negotiated. Any of the
other thirty-three countries that might want to block final agreement could bolster its
position simply by demanding that the talks be put on hold until the U.S. president
can provide a credible promise that congressional approval of the trade pact as written will be forthcoming.

Passage of fast-track authority would sharply reduce the ability of another country
to disrupt these negotiations. It is no secret that Brazil, for example, does not consider the FTAA a priory. It has voiced a preference for first building and expanding
Mercosur, and it has sought a united, hard-line stance by Latin American countries to
make heavy demands on the United States for trade concessions (e.g., reforms in its
antidumping regime). If and when fast-track negotiating authority is renewed, Brazil
or any other opponent of the FTAA would quickly lose leverage in trying to scuttle
the negotiations. Several Latin American countries have indicated that they would
seek a free trade arrangement directly with the United States if the FTAA talks failed
and (presumably) if fast-track "authority" was renewed. Under such a scenario, Brazil
or any other country vetoing an FTAA agreement could expect to find itself left out
of a patchwork of bilateral free trade agreements involving the United States.

Renewal of fast-track authority ("trade promotion authority" in current
Washington parlance) is not a guarantee of launching the FTAA. Final congressional
action on such a bill is likely to be conditioned on compromise language requiring
future trade agreements to include labor and environmental standards (see Chapter
13). Like developing countries everywhere, Latin American countries worry that such
standards would discriminate against them by reducing their international competitiveness and prompting excessive foreign intervention into their domestic affairs.

As with NAFTA, negotiating the FTAA agreement may be the relatively easy part.
Inevitably, those U.S. companies and workers that see themselves vulnerable to
increased imports of labor-intensive goods will oppose U.S. membership. Inevitably,
some labor and environmental groups will denounce the potential damage to workers' rights and the environment that could be caused by further trade liberalization, a

policy they see as being promoted by big corporations to increase their profits. Concerns will again be raised that the terms of a regional free trade agreement will increase the ability of MNCs to challenge government regulations and encourage companies to shift production to countries that don't strongly enforce labor and environmental standards. In sum, the FTAA is squarely in the sights of the antiglobalization movement, as seen in the demonstrations held at the 2001 Summit of the Americas held in Quebec City.

## Negotiating an Asia-Pacific Free Trade Area

What is potentially the world's largest regional free trade agreement—in both economic and geographical terms—is being discussed in a uniquely informal manner. An Asian-Pacific trade bloc is the (very) long-term goal of countries interacting so unofficially that they convene in what is called "Asia-Pacific Economic Cooperation" (APEC), an incomplete name that has been derided as being four adjectives in search of a noun. This omission is by design because some participating countries have firmly declined to recognize it as a formal international negotiating body. (Scholars and journalists have reduced the awkwardness by taking it upon themselves to add the lower-case noun "forum" when discussing APEC.) If a free trade area is eventually created, it likely will be a web of unilateral and bilateral commitments rather than a formal multilateral agreement. The economic logic of free trade in the Pacific Basin is the same as anywhere else. The most important difference is that the degree of political cohesion among the countries involved falls far short of the sense of community prevailing in Western Europe and the Western Hemisphere. Even the idea of a purely Asian common market has not progressed very far mainly because national sovereignty is jealously guarded and there is no mutually acceptable country to assume a leadership role.

If the efforts of the APEC forum successfully create the equivalent of an Asia-Pacific free trade area, the impact on the international trading system will be unprecedented. Such an arrangement would encompass nearly half the world's population, about 60 percent of the world's GDP, and about 40 percent of world trade. Sheer size was only one of many reasons that trade officials in the Clinton administration unequivocally viewed participation in efforts to create such a regional trade group as a means of advancing the U.S. national interest. As was the case with the FTAA proposal, the potential for the spread of subregional economic groups suggested that the United States either could be involved in the design of an inclusive free trade group covering both sides of the Pacific Ocean or could risk being left out of exclusionary groups. The ten-country Association of Southeast Asian Nations (ASEAN) initiated a limited free trade area in 1992, and the idea has been floated of ASEAN's joining Japan, China, and South Korea to form a larger Asian trading bloc. Malaysia (acting somewhat like the counterpart to Brazil in Western Hemisphere trade bloc efforts) has advocated creation of the East Asian Economic Caucus that would exclude the United States. More recently, the EU encouraged enhanced Asian-European economic consultations, an idea that has produced regularly scheduled gatherings among government officials in what is known as the Asia-Europe Economic Meeting.

The scenario of a patchwork of subregional free trade agreements spreading across Asia and excluding American participation—or even more dramatic, an Asian-EU coalition—

is anathema to U.S. trade policymakers. The value of two-way American trade with Asia since the 1980s has been far larger than it has been with Europe. In addition to reducing the risk of trade diversion, an all-inclusive Asia-Pacific free trade area presumably would further enhance U.S. trade interests by providing exporters with greater access to Japan and China, the sources of the two largest U.S. bilateral trade deficits. The pursuit of such a trade bloc also provides the United States (and every other APEC member) with leverage in dealing with the multimember European Union. The most vivid example of this occurred in 1993, when U.S. negotiators sent clear signals to their EU counterparts that if the Uruguay Round of multilateral talks collapsed because the Europeans would not adequately reduce agricultural trade barriers, the United States would simply turn its energies to seeking an Asian-Pacific discriminatory free trade bloc.

An APEC forum that became even an unofficial overseer of Asia-Pacific free trade is attractive to U.S. foreign policy planners, most of whom believe that increased trade and foreign direct investment improve political relations among countries. Building effective trans-Pacific institutions would closely parallel long-standing U.S. efforts to build transatlantic institutions. For all these reasons, APEC has become the cornerstone of U.S. economic policy in the region. In addition to endorsing the goals of free and open trade and investment in the Pacific Basin, the United States supports APEC because it is "about building a 'community' of economies . . . ; and about building shared security, shared prosperity and a shared future for that community."[41]

The American private sector is not unanimous in supporting Asia-Pacific free trade. APEC's trade liberalization efforts are opposed in the United States by the same groups having problems with trade liberalization in general. Most notable are the relatively few sectors, such as apparel and steel, that are most vulnerable to increased foreign competition, environmental groups that do not want to encourage more trade until better environmental protection standards are adopted worldwide, and unions that want implementation of global labor standards. As long as these groups are successful in delaying the restoration of fast-track authority, the odds are against the launching of an Asia-Pacific free trade area and U.S. participation in it.

The twenty-one Pacific Basin countries discussing the elimination of mutual barriers to trade and investment are an unusually disparate group. They include industrial giants such as the United States and Japan; newly industrialized countries such as Korea, Singapore, and Malaysia; regional political powers such as Russia and China; intermediate economic powers such as Canada and Australia; relatively small, less-developed economies such as Peru, Papua New Guinea, and Vietnam; and two "non-countries," Hong Kong and Taiwan.[42] The governmental systems and cultures of Asian, North American, and Latin American countries are so varied and the physical distance between them is so great that it is a stretch to label the trade bloc that might emerge as "regional," especially if non-Asian countries willing to adhere to APEC's free trade rules are allowed accession.[43]

APEC operates on a consensus basis and in conformity with WTO rules. No decisions are legally binding; participants respond to agreements voluntarily. APEC deliberations on dismantling trade barriers are not even officially designated as "negotiations." As a result, the process is sometimes described as "concerted unilateral action" in which an unofficial, amorphous framework guides the voluntary behavior of members, not organizationally mandated rules.

APEC had a humble beginning. Created in 1989 at the initiative of the Australian prime minister, it was originally meant to be an informal consultative group that would discuss economic issues of importance to a select few countries in the Western Pacific. As originally conceived, APEC was not going to include the United States or any other country in the Western Hemisphere as members.[44] The original twelve members (which did include the United States and Canada) gradually increased to twenty-one as the scope and ambition of the originally modest agenda increased far beyond what had been expected. The metamorphosis of APEC into a force for trade liberalization became visible in 1993. President Clinton elevated the importance of the group by hosting the first ever meeting of the APEC forum's political leaders, and a meeting of its trade ministers received a report from outside the advisory body, the Eminent Persons Group. The report enthusiastically recommended adopting free trade and investment.

At the political leaders' meeting held in 1994, the determined effort of the host, Indonesian President Suharto, was instrumental in producing the Bogor Declaration, which informally (not legally) committed the participants to the goal of open trade and investment in the region by 2010 for industrialized economies and 2020 for developing economies. One reason for the ready acceptance at the highest political levels of the pursuit of free trade in the Pacific Basin was that the Bogor Declaration was carefully hedged. It spoke only of the principle of regional free trade and did not include a specific reference to a free trade agreement. In addition to the continued success of the EU, there was the indisputable record of increased economic development and growth that followed in the wake of decisions by Korea, Singapore, and Taiwan in the late 1960s to switch from a protectionist import substitution strategy to an export promotion policy. As discussed in Chapter 10, China also had come to the conclusion that a market-based trade policy was the most effective means to improved standards of living. Furthermore, in the early 1990s many East Asian countries were confident that they would perennially enjoy above average economic growth and increasing prosperity. No one had an inkling that a regional financial crisis would erupt just a few years later and swiftly end East Asia's run as the world's fastest growing region.

The Osaka Action Agenda adopted at the 1995 APEC leaders' meeting set forth a specific agenda to translate the free trade vision into reality. Fifteen issue areas were identified for the discussions, which continued into the new millennium. Many of them overlap the FTAA negotiating agenda: eliminating tariff and nontariff barriers; liberalizing restrictions on trade in services and foreign direct investment; protecting intellectual property rights; and adopting more transparent government procurement provisions.

## Conclusions and Outlook

The embrace of regional free trade areas by U.S. trade policy has been more a matter of pragmatism than of philosophical preference. Regional free trade groups are not preferable to the global, nondiscriminatory removal of trade barriers. Only time will tell whether they are building blocks or stumbling blocks to an international trade regime based on free trade. The two approaches to import liberalization may prove to be mutually exclusive or (more likely) they may develop a positive symbiosis, that is, each helping to promote the other. For advocates of free market economics, the inclusion of many emerging markets in newly formed trade blocs is an important means of locking in economic reforms and avoiding a reversion to protectionism when economic problems develop, as exemplified by Mexico's restraint at the height of its peso crisis in 1995. A series of interlocking free trade agreements among major regional trade blocs may someday provide the bridge to global free trade. Until more definitive data are available, perceptions will define the realities of regionalism.

Although U.S. participation in regional trade blocs is a relatively new phenomenon, for the most part the relevant considerations replicate the political economy of U.S. trade policy in general. There is the usual predisposition of most U.S. trade policymakers in the executive branch to equate any kind of trade liberalization exercise with positive economic progress. A second familiar dynamic is the need for the administration to convince Congress of two things. One is that the upside benefits so outweigh the costs that passage of membership-enabling legislation will benefit the vast majority of their constituents; the other is that Congress must be convinced that consideration will be given to relieving the problems of those injured by the elimination of trade barriers. A third repetitive pattern is that interest groups opposed to trade liberalization in general oppose U.S. participation in regional groups. Import-induced damage to workers' interests and the environment are perceived by these groups as the inevitable fallout of *any* major reductions in U.S. trade barriers. The biggest inconsistency between the U.S. government's embrace of regional and multilateral free trade is the discrimination inherent in trade blocs and their potential for trade diversion, two factors inconsistent with modern U.S. trade ideology. Thus U.S. policymakers will probably promote and join regional trade agreements only as a means to a larger, multilateral end.

If it becomes a member of the FTAA and the APEC free trade area, the United States will have abolished trade barriers to so many countries and on so many goods that it will be close to having achieved de facto free trade status. As dramatic as this would be, the impact of progressive free trade regionally will still remain a distant second to macro factors in determining domestic economic growth rates and the size of the labor force. Intense opposition will continue to confront U.S. efforts to promote regional and multilateral free trade. Legitimate concerns will always exist about the equity of trade-induced changes in the composition of the labor force as some workers suffer lost or diminished incomes while being unable to influence U.S. trade policy. The antiglobalization backlash has taken these concerns to a new level of intensity—one that has already altered the course of U.S. trade policy. This phenomenon is the subject of the next chapter.

## For Further Reading

Economic Policy Institute, *NAFTA at Seven: Its Impact on Workers in All Three Nations,* April 2001. Available at www.epinet.org/.

Joint Economic Committee. *Potential Economic Impacts of NAFTA: An Assessment of the Debate.* October 1993.

Krugman, Paul. "The Uncomfortable Truth About NAFTA." *Foreign Affairs* 72 (November–December 1993): 13–19.

Lawrence, Robert Z. *Regionalism, Multilateralism, and Deeper Integration.* Washington, D.C.: Brookings Institution, 1996.

Mayer, Frederick W. *Interpreting NAFTA.* New York: Columbia University Press, 1998.

Perot, Ross, and Pat Choate. *Save Your Job, Save Our Country: Why NAFTA Must Be Stopped—Now.* New York: Hyperion Books, 1993.

Salazar-Xirinachs, Jose, and Maryse Robert, eds. *Toward Free Trade in the Americas.* Washington, D.C.: The Organization of American States and the Brookings Institution, 2001.

*Study on the Operation and Effects of the North American Free Trade Agreement.* Report of the president to Congress, July 1997.

U.S. International Trade Commission. *The Impact of the North American Free Trade Agreement on the U.S. Economy and Industries: A Three Year Review.* Washington, D.C.: U.S. International Trade Commission, June 1997.

The World Bank, *Trade Blocs.* New York: Oxford University Press, 2000.

## Notes

1. Data source: Web site of the World Trade Organization; accessed at www.wto.org/.

2. The World Bank, *Trade Blocs* (New York: Oxford University Press, 2000), 1.

3. Jacob Viner, *The Customs Union Issue* (New York: Carnegie Endowment for International Peace, 1950), 52.

4. U.S. International Trade Commission, *The Likely Impact on the United States of a Free Trade Agreement with Mexico* (Washington, D.C.: U.S. International Trade Commission, February 1991), 1–2.

5. The addition of Mexico's small GDP to the preexisting U.S.-Canada Free Trade Agreement did little to enlarge what technically was already the world's largest free trade area when measured by GDP.

6. U.S. International Trade Commission, *Likely Impact of a Free Trade Agreement with Mexico,* 2–1.

7. Frederick A. Mayer, *Interpreting NAFTA* (New York: Columbia University Press, 1998), 272.

8. Abraham Lowenthal, "Recasting the NAFTA Debate," text of an address delivered at a conference on NAFTA held in Washington, D.C., 28–29 June 1993, 3.

9. *Weekly Compilation of Presidential Documents* 9 (20 September 1993): 1758.

10. Joint Economic Committee, *Potential Economic Impacts of NAFTA: An Assessment of the Debate,* October 1993, vi.

11. Robert A. Blecker, as quoted in ibid., 34.

12. U.S. International Trade Commission, *Likely Impact of a Free Trade Agreement with Mexico* (Washington, D.C.: U.S. International Trade Commission), 2–2.

13. Arlene Wilson, *NAFTA: How Many Jobs Are At Risk?* Congressional Research Service report, 18 May 1993, 3.

14. Robert A. Blecker and William E. Spriggs, *On Beyond NAFTA: Employment, Growth, and Income Distribution Effects of a Western Hemisphere Free Trade Area,*" IDB-ECLAC working paper no. WP-TWH–28, March 1993, 35–36.

15. Joint Economic Committee, *Potential Economic Impacts of NAFTA,* 31.

16. Congressional Budget Office, *A Budgetary and Economic Analysis of the North American Free Trade Agreement* (Washington, D.C.: Government Printing Office, 1993), xiii, 13.

17. George Ingram, *NAFTA: Evaluating the Arguments* (Washington, D.C.: Foreign Policy Institute of the Johns Hopkins University School of Advanced International Studies, 1993), 5.

18. As quoted in the *New York Times,* 17 November 1993, 1.

19. Patrick J. Buchanan, "America First, NAFTA Never," *Washington Post,* 7 November 1993, C1, C2.

20. William A. Orme, Jr., "The NAFTA Debate—Myths Versus Facts," *Foreign Affairs* (November–December 1993), 2.

21. See, for example, *New York Times,* 16 November 1993, A1; *Washington Post,* 16 November 1993, A23.

22. This assertion was demonstrated when the public sector advisory groups submitted to the Bush (I) administration their assessments of NAFTA; favorable findings came from the senior committee, the Advisory Committee for Trade Policy and Negotiations (ACTPAN), as well as the advisory committees on industry, services, and agricultural policies.

23. *Washington Post,* 8 November 1993, A10.

24. *Wall Street Journal,* 20 May 1993, A18, and 15 November 1993, A14.

25. Ibid., 15 November 1993, A14.

26. Quoted in the *Wall Street Journal,* 19 November 1993, A7.

27. Some newspapers printed suggestions that some representatives from tobacco-growing states were promised that the administration would accept a lower increase in taxes on cigarettes in return for their favorable vote on NAFTA; although there was absolutely no proof to document this supposition, it sounded credible enough to warrant its being reported. See, for example, "How a Sense of Clinton's Commitment and a Series of Deals Clinched the Vote," *Wall Street Journal,* 19 November 1993, A7.

28. Data source: U.S. Department of Commerce; accessed at www.ita.doc.gov/.

29. "NAFTA at Age Seven—Building on a North American Partnership," joint statement of the United States, Canada, and Mexico, dated 2 August 2001; accessed at www.ustr.gov/.

30. Text of a speech by Robert Zoellick, 26 July 2001; accessed at www.ustr.gov/.

31. Senate Committee on Foreign Relations, statement of Richard Fisher, Deputy U.S. Trade Representative, *Trade Versus Aid: NAFTA Five Years Later,* 13 April 1999, 13. Ambassador Fisher did add that the administration was not claiming that NAFTA alone created all the new jobs and exports.

32. Mary Jane Bolle, *NAFTA: Estimated U.S. Job 'Gains' and 'Losses' by State over 5 1/2 Years,* Congressional Research Service report, 2 February 2000, 3; data for fiscal 2000 provided by the Labor Department directly to the author.

33. "Derail Fast Track"; accessed at www.uaw.org/.

34. Robert Scott, "Distorting the Record—NAFTA's Promoters Play Fast and Loose with Facts," Economic Policy Institute Issue Brief No. 158, July 2001; accessed at www.epinet.org/.

35. Statement of Dr. Kate Bronfenbrenner to the U.S. Trade Deficit Review Commission, 29 October 1999; accessed at www.ustdrc.gov/.

36. Introduction and chapter 3 of "North American Integration Three Years After NAFTA: A Framework for Tracking, Modeling and Internet Accessing the National and Regional Labor Market Impacts, December 1996; accessed at www.naid.sppsr.ucla.edu/nafta96/introduction.html/.

37. U.S. International Trade Commission, *The Impact of the North American Free Trade Agreement on the U.S. Economy and Industries: A Three-Year Review* (Washington, D.C.: U.S. International Trade Commission, June 1997), xxi, xxii, and 3–8.

38. Data source: speech of the U.S. Trade Representative, Robert H. Zoellick, 26 July 2001; accessed at www.ustr.gov/.

39. The first deviation in the unequivocal U.S. stand in favor of multilateralism and against regional preferential arrangements came about in the early 1980s for foreign policy reasons. The Reagan administration convinced the Congress to pass legislation (the Caribbean Basin Economic Recovery Act) to provide preferential access to the U.S. market for countries in Central America and the Caribbean. Increased exports to the United States were seen in Washington as a means of encouraging political stability and reducing the internal conflicts that had engulfed several Central American countries.

40. U.S. General Accounting Office, *Free Trade Area of the Americas—Negotiations at Key Juncture on Eve of April Meetings* (Washington, D.C.: U.S. General Accounting Office, March 2001), 4.

41. Congressional testimony of Ambassador John Wolf, U.S. Coordinator for APEC, 6 November 1997; accessed at www.state.gov/wwwpolicy_remarks/971106_wolf_us_and_apec.html.

42. There are no APEC "summits" because Taiwan does not have a head of government recognized by China and some other APEC participants; Hong Kong participates even though it is an administrative region of China. Sessions at the highest political level are called "leaders meetings."

43. The size and sophistication of the economies participating in the APEC forum are also extremely varied, but not necessarily more so than among the Western Hemisphere countries negotiating the FTAA.

44. Dick K. Nanto, *Asia Pacific Economic Cooperation (APEC) and the 2000 Summit in Brunei,* Congressional Research Service report, January 2000; accessed at www.cnie.org/nle/econ–130.html/.

# 13 Consensus Cracks:
# The Anti-Globalization Backlash

The content and character of U.S. trade policy discussions took a dramatic turn at a most unlikely time: the prolonged national prosperity of the 1990s. A dramatic reconfiguration in the politics of U.S. trade policy shook the foundations of the relatively sedate world of policymaking. A new breed of political activism advanced a populist agenda that challenged many of the core, seemingly inviolate tenets and goals of post-1930s U.S. trade policy. This happened in the midst of what in some respects was capitalism's finest hour. Communism had collapsed. Invasive government control of the domestic economy was being disavowed by one country after another. Positive economic results were appearing in many of the developing and ex-Communist countries that had embraced market forces, deregulation, and privatization. The relatively free-market-oriented U.S. economy was enjoying a record peacetime economic expansion with near full employment and low inflation. The Uruguay Round of trade liberalization negotiations had been successful. In sum, the American preference for liberal trade seemed to be solidly entrenched.

Paradoxically, nascent strands of opposition to six decades of U.S. leadership in the international effort to reduce trade barriers were on their way in the early 1990s to becoming a major domestic force to be reckoned with. Originally spurred on by a growing disenchantment with the nature, effects, direction, and management of the world economy and then galvanized by fury directed against NAFTA, a growing number of nonprofit interest groups in the United States (and abroad) became increasingly effective in making their protests heard. To its surprise, the "establishment" found itself on the defensive against a privately organized, multilateral offensive directed at a relatively new set of economic, political, and social grievances collectively packaged as a protest against "globalization."

Two procedural dilemmas go along with the substantive disagreement on how to manage the world economy. The first is the extraordinary complications that have followed expansion of the trade agenda to include nontraditional concerns. The second problem has been the inability, or unwillingness, of both sides in the globalization debate to compromise and reconcile their differences. The result of an unusually intractable trade policy impasse is fully consistent with this book's emphasis on the three dimensions of U.S. trade policy. When there is a flashpoint in the *political* process of determining what trade strategy best serves the *economic* interests of the United States, the next step is a struggle on Capitol Hill about *laws:* how to revise an old trade statute, what needs to be included in new ones, and what objectives should be conveyed to the administration for an upcoming trade negotiation.

The subject matter of this book and space limitations necessitate a narrow focus on the trade-related aspects of the antiglobalization backlash. It should be noted that a substantial portion of the accusations of misguided, harmful policies and programs has been and still is directed to other sectors and institutions of the international economic order. These include the international financial system and the International Monetary Fund, the development sector and the World Bank, and the international investment system and multinational corporations.

The first part of this chapter explains *why* discontent with the trade policy status quo grew into a politically potent force in the 1990s and produced a major modification in the evolution of U.S. trade policy. *Who* the new actors are and *what* their agenda is comprise the second part. Finally, the chapter examines *how* contemporary U.S. trade policy was tangibly affected by protests from a new cohort of interest groups and the inability of policymakers to forge consensus on an appropriate response.

## What Is Globalization and Why Are People Opposed to It?

The private sector input into the formulation of U.S. trade was historically monopolized by businesses affected by trade flows and, beginning in the 1960s, by labor unions that believed their members were hurt by intensifying import competition. The "public opinion" factor grew significantly in the 1990s as nongovernmental organizations (NGOs) emerged as influential voices having a direct impact on U.S. trade policy substance. NGOs can be defined as nonprofit groups operating in one or more countries[1] that are organized around an issue of common concern to its members that is not related to personal profit (a definition that outright excludes only business groups and political parties). NGOs are an integral part of civil society, in turn defined as affinity groups operating between the levels of individual citizen and the government.

Whereas *economic* trends in the 1990s reinforced the notion held by most U.S. government officials and business executives that existing trade priorities were effectively serving the overall national interest, the *politics* of trade policy were quietly entering the initial stage of a radical transformation. Many NGOs, though dealing with different kinds of policy issues and sometimes embracing beliefs at opposite ends of the political spectrum, found common ground in perceiving harmful trends in the direction and management of the international economic order. The result was the coalescing of an informal but determined coalition that ranged from large, often well-financed nationwide organizations to small grassroots groups operating on a shoestring. It did not take long for the coalition to hit critical mass within the United States in terms of influencing Congress and stirring public opinion, or to link up with NGOs in other countries that had parallel agendas. Although their primary missions fell into several unrelated areas, the interests of their respective policy agendas and constituencies were perceived as being incompatible with the decades-old U.S. government push to systematically reduce trade barriers and construct a more market-based international trading system.

As the organized voices opposed to free trade and the free movement of international capital intensified and refined efforts to upset the international economic policy status quo, their demands became too loud (literally, sometimes) for U.S. policymakers to ignore. When their tactics were replicated by foreign counterparts, other governments were similarly affected. By the mid-1990s, it was no longer business as usual. Not since the Roosevelt administration's 1934 initiative generated history's first sustained, worldwide assault on protectionism was conventional wisdom on what constituted "good" trade policy dealt such a quick, forceful blow. Trade policy deliberations quickly moved past the long-established core question of the proper extent of government intervention to determine import and export flows. In the United States and elsewhere, the once transcendent issue of the economically appropriate and politically acceptable levels of trade barriers and distortions was eclipsed by the introduction of new kinds of demands from civil society. One was that the international trading system be administered in a more "democratic" manner to protect the right of the majority to determine domestic policies and regulations. A second major demand was that future trade agreements include the "social issues" of advancing and enforcing environmental and labor standards, two subjects that previously had been considered domestic matters only tangential to the international trade regime.

The bottom line is that the "trade and . . ." phenomenon linking trade to social issues involves not the traditional balance to be struck *among* competing commercial interests but the proper balance *between* economic interests and nontrade goals that society values.[2] Joining the technical terminology of trade policy discussions was a new array of nontraditional subjects such as the destruction of rain forests, the depletion of the ozone layer, the disposal of toxic wastes, sweatshops, child labor, dolphins, and sea turtles. Those believing that gains from trade flowing from comparative advantage were the most potent means of enhancing the overall welfare of all countries were challenged for the moral high ground.[3] Concerns expressed by economists about efficiency and competitiveness were now being countered by denunciations of a nondemocratic global economic order and an unequal distribution of gains from trade. Equally prominent were complaints that existing trade rules failed to provide adequate protection to the environment and endangered species. The protection of corporate and investor interests were attacked for being excessive.

The political dynamics that created a major new phase of U.S. trade policy emanated from the intensifying and widening backlash against "globalization." Supporters and critics of this concept share one noticeable trait: advocacy of their viewpoint is clouded because it lacks a standard, precise definition of what this generic term entails as well as a universally accepted conceptual framework in which to analyze it. Some elements of globalization are tangible, others are abstract. It has been suggested that globalization is inherently two-sided: It is "everything and its opposite. It can be incredibly empowering and incredibly coercive." It can make countries fall faster and faster behind the norm of economic achievement, and it can help countries catch up faster and faster with international standards.[4]

Globalization usually, but not always, refers to trends related either to economics or politics. Less frequently, the term is equated with cultural factors that inevitably involve concerns about pervasive Americanization through the export of consumerism, movies, music, fast food, pop fashion, free market capitalism, and so on. When discussed as an economic phenomenon, globalization is usually a synonym for three interchangeable terms: internationalization, international economic integration, and interdependence.

These three terms refer to accelerating flows of goods, services, people, capital, ideas, and technology across national boundaries, as well as increased sensitivities of individual national economies to global economic conditions. In short, a growing percentage of all economic transactions is being conducted between companies and people residing in different countries. The main driving forces of increased international economic interdependence are technological advances in telecommunications and information technology; reduced transportation costs; and the growing number of increasingly large multinational companies producing, selling, and dominating markets for their products on a global basis. The progressive dismantling of trade barriers and capital controls in the post-World War II era is another important contributing factor to economic integration.

Reliance on free market forces is more compatible with liberal trade policies than with protectionism. It was for this reason that the trading system was progressively based on an international specialization of labor determined by the comparative advantage of nation-states and the reduction of official obstacles to trade. The guiding principle, as discussed in previous chapters, is the mutual benefits derived from utilizing the world's resources in the most efficient manner possible to maximize output and minimize costs. If the subject matter of this book had included U.S. international financial policy, it would have included a parallel discussion of the economic theory outlining the benefits of allowing market forces to decide in which sectors and in which countries to allocate capital resources. A widely held view among American economists is that private investors, risking their own money and being relatively well informed on evolving market conditions, are better able than civil servants or politicians to determine where to obtain the maximum return on investment, that is, how to utilize capital in the most efficient manner.

In a slightly larger sense, globalization can be equated to a confluence of policy phenomena that became more pronounced in the later years of the twentieth century and directly or indirectly were aimed at lifting restraints on entrepreneurial initiative. They include deregulation of national markets, privatization of state-owned enterprises, restrained governmental spending (often on the social safety net), reductions in taxes, more liberal import policies, and reduced controls on private international capital flows. The desirability of such phenomena is a subjective issue because a largely unregulated private sector is often associated with unequal income distribution (even though everyone's income may be rising in absolute terms).

A different school of thought downplays the idea of globalization as a new or seismic change in the world economy. Instead, some analysts argue that current trends are merely the resumption of the integration of national economies that began as far back as the early 1800s. Integration reached an advanced stage at the beginning of the twentieth century, but was temporarily reversed by two world wars and a depression that triggered a global retreat into protectionism. The "nothing radically new" approach points to data showing that foreign trade as a percentage of the GDP of major industrialized countries was roughly the same at the beginning and end of the twentieth century. In addition, international labor migration reached a peak in the late nineteenth century.[5]

A broader intellectual framework for defining globalization goes beyond the quantitative economic indicators and emphasizes political phenomena in general and fundamental changes in governance induced by globalization in particular. The usual conclusion is that, worldwide, there has been such a large increase in corporate power relative to state power that the autonomy of sovereign nation-states has been significantly infringed. Senator Jeff Bingaman (D., N.M.) has argued that globalization involves the blurring of borders and the weakening of governments as the result of several new and significant factors: "the flow of information, the integration of technologies, the liberalization and deregulation of economies, the free movement of people, [and] the rise in power of non-governmental organizations."[6]

However one defines it, a critical question is whether the changes wrought by globalization, now and in the foreseeable future, are positive or negative on balance. A second important question is whether globalization is distributing costs and benefits relatively equitably or whether it inevitably increases the gap between rich and poor within countries and among countries. That diametrically different answers have been given to these core questions is indicative of the inevitability of value judgments when evaluating a very complex and abstract concept. The conclusion one reaches about globalization is invariably shaped by, and is consistent with, one's larger philosophical beliefs concerning, among other things, the virtue of free markets versus government regulation and to what extent workers should be rewarded relative to capital (entrepreneurs and corporate shareholders) for the output of goods and services.

The inherent content of "globalization" in its various forms makes inevitable at least some controversy. First, it is an imprecise, inclusive term that means different (but important) things to different people. Second, the specific issues associated with it are symbols of major differences in economic ideology; in short, there is a deep philosophical divide. Third, the pursuit of a market-based international trading system inevitably increases trade and is thereby constantly creating winners and losers. There is nothing out of the ordinary when workers, threatened either with losing their jobs or with cuts in wages and benefits because of increased import competition, are unwilling to make personal sacrifices in the name of economic theory or for the greater good of their fellow citizens. Two things are new, however. The first is the intensity of the perception among American workers in a number of industrial sectors that increased globalization of production poses a serious danger to their welfare. The second is the number of nonlabor activists allying themselves with this diagnosis and supporting labor's demands for a revised list of U.S. trade policy priorities and values.

Another major source of controversy involves distributional issues. Some people's political beliefs lead them to believe that the free-market-oriented nature of the world economy is responsible for the unconscionably large share of international economic prosperity that continues to go to a few already wealthy countries and a relatively few very wealthy individuals. Few rich countries or individuals are said to demonstrate adequate desire or ability to correct the highly skewed international distribution of income. The statistic that at least half the earth's population lives on the equivalent of $2 a day or less raises the highly contentious question of whether underdevelopment is a self-inflicted malady or whether it is imposed by external forces. Some assert that the underdevelopment is attributable to the detrimental effects of globalization. Others argue that sub-par economic performances are mainly due to the choice of nonmarket policies that prevent some countries from receiving the benefits that come from being integrated into the global economy. This diagnosis leads to the inevitably controversial suggestion that LDCs should adopt more globalization-friendly policies.

Concerns about the environment are another important factor perpetuating intellectual dissonance in the effort to measure the cost-effectiveness of a global economy whose priority is growth. Critics link economic growth with increased air, land, and water pollution as well as depletion of natural resources. They also decry what they see as a pattern of international trade law decisions favoring free trade over environmental protection polices (discussed in Chapter 8 and below). The opposite view points to data that suggest a correlation between increased wealth—something that globalization allegedly promotes—and the ability to afford more vigorous environmental protection standards and enforcement techniques.

Most of the furor surrounding globalization is therefore explainable. The ambiguities of this term do not, however, fully explain why the opposing sides have such different intellectual centers of gravity and mutual mistrust that they have been unable to make significant progress in reaching a harmonious common ground that allows each side to achieve at least some of its objectives. The polarization between organized supporters and detractors of globalization is unusual in its intensity and duration. A softening of rhetoric and crafting of compromises on how to deal with the foreign trade aspects of globalization have been so limited that one can speak of a dialogue of the deaf. To quote Robert Gilpin, "Many of the assertions of both proponents and opponents of globalization are either untrue, exaggerated, or just plain silly." Although globalization is very important, "the world is not nearly as integrated as many believe, nor is globalization irreversible."[7] Neither side can escape charges of occasional "short-cut" methodology in efforts to "prove" their assertions.[8]

A favorable evaluation of globalization comes from those who believe that market-oriented economic policies are major contributing factors to higher growth rates, rising standards of living, and higher incomes. Advocates argue that no relatively poor country has achieved prosperity by shutting itself off from foreign markets. Alan Greenspan, chairman of the Federal Reserve Board, argued that the broadening of markets has enhanced competition and nurtured what Joseph Schumpeter called the "creative destruction" of capitalism, that is, the continuous scrapping of old technologies to make way for the new: "Through its effect on economic growth, globalization has been a powerful force acting to raise standards of living. More open economies have recorded the best growth performance."[9] A World Bank study estimated that a group of twenty-four developing countries characterized as "globalizers" (i.e., those more open to international trade), averaged 5 percent annual growth in per capita GDP in the 1990s compared to 1.4 percent for nonglobalizing LDCs. The former also enjoyed a greater relative reduction in poverty and increased life expectancy. According to the authors of the study, the real losers from globalization are those developing countries "that have not been able to seize the opportunities to participate in this process."[10]

The unofficial guidebook to the benefits and inevitability of globalization is *The Lexus and the Olive Tree,* a best-selling book by Thomas Friedman, a *New York Times* foreign affairs columnist. He enthusiastically endorses globalization because on balance it

> is the inexorable integration of markets, nation-states and technologies to a degree never witnessed before—in a way that is enabling individuals, corporations, and nation-states to reach around the world farther, faster, deeper and cheaper than ever before. . . . The driving force behind globalization is free-market capitalism—the

more you let market forces rule and the more you open your economy to free trade and competition, the more efficient and flourishing your economy will be. . . . [Globalization] has its own set of economic rules . . . that revolve around opening, deregulating, and privatizing your economy to make it more competitive and attract foreign investment.[11]

If globalization is viewed as a virtuous end having no cost-effective alternative, the resulting pressure on countries to adopt "appropriate" economic policies as means to increased prosperity can be viewed as a good thing in the long-term. Friedman's enthusiasm over what he calls the "Golden Straightjacket" of policy conformity required for national economic success in the "new world order" brings us to the so-called Washington Consensus. The latter is the unofficial credo of a school of thought identifying an agenda of market-oriented reforms as the sine qua non for developing countries to achieve sustained growth and reduced poverty.[12] To the opposing school of thought, it is the symbol of a wrong-headed refusal to recognize the harsh effects of problems caused by market failures.

Although it once dominated conventional wisdom, the pro-globalization approach is now more often than not on the defensive, responding to a more vociferous opposition. A completely different assessment comes from a growing number of critics around the world who look at the same trends as do Messrs. Greenspan and Friedman, but conclude that an overwhelmingly negative phenomenon has been unleashed. While the U.S. government and the International Monetary Fund argue that these policies have a proven track record of success in countries around the world, others criticize free markets as being too prone to crises and not equitably distributing the gains from economic growth and technological progress. "Globalization is a way of forgetting all this. . . . It is capitalism in denial."[13] As seen by Dani Rodrik, the biggest problem is that while markets are becoming increasingly global, the institutions needed to support them remain by and large national. The "desire by producers and investors to go global weakens the institutional base of national economies. This inhibits equity and legitimacy."[14]

A more ominous warning issued by opponents is their perception of a clear and present threat to national sovereignty. They believe that the increased international mobility of production and of capital inexorably diminishes the ability of nation-states to adopt internal economic policies without undue concern for external consequences. Governments are allegedly coerced into adopting a least-common-denominator array of economic policies that seek to keep corporations' production costs down, e.g., relatively few business regulations and low corporate taxes. National and local governments, in their anxiety to attract new foreign direct investment, keep local companies from moving to lower-cost countries, and retain the confidence of the international investment community, are allegedly placing too high a priority on staying competitive. Allegedly, official policies lean too far in the direction of accommodating business. What results, say globalization critics, is a shrinking commitment by governments to maintain an effective social safety net, enforce fair labor standards, and protect the environment. They have dubbed the process a "race to the bottom."

These beliefs lead to the conclusion that the continued economic integration of nations causes domestic groups, and even entire countries, to lose control over their own destinies to more powerful outside economic and technological forces.[15] Stated another way, democracy allegedly cannot function properly because democratic governing institutions function in a world economy characterized by unchecked power "where markets in currency, labor, and goods run like engines without governors."[16] Ralph Nader has expressed fears of a global autocracy in more extreme terms:

> Globalization's tactic is to eliminate democratic decision-making and accountability over matters as intimate as the safety of food, pharmaceuticals and motor vehicles or the way a country may use or conserve its land, water and minerals, and other resources. What we have now . . . is a slow-motion coup d'etat, a low-intensity war waged to redefine free society as subordinate to the dictates of international trade—i.e., big business *uber alles.*[17]

These concerns lead to another concern that is common to the anti-globalization message: the "democracy deficit." If elected governments do feel compelled to conform to the demands of globalization at the expense of the people who elected them, a basic tenet of democracy is thwarted. To those opposed to globalization, the voice of the world's majority is being stifled by a powerful minority: executives of big multinational companies and senior officials of international economic organizations. By having disproportionate say in setting the international economic rules and influencing markets, a relative handful of people can impose their wills, values, and self-interests on the global commons. The conclusion is that only by halting the encroachment of profit-driven globalization can there be a correction to a balance of power that has shifted too far against national political leaders directly accountable to the voting public.

Opponents see the existing international economic order as one that aids and abets the elites in systematically exploiting the majority. Specifically, they denounce the inequity of a global system that embraces market principles and has caused, in their opinion, a pronounced tilt in favor of rewarding and protecting investors at the expense of workers and the environment. Globalization is seen as having exposed a "deep fault line" between groups that possess the skills and mobility to flourish in global markets and those that do not.[18] Allegedly, the primary purpose of NAFTA and other recently signed free trade agreements is "to dismantle social protections and financial regulations in order to allow capital to invest across borders rapidly and unhindered."[19] The recurring financial crises that have caused misery and instability in various emerging market countries since 1995 are seen as further evidence of the toll inflicted on everyday citizens by unrestrained international capital flows by investors and speculators. The anti-globalization argument attributes China's ability to escape the economic carnage of the Asian Contagion crisis to the nonconvertibility of its currency, government control of the financial system, and other non–Washington Consensus economic measures limiting the impact of external influences on the country.

The unions comprising the AFL-CIO represent many of the moderately and low-skilled factory workers who believe they are among the most victimized constituencies of an integrating global economy. Their insecurity is fueled by the conviction that they are the most vulnerable to being replaced by lower paid, nonunionized foreign workers working for U.S. companies or their contractors that have moved production offshore. Hard data and economic theory support the claim that relatively low-skilled American workers in the manufacturing sector have long accounted for most of the jobs lost to import competition. Less clear are the data advanced in support of labor's contention that wages and benefits are being held down throughout the United States by the pressure to compete with a virtually inexhaustible supply of low-paid labor in developing countries. An AFL-CIO official has said that U.S. trade policy "is lopsided: it protects copyrights, but not workers' rights. It takes care of international investors, but not the environment. We are opening markets abroad in financial services and agriculture, but we are not taking care of displaced workers at home."[20]

Statistical evidence indicates that labor has had to contribute a higher share of total tax revenue as the relative share paid by corporations drops in the United States and elsewhere. Large manufacturing companies appear less able to provide job security to their workers partly because of increased competition but also because their enhanced global mobility makes them less dependent on the allegiance of the local labor force. It has been argued that this situation results in governments' being "less able to sustain social safety nets, because an important part of their tax base has become footloose because of the increased mobility of capital."[21]

## New Actors; New Issues; New Trade Politics

The lobbying effort mounted by anti-globalization NGOs in pursuit of fundamental changes in the international trading system and U.S. trade policy has produced fundamental changes in the politics of the policymaking process. Until the mid-1990s, to pass legislation authorizing further reductions in U.S. trade barriers, it sufficed to create coalitions of export interests for which gains outweighed import-competing interests. For the most part, the major players were companies and workers with relatively narrow economic interests. "And generally, while there were always opponents of liberalization in the Congress, they tended to reflect narrow, often regionally based, economic interests."[22] It was therefore possible and customary for pro-liberal trade forces to craft bipartisan majorities. With hindsight, we now know that the beginning of the end of this era in U.S. trade policy materialized when the NAFTA debate (discussed below and in Chapter 12) energized not only opposition to its foreign direct investment provisions but also a demand for expanding the ambits of trade policy to include social issues. By expanding to give serious consideration to nontraditional issues and to hundreds of NGOs newly interested in foreign trade, the U.S. policymaking process became a much more contentious arena for resolving conflicting views on what constitutes "good" trade policy.

The sharp disagreement about the substantive merits of attacks on the various consequences of globalization carries over to an equally animated disagreement on the net virtues of the activists delivering the message. To provide a nonjudgmental examination of the new actors and their agenda is far more difficult than a one-sided defense or condemnation. In the first place, few people who have thought through the pro and con arguments regarding globalization remain neutral. Value judgments, not scientifically proven truths, are the norm. A scholarly overview is also difficult because the multiple goals of the anti-globalization movement and the distinct tactics used to advance them have different degrees of merit, distortion, and relevance. There are differences between making a statement through the written word, marching by the thousands in the street, and hurling Molotov cocktails at police or through store windows. The disproportionate media coverage accorded the violent forms of protest gives a distorted picture of the diverse, largely peaceful anti-globalization movement.

The campaign against globalization and, by implication, against the trade policy status quo is being pressed by informal coalitions of convenience among myriad organizations and individuals whose common estrangement with the international economic status quo is the outgrowth of a variety of policy concerns and priorities. Shared antipathy toward globalization in general and freer trade in particular unites political activists from across the entire ideological spectrum who agree about little else; many have never before even considered working together. At one end of the spectrum are established entities that conduct an ongoing intellectual dialogue with policymakers to convey specific concerns and recommendations. At the other end are small grassroots efforts that, in varying degrees, viscerally dislike and distrust all capitalist institutions. They feel that it is necessary to work outside the system. Many of these groups believe that massive, sometimes violent, confrontations in the streets are the most effective means of convincing senior officials in national governments and international economic organizations to change existing policies. Some political scientists have suggested that, as repugnant as violence may be, street demonstrations have had the positive effect of persuading policymakers to establish closer working relationships with the more mainstream NGOs. The WTO, IMF, and World Bank have revised their procedures and created new offices specifically to work more close-ly with civil society. They have done this in part because of a genuinely greater will-ingness to listen, in part because it is good public relations, and in part to isolate the more radical groups.

Virtually all the NGOs protesting against globalization at the beginning of the twenty-first century were originally created for another purpose. The great majority of these organizations seek to advance what generally would be categorized as liberal, or left-of-center, political causes in such diverse areas as environmental protection, labor rights, human rights, humanitarian relief, consumer protection, preservation of cultural values, and animal rights. Yet in pushing to curb what they see as the excess-es of globalization, they have shed the traditional liberal distrust of nationalism. In the larger sense, they advocate restoring sovereign control over economic policies and human and natural resources that allegedly have come excessively under the influence of self-serving, unelected leaders of international organizations and multinational cor-porations. These groups also insist that international organizations become more transparent. Instead of negotiating behind closed doors, they should be more account-able and responsive to the views of the general public in their member countries.

The tangible trade policy changes most eagerly sought by the new NGO activists are the inclusion of environmental and labor standards as standard provisions in future trade agreements. Few clear-thinking Americans are in favor of devastating the earth's environment, forcing children to work against their will, or condoning patent-ly unsafe working conditions. Nevertheless, there are sharp differences of opinion, first, about what should be the exact wording of more vigorous environmental and labor standards, and second, about the nature of the link between those standards and the rules of international trade (see Boxes 13.1 and 13.2).

BOX 13.1   **The Pros and Cons of Including the Promotion and Enforcement of Labor Standards in International Trade Agreements**

Widespread agreement exists in principle that core labor standards should be respected worldwide. The problem is that consensus breaks down once beyond this generality. The critics and supporters of globalization in the United States and elsewhere have diametrically opposed policy prescriptions on the extent— if any—to which the provisions of future trade agreements specifically promote these standards, how to define them, what kinds of enforcement measures should be provided, and who judges accusations of violations. Prior to the emergence of the anti-globalization backlash, multilateral discussions of labor standards were held solely in the International Labor Organization (ILO), a specialized United Nations body. The ILO has adopted a number of conventions (only a few of which have been ratified by the United States) that enunciate internationally recognized rights of workers: freedom of association; freedom to organize and bargain collectively as a group; prohibition of forced labor; prohibition of employment discrimination on the basis of race, gender, and so forth; and a minimum working age to provide the "effective abolition of child labor." In 1999, the ILO approved a new convention designed to eliminate the "worst forms" (i.e., compulsory and exploitative) of child labor.

Disagreement centers on the question of the extent, if any, to which protection of labor standards on a global basis should be incorporated directly into international trade law. The wisdom of requiring them as components of future trade agreements is the focal point of the ensuing policy debate.

Advocates of strong linkage argue that core labor standards are the moral equivalent of basic human rights and therefore deserve the strongest possible backing. Trade sanctions are seen as a highly effective means of maintaining an effective multilateral enforcement mechanism. Countries not respecting these values should have their access to foreign markets restricted. To pro-labor groups, the potential costs inflicted by these sanctions would increase the likelihood that exploitative practices are slowly relaxed; the likely end result would be a gradual rise in the political and economic status of workers in LDCs. In the meantime, American workers see no justification for enduring the financial hardships—loss of jobs and lower wages—that might follow from being forced to compete against foreign labor having unfair competitive advantages.

The counterargument to these views is that advocacy of a hard linkage between labor standards and trade agreements is based either on misplaced moral principles or simple protectionism. Most countries with an unskilled labor force and a weak physical infrastructure will feel compelled to ignore the standards in order to remain internationally competitive. The resulting external commercial retaliation by industrialized countries allegedly would keep tens

**BOX 13.1 (continued)**

of millions of workers mired in poverty and deny hundreds of millions of consumers the benefit of relatively low-priced, labor-intensive imports. Believing that bad jobs are preferable to no jobs at all, the noted economist Paul Krugman argues that the only reason developing countries have been able to compete with industrial countries in manufactured goods is their ability to offer cheap labor to employers. As long as countries have no realistic alternative to industrialization based on low wages, "to oppose it means that you are willing to deny desperately poor people the best chance they have of progress for the sake of what amounts to an aesthetic standard—that is, the fact that you don't like the idea of workers being paid a pittance to supply rich Westerners."[23]

Those who accuse globalization of tilting too much in favor of protecting capital and too little in protecting workers point to the Uruguay Round agreement on Trade-Related Aspects of Intellectual Property Rights as an example of incorporating within trade agreements and the WTO a legal framework for protecting the rights of resource holders. Intellectual property rights and workers' rights are seen by some to be similar in principle. So why is it that rules to protect property and copyrights are considered "part of a free market system" and included in trade agreements, "but those that protect worker and human rights are labeled reactionary," asked John Sweeney, president of the AFL-CIO.[24] The answer given by the opposing perspective is that the violation of American intellectual property directly hurts the economic well-being of American citizens, while denial of core labor rights directly hurts the foreign worker, not someone subject to U.S. laws and moral standards.

There are even two sides to the story of placing limits on child labor, an issue that seems fairly straightforward to most people in industrialized countries. Foreign children clearly deserve some protection from unscrupulous bosses, but there is no consensus on where to draw the line. Families in the poorest countries are often heavily dependent on the earnings of children who may have limited or no access to education. Inflexible import retaliation against goods made by young children could drive many or all of them to far worse jobs, or even to begging and prostitution.

U.S. efforts to convene a permanent working group in the WTO to consider labor standards have been repeatedly rebuffed by other countries on the grounds that the WTO lacks jurisdiction in the matter.

Opponents of globalization place a high priority on adopting a strong set of environmental and labor standards worldwide and using trade sanctions to convince countries to comply with them. Enforcement of these standards is seen as the most effective means to prevent a so-called race to the bottom. Sometimes called *downward harmonization,* this term describes the presumed chain of events that follows when countries feel pressured to keep their exports price-competitive and to attract foreign direct investment by advertising themselves as low-cost producers. Gradually, environmental

BOX 13.2   **The Relationship Between Environmental Standards, International Trade Flows, and International Trade Rules**

Widespread agreement exists about the need to prevent large increases in air, water, and land pollution, be it through voluntary or government-directed methods. There is also widespread agreement in principle about the need to protect endangered species of animals. The principle that overlap exists between trade and environmental policies is not in dispute.

Deep-seated disagreement does exist on the larger question of which is the greater danger: increasing trade flows that frustrate efforts to protect the environment or the proliferation of environmental regulations and enforcement mechanisms that could result in new barriers to trade. Also in dispute is whether the absence of comprehensive standards encourages companies to engage in "eco-dumping" by shifting production to lax-enforcement countries (no hard evidence has been produced to demonstrate that this has yet occurred to any significant degree). Nor is there agreement on whether economic growth and increased trade flows inevitably lead to more environmental degradation, or whether increased growth provides countries with the financial resources to support enhanced protection efforts and therefore a healthier environment.

The anti-globalization side of the argument believes it necessary to weave direct links between environmental standards and trade rules. It sees the threat of trade sanctions as a highly effective, proactive means of achieving and enforcing these standards. The opposing side argues that trade barriers are inefficient means of protecting the environment and recommends focusing directly on the physical sources of pollution. This view urges extreme caution in allowing the use of trade policy for advancing "green" objectives in order to preclude a resort to disguised protectionism and prevent a reduction in trade flows.

International consensus on the dangers of certain kinds of pollution has led to the signing of several multilateral environmental agreements (MEAs). Thus far they have been concluded on an ad hoc basis; no single institutional framework exists for promoting and protecting environmental standards as it does with core labor standards in the ILO. Some have suggested creating an international environmental organization to remedy this omission. Of the approximately two hundred MEAs in force at the end of 2001, fewer than 10 percent contain provisions directly dealing with trade. The most important ones that do are the Convention on International Trade in Endangered Species of Fauna and Flora, the Montreal Protocol on Substances that Deplete the Ozone Layer, and the Basel Convention on the Control of Transboundary Movements of Hazardous Wastes and Their Disposal.

No GATT or WTO dispute has arisen (at least through early 2002) on the use of retaliatory trade measures to punish an offender of an MEA. Still, the environmental lobby worries about the possibility that future decisions by the

**BOX 13.2 (continued)**

WTO's dispute settlement mechanism could rule that sanctions taken under one of these agreements violate trade rules. It therefore urges a formal international agreement to specify that the WTO would not have primary jurisdiction when MEA issues are involved. To support the thesis that the WTO is naturally predisposed to overrule domestic environmental protection laws, critics of globalization can point to a GATT panel's ruling against the legitimacy of U.S. restrictions imposed on imports of tuna from Mexico because its fishermen were using nets that inadvertently killed dolphins, and to decisions by WTO dispute settlement panels seemingly unsympathetic to the killing of endangered sea turtles and to U.S. clean air regulations (see Chapter 8). NGOs complain that the WTO has consistently undermined environmental, health, and safety laws, and in doing so has taken decisions about national laws "out of the hands of the public, their elected representatives, and national courts." Even worse, say the critics of globalization, the WTO has done so behind closed doors.[25]

The counterargument to these positions is that the WTO was designed from the outset to be compatible with international environmental standards and has acted accordingly. According to the preamble to the agreement creating it, the organization is supposed to seek "the optimal use of the world's resources in accordance with the objective of sustainable development," and should not intervene in national or international environmental policies. From its inception, the WTO has had an active Committee on Trade and the Environment to study the interactions between these issues and make recommendations if modifications to institutional structure or procedures are deemed necessary. The pro-WTO view asserts that its rules are fully compatible with existing MEAs and that it is unlikely that actions taken in connection with one of them would ever be challenged in the dispute settlement mechanism. Furthermore, the controversial rulings by the GATT and WTO can be interpreted as being directed at relatively narrow, technical aspects of how domestic environmental laws were applied to other countries, not at their overall intent or validity.

In a 1999 study, the WTO Secretariat rebutted the contention that increased economic growth leads to increased environmental problems. The latter were said to be best addressed by going to their source, not by targeting peripheral causes such as exports and imports that "can only partially correct market and policy failures, and at a higher price to society." Because most damage to the environment results from pollution-heavy production processes, the disposal of waste products, and certain kinds of consumption, the WTO asserted that "trade as such is rarely the root cause of environmental degradation."[26] In sum, supporters of globalization claim they do not oppose environmental protection standards and treaties, and they do not deny that trade-related aspects of this subject (e.g., rules for invoking trade barriers on environmental protection grounds)

**BOX 13.2** **(continued)**

ought to be considered in the WTO. However, they make it clear that they oppose requirements that all new trade agreements contain specific provisions advancing environmental standards. They think an organization that has greater technical expertise and clearer jurisdiction than the WTO should be responsible for drafting such standards and ruling on accusations of violations.

protection efforts and incomes would ratchet down. Those who see events unfolding in this manner believe that the existing international trading system is unwilling to place either environmental concerns (including preservation of endangered species) or safeguards to protect workers' rights on a par with, or ahead of, economic efficiency and the expansion of trade. At a time when some think that workers and the environment need the nation-state more than ever as a buffer from rising demands for profits by "corporate-defined internationalism," globalization may be causing governmental attitudes to move in the opposite direction.

The specter of diminished U.S. sovereignty prompts some ultraconservatives to publicly criticize the same trade policies that their left-of-center counterparts negatively associate with globalization. The perceived need for a return to economic nationalism causes those who would ordinarily endorse free market policies to oppose U.S. participation in new multilateral or regional agreements to further reduce government-imposed barriers to trade. A neoisolationist stance is especially evident when they warn of a serious diminution of U.S. sovereignty occurring at the hands of "invisible" international civil servants who run the WTO and other international organizations. Instead of advocating a trade regime based on a free flow of goods, services, and capital unfettered by government fiat, arch-conservatives such as Patrick Buchanan urge trade and tax policies that put American interests ahead of the global economy "and the well-being of our own people before what is best for 'mankind.'" Buchanan, the one-time Reform Party presidential candidate, expressed solidarity with his ideological opposite, Ralph Nader, in advocating that "whatever the decisions about the economic destiny of Americans are, they [should] be made by the American people and not by the transnational corporations in collusion with the embryonic institution of world government."[27]

The NGOs' offensive against the trade policy status quo did not arise in a vacuum. Two important events were key catalysts. The first was the bitterness shared by American environmental groups and labor unions about their failure in 1993 to defeat the legislation approving U.S. participation in NAFTA (see Chapter 12). Until they bonded in their common campaign to thwart a free trade agreement with Mexico, the two sides had pursued different missions that kept them operating in separate political universes. The proposal to initiate free trade with Mexico alarmed environmental NGOs because they predicted an upsurge of pollution along the Mexican side of the border. Organized labor was alarmed by threats to jobs, fringe benefits, and working conditions for workers in general and union members in particular. After losing the NAFTA political battle, the two groups channeled their mutual anger into a commitment not to lose the larger war. They then started what they saw as the good fight against the larger target: globalization-tinged trade policies that appeared to be inflicting unacceptable damage on their respective causes.

In retrospect, pro-NAFTA forces oversold the potential of the agreement to generate incremental exports and jobs, prompting opponents to bellow "we told you so." In addition, the pathbreaking, but loophole-heavy enforcement provisions of the side agreements on environmental and labor standards came under scathing criticism from globalization skeptics.[28] They believed that the very limited effectiveness of the two side agreements demonstrated that lobbying leverage can quickly disappear and political goals can be undermined if NGOs are too quick to reach accommodation with the liberal trade–minded U.S. executive branch.

The newly created World Trade Organization was the other principal catalyst accelerating the intensity and tenacity of the anti-globalization backlash. A number of NGOs and conservative politicians looked at the WTO's objectives and rules as well as subsequent rulings by its dispute settlement mechanism (see Chapter 8) and became convinced that many of their worst fears had materialized. Many decisions over public health, safety, and social concerns would be shifted to the secretive adjudication process for resolving trade disputes. It was also assumed that laws providing remedies for import-induced injury to workers would be challenged, and that national environmental protection laws would be overruled because they violated the WTO's predilection for encouraging free trade. Environmental NGOs, for example, were infuriated with the WTO judgment that initially ruled against U.S. efforts to restrict imports of shrimp from countries where fishermen used harvesting methods that killed large numbers of endangered species of sea turtles. The ruling turned sea turtles into a popular symbol that embodied the helpless victims of globalization. The Friends of the Earth spoke for many when it wrote:

> Imagine how you'd feel if your organization managed to convince your city council, state legislature, or Congress to enact a decent law, then a foreign government or corporation challenged the law as illegal under international trade rules. The next thing you know, a special trade court closed to the public could decide that the law should be eliminated or weakened. It can happen. It has happened. It's called the World Trade Organization.[29]

Visions of lost American jobs, unrestrained pollution, and avaricious multinational corporations playing governments off against one another encouraged groups concerned about health, human rights, and many other causes to stand shoulder-to-shoulder with labor and environmental NGOs in opposing globalization and the trade policies that sustain it. The WTO then became the lightning rod for any number of grievances.

The "Battle in Seattle" in December 1999 was a major turning point in the anti-globalization backlash. The "anti" movement mobilized some 40,000 demonstrators to simultaneously display the breadth and depth of its convictions and physically hinder the ability of international officials to conduct a WTO ministerial meeting. The resulting chaos in the streets of downtown Seattle and the media attention it generated unquestionably played *a* role in causing the unprecedented failure of a high-level meeting convened to approve the initiation of a new round of multilateral trade negotiations. The precise extent to which NGOs and self-styled anarchists caused the diplomatic impasse is a hotly contested issue that is unlikely ever to be resolved. A good argument can be made that the breakdown of the talks was mainly self-inflicted because of inadequate staff preparation; unrealistic or inconsistent negotiating positions by several major countries; and President Clinton's public expressions of sympathy for some of the demonstrators' demands, which infuriated other delegations.[30] Concern about the embarrassing if not disruptive effect of future massive anti-globalization demonstrations became an intimidating factor to senior trade negotiators. When the new reluctance of most cities to bear the costs and danger of hosting what were once prestigious high-level international economic meetings was added to the equation, decisionmakers could not logically dismiss the need to respond to at least some of the demands advanced by the environmental and labor lobbies.

Those supportive of globalization, however the term is defined, include the vast majority of government officials in the industrialized world, large corporations and agribusiness, and academic economists. Seeing the world differently, they still support liberal trade in general, and view NAFTA and the WTO positively. They argue that labor and environmental standards, as well as the protection of human rights, are inherently desirable objectives, but do not belong as integral parts of trade negotiations in the WTO or in trade agreements. Instead, the pursuit of social issues would allegedly be better served if they were discussed in more specialized international organizations, namely, the International Labor Organization and a newly created international environmental agency. They would presumably possess greater technical knowledge about drafting workable workers rights and environmental protection standards and how to rule on charges of noncompliance.

The so-called blue (as in blue-collar workers) and "green" (environment) issues are mainly seen through a prism that focuses on the need to prevent the imposition of new trade barriers and discrimination against poorer countries that do not maintain the higher, "state of the art" labor and environmental standards of the industrialized countries. The proposed authorization of retaliatory sanctions for noncompliance is a special target of opposition. This negativism is usually motivated by belief in the virtues of liberal trade and fear that governments would cynically manipulate these subjective standards into implicit devices to restrict unwanted imports. Those concerned about less-developed countries see them as the prime targets of potential neo-protectionism. Poor countries judged not to be maintaining "satisfactory" international labor and environmental standards would be subject to sanctions against their exports by their trading partners. LDCs that did try to meet higher standards mandated by industrialized countries would lose some or all of the cheap labor and low production costs that are sources of their comparative advantage in producing labor-intensive goods. One way or the other, many manufactured goods currently or potentially produced by LDCs would be priced out of the U.S. market (as well as markets in other countries). Most American business executives, especially those in multinational companies, also oppose direct linkage between social issues and trade agreements, but for different reasons. They generally dislike legislative provisions that portend additional regulations and increased costs.

A good summary of the pro-liberal trade, pro-free-market point of view—one that speaks of a "race to the top"—is provided by Daniel Griswold:

> By discouraging trade and foreign investment, sanctions would retard economic growth, making it more difficult for poor countries to raise environmental, labor, and overall living standards. . . . Openness to trade and investment encourages faster growth, which leads to rising incomes and higher labor and environmental standards. As a result, those nations with the highest social standards in the world today are also among the most open to the global economy."[31]

Several policy options exist that might eventually form the basis of a common ground between these contradictory, seemingly irreconcilable visions of the world economy. These include "eco-labeling," a system that would inform consumers about the environmental impact of the production of specific goods. Another possible compromise is to make individual countries responsible for enforcing their own "reasonably" vigorous environmental and labor standards and be subject to punishments short of trade sanctions, such as externally imposed fines, for inadequate compliance. NGOs might also systematically organize consumer boycotts against goods from countries that are viewed as grossly violating basic human rights or failing to maintain "acceptable" levels of labor and environmental standards. Another option attracting attention in the United States is federal funding of a wage insurance program. It would provide extended unemployment benefits approximately equivalent in value to the last salary of a worker who had lost his or her job because of imports or domestic reasons such as corporate cutbacks.

## U.S. Trade Policy Relegated to the Slow Track

One of the most important manifestations of the anti-globalization backlash on U.S. trade policy was the extraordinary difficulty faced by two administrations in obtaining congressional passage of what previously had been uncontroversial trade legislation. The statutes subjected to delay and opposition on Capitol Hill almost certainly would have been approved with little fanfare or controversy in earlier years when the liberal trade coalition was still a dominant force. Another big change beginning in the early 1990s was that presidents could no longer use Cold War rhetoric to convince wavering members of Congress to vote in favor of trade-liberalizing legislation. The old sales pitch had been simple but effective: Enhanced international economic integration and cooperation would make non-Communist countries more economically prosperous and politically stable. Communist bloc countries, being outside the market-oriented trading system, would be left further behind.

From the late 1990s into the new century, the legislative machinery enabling the executive branch to advance the goal of world trade liberalization uncharacteristically ground to a near halt. First, this shutdown was caused by the seismic shift in the domestic politics of trade policy. Never before had there been such an unrelenting offensive waged by so broad a range of influential elements of civil society. Never before had social reasons been used to justify opposition for *every* major trade initiative proposed during the eight years of the Clinton administration and the first year of the Bush II administration. It was extraordinary that voices were raised against all proposed legislation that would result in *any* kind of increased imports.

The most important instance of "statutory stall" was the more than eight-year failure of Congress to approve the requests of two presidents to renew fast-track negotiating authority. As explained in Chapter 7, fast-track (renamed "trade promotion authority" by the Bush II administration) is the procedure devised to reconcile Congress's ultimate authority over trade policy with the perceived need to provide the executive branch credible authority to negotiate reductions in or elimination of U.S. tariff and nontariff barriers. Fast-track advocates equate credibility in this instance with the executive branch's ability to convince other governments of the high probability that a trade agreement signed with the United States will not come undone by deal-breaking amendments inserted into the implementing legislation by a Congress seeking to protect constituents. The fast-track provision requires that throughout the course of trade negotiations the administration keep congressional leaders fully informed. This arrangement provides members with early opportunities to convey their reactions to the administration about the concessions being offered by and to the U.S. negotiating team. The most distinctive feature of the statute is that it changes lawmaking procedures by stipulating that Congress can neither bottle up in committee the legislation implementing the trade agreement nor amend it when voting on it. The provision was originally enacted in 1975 and routinely renewed on three occasions.[32]

Fast-track negotiating authority expired in 1994. This lapse was of no immediate concern because U.S. trade policy at the time was focused on digesting the completion of the Uruguay Round and the beginning of NAFTA, not looking to inaugurate new negotiations. Soon, however, the Clinton administration wanted to conclude a free trade agreement with Chile to open the door for its membership in NAFTA. The administration also moved quickly in its efforts to create regional free trade areas in the Western Hemisphere and in the Asia-Pacific region (see Chapter 12). Fast-track authority would greatly increase the odds that these negotiations were successfully completed and the agreements signed would be implemented. Opponents of further trade liberalization naturally saw their agenda being served by an indefinite hiatus for fast-track.

Renewal of fast-track authority languished because of irreconcilable differences between the opponents and supporters of globalization. For reasons explained above, the former were adamant that the legislation specifically require strong international labor and environmental standards to be a core U.S. negotiating objective for all trade

## Box 13.3  How Important Was Renewal of Fast-Track Authority?

The importance and desirability of lapsed fast-track negotiating authority in the late 1990s and early 2000s are subject to different interpretations. Its absence represented a legal impediment—not an absolute prohibition—to the signing of new trade-liberalizing or regional free trade agreements. The larger question of whether this authority should even exist is a value judgment based on one's support for, or opposition to, further reductions in import barriers. If one prefers either to limit further trade liberalization or to assure that Congress has maximum leverage over the terms of future agreements signed by the president, fast-track is undesirable. Conversely, most advocates of trade liberalization consider it a highly desirable legislative tool.

The president needs statutory authority, not to negotiate and reach agreement with other governments but to legally adopt the reductions in trade barriers the U.S. government has agreed to. New trade initiatives are possible to the extent that other countries are willing to undertake the laborious effort of hammering out a trade agreement with the United States even at the risk of Congress's adding crippling amendments to the implementation legislation. The odds are high—though not 100 percent—that members of Congress will introduce so many amendments to such bills that the administration will have to demand a reopening of negotiations to comply with Congress's dictates. Most foreign governments do not want to invest the time and energy in the face of such uncertainty. Another concern of liberal traders is that an amendable trade bill could become a vehicle for legislating protectionist measures in other areas of U.S. trade policy. It has also been argued that some countries would not put their best liberalization offer on the table if they feared that congressional rejection of a completed agreement would require reopening negotiations.

The widely accepted contention that free trade agreements are so far-reaching that fast-track authority is absolutely essential was belied by congressional approval in 2001, with minimal changes, of a free trade agreement signed with Jordan. The lack of congressional desire to tinker with the bill was partly due to minimal U.S. imports from that country and partly to the provision that obligated both countries to enforce their existing labor and environmental protection laws and not to relax either for the purpose of promoting their exports or discouraging imports. Chile and Singapore were discussing terms of bilateral free trade agreements with U.S. trade officials in early 2002, undeterred by lapsed fast-track authority.

---

agreements concluded under fast-track. The opposing side, for reasons also discussed above, wanted either tenuous, highly qualified references or none at all.

Inability to resolve the conflict precluded assembling a majority in the House for passage of *any* version of renewal legislation during the Clinton administration. (The more pro-trade Senate was seen as likely to approve a fast-track bill containing limited references to the "green" and "blue" issues.) Any proposal containing strong labor and environmental provisions was unacceptable to most House Republicans and the relatively few Democrats who were committed supporters of liberal trade. Any bill not containing strong provisions was unacceptable to labor and environmental groups and therefore unacceptable to the vast majority of Democrats.

These obstacles notwithstanding, it is still conceivable that the two sides could have been pressured to accept vague but mutually satisfactory statutory language *if* the Clinton White House, industry, and agriculture had descended en masse on Capitol Hill and executed a smart, sustained, and well-coordinated lobbying effort. Instead, the liberal trade lobby just went through the motions. Distracted by other priorities and not yet aware that a once relatively pro forma legislative process was being undermined by the new politics of U.S. trade policy, the Clinton administration conducted lobbying efforts on Capitol Hill that many neutral political observers judged to be inadequate to what was needed to assure renewal of fast-track.[33] The problem of different political parties controlling the two ends of Pennsylvania Avenue was compounded because many Republican members of Congress, especially in the House, had developed an intense personal antipathy towards President Clinton and an aversion to legislative actions that would enhance his political stature. The business sector seemed to be operating on the belief that it was not cost-effective to expend a large amount of political capital for an uphill effort on a nonpriority trade policy goal that had become hotly contested.

Getting fast-track authority renewed was one of the few Clinton legislative goals that was shared by his successor. The Bush administration's proposed bill had several things going for it. The president and the House majority were now members of the same party, and industry (minus steel and textiles) and agriculture were still in favor of renewal. The ultrasensitive issues of environmental and labor provisions were dealt with in a middle-of-the-road fashion that mollified some but fully satisfied few. Respect for core labor standards was designated as a U.S. trade negotiating objective, but self-enforcement of a country's workers' rights legislation was called for in lieu of externally imposed sanctions. Ensuring that trade and environmental policies are mutually supportive was also designated as a negotiating objective, but again the self-enforcement of each country's environmental protection laws was stipulated. Nevertheless, the prospects for approval remained so uncertain that some supporters wanted the vote on the administration's bill delayed until a headcount indicated a firm majority existed.

Passage of the bill in the House on December 6, 2001, could not have been any closer. Upon completion of the initial roll call, the bill had been defeated by a couple of votes. With Democrats calling for a gavel to officially end the vote, the Republican leadership held off and bargained frantically to gain a handful of converts. They succeeded, and the bill officially passed, 215–214. To eke out even this narrowest of majorities, the White House and House leaders had needed to use both carrot-and-stick tactics. With only twenty-one Democrats voting in favor of the fast-track bill, every Republican vote was important. Among the incentives promised literally at the last-minute were more restrictive criteria for granting free access to textile imports from Caribbean, Central American, and Andean countries; in addition, the administration promised limits on imports of duty-free citrus fruit from Latin America if a Western Hemisphere free trade area is created. These carrots were added to earlier administration promises to respond to the import-related problems of the domestic steel industry.[34] Some avid liberal traders complained that the administration had made too many protectionist concessions.

Absent the tragic events of September 11, 2001, and their aftermath, the fast-track bill still might have been defeated. The "stick" tactic consisted of pressure applied to several uncommitted House Republicans to demonstrate solidarity with the president in the midst of a shooting war and a global political war against terrorism, both of which needed assistance from an international coalition. Just before the vote, House speaker Dennis Hastert implored the rank and file not to undermine the president at "the worst possible time." The plea to defend urgent national security considerations, by definition, is a seldom used trump card, but one that consistently beats parochial commercial interests.[35] The U.S. Trade Representative at the time, Robert Zoellick, had been arguing for weeks that there was a link between trade liberalization and the war against terrorism. He urged Congress "to send an unmistakable signal to the world that the United States is committed to global leadership of openness and understands that the staying power of our new coalition depends on economic growth and hope. . . . America's trade leadership can build a coalition of countries that cherish liberty in all its aspects."[36] The House's approval of the bill by the narrowest of margins immediately raised doubts about fast-track's long-term ability to produce additional trade liberalization. Some analysts noted that if the "easy" part was so hard-fought, congressional passage of legislation implementing far-reaching trade liberalization agreements was uncertain at best.

The trade-legislation-at-risk syndrome also played out through a proposed bill that had far fewer implications for the U.S. economy than the renewal of fast-track authority. The Africa Growth and Opportunity Act was originally introduced in 1997 by a bipartisan group of congressional members and was at least as much an effort to promote economic development in the poorest region of the world as it was a trade measure. The intent was to delegate authority to the president to promote private sector activity on various fronts in the long-troubled economies of sub–Saharan Africa. Improved market access for goods from these countries could be provided through more extensive tariff-free treatment, and the administration could allocate funds and official guarantees to encourage additional American foreign direct investment there. The all-important quid pro quo for eligibility for these benefits was certification by the U.S. government that a country was embracing economic reform, and more specifically, that it was making concrete progress toward establishing (or had already achieved) a market-based economy. This prerequisite was denounced by NGOs that opposed the free market strategy associated with the Washington Consensus and the tactic of forcing LDCs to embrace it.

Even though non-oil imports from sub–Saharan African countries account for less than one-half of 1 percent of total U.S. imports and despite the failure of decades of foreign aid to reduce poverty in the region, the bill attracted serious opposition. What seemed like a quick and simple process became prolonged and complicated. U.S. apparel and textile companies and unions voiced their traditional opposition to reducing trade barriers on the grounds that lost sales and jobs would ensue, even though the U.S. International Trade Commission estimated in 1997 that less than seven hundred American textile and apparel jobs would be lost in the short- to medium-term.[37] Less traditional, more strident opposition came from what would be considered politically liberal NGOs in the anti-globalization camp. They denounced the Africa bill as foisting the evils of IMF-style forced budget cuts and privatization on countries in danger of having their sovereignty subverted by a new kind of colonial master: the multinational corporation. Global Trade Watch adopted shrill rhetoric to argue that the act was "lethal medicine" being surreptitiously promoted by an unnamed coalition of U.S. oil and manufacturing companies that wanted to "promote U.S. corporate control of African economies and natural resources."[38] The bill was eventually passed and signed into law in May 2000.

Human rights NGOs led the opposition to legislation granting permanent MFN status to China, even though the bilateral trade agreement that preceded it consisted entirely of Chinese market-opening measures (see Chapter 10). Lobbying against the bill was so intense that prospects for passage in the House of Representatives remained uncertain until days before the floor vote in 2000. The anti-globalization movement does not have as one of its goals increased commercial engagement with a country that, among other things, denies its citizens due process, has the potential of exporting massive amounts of manufactured goods that could displace domestic U.S. production and jobs, allegedly uses prison labor to make some exported goods, and threatens military action against Taiwan.

A more definitive display of influence by opponents of globalization was their role in helping to bring about the collapse of efforts in the Organization for Economic Cooperation and Development (OECD) to negotiate the Multilateral Agreement on Investment (MAI). The principal objective here was to consolidate into one treaty many of the guidelines, as contained in numerous bilateral agreements already in force, that are designed to limit government-imposed limitations on inward foreign direct investment. Few outsiders had even heard of this relatively obscure effort until the draft treaty was posted on the Web site of Public Citizen. Linked by the Internet, some six hundred trade, development, environment, labor, human rights, and consumer NGOs in more than seventy countries launched a scathing denunciation of the proposed treaty, both in procedural and substantive terms.

The closed-door secrecy of the negotiations was attacked. So, too, was its alleged tilting of the playing field too heavily in favor of multinational companies to the detriment of governmental ability to regulate in the health, environment, and workers' rights sectors. Opponents were especially angry with the open-ended potential of a new provision that would have enabled companies to demand financial compensation from a host government for a wide range of reasons, including "a lost opportunity to profit from a planned investment." "License to Loot" was the title of the anti-MAI message on the Friends of the Earth Web site. The investment treaty was also considered unacceptable because it would allegedly encourage the shift of production facilities from one country to another, something that is viewed by some as not providing net benefits to the majority of the world's peoples. Embarrassed by the unrelenting barrage of public criticism from NGOs and unable to resolve the deadlock on a few sensitive points (such as exceptions in the application of the proposed rules for certain industries), the OECD negotiators indefinitely suspended negotiations in 1998 on the proposed multilateral investment pact after three years of effort.

## Conclusions and Outlook

The anti-globalization backlash is not going to fade away in the foreseeable future. To the cheers of some and the dismay of others, it appears to be in an early stage of having a significant long-term impact on the process and substance of trade policy in the United States and elsewhere. The trade policy debate may well have permanently expanded beyond the traditional pursuit of economic efficiency to include issues of fairness and quality of life. The larger belief that unregulated markets are the optimal economic strategy will be subject to recurring challenges. Civil society and street protesters have joined the leaders of major corporations (and their lobbyists) in the ranks of critical private sector inputs to trade policymaking. As a result of the changed political landscape, U.S. trade policy could become less committed to the further liberalization of trade barriers.

Whether an individual praises or condemns globalization is a function of his or her belief system and economic ideology. The opposition camp has been positively depicted as an "alternative globalization movement—one that seeks to eliminate inequalities between rich and poor and between the powerful and the powerless, and to expand the possibilities of self-determination."[39] Another effort to depict the movement in a positive manner argues that the economic virtues of trade and the appropriate ground rules for trade are two different things. The struggle for a decent, democratic, and humane society may have relatively little to do with international trade; it "exists in an entirely separate realm—the realm of democratic citizenship."[40] Critics of anti-globalization activism argue that, no matter how noble their goals, NGOs are still special interest groups. Supporters of globalization ask "who elected the NGOs" to demand policy changes on behalf of the public at large? Many NGOs are alleged to operate in a similar manner as the targets of their criticism: on a multinational basis, behind closed doors, and often suffering "from tunnel vision, judging every public act by how it affects their particular interest."[41] In another example of the "backlash against the backlash," the then Mexican president, Ernesto Zedillo, told an international forum that a "peculiar" alliance including the extreme right and left, environmentalist groups, labor unions in industrial countries, and "some self-appointed representatives from civil society" has gathered around a common endeavor: "to save the people of developing countries from . . . development."[42]

Given the clash of values, the lawmaking process is and will continue to be the focal point in the United States for competing factions seeking to determine trade policy substance. This is not a new phenomenon, but the volume of the many voices opposing a liberal, that is, market-based, trade policy is without precedent in the post–World War II era. The inability to devise mutually acceptable compromise language for constructive means of incorporating social issues, principally labor and environmental standards, in the international trade agenda reflects systemic problems that are far from being resolved. Opponents of globalization are deeply committed to their concerns, but their message and how it is delivered are often fragmented. The side defending globalization is less divided, but it has been ineffective in conveying a popular message that resonates among the public at large.

The Clinton administration liked to say that the best way to resolve the impasse was to put "a human face" on globalization. The problem with this catchy slogan is that there is no consensus about whose face would best represent globalization; the candidates include Bill Gates, a peasant in Central America, Ronald McDonald, an international banker who lends to LDCs, and a child in an Asian sweatshop. Meaningful convergence between the two opposing views of globalization will be many years in coming.

## For Further Reading

Burtless, Gary, Robert Z. Lawrence, Robert Litan, and Robert Shapiro, *Globaphobia: Confronting Fears About Open Trade*. Washington, D.C.: Brookings Institution Press, 1998.

Deardorff, Alan V., and Robert Stern, eds. *Social Dimensions of U.S. Trade Policies*. Ann Arbor, Mich.: University of Michigan Press, 2000.

Destler, I. M., and Peter J. Balint. *The New Politics of American Trade: Trade, Labor, and the Environment*. Washington, D.C.: Institute for International Economics, 1999.

Esty, Daniel. *Greening the GATT: Trade, Environment, and the Future*. Washington, D.C.: Institute for International Economics, 1994.

Friedman, Thomas. *The Lexus and the Olive Tree*. New York: Anchor Books, 2000.

Graham, Edward M. *Fighting the Wrong Enemy: Antiglobal Activists and Multinational Enterprise*. Washington, D.C.: Institute for International Economics, 2000.

Gray, John. *False Dawn: The Delusions of Global Capitalism*. New York: New Press, 1998.

Greider, William. *One World, Ready or Not: The Manic Logic of Global Capitalism*. New York: Simon & Schuster, 1997.

Micklethwait, John, and Adrian Wooldridge. *A Future Perfect: The Challenge and Hidden Promise of Globalization*. New York: Times Books, 2000.

Morici, Peter. *Reconciling Trade and the Environment in the World Trade Organization*. Washington, D.C.: Economic Strategy Institute, 2002.

Rodrik, Dani. *Has Globalization Gone Too Far?* Washington, D.C.: Institute for International Economics, 1997.

Steger, Manfred B. *Globalism: The New Market Ideology*. Lanham, Md.: Rowman & Littlefield Publishers, 2002.

## Notes

1. The number of NGOs operating internationally was estimated to be 26,000 in 1999, up from about 6,000 in 1990. Data source: *Foreign Policy* 126 (September/October 2001): 24.

2. I. M. Destler and Peter J. Balint, *The New Politics of American Trade: Trade, Labor, and the Environment* (Washington, D.C.: Institute for International Economics, 1999), 9.

3. Ibid., 42.

4. Thomas L. Friedman, *The Lexus and the Olive Tree* (New York: Anchor Books, 2000), 406.

5. For good historical data on globalization, see Paul Masson, *Globalization: Facts and Figures*, IMF policy discussion paper 01/4, accessed at www.IMF.org/.

6. Senate Committee on Finance, testimony in *Globalization and American Trade Policy: Hearing before the Committee on Finance,* 27 February 2001, 40.

7. Robert Gilpin, *The Challenge of Global Capitalism* (Princeton: Princeton University Press, 2000), 294.

8. For example, some supporters of globalization are inclined to oversimplify statistical evidence allegedly showing close links between prosperity and adherence to an outward-looking trade policy. Some critics frequently distort the limitations on U.S. sovereignty resulting from membership in the WTO and exaggerate the net loss of jobs in the United States from free trade with Mexico.

9. Federal Reserve Board press release of speech by Alan Greenspan, 24 October 2001, 1.

10. David Dollar and Aart Kraay, "Trade, Growth, and Poverty," *Finance and Development* (September 2001); accessed at www.IMF.org/external/pubs/.

11. Friedman, *Lexus,* 9.

12. The agenda includes disciplined fiscal and monetary policies (including fewer government subsidies), financial and trade liberalization, deregulation and privatization of business, protection of commercial property rights, and a smaller bureaucracy.

13. Mark Weisbrot, "Globalization for Whom?"; accessed December 2001 at www.cepr.net/globalization.html/.

14. Dani Rodrik, "Governance of Economic Globalization," in Joseph Nye, Jr., and John Donahue, eds., *Governance in a Globalizing World* (Washington, D.C.: Brookings Institution Press, 2000), 348.

15. Gilpin, *Global Capitalism,* 315.

16. Benjamin R. Barber, "Globalizing Democracy," *The American Prospect,* 11 September 2000, 19.

17. As quoted in Manfred Steger, *Globalism: The New Market Ideology* (London: Roman & Littlefield Publishers, 2002), 106–107.

18. Dan Rodrik, *Has Globalization Gone Too Far?* (Washington, D.C.: Institute for International Economics, 1997), 2, 85.

19. Jeff Faux, "Whose Rules for Globalism?" *The American Prospect,* 5 June 2000, 14.

20. Testimony of Thea Lee, 9 July 1997, to the House Committee on International Relations, accessed at www.aflcio.org/stopfastrack/lee.htm/.

21. Dani Rodrik, "Sense and Nonsense in the Globalization Debate," in Jeffry A. Frieden and David A. Lake, eds., *International Political Economy: Perspectives on Global Power and Wealth* (Boston: Bedford/St. Martin's, 2000), 464.

22. Robert Z. Lawrence, "International Trade Policy in the 1990s," accessed December 2001 at www.ksg.harvard.edu/cbg/lawrence725.pdf/.

23. Paul Krugman, "In Praise of Cheap Labor," *Slate Magazine,* 20 March 1997, accessed at www.mit.edu/krugmanwww/smokey.html/.

24. Text of a speech delivered 1 April 1998, accessed at www.aflcio.org/publ/speech98/sp0401.htm/.

25. See, for example, the Web site of Friends of the Earth at www.foe.org/international/wto/.

26. The report, *Trade and Environment,* was accessed from WTO Web site at www.wto.org/english/tratop_e/envir_e/stud99_e.htm/.

27. As quoted in Steger, *Globalism,* 88, 143.

28. See, for example, Jerome I. Levinson, "Worker Rights and Foreign Direct Investment," in Daniel Bradlow and Alfred Escher, eds., *Legal Aspects of Foreign Direct Investment* (The Hague: Kluwer Law International, 1999), 149.

29. Friends of the Earth, accessed December 2001 at www.foe.org/. A list compiled by Global Exchange of ten harshly phrased reasons to oppose the WTO, including the allegations that it "is killing people" and "destroying the environment," was accessed at www.thirdworld-traveler.com/WTO_MAI/TopTenReasons_Oppose.html/.

30. See "After Seattle: A Global Disaster," *The Economist,* 11 December 1999, 19; and Jeffrey J. Schott, "The WTO after Seattle," in Jeffrey J. Schott, ed., *The WTO After Seattle* (Washington, D.C.: Institute for International Economics, 2000), 3–5.

31. Daniel T. Griswold, *Trade, Labor, and the Environment: How Blue and Green Sanctions Threaten Higher Standards,* Cato Institute Trade Policy Analysis No. 15, August 2001, 14, 18.

32. As noted in Chapter 6, it is standard procedure for Congress to delegate all trade liberalization authority to the president only for a fixed period of time, that is, not permanently. This practice facilitates the termination of such authority if Congress changes its mind or deems the president to have abused his authority and exceeded the intent of the legislation.

33. See, for example, Bruce Stokes, "An Erratic Hand At the Helm," *National Journal,* 16 January 1999, 119.

34. "Trading Nations Count the Cost of Fast-Track," *Financial Times,* 10 December 2001, 8.

35. Voting on fast-track in the middle of military actions in Afghanistan was a timing variable that suggests the impossibility of constructing one enduring model of trade policy decisionmaking.

36. Robert Zoellick, "Countering Terror with Trade," *Washington Post,* 20 September 2001, A35.

37. As cited in Chailendu K. Pegues, *The Africa Trade Bill: Bringing Africa Into the Global Economy,* report issued by the Progressive Policy Institute, March 1998, 3. The ITC report was accessed at www.usitc.gov/wais/reports/arc/w3056.html/.

38. Accessed June 2000 from Public Citizen at citizen.org/pctrade/Africa/stopthe/html/.

39. Michael Hardt and Antonio Negri, "What the Protesters in Genoa Want," *New York Times,* 20 July 2001, A3.

40. Robert Kuttner, "The Seattle Protesters Got It Right," *Business Week,* 20 December 1999, 25.

41. Jessica T. Matthews, "Power Shift," *Foreign Affairs* 46 (January/February, 1997): 64.

42. Text of speech delivered to the World Economic Forum, 20 January 2000, accessed at the International Chamber of Commerce Web site: www.iccwbo.org/.

# 14 A Look Ahead

Efforts by U.S. policymakers to reduce barriers to the flow of international trade, establish rules of acceptable behavior among nations, and recognize the need to provide those financially harmed by the emphasis on trade liberalization with an opportunity to petition for relief have entered their seventh decade. A record of significant accomplishment has been amassed, but much still needs to be done. The workload for U.S. trade policymakers and negotiators is likely to continue expanding indefinitely. New challenges for U.S. trade policy and a significant portion of its new content can be identified in general terms. Beyond traditional decisions on whether to increase or reduce restrictions on individual categories of imports and exports, the future agenda will include (1) responses to recent, unresolved problems, whose final dispositions are currently in doubt; and (2) original policy initiatives required by the need to respond to unforseen trends and events, newly invented products and technologies, extraordinary actions by other countries, and so on.

Despite the extensive array of policies, laws, programs, and procedures discussed in previous chapters, the policy agenda will never stop expanding, either in content or in complexity. Perhaps the only event that could thwart this scenario would be the highly unlikely decision by the U.S. government to delegate full responsibility to the market mechanism for determining which goods are or are not imported and exported. Any country can opt out of having a trade policy and simply refuse to do anything to alter international business activities carried out by the private sector. No country is seriously contemplating going this route.

Having dismissed the notion that trade policymaking is about to reach a plateau, this chapter will first provide a brief overview of which elements of U.S. foreign trade policy are likely to remain relatively unchanged in the future and which are likely to experience change. Then, after a look at the newly emerging issues, the dimensions and consequences of which are still not fully defined, a few educated guesses will be advanced on the issues that are likely to make their presence felt in the longer-term.

## What Should Remain the Same and What Is Changing

The old French aphorism that the more things change, the more they remain the same is largely, but not totally, applicable to the content and goals of U.S. trade policy in the near to intermediate term. Continuity should be the dominant theme in the future, overshadowing a few genuinely new issues and the disappearance of existing ones.

The continued absence of consensus about the best strategy and the appropriate goals for U.S. trade policy almost certainly will endure, as will the consequences of factional disagreement. Since the end of the immediate post–World War II period, in which national security concerns drove its trade policy (see Chapter 2), the United States in literal terms has not had *a* trade policy. Instead, it has adopted multiple trade *policies* that not infrequently are inconsistent with one another. U.S. international economic hegemony in the twenty-year period beginning in 1945 contributed to an unusually broad-based consensus on import and export strategies. Virtually uncontested U.S. priorities included opening the American market wider to its new allies in the Cold War, accepting their limited ability at that time to import American goods, and imposing blanket restrictions on exports of military and high-technology goods to Communist bloc countries. The broad consensus began fading in the mid-1960s because of major structural changes, principally domestic problems in the U.S. economy, the return of Western Europe and Japan to the ranks of international commercial superpowers and, later, the disintegration of the Soviet empire and the end of the Cold War. If anything, the ability to construct broad-based support even for limited initiatives has been more elusive than ever since the early 1990s (see Chapter 13). With agreement on the nature of "first-best" policy so elusive, U.S. trade policies in the future might display even more shades of gray than they have in the recent past.

No matter how rapid the pace of change in the world economy, U.S. trade policymakers, like their foreign counterparts, will still face the repeated need to make difficult decisions. Easy answers will never exist in a policy sector dominated by perceptions instead of hard truths and the presence of at least two points of view in all major decisions. Decisions will still need to be made among conflicting priorities, loyalties, and values. Virtually no major policy stance will win unequivocal approval among competing domestic interest groups (or among trading partners). Trade policymakers will still rely mainly on value judgments to weigh the benefits of making further reductions in trade barriers against such factors as dislocations—real or imagined—inflicted on import-sensitive sectors and the inevitable desire of politicians to avoid antagonizing powerful interest groups. The lack of homogeneity or simplicity in the issues that need to be faced make it unlikely that U.S. trade policy will be able to abandon its multitrack approach incorporating bilateral, regional, and multilateral talks seeking reductions in distortions to trade.

The process of making trade policy cannot shed the inescapable balancing act that seeks to accommodate the differing needs of its four components: domestic economics, domestic politics, international economics, and international politics. Reduced to its lowest common denominator, U.S. trade policy will always be imperfect in determining how best to serve these four policy spheres, an uphill task given that the objectives of these areas can seldom be simultaneously achieved through any one policy or action. For example, as long as it is a global superpower, the United States will have the special dilemma of determining the right balance between the goal of export promotion and a perceived need, not equally shared by any other government, to impose trade sanctions for reasons of foreign policy or humanitarian concerns. The process of reconciling priorities will continue to be brokered by a partnership between an executive branch predisposed to a global perspective and a legislative branch predisposed to responding to the demands of domestic constituents.

The economics of trade will continue to be subsumed in the politics of trade, and much of the process of formally reconciling different viewpoints and achieving concensus will take place in the context of writing and administering trade laws.

One source of change in the future conduct of U.S. trade policy will be the expanded use of the WTO's dispute settlement mechanism; indeed, the net desirability of this new reliance on multilateral tribunals will be debated for years to come. For better or worse, the direct, unilateral application of the provisions of Section 301 (see Chapter 7) to pressure trading partners into reducing or eliminating their barriers to U.S. exports will all but disappear. This change will please the many U.S. trading partners who intensely disliked Section 301 because they resented and feared unilateral threats of retaliation. Requesting a WTO dispute settlement panel (see Chapter 8) to rule that another country is violating its trade commitments can provide a veneer of multilateral legitimacy for efforts to change foreign behavior. But some would say legitimacy is for naught if the U.S. position is rejected by the neutral panel. To some extent, the option of using the services of the WTO's Dispute Settlement Body (DSB) will virtually eliminate the often vexing debate in U.S. government circles about how aggressive to be in demanding that other countries modify their trade policies to conform to U.S. definitions of fair trade.

The other side of the coin is that U.S. government trade lawyers will probably be spending more time defending the U.S. position before the DSB. Countries that once would have been loathe to make unilateral trade demands on the United States, or to threaten retaliation, are less hesitant to take their grievances against U.S. trade practices to a respected international dispute settlement body. The potential for another major change in U.S. trade relations is suggested by the unprecedented series of challenges in the WTO to actions taken under various U.S. import remedy laws. Beginning in the late 1990s and continuing into the new century, various trading partners demonstrated a near-zero tolerance for the imposition of higher duties by the United States following investigations in connection with the escape clause and antidumping statutes. Countries whose exports were the subjects of these investigations had a high success rate in convincing dispute settlement panels that the manner in which the United States determined that higher duties were warranted violated international rules and needed to be rescinded. If aggressive actions taken against U.S. efforts to protect domestic constituents by other countries continue and the dispute settlement mechanism continues to rule against it, the U.S. government will come under pressure to reassess its import policy, its trade laws, its association with the WTO, or all the above.

To a limited extent, the domestic discussions of U.S. trade policy goals will change substantially with the growing integration of social issues (see Chapter 13 and below) into the negotiating agenda. Historically, the debate about the utility of import barriers centered almost entirely on weighing the need to protect the economic interests of domestic producers and workers from import competition against the interests of consumers and efficiency. The introduction of quality of life concerns—environmental and labor standards—alters the traditional equation by introducing some genuinely new, quasi-economic concepts into the world of trade policy negotiations.

# Unfinished Business and Upcoming Tasks

All discussions of future directions for U.S. trade policy would benefit from short-term success in reducing the ambiguity that envelops the relatively large, persistent U.S. merchandise trade deficit and the declining surplus in trade in services. It is unclear to what extent, if any, the goal of reducing the deficit should be given high priority. Before trying to fix something, it is logical first to confirm that something is seriously wrong and then determine its source, severity, and how to deal with it. As discussed in Chapter 4, some uncertainty is inevitable when calculating how serious a problem the U.S. deficits are. Only the mathematical size of the trade deficit is an absolute certainty. No incontrovertible determination can be made as to what is "too big" and unsustainable (in part because that number would change over time). Is the size of the deficit relative to U.S. GDP a better statistical benchmark than its absolute size? Is the large deficit a derivative of the mix of the domestic saving-investment imbalance, a secular decline in U.S. industrial competitiveness, and an "overvalued" dollar? If these are the principal causal factors, the scope for trade policy to shrink the deficits is limited, despite the individual sectors that would benefit if other countries reduced barriers to imports of American goods. There are no definitive answers to any of these questions, but better insights would contribute to more informed judgments and decisions.

An important piece of unfinished business for U.S. trade policy is preparation of detailed negotiating positions for the large and ever-expanding number of issues that will be discussed in the upcoming round of multilateral trade negotiations. (The nature of this task will be strongly influenced by whether Congress delegates fast-track authority to the administration during the critical years of these negotiations.) Some agenda items will be of more importance than others. For example, the U.S. economy would reap disproportionate benefits from advancing the still rudimentary liberalization of restrictions on trade in services and agriculture. Also on the agenda of the upcoming MTNs is the difficult question that has recently arisen for U.S. trade policy: how to reconcile the traditional commitment to protect the intellectual property rights of pharmaceutical companies with the need to respond to the demands by LDCs that they have access to cheap medicines to prevent epidemics and soaring death rates from AIDS and other diseases. On the one hand, there are life and death consequences associated with the availability of cheap substitutes, licensed or not from the patent holders, for expensive proprietary drugs. On the other hand, pharmaceutical companies may not be willing to continue spending billions of dollars to develop new drugs if they lack reasonable assurances of recouping their investment.

In the new round of trade negotiations, the U.S. government will expend considerable energy dealing with efforts to draft effective protocols establishing the appropriate means of linking trade rules with the goals of promoting environmental and labor standards. Agreement is needed on guidelines to decide when imposing import barriers in the name of environmental policy is a legitimate policy act, exempt from external challenges, designed to enforce a country's environmental and health standards and when it is a disguised form of protectionism subject to the rules of the WTO. Similarly, agreement needs to be reached on the WTO-legality of a country's imposing trade sanctions against the violator of a multilateral environmental agreement. A related issue will be whether the WTO is the appropriate primary forum for dealing with international efforts to protect the environment and prevent lax-enforcement countries from attracting large amounts of foreign direct investment in a "race to the bottom." A similar set of dilemmas exists for labor standards. They have been praised for their humanitarian objectives, and these standards have been denounced for their potential to undermine the competitiveness of LDCs in producing labor-intensive products. In this instance, engaging the International Labor Organization is an alternative to giving the WTO the responsibility of promoting and enforcing labor standards.

U.S. trade policymakers may face more nuanced complaints from domestic workers about the alleged unfairness of their having to compete with foreign workers who, by American values, are being exploited by poor wages and working conditions and the lack of the right to unionize. Defenders of liberal trade in the past have countered such complaints by arguing that the United States does not have a comparative advantage in labor-intensive, low-tech goods, and that workers in LDCs are paid less because they are less productive on average than American workers. As U.S. multinational corporations move their U.S.-originated managerial skills, capital equipment, and worker training programs to Mexico and other developing countries, an increase in imports of more sophisticated manufactured goods can be expected. With the right training, supervision, and state of the art equipment, relatively low-paid foreign labor can be brought up to, or near, U.S. levels of productivity (the output per hour of work) in some product lines. Using cheaper foreign labor with no sacrifice in productivity gives a multinational corporation the choice between lowering its prices or raising its profits.

Another emerging issue in import policy is how to disentangle the self-serving demands from legitimate grievances that comprise foreign criticism of U.S. trade remedy laws. Once again, U.S. trade negotiators are caught between two equally intense desires. One is the escalating demands by several trading partners that U.S. laws be revised to reduce the effects of their alleged "procedural protectionism." The other is the adamant refusal of many domestic interest groups to relinquish any of their legal rights to appeal for import relief, especially from unfair foreign trade practices.

Major unfinished business exists in the export policy sector. After years of failure, the executive branch, Congress, and the private sector need to agree on the provisions and broad standards of an updated U.S. export control strategy. If no common ground is found between those who advocate controls and sanctions to promote foreign policy and humanitarian objectives and those who believe them to be mostly futile and an expensive burden on American industry, U.S. export policy will continue to drift and operate on a mostly ad hoc basis. The familiar pattern in U.S. trade policy of finding and enunciating policy consensus through the legislative process has failed to materialize, leaving the U.S. government unable to pass a new version of the Export Administration Act many years after it expired (see Chapter 9).

## Longer-Term Additions to the Trade Agenda

Significant changes in the conduct of U.S. trade policy will result if and when the proposed free trade areas in the Western Hemisphere and the Asia-Pacific region are created (see Chapter 12) and the United States becomes a member. If history is any guide, the phasing out of trade barriers on such a large scale will lead to relatively rapid increases in imports and exports—thereby creating new groups of winners and losers. Besides moving the United States closer to a free trade position, membership in these two large regional trading blocs would likely lead to a decline in the relative importance of trade with Europe to the United States. As the EU continues to add member countries, the international trading system might indeed begin to cluster around three regional "super blocs." Should this somewhat unlikely scenario materialize, U.S. trade strategists, as well as foreign policy planners, would have to deal with a host of new issues. A completely different set of concerns will face U.S. trade policy in the future if the Western Hemisphere and Asia-Pacific free trade areas fail to materialize or the United States does not join. Under this scenario, the United States could find itself an outsider, its goods placed at a disadvantage because of exclusion from free market access to those Latin American and Asian countries belonging to regional or subregional trade blocs.[1] To reduce discrimination against its exports of goods and services if this scenario materializes, the United States probably would actively seek bilateral free trade agreements with all those countries interested in securing preferential access to the American market.

Trade policy will also be affected in the long-term by the further withering away of three traditional "boundaries," the common effect of which is that many old trade concepts will face obsolescence and require a fresh policy approach. The first fading boundary involves the rising irrelevance of most tariff and nontariff barriers imposed by governments at their borders. For most of history, they were what prevented free trade. By the 1970s, trade liberalization agreements had been so successful in reducing them that trade negotiators began moving further and further "inland." Foreign trade issues followed and moved further and further into the inner sanctum of national sovereignty as the informal boundary between external and internal faded. The new primary targets are what had previously been considered domestic measures off-limits to outside interference, even though they deliberately or inadvertently distorted international trade. What then occurred was a graduated climb, still in progress, from relatively less politically sensitive issues to more sensitive ones. The first round of agreements on internal measures discriminating against imports came in the 1970s and imposed general codes of conduct on national health and safety standards and on government procurement procedures. National environmental and labor policies comprised the second round.

The newest phase in the "creeping domestication" of trade policy is looking at the trade-distorting aspects of regulatory and competition policies. The thought of consolidating disparate national policies into a common global set of standards appears to be an unrealistic goal for the foreseeable future. However, it would be feasible to seek international agreements to ban or limit specific kinds of identifiable national regulatory measures that affect production, distribution, pricing, and other functions in ways that favor domestic companies. Regulatory reform is especially important for future efforts in liberalizing trade in services (e.g., telecommunications and airlines).

Competition policy can have international implications when a government has a lax attitude towards enforcing antitrust laws. Such a posture carries a high risk of encouraging market failures. Domestic competition policy can impede imports by permitting companies and their trade associations to establish product standards, distribution rules, and enforcement procedures; other measures include condoning collusive practices by private cartels, including price fixing and market share arrangements among companies and allowing the operation of private monopolies (such as telecommunications companies). Allowing rigged bidding practices in the private sector is another aspect of competition policy that discriminates against foreign exporters and consequently is a legitimate target for future inclusion in the growing body of international trade rules. When competition and regulatory policies become mainstream components of trade negotiations, they will affect the institutional aspects of U.S. decisionmaking. Agencies having primary trade policy jurisdiction, such as the USTR and the Commerce Department, will have to work more closely with a growing number of domestic regulators—and sometimes defer to them—for example, the Justice Department's antitrust division, the Food and Drug Administration, and the Federal Trade Commission. (The Environmental Protection Agency for many years has been a significant participant in U.S. trade policymaking.)

The "fading of boundaries" concept can also be applied to the blurring distinction between international trade and foreign direct investment. The data demonstrating the increasingly significant role of multinational corporations in the international flow of goods presented in Chapter 4 suggest the long-term desirability of fleshing out the very general current outline of the agreement on trade-related investment measures concluded in the Uruguay Round. Trade distortions emanating from discriminatory limitations and national regulations on foreign companies appear destined to become more significant in the long-run if the trading system is not more formally treated as being part of a combined international trade and investment order. As the world's largest home country and host country for foreign direct investment, the United States should have more interest than any other country in new international trade rules affecting governmental behavior at the nexus between trade and multinational corporate activity.

A third breakdown in traditional trade boundaries is the "national identity" of many technology-intensive goods. The growing reliance of companies, especially in the electronics sector, on outside contractors throughout the world for components (known as vertical specialization) and their increased use of outsourcing for the entire manufacturing process are hastening the globalization of production, as well as accelerating the growth of trade. Computers and automobiles exemplify the trend in which sophisticated goods are becoming an "amalgam" of parts made in so many countries that, despite the corporate name that appears on the label, designating a single country of origin is misleading. When foreign content is nearly as great as local content, branding goods as American-, Japanese-, or Korean-made becomes less relevant to traditional trade statistics and rules. As multinational companies expand to more countries and seek to promote a global image, even low-tech goods such as athletic shoes will experience a diminished national identity among consumers and government officials.

Appropriate international rules affecting the conduct of electronic commerce are just beginning to enter discussions among government trade officials. This is an idea whose time has come because technological breakthroughs in information processing and telecommunications are in an early stage of radically altering relationships between individual consumers and producers of goods and services, and between businesses and their suppliers. The complexity of the issues, together with the potentially enormous amounts of money associated with the presumed rapid growth of business transactions conducted over the Internet, suggest a staggering set of negotiating problems that are unlikely to be resolved in this decade. Consensus will not easily come to the question of whether a government can impose a tariff or sales tax on its citizens when they order a product online from a company in another country. Beyond that are such divisive questions as whether and what kinds of global content and security standards should be established. At the highest level of generalization, the unique economic questions surrounding the advent of the information technology revolution involve the centuries-old tendency of countries to adopt a zero-sum gain mentality and then attempt to maximize their share of the perceived benefits accruing from international commerce.

## In Conclusion

The guidelines presented in this book should remain an accurate guide to the "hows" and "whys" of the U.S. trade policy well into the future. We should expect evolution, not revolution. The perennial need to seek compromise among different interpretations of the national interest will discourage dramatic changes in strategy—except in the most severe and unexpected changes in economic or political circumstances. U.S. trade policy will always represent the end product of choices that must be made between conflicting yet legitimate values. In other words, politics will shape economic policy. Differing self-interests will invariably continue to produce conflicting policy recommendations, each having some degree of wisdom and truth but not enough of either to attract universal support. The allure of moving closer to free trade will continue its uneasy coexistence with the desire of politicians to be reelected. This means that future administrations, like their predecessors, will be genuinely committed to further trade liberalization but will deviate from that quest by periodically granting protection from imports to an industry because of its political clout, not its economic need.

The bottom-line is that paradoxes, inconsistencies, strengths, weaknesses, successes, and failures will continue to collectively reside within the totality of U.S. trade relations. The future trade policy of the United States will still be simultaneously praised and criticized. Its overall substance is unlikely to be exceptionally better or worse, or to have more continuity than the trade policy of the average country or customs union. What will stay exceptional is the importance of the United States in playing a leadership role in developing a global consensus on future directions in the trading system.

### For Further Reading

Feketekuty, Geza, and Bruce Stokes, eds. *Trade Strategies for a New Era: Ensuring U.S. Leadership in a Global Economy.* New York: Council on Foreign Relations, 1998.

Lawrence, Robert Z., Albert Bressand, and Takatoshi Ito. *A Vision for the World Economy: Openness, Diversity, and Cohesion.* Washington, D.C.: Brookings Institution, 1995.

### Notes

1. In the fall of 2001, more than 130 free trade agreements existed in the world, of which the United States belonged to two. Of the 30 free trade agreements within the Western Hemisphere at that time, the United States belonged to only one. Data source: USTR press release of a speech by Ambassador Robert B. Zoellick, 24 September 2001, 5.

# Appendix
## Selected Web Sites on International Trade*

### U.S. Government

| | |
|---|---|
| U.S. Trade Representative | USTR.gov |
| Department of Commerce | |
|   Bureau of Economic Analysis | Bea.gov |
|   International Trade Administration | Ita.doc.gov |
|   Office of Trade and Economic Analysis | Ita.doc.gov/td/industry/otea |
| | [Note: This is an excellent site for U.S. trade statistics] |
| U.S. International Trade Commission | USITC.gov |
| House Ways and Means Committee | Waysandmeans.house.gov |
| Senate Finance Committee | Senate.gov/%7efinance |

### International and Regional Organizations

| | |
|---|---|
| World Trade Organization | WTO.org |
| World Bank International Trade Grou: | Worldbank.org/research/trade/index.htm |
| European Union | Europa.eu.int |
| Organization for Economic Cooperation and Development | OECD.org |
| United Nations Conference on Trade and Development | Unctad.org |

### Nongovernmental Organizations

| | |
|---|---|
| Friends of the Earth | Foe.org |
| Global Trade Watch | citizen.org/trade/index/cfm |
| USA Engage (export controls) | Usaengage.org |

### Research Organizations

| | |
|---|---|
| American Enterprise Institute | Aei.org |
| Brookings Institution | Brookings.org |
| Cato Institute | Cato.org |

## Research Organizations (continued)

Economic Policy Institute                          Epinet.org
Economic Strategy Institute                        Econstrat.org
Heritage Foundation                                Heritage.org
Institute for International Economics               IIE.com

## Miscellaneous

Global Macroeconomic and Financial
   Policy Site                                      Stern.nyu.edu/globalmacro

Harvard Center for International Trade
   and Development                                 Cid.harvard.edu/cidtrade

National Association for Business
   Economics, International Links                  Nabe.com/publib/intllink.htm

Yahoo Global Economy                               dir.yahoo.com/Social_Science/Economics/
                                                Global_Economy

Glossary of International Economics                 www-personal.umich.edu/~alandear/glossary

The Language of Trade (dictionary of
   trade terms, acronyms, and chronology
   of trade events)                               Usinfo.state.gov/products/pubs/trade/
                                                homepage.htm/

*"www." omitted

# About the Authors

**Stephen D. Cohen** is professor of international relations at the School of International Service of American University. Prior to joining the faculty in 1975, he served as a senior staff member on the White House–Congressional Commission on the Organization of the Government for the Conduct of Foreign Policy, and as an international economist at the U.S. Treasury Department and the U.S.-Japan Trade Council. Among Dr. Cohen's books are *The Making of U.S. International Economic Policy* (now in its fifth edition); *An Ocean Apart: Explaining Three Decades of U.S.-Japanese Trade Frictions;* and *International Monetary Reform, 1964–69: The Political Dimension.* His articles have been published in *International Affairs, Journal of World Trade, World Development, The International Economy,* and other journals. He received his B.A. and Ph.D. from American University and an M.A. from Syracuse University.

**Robert A. Blecker** is professor of economics at American University and a research associate of the Economic Policy Institute, both in Washington, D.C. He received his B.A. from Yale University and his M.A. and Ph.D. from Stanford University. He has participated in working groups on international trade and financial issues at the Center for Economic Policy Analysis at New School University, the Economic Strategy Institute, and the Council on Foreign Relations. He is the author of *Taming Global Finance: A Better Architecture for Growth and Equity,* and *Beyond the Twin Deficits: A Trade Strategy for the 1990s,* and is the editor of a volume on *U.S. Trade Policy and Global Growth.* His articles have appeared in the *Cambridge Journal of Economics, Economica,* and *Weltwirtschaftliches Archiv.*

**Peter D. Whitney** is Economist in Residence at American University in Washington, D.C.; Senior Advisor on Latin America for Control Risks Group, an international management consulting company; Adjunct Professor at the Fuqua School of Business at Duke University; and Instructor for the State Department on the WTO and Trade Dispute Resolution. Previously, he served in the U.S. Foreign Service as Deputy Chief of Mission, Economic Counselor, Consul and Economic Officer to Argentina, Brazil, Chile, Jamaica, Japan, and Portugal. At the State Department he served as Director of Economic Policy for Latin America and the Caribbean. He received a B.A. from Princeton (history), an M.A. from Vanderbilt (economics), and an M.P.A. from Harvard (administration). He is a graduate of the National War College. He has also taught economics at Sophia (Tokyo) and UNC Chapel Hill.

# Index